Generation Z Marketing and Management in Tourism and Hospitality

Nikolaos Stylos · Roya Rahimi ·
Bendegul Okumus · Sarah Williams
Editors

Generation Z Marketing and Management in Tourism and Hospitality

The Future of the Industry

Editors
Nikolaos Stylos
School of Management
University of Bristol
Bristol, UK

Bendegul Okumus
Rosen College of Hospitality Management
University of Central Florida
Orlando, FL, USA

Roya Rahimi
University of Wolverhampton
Wolverhampton, UK

Sarah Williams
University of Wolverhampton
Wolverhampton, UK

ISBN 978-3-030-70697-5 ISBN 978-3-030-70695-1 (eBook)
https://doi.org/10.1007/978-3-030-70695-1

© The Editor(s) (if applicable) and The Author(s), under exclusive license to Springer Nature
Switzerland AG 2021
This work is subject to copyright. All rights are solely and exclusively licensed by the Publisher,
whether the whole or part of the material is concerned, specifically the rights of translation, reprinting,
reuse of illustrations, recitation, broadcasting, reproduction on microfilms or in any other physical
way, and transmission or information storage and retrieval, electronic adaptation, computer software,
or by similar or dissimilar methodology now known or hereafter developed.
The use of general descriptive names, registered names, trademarks, service marks, etc. in this
publication does not imply, even in the absence of a specific statement, that such names are exempt
from the relevant protective laws and regulations and therefore free for general use.
The publisher, the authors and the editors are safe to assume that the advice and information in this
book are believed to be true and accurate at the date of publication. Neither the publisher nor the
authors or the editors give a warranty, expressed or implied, with respect to the material contained
herein or for any errors or omissions that may have been made. The publisher remains neutral with
regard to jurisdictional claims in published maps and institutional affiliations.

This Palgrave Macmillan imprint is published by the registered company Springer Nature Switzerland
AG
The registered company address is: Gewerbestrasse 11, 6330 Cham, Switzerland

Preface

Generation Z (Gen Z) is the demographic cohort that has attracted scholars' worldwide attention due to the fundamentally different ways of thinking, doing, and living. Gen Zers represent a primarily digital generation that has been affected to the highest degree by their voluntary engagement with various online applications. There are some unique characteristics of Gen Zs in addition to driving the fourth industrial revolution and smart technologies, which are: (a) their advanced consciousness of protecting the natural environment and supporting sustainability, (b) their active engagement with sharing economy applications, (c) their different consumption patterns as affected by social and ethical concerns, (d) and their strong will to pursue meaningful careers to serve personal aspirations and collective/communal goals.

Consequently, scholars engaging in interdisciplinary research have well acknowledged the importance of exploring Gen Zs' behavioral patterns and decision-making separate to other demographic cohorts, as in various occasions different than usual theorizations emerge from empirical research. In the field of tourism management and marketing, some work has been recently published trying to decode how Gen Zers choose, plan, experience, and communicate their involvement either as tourists or professionals of the tourism sector. Nevertheless, there is still a lack of Gen Z research across the different branches of tourism sector (e.g., accommodation/hospitality, restaurants, aviation/airliners, and other means of transportation), attractions/events, and tourism information services), and with respect to the various managerial disciplines (e.g., from digital marketing to human resource management and entrepreneurship).

Therefore, this is the first book offering a collection of selected topics aiming to better understanding how Gen Zers shape as tourists and lead as managers in the global tourism sector of our times. This should be of interest to managers, scholars, and students interested in acquiring a more concrete knowledge on Gen Zers' crucial role in the marketing and managing of tourism-related services.

The editorial team would like to thank very much all the authors contributing to this book, and Palgrave Macmillan publishers for their invaluable support in materializing this publication.

We wish you all find this as a useful companion and reference point in the new world of digital natives/Gen Zers.

Bristol, UK
Wolverhampton, UK
Orlando, FL, USA
Wolverhampton, UK
December 2020

Nikolaos Stylos
Roya Rahimi
Bendegul Okumus
Sarah Williams

Introduction

Generation Z (Gen Z), also known as Post-Millennials, the iGeneration, or the Homeland Generation, is the demographic cohort following Generation Y also called 'The Millennial Generation'. Gen Y has been the subject of much research, the next generation, Generation Z is still an underexplored issue. This generation has evolved in an environment increasingly permeated by ICT and can be defined as a hyper-connected generation (Haddouche & Salomone, 2018). There are no precise dates for when this cohort starts or ends; demographers and researchers typically use starting birth years ranging from the mid-1990s to early 2000s and ending birth years ranging from the late 2000s to early 2010s (Williams & Page, 2011). For this book, we define generation Z as a group of individuals born during the same temporal period of the time (mid-1990s to the late 2000) in which they shared unique events created by their common age situation in history. Generation Z is growing up in a world intertwined with new technologies, internet, smartphones, video games, and screens. They live ubiquitously because they are hyper-connected and their playing field is global. They can start a video game with their neighbor and pursue it with another player on the other side of the planet (Haddouche & Salomone, 2018). Generation Z consists of the youth and young adults, i.e., they are our youngest consumers, students, colleagues, constituents, voters, and neighbors. Being able to better understand who they are and how they understand the world is essential for being able to effectively work with, support, and lead them.

Hospitality and tourism is the second largest industry in the world and is a driver of job growth and economic prosperity, accounting for 1 in 10 jobs worldwide. In 2019, Travel & Tourism directly supported 330 million jobs (WTTC, 2020). The direct, indirect, and induced contribution of travel and tourism is US$ 8.9 trillion to the world GDP (i.e., 10.3% of world GDP), US$1.7 trillion visitor exports, and US$948 billion in capital investments (WTTC, 2020). As Gen Z individuals are the future employees and consumers of tourism services, demographic changes can affect tourism directly or indirectly in various ways. Direct impacts relate to demand (volume and structure) and the labor market (number of workers and their qualification) while the indirect impacts relate to jobs within the tourism industry, and tourism services (Robinson & Schänzel, 2019). Gen Z tourists are often presented as mastering computer science and ICT and are described as difficult to retain. This young generation has prescribing power and expect a great deal from their travels and for them, tourism is at the same time a moment of conviviality, of socialization, of implication, and of empowerment. They are not only influencing consumption patterns, but also bring their values to work life, thus changing the attitudes toward the employee–employer relationship and how work is being done.

Although the literature exploring how Gen Zers perceive, engage, and link to tourism and hospitality services steadily grows during the last few years, a book that would set strong foundations on both the managerial and marketing aspects is actually missing from the bibliography. As Gen Zers may hold various roles in the tourism economy—i.e., as visitors, guests, consumers, employees, and entrepreneurs—trying to encapsulate individuals' aspirations, expectations, preferences, and behaviors would offer key insights and improve our understanding to the important contributions they make to this sector.

Consequently, through a collection of twelve chapters that are split into two sections, this book offers key insights into numerous aspects of the management and marketing of the hospitality and tourism industry with respect to Generation Z.

The management section of the book consists of four chapters. In Chapter 1, Digital Natives Leading the World: Paragons and Values of Generation Z, the authors aimed to understand the characteristics and the details of the ways Gen Z members are acting as social influencers. The study also casts light on the value systems and leadership styles of generation Z. Recent examples and paragons of Gen Z have also been discussed to provide insights to the organizations on ways to manage their workforce. In Chapter 2, Mejia and Pinto provide a comprehensive view of all five-generation cohorts, i.e., Traditionalists, Baby boomers, Gen X, Gen Y, and Gen Z, who contribute to the development of tourism and hospitality through a variety of managerial roles in their respective organizations. After discussing basic characteristics for each cohort, the authors compare these five generations by delineating their contribution to the work environment, revealing important managerial aspects for the tourism and hospitality industry. Finally, a set of strategies are provided, aiming at solutions for successful knowledge transfer and engagement toward enhanced intergenerational relationships within organizations and across the tourism and hospitality industry. In Chapter 3, Generation Z's career path in Tourism Entrepreneurship is presented, and the authors discuss the role of tourism entrepreneurs who concentrate more on their quality of life while living in their desired destination. Similar to other studies which classified tourism entrepreneurs as growth-oriented, this chapter states that new generations are changing their mindsets from lifestyle entrepreneurs to growth-oriented entrepreneurs. It is also stated that Gen Z entrepreneurs are not locked into a traditional corporate mindset, they have advance technological knowledge, and they are risk-takers with strong leadership abilities. It examines entrepreneurship paths for Gen Z across four sections. The first part of the chapter provides some information about tourism entrepreneurship. The second part discusses the role of a person as an entrepreneur and as an intrapreneur within the tourism industry concept. The third part examines the details about Gen Z's characteristics, lifestyle, and business choices. The final part explains the question of 'Will Gen Z prefer to be an entrepreneur or an intrapreneur in the tourism industry?'. In Chapter 4, Olson and Ro discuss Generation Z tourists and their perceptions of well-being within the context of hospitality and tourism experiences, focusing on the following areas of well-being: physical, mental/health, social, technology, and environmental. Throughout the chapter, examples and implications are provided for hospitality and tourism practitioners who are navigating the complexities of an emerging cohort of tourists.

The marketing section of the book consists of eight chapters. Starting from Chapter 5, Kamenidou, Vassilikopoulou, and Priporas, explore and critically discuss the tourist behavior of Generation Z cohort. The authors discuss that as independent travellers, Gen Zers are active during their trip and get involved in many activities. Their key motivations to travel include among others socialization, escape from the everyday routine, and gaining a unique and memorable experience that they could share with their peers (e.g., in social media). They also mention that Gen Zers, as family tourists, enjoy being engaged in physical activities and having fun. Thus, tourism providers could include such activities when targeting family vacations, whereas unique cultural and sports events could also be attractive for Gen Zers who travel independently. In Chapter 6, Gen Z tourists' involvement with smart devices is discussed with the focus being on the technology acceptance of this generation, as they tend to use smart devices and applications in all their activities, thus forming an important target group for the future of the tourism sector. The authors refer to the technology Gen Zers use in light of the current advances in smart devices and applications and related tourism experiences. The effect of smart devices and applications on the tourism experience of the Z generation is scrutinized by taking into consideration the use of pre-travel technologies, on-site technologies, and post-travel technologies in the tourism sector. Moreover, the tourism experiences of the Z generation are examined and their possible effects are evaluated within the framework of digitalization of the device and applications such as AR, NFC, Wearable technologies, QR codes, and IoT (internet of things). In Chapter 7, Barbe and Neuburger critically discuss influencer marketing and the effects of digital influencers on Generation Z followers and the implications for the tourism and hospitality industry. The authors exemplify influencer marketing as an effective way for reaching and persuading Gen Z individuals across the specific sectors of the hospitality and tourism industry. By reviewing the latest literature in tourism destinations, hospitality, events & festivals, and transportation, Barbe and Neuburger provide a state-of-the-art review of academic publications, analyze case studies, and highlight key points of implementing influencer marketing for Gen Z for these sectors. Finally, recommendations and managerial implications are offered for how to best leverage the power of digital influencers to the benefit of this growing market. In Chapter 8, Le and Arcodia, by using an online survey, investigate Generation Z's perceptions of safety, security, and risks on cruise ships. The findings highlight this market is concerned about cruise-related accidents, terrorism, piracy and crime, and motion sickness, and to a lesser extent about infection outbreaks and sexually transmissible infections. The findings suggest significant implications of how cruise operators can develop policies, customize on-board mitigation strategies, and develop marketing communications to fulfil this market's demand. In Chapter 9, the new foodie generation: Gen Z, Kılıç, Bekar, and Yozukmaz discuss food-related behaviors and preferences of this generation. Although the term 'foodie' has been recently promoted by popular culture and then gastronomy literature, as a niche market, foodies have to be studied from a theory-based perspective in terms of market research. The authors state that Gen Z foodies are necessary for marketing activities, because they will change food and beverage industry and thus tourism industry with their technology addiction. As a result, the foodie behaviors and characteristics of Generation Z are explained and discussed in detail and some practical implications are suggested. In Chapter 10, Lee, Chen, and Chan examine Gen Z tourists' perceptions on patronizing street food in Hong Kong. A questionnaire was distributed and a total of 161 valid samples were collected from Chinese tourists and Western tourists. Factor analysis, series of independent sample t-tests, and chi-square tests were conducted. The study identified five factors: etic destination image, local emersion, e-WOM, emic food characteristics, and safety/hygiene. Further investigation revealed no significant difference between both groups of respondents based on the five factors.

The chi-square results suggest that Chinese Gen Zs are more knowledgeable and receptive to patronize street food in Hong Kong. Implications for promoting street food for the future development of Hong Kong food tourism are discussed. Then, in Chapter 11, Raggiotto and Scarpi propose a theoretical conceptualization and offer theoretical and managerial insights into Gen Z individuals' engagement with action sports tourism events. A very comprehensive demonstration of the relevant thematic tourism field is provided, a model is proposed, and empirical evidence is offered about Gen Z tourists' intention to revisit and repeat attendance of this type of event. The influence of key behavioral constructs on Gen Z's relevant behavioral aspects are tested, and managerial insights may advance academics' and sport tourism managers' understanding and planning, respectively, of strengthening this type of tourism area. Finally, in Chapter 12, Penny Walters sets the foundations and presents the latest on Ethical Consumerism, focusing on Generation Z consumers. In addition to defining ethical consumerism and relevant theoretical underpinnings, Walters provides great coverage of the various types of it. She also summarizes the role of Generation Z tourists in promoting ethical consumerism in the UK tourism and hospitality industry. Finally, the author offers managerial recommendations to governments, DMOs, and private tourism organizations on how to best leverage the power of ethical consumerism in light of the COVID-19 pandemic crisis, given the particular behavioral characteristics, attitudes, trends, preferences, and aspirations of Generation Z tourists.

Nikolaos Stylos, Ph.D.
Roya Rahimi, Ph.D.
Bendegul Okumus, Ph.D.
Sarah Williams

References

Haddouche, H., & Salomone, C. (2018). Generation Z and the tourist experience: Tourist stories and use of social networks. *Journal of Tourism Futures*, *4*(1), 69–79.

Robinson, V., & Schanzel, H. (2019). A tourism inflex: Generation Z travel experiences. *Journal of Tourism Futures, 5*(2), 127–141.

Williams, K. C., & Page, R. A. (2011). Marketing to the generations. *Journal of Behavioral Studies in Business, 3*(1), 37–53.

WTTC. (2020). *Economic impact reports.* Retrieved from https://wttc.org/Research/Economic-Impact, on October 29, 2020.

Contents

Part I   Management Section

**1 Digital Natives Leading the World: Paragons
and Values of Generation Z**   3
Rohan Bhalla, Pinaz Tiwari, and Nimit Chowdhary

**2 Generation Z and Managing Multiple Generational
Cohorts Simultaneously in Tourism and Hospitality**   25
Cynthia Mejia and João Pinto

**3 Generation Z and Tourism Entrepreneurship:
Generation Z's Career Path in the Tourism Industry**   53
Senem Yazici and Reyhan Arslan Ayazlar

**4 Generation Z and Their Perceptions of Well-Being
in Tourism**   101
Eric D. Olson and Heejung Ro

xvi   Contents

Part II   Marketing Section

5   New Sheriff in Town? Discovering Generation Z as Tourists   121
Irene (Eirini) Kamenidou, Aikaterini Vassilikopoulou, and Constantinos-Vasilios Priporas

6   Gen Z Tourists and Smart Devices   141
Serap Ozdemir-Guzel and Yonca Nilay Bas

7   Generation Z and Digital Influencers in the Tourism Industry   167
Danielle Barbe and Larissa Neuburger

8   Generation Z: Young People's Perceptions of Cruising Safety, Security and Related Risks   193
Truc H. Le and Charles Arcodia

9   The New Foodie Generation: Gen Z   223
Burhan Kılıç, Aydan Bekar, and Nisan Yozukmaz

10   Perceptions of Gen Z Tourists on Street Food in Hong Kong   249
Derrick Lee, Tingzhen Chen, and Wilco Chan

11   Generation Z Active Sports Tourism: A Conceptual Framework and Analysis of Intention to Revisit   281
Francesco Raggiotto and Daniele Scarpi

12   Are Generation Z Ethical Consumers?   303
Penny Walters

Index   327

Editors and Contributors

About the Editors

Dr. Nikolaos Stylos is Senior Lecturer/Associate Professor of Marketing, Postgraduate Research Director, and 'Innovation & Digitalization' research group Lead at School of Management, University of Bristol, UK. He has also been appointed as Honorary Professor of Hotel Management at Tainan University of Technology, Taiwan. He has a Ph.D. in Business Administration (Marketing), an M.B.A, an M.Sc. in Mechanical Reliability Engineering, and a Post Graduate Diploma in Mechanical Engineering. His research projects focus on decision-making in tourism marketing, consumer behavior, digital marketing, Industry 4.0 management applications, Big Data and AI, and environmental management. Dr. Stylos has published in various world-leading journals including *Tourism Management, Journal of Travel Research, Psychology & Marketing, Journal of Business Research, International Journal of Contemporary Hospitality Management, Computers in Human Behavior, Technological Forecasting and Social Change, and Journal of Cleaner*

Production. Dr. Stylos has served as a professional management and technical consultant for more than a decade.

Dr. Roya Rahimi is a Reader in Marketing and Leisure Management. She teaches across tourism, hospitality, and marketing subject areas and supervises undergraduate/postgraduate dissertations as well as Ph.D. students. Her research interests are Innovation, Big data, CRM, Organizational Culture, Gender Equality, and Tourism Higher Education. Her research work has been published in top-tier journals such as *Annals of Tourism Research, Journal of Tourism and Hospitality Research, Journal of Travel & Tourism Marketing, International Journal of Contemporary Hospitality Management, and Anatolia.* Her work has been also presented at various international conferences and appears in book chapters released by Routledge, CABI, Emerald, and IGI. She has been published in a variety of languages. She sits on the editorial board of different leading journals and her industry experience includes seven years working in the hotel industry in a number of international hotels in various countries.

Dr. Bendegul Okumus has an undergraduate degree in Nutrition and Home Economics, master's and Ph.D. degrees in Food Hygiene and Technology, and a second master's degree in hospitality and Tourism Management. She worked for the Florida Department of Health in Orange County WIC program, which is a federally funded nutrition program for Women, Infants, and Children. She also has work experience in the hospitality industry, particularly in food preparation, food services, and event management areas. Her primary teaching areas include Nutrition Concepts and Issues in Food Services, International Cuisine and Culture, Sanitation in the Food Service Industry, and Health and Wellness in Hospitality and Tourism. Her research focuses on food safety, eating behavior and eating habits, food and culinary tourism, food waste and health & wellness in hospitality and tourism. Dr. Okumus has worked in multidisciplinary research teams, secured and completed research grants. She has authored/co-authored numerous academic journal articles, conference presentations, book and book chapters.

Ms. Sarah Williams is Associate Director of the Business School at the University of Wolverhampton. Following a career in public relations and marketing communications spanning 11 years, Sarah has been teaching and researching in the area of public relations, marketing, and digital marketing communications for over 16 years. She has previously worked for international marketing agencies, including McCann Erickson and IMG Connect. This practical experience underpins her approach to the teaching and research of public relations, advertising, and marketing. Her research interests include the impact of social media on PR practice, as well as investigating professional practice in public relations. She has recently contributed chapters to 'Experiencing Public Relations' by Bridgen and Verčič (2017) and 'Promotional Strategies and New Service Opportunities in Emerging Economies' by Nadda, Dadwal, and Rahimi (2017).

Contributors

Professor Charles Arcodia is an experienced tertiary educator having taught and researched in the tertiary sector for over 20 years. He has held leadership positions in a variety of educational and business service contexts. Before he joined the higher education sector he was directly involved in industry in a variety of organizational and management roles. His primary areas of teaching and research interest are event management, tourism and hospitality education, and various tourism and related cultural issues. He is currently the Deputy Head of the Department of Tourism, Sport and Hotel Management at Griffith University, Australia.

Dr. Reyhan Arslan Ayazlar received her Ph.D. from Adnan Menderes University in 2015. She is an Associate Professor in the Department of Tourism Management at Mugla Sitki Kocman University. Her research interests include tourism marketing and tourist behavior. She has published studies focusing on tourist experience, local residents' role in the tourism industry, and alternative tourism types such as rural tourism, festivals, VFR tourism, and wildlife. She also has national and international conference papers in Turkish and English.

Dr. Danielle Barbe is a Lecturer in Digital Marketing at Newcastle Business School, Northumbria University. Danielle earned her Ph.D. in Tourism, Hospitality, and Event Management and a minor in Communications from the University of Florida in Spring 2020. Danielle's research examines the capabilities of digital communication tools in the context of tourism, with the goal of developing theoretically driven and empirically tested strategies that incorporate web, social, and mobile technologies to enhance the communications efforts between tourists and tourism suppliers.

Dr. Yonca Nilay Bas graduated from Istanbul University, Faculty of Economics, Department of Business Administration (2010). Received an M.A. degree (2012) and a Ph.D. (2020) from Istanbul University Institute of Social Sciences, Department of Business Administration. She is currently a Lecturer at Istanbul University-Cerrahpaşa, Business Administration program. Basic working areas: Strategic Marketing and Brand Management, Consumer Behaviour, Customer Relationship Management.

Dr. Aydan Bekar is an Associate Professor in the Department of Food and Beverage Management at the Faculty of Tourism at Mugla Sıtkı Koçman University, Turkey. She completed her Ph.D. in the Department of Education of Household Economics and Dietetics at Gazi University, Ankara, Turkey. Her research interests cover fields of gastronomy, tourism marketing, and food and beverage management. She has published many articles as well as books or book chapters on menu planning in food and beverage enterprises, popular culture and gastronomy and foodies.

Mr. Rohan Bhalla is a Senior Research Fellow, pursuing his Ph.D. from Department of Tourism and Hospitality Management, Faculty of Humanities and Languages, Jamia Millia Islamia (a central university). He is a Gold Medallist in PGDM (International Business) from Indian Institute of Tourism and Travel Management and has completed his graduation in Business Administration from Jiwaji University, India. He has also completed an advanced course in research from Mid-Sweden University, Sweden. He has academic experience of two years at all levels of imparting education, including his association with Indian Institute of

Management, Indore. He has contributed to nine publications, including chapters in edited books and research articles in National and International Journals including *ABDC indexed Journal*. His area of expertise is qualitative research, and he works in a multidisciplinary approach, particularly in real-time social sciences projects. His interest lies in Philosophy of Science, Spirituality, Transformational, and Rural Tourism studies. He also takes an interest in HRM, Behavioural Sciences, Social Psychology, Communication, and Personality Development Programs.

Dr. Wilco Chan is the Visiting Professor of Institute for Tourism Studies (IFT), Macao. Besides teaching and research, Prof Chan is the Vice Director of Global Training Center for Tourism Education and Training under IFT and handles the forums plus workshops referred by United Nation WTO and Greater Bay Area's Initiatives. Prior to joining the teaching career, Prof. Chan had worked as manager in international hotel chains and had been stationed in Shanghai, Beijing, Guilin, and Guangzhou. His teaching specialism covers the subjects—Hospitality Technology, Environmental/CSR Management, Hotel Planning & Design, Consultancy Projects, Financial Management and Food Supply Chain at postgraduate level. He had also served as panel chairman/member on behalf of HKCAAVQ for accrediting academic or vocational programs.

Dr. Tingzhen Chen is a Senior Lecturer in Tourism at James Cook University, Australia. She studied at Xi'an International Studies University in China and then at James Cook University, Australia, where she completed an Honours degree and her Ph.D. Her research interests include tourism seasonality and the experiences and behaviors of the Chinese market. She has also published in areas of marketing and economics related to China.

Dr. Nimit Chowdhary is an Engineer, M.B.A., and Ph.D. in Management. He is Professor and ex-Head of the Department of Tourism and Hospitality Management at Jamia Millia Islamia who has more than 27 years of academic experience. Of which close he has been a full professor for 14 years in India, China, and Mexico. He is a recipient of AICTE Career Award for Young Teachers; SIDA Fellowship, Sweden; Guest xxii Editors and Contributors

Scholarship, Sweden; Linnaeus Palme Exchange Programme Grants, Sweden; PIMG Research Excellence Award, Gwalior; Scholars' Grant (EMTM), Erasmus Mundus, Europe among others. Recently he was chosen for prestigious LEAP programme at Oxford University. He has supervised 15 Ph.Ds., authored eight books, edited four books, and contributed more than 125 papers. He has travelled extensively to around 40 countries.

Dr. Irene (Eirini) Kamenidou is Professor of Marketing at International Hellenic University, Greece. She holds a Ph.D. in food marketing and has more than ten years of working experience in the public and private sector on agricultural and food marketing. Her works have been part of various international academic journals and conferences such as *Journal of Business Research* and *International Marketing Review*. Her research interests focus on agricultural and food marketing, tourism, retailing and social marketing. Irene has participated in several EU-funded projects and served as Dean of the Business School at Eastern Macedonia and Thrace Institute of Technology.

Dr. Burhan Kılıç is an Associate Professor and the Head of Department of Food and Beverage Management at the Faculty of Tourism at Mugla Sıtkı Kocman University, Turkey. He completed his Ph.D. in the Department of Tourism Management Education at Gazi University, Ankara, Turkey. His research interests are tourism marketing, food and beverage management, tourist behavior, social media marketing, and gastronomy. He has published or edited many articles, books, and book chapters on dark tourism, gastronomy tourism, menu planning, marketing in tourism, and consumer behavior.

Dr. Truc H. Le is a recent Ph.D. graduate from the Department of Tourism, Sport and Hotel Management at Griffith University, Australia. She was awarded Griffith University Medal in Bachelor of Business (Hons I) in 2016. Her research focus includes risks and risk perceptions, cruise tourism, authenticity, user-generated content analytics, and machine learning. She has published in top international tourism and hospitality journals such as *Tourism Management, International Journal* *of Hospitality Management*, *Current Issues in Tourism*, and *Tourism Recreation Research*.

Dr. Derrick Lee is a Senior Lecturer in the Academic Division, Singapore Institute of Management, with interests in destination marketing, gastronomy, integrated resorts, and tourism management. He holds a Ph.D. from James Cook University, Townsville. He has published in areas of tourism management and casino tourism. His teaching specialism covers the areas of tourism, hospitality, events, and business management.

Dr. Cynthia Mejia is an Associate Professor and the Interim Chair of the Department of Foodservice and Lodging Management at the University of Central Florida Rosen College of Hospitality Management. Dr. Mejia's industry experience is in F&B and hotel operations management, primarily working for luxury brands both in the USA and in Singapore. Her publications and areas of research include human resource management, cross-cultural organizational management, technology acceptance in hospitality organizations, green facilities management, and hospitality education.

Ms. Larissa Neuburger is a Ph.D. Candidate and Graduate Teaching Assistant at the Department of Tourism, Hospitality, and Event Management at the University of Florida. Her research interests are in the area of Technology in Tourism and in particular immersive technologies such as Augmented and Virtual Technology as well as tourist experience.

Dr. Eric D. Olson is currently an Associate Professor, Program Director for the Event Management Program, and Event Management Director of Graduate Education at the Department of Apparel, Events, and Hospitality Management at Iowa State University. His research interests are in the area of LGBT+ tourism and events. His work has been published in *Annals of Tourism Research*, *Tourism Management*, and *Journal of Hospitality Management*.

Dr. Serap Ozdemir-Guzel Graduated from Dokuz Eylul University, Faculty of Business, Department of Tourism Management (English) (2010). Received M.A. degree from Dokuz Eylül University Institute of Social Sciences, Department of Tourism Management (2013), Ph.D.

xxiv   Editors and Contributors

degree from Istanbul University, Institute of Social Sciences, Department of Tourism Management. She is currently a Lecturer at Istanbul University-Cerrahpaşa, Tourism and Hotel Management program. Basic working areas: *Tourism Marketing, Destination Marketing, Tourism Management.*

Mr. João Pinto completed a dual master's degree in hospitality and Tourism Management from ISCTE-IUL in Portugal and UCF Rosen College of Hospitality Management in Orlando, Florida after the conclusion of his bachelor's degree in Management from ISCTE-IUL. While studying at UCF Rosen College, João worked as a graduate research assistant, which allowed him to further develop his knowledge on issues affecting the hospitality and tourism industry, such as multigenerational workforces.

Dr. Constantinos-Vasilios Priporas is a Senior Lecturer in Marketing at Middlesex University Business School, UK. His research interests include consumer behavior and strategic marketing with main emphasis on tourism, retailing, and food. He has published in several international academic journals and conferences, including *Tourism Management, Journal of Travel Research, Journal of Business Research, International Marketing Review, International Journal of Contemporary Hospitality Management, Computers in Human Behavior*. In addition, he co-authored a textbook on *Technology and Innovation for Marketing* and co-edited a book on *Market Sensing*. He is member of several professional bodies and he is editorial board member of the *Journal of Customer Behaviour* and has acted as a guest editor, reviewer, and track chair in academic journals and conferences.

Dr. Francesco Raggiotto is a Research Fellow in Marketing at the Department of Economics and Statistics at the University of Udine, Italy. His current research interests are in consumer behavior and sport management. He has published in *Tourism Management, Journal of Business Research, Journal of Retailing and Consumer Services*, and others.

Dr. Heejung Ro has been a faculty member of UCF's Rosen College of Hospitality Management since 2007. She earned her Doctorate in Hospitality Management from Pennsylvania State University. Her research interests include service encounters in the services marketing and management context, with a focus on customer complaining behavior, service recovery, consumer emotions, and gay and lesbian customers' service evaluations. Her work has been published in the *International Journal of Hospitality Management*, *Journal of Hospitality & Tourism Research*, and *Journal of Business Research*. She teaches Guest Services Management and Research Methods in Hospitality & Tourism.

Dr. Daniele Scarpi is Associate Professor of marketing at the Department of Management at the University of Bologna, Italy. His current research interests are in consumer behavior, decision-making, and retailing. His papers have been published in *Tourism Management*, *Marketing Letters*, *Journal of Retailing*, *Journal of Business Research*, *Journal of Advertising Research*, *Economic Psychology*, *Industrial Marketing Management*, and others.

Ms. Pinaz Tiwari is a Doctoral Researcher in the Department of Tourism and Hospitality in Jamia Millia Islamia, New Delhi, India. She has worked in the tourism sector for two years and gained expertise in customer management. She has done her graduation in Commerce from Delhi University and completed her M.B.A. in Tourism with specialization in International Tourism Business. She looks forward to making a career in teaching and creating a difference in the tourism industry with her research works. Her interest areas are tourists' behavior, tourism marketing, destination management, and tourism education. She has ten publications to her credits including book chapters in edited books published by Routledge, Palgrave Macmillan, IGI Global Edition and Emerald, SCOPUS-listed research articles, and conference papers.

Dr. Aikaterini Vassilikopoulou received her Ph.D. in Marketing from the Athens University of Economics and Business (AUEB). She also holds an M.Sc. in Economic Psychology from the University of Exeter, UK and an M.B.A. from AUEB. For the past 17 years, she has been teaching various marketing courses in higher education. She has also worked as a Marketing Manager in a wine industry company. Her academic work has been published in journals including the *Journal of Business Research*, *The European Journal of Marketing*, *Journal of*

Contemporary Hospitality Management, and The Journal of Consumer Behaviour. She is also the co-author of two books (marketing research and e-marketing).

Dr. Penny Walters is the Unit Director of the Marketing Management and Consumer Behaviour Masters' modules at the University of Bristol, serves on the School of Management Ethics Committee, and is a member of 'staff in attendance' at the University Court. Penny is the Business Studies External Examiner for Cambridge Education Group (CATS) University Foundation Programme (UFP). Penny is a facilitator for 2 'taster' MOOCs: 'Growing as a Manager' (The Chartered Management Institute (CMI)/ OU), and 'The Digital Economy, Selling Through Customer Insight' (OU Faculty of Business & Law). Penny guest lectures internationally in-person and via webinars, and writes articles on a number of topics within genealogy. Penny is the author of Ethical Dilemmas in Genealogy (2019) and The Psychology of Searching (2020) and is the founder of University of Bristol Family History Club (2019), and has designed and run a new online University of Bristol module, Back to the roots: Understanding your history through genealogy research (2020). www.searchmypast.co.uk.

Dr. Senem Yazici received both her M.Sc. and the Ph.D. degree in Tourism Management at the University of Surrey in 2010. Her research area covers entrepreneurship, tourism technology, hotel management, and intrapreneurship in tourism. Dr. Yazici published several articles in academic journals and book chapters related to strategic management, entrepreneurship, and tourism technology. Dr. Yazici is an Assistant Professor in the Department of Tourism Management at the Faculty of Tourism, University of Mugla Sitki Kocman University, Turkey.

Dr. Nisan Yozukmaz is a Researcher in the Department of Tourism Management, Pamukkale University, Turkey. She completed her Ph.D. education in the Department of Tourism Management in Mugla Sıtkı Koçman University, Turkey with a doctoral dissertation on tourism heterotopias and visitors' feeling of being. Her research interests include tourism anthropology, tourism sociology, tourist psychology, tourist behavior, and tourism marketing.

List of Figures

Fig. 6.1	Gen Z tourists' most used application	150
Fig. 6.2	Smart devices usage in pre-travel, on-site, and post-travel	156
Fig. 6.3	Gen Z tourist and smart device usage	159
Fig. 7.1	Timeline of digital influencers	172
Fig. 7.2	Summary of influencer marketing for each hospitality and tourism sector	184
Fig. 8.1	Percentage distributions of overall perceived risk	209
Fig. 11.1	The conceptual model	290
Fig. 11.2	Results of model estimation	293
Fig. 12.1	The recent generations (*Source* The Author)	304

List of Tables

Table 1.1	Generations chronological classification	7
Table 2.1	Generational cohort comparisons and integrated managerial strategies	39
Table 3.1	Tourism entrepreneurs' typologies and definitions	59
Table 3.2	Entrepreneurship vs Intrapreneurship	69
Table 3.3	The rate of stereotypes of the other generations	73
Table 3.4	Generation Y vs. Generation Z	75
Table 3.5	The features and thoughts of Gen Y and Gen Z about business	77
Table 7.1	Classification of digital influencers	173
Table 8.1	The relationship between uncertainty and adverse consequences (adopted from Le and Arcodia 2018)	199
Table 8.2	Construct and selection of its measures	203
Table 8.3	Perceived risk rating	205
Table 8.4	Characteristics of respondents	205
Table 8.5	Perceived safety in selected cruising situations	206
Table 8.6	Means and standard deviations of perceived probability, perceived severity and overall perceived risk	208

xxx **List of Tables**

Table 10.1	Different modes of street food provision in Hong Kong	255
Table 10.2	Demographic characteristics of the respondents ($N = 161$)	259
Table 10.3	Results of the EFA (N = 161 Gen Z Tourists)	260
Table 10.4	Results of independent t-test on five factors between Chinese and Western Gen Z's	265
Table 10.5	Chi-Square results of the 14 HK street food items	266

Part I
Management Section

1

Digital Natives Leading the World: Paragons and Values of Generation Z

Rohan Bhalla, Pinaz Tiwari, and Nimit Chowdhary

Introduction

In the twenty-first century, smart technological advancements, the progression of the globalisation process, and societal transformations have led to the evolution of workplaces globally. Organisations are investing their capital in creating innovative systems based on knowledge management (Riad Shams and Belyaeva 2019). To be effective and efficient, organisations must understand the characteristics, capabilities, and working styles of the people employed with them. This realisation requires an in-depth understanding of the process of massive personnel replacement, known as 'demographic metabolism' (Ryder 1985), to lead

---

R. Bhalla (✉) · P. Tiwari · N. Chowdhary
Department of Tourism and Hospitality Management, Jamia Millia Islamia, New Delhi, India

N. Chowdhary
e-mail: nchowdhary@jmi.ac.in

© The Author(s), under exclusive license to Springer Nature
Switzerland AG 2021
N. Stylos et al. (eds.), *Generation Z Marketing and Management in Tourism and Hospitality*,
https://doi.org/10.1007/978-3-030-70695-1_1

the upcoming generation in the workplaces. Generation Z (alongside with the youngest Generation Alpha) is one of the newest additions in the world which will be entering the workforce by mid-2020 and 2021. Their attitudes, lifestyle, thought process, working styles, and behaviours are undoubtedly different compared to the previous generations (Arsenault et al. 2008). These differences are valuable because they are idiosyncratic and originate from different values and mind-sets of people (Zemke et al. 2000). Due to these differences, the existing leadership and corporations would require a shift in the work culture. Therefore, Murphy et al. (2004) suggest acknowledging the gaps between different generations and adopting suitable management practices.

Born in the late 1990s and raised in 2000s, Gen Zers are bringing the most significant generational shift in the world. Generation Z will fill the gap created after the retirement of 30 million ageing baby boomers, also termed as youth bubble. The significance of developing the understanding of Generation Z was reported by Bloomberg which emphasised that the population of Generation Z is 32% of the world's population and they will outcast the millennials in the coming years (Petsko 2018). Currently completing their education, Generation Z is going to form a significant part of the workforce across the world in a few years' time. As studied by Deloitte (2017), Generation Z is going to be 20% of the workforce by the beginning of the year 2020. However, the new cohort of the workforce will set forth a decent number of challenges to the existing leaders and managers working in different sectors (Tulgan 2013). Further, it is observed that Gen Z people are more tech-savvy, efficient with machines, and highly ambitious. Thus, the lack of understanding may prevent organisations from capitalising on the strengths of the youngest generation (Arsenault et al. 2008).

The very base of the differences between Generation Z and the previous generations exists in the developments made between the 1990s and 2000s. The twenty-first century predominantly has experienced advanced technology and data loaded information in every sphere of business and non-business life. Further, the rise in the speed of the internet gave access to vital information to Gen Z at the initial stages of their lives. Bateh (2018) has rightly considered this modern era as an 'Information era' wherein the people are surrounded by innovative technology and embracing automation, machine learning, virtual reality, robotics, and artificial intelligence. Owing to the technological advancement and convenience of getting the required information on smartphones, Bako (2018) has characterised Gen Z as technically proficient, and multi-cultural with the right educational qualifications. Owing to their higher technical familiarity, Gen Z is also known as I-Gen, App Generation, Centenaries (Gardner and Davis 2013), and even digital natives.

The Tourism and Hospitality sector is one of the critical drivers of economic growth, job opportunities, and economic prosperity as a whole. According to the World Tourism and Travel Council Report in 2019 (WTTC 2019), travel and tourism accounted for 319 million jobs across the world with the global GDP of 10.4%. Due to the involvement of several other sectors like accommodation, entertainment, transportation, etc. the presence of diverse small- and large-scale companies is much evident. With unprecedented growth in the tourism and hospitality industry, more jobs would be created, and thus, the demand for effective leadership emerges. Employee motivation and satisfaction are of the utmost priority for working with Generation Z, as they are more likely to switch their jobs (Ozkan and Solmaz 2015).

Moreover, Bencsik et al. (2016) argued that I-Gen is less optimistic as compared to the previous generations at the workplace. However, Goh and Lee (2018) reported an exception that Gen Z has a positive attitude about working in the hospitality and tourism industry due to travelling prospects. Undoubtedly, the emergence of Generation Z is the next important thing from a societal transformation point of view. Even though a lot of studies drawn a comparison of diverse generations (Baby boomers, X, Y, and Z) and their related working styles (Zemke et al. 2000; Berkup 2014; Bako 2018), fewer studies have discussed suitable leadership styles and value system to be adopted while working with the newest generation. Since different generation requires different leadership styles (Al-Asfour and Lettau 2014), the authors focus on highlighting values and ideals for justifying the suitable leadership style to be adopted while managing a team of people belonging to the next generation.

The Emergence of Generation Z

The study of generations is a multidisciplinary approach, and generations are decided based on their birth years. To comprehend the emergence of Generation Z and their characteristics, we need to understand the term "generation," the chronological order of the generations and the features of each generation which makes them distinct from each other. While describing a generation, Ryder (1985) stated that a generational cohort is "*a group of people who have experienced the same events during the same period.*" A birth cohort includes individuals who age together, have similar life experiences in the future, which will shape their lives, and each cohort differentiates from another (Hung et al. 2008).

The generation theory implicitly states that one can generalise the group differences to the average group level of each generation to create a better understanding of the personality traits and profile of the individuals of a specific generation (Twenge et al. 2010). As described by various researchers, the generational classes differ from each other about the varied historical events and their consequential impacts. The distribution of ages between two cohorts differ, primarily because of migration and mortality (Ryder 1985). In the majority of the generational theories and research, the main distinctive characteristic is years of birth(Strauss and Howe 1991; Berenda and Mannheim 1953; Arsenault et al. 2008; Zemke et al. 2000). For instance, there are four significant generations recognised by Zemke et al. (2000), namely: Veterans (1925–1945), Baby Boomers (1946–1960), Generation X (1961–1980), Generation Y (1981–1995), and Generation Z (1996–2010). However, researchers on generational studies have relied on a birth date along with demographic traits to describe the characteristics of a specific generation (Cogin 2012). Parry and Urwin (2011) argue that age effects might not be mutually exclusive. Pragmatic observations are indeed done based on age groups.

Nevertheless, the authors stated that similar personality traits might occur concerning the end of one generation (say, generation Y) and the start of another generation (say, Generation Z). It means that a person born in 1994 of Generation Y may illustrate similar characteristics of those born in 1995 in Generation Z, also termed as cross-over effect (Ryder 1985). The widely accepted age group for Generation Z is people who are born from 1995 till 2010 (Berkup 2014; Goh and Lee 2018; Bako 2018; Randstad 2017) and are children of Generation X.

Interestingly, the essence of different definitions of generations is based on a specific period in which they are born, raised and usually share similar characteristics and viewpoints as they carry the memories and experiences which are affected by events that happened in that period. However, the debate of the chronological sequence of the years falling under every generation, setting their lower and upper limits continues (Berkup 2014). One more line was marked in another classification which sets apart Generation Y, popularly known as Millennials, from Generation Z. The cut of the line was drawn after extensive study of the content in 1998. The line segregated Generation Y and Z by stating that anyone born between 1981 and 1996 is known as Millennials and the people born after 1997 and onward should be considered under Generation Z. The very concept of generations stands on the foundation of the period. However, there is no conclusion or formula to determine how long the period of one generation should be fixed (Dimock 2019). Although, based on the experts' views and assessment of the historical events, these generations have been considered and reviewed differently in both national and international diaspora. However, Berkup (2014) used the following classification (Table 1.1).

A lot of studies have indicated that Digital Natives are different from Generation X and Generation Y in various aspects (Shatto and Erwin 2016; Betz 2019; Berkup 2014; Bako 2018; Arsenault et al. 2008; Zemke et al. 2000; Bencsik et al. 2016). For instance, Bako (2018) found that Generation Z gives importance to attributes like risk-taking, career-oriented, self-sacrificing, normative, and secretive ineffective leadership,

Table 1.1 Generations chronological classification

Generation name	Chronological generation classification
Traditionalists	1900–1945
Baby Boomers	1946–1964
Generation X	1965–1980
Generation Y	1981–1995
Generation Z	1996–2010

which are considerably different from the attributes preferred by Generation X. Similarly, Bencsik et al. (2016) noted that people of Generation Z rely more on simple techniques of learning, especially which comes under the realm of their interest areas. In contrast, Generation Y is quick to develop their skills related to Information Technology. Indeed, generation Z will be the largest cohort of consumers; thus, market researchers, industries, and academicians are putting a lot of emphasis on digging the information related to them. Any information, characteristics, traits, values, behavior, and trends related to Generation Z are being extracted, used, and treated as business intelligence (Hamed 2017). The reason behind keeping Generation Z at the focal point is the immense potential and opportunities that it carries for the world. Gathering information about Generation Z will enable the industries to develop marketing strategies to unveil and harness the opportunity of one of the most significant sections of the population.

Characteristics of Generation Z

Every generational cohort is heterogeneous (Ryder 1985), and so are digital natives. They are curious, hardworking, careful, and futuristic. Gen Z is unique in the sense that they develop relationships with people over the social media platforms more comfortably as compared to the predecessor cohort. The obsession of Instagram, YouTube, Snapchat, Tumblr, and many other social media networks amongst Generation Z makes them believers in virtual reality. Furthermore, Gardner and Davis (2013) called Generation Z, 'The App Generation' mainly because of their ability and understanding of the latest technology such as smartphones, laptops, a variety of applications, and tablets. The rise of mobile apps and social media is popular amongst the newest generation across the world. The authors also consider this generation as "digital natives" as Gen Z is born in the information era where technology is present in every sphere of their lives along with the free flow of information. They may not think of a world without technology, especially their smartphones.

Digital natives view educational qualifications merely as a task, which is a pre-requisite to get a good job and reasonable remuneration. Levine and Dean (2012) reveal that nowadays, youth is career-focused, and their behaviour is more rational and pragmatic. As the newest generation tends to become more pragmatic, they are likely to move towards being individualistic and less community-minded. Features like individualism, seclusion, and non-participation are shared amongst the members of Generation Z (Gardner and Davis 2013; Twenge et al. 2010). From the workplace point of view, the research conducted by Deloitte (2017) revealed that Gen Z appreciates honesty and integrity. Thus, based on previous literature, the following characteristics of Gen Z are identified:

1. **Diverse:** One of the primary characteristics that make digital natives different from other generations is their openness to diversity (Dimock 2019; Al-Asfour and Lettau 2014; Shatto and Erwin 2016). Diversity in terms of culture, nationalities, opinions, and working patterns and Bateh (2018) defines this characteristic as Pluralistic. The study conducted by Pew Research, as mentioned in Dimock (2019), reported that the majority of bi-racial and multi-racial children are found in Generation Z. They are the fastest-growing in the United States of America as well as other countries. The report also found that exposure to various cultures and people make them open-minded and accepting as compared to Generation Y. This attribute of Generation Z can be utilised constructively by organisations to create a pool of individuals and promote creativity at the workplace.

2. **Exposed to Media:** Another essential characteristic of digital natives is exposure to media. The generation has been brought up with facilities like the internet, Wi-Fi, and high broadband cellular services (Dimock 2019; Shatto and Erwin 2016). This generation has grown up in a technical environment which makes them exposed to media at a larger scale in comparison with previous generations. Previous research on continuous exposure to media has shown that the attention span of Generation Z is also low when compared to Generation Y, for instance, the people in this generational cohort spend an average of 09 hours a day on their mobile phones (Pew Research Centre, 2014). According to the Kaiser Family Foundation, the youth of

Generation Z uses the internet more than any other previous generation, and they play a crucial role in generating content on social media platforms.

3. **Self-driven learners**: Digital natives are considered the most educated workforce generation (Bako 2018) along with advanced technical knowledge. Shatto and Erwin (2016) found that Generation Z is self-directed learners who thrive on technology at a higher level. Similarly, Betz (2019) also noticed that digital natives preferred the informal style of training at the workplace and want to take charge of their future (Bateh 2018). It is common to find people in Generation Z who have learned various skills through the internet (probably from YouTube).

4. **Lack of Consequential Thinking**: Researchers have found that, though collaborative and hardworking (Bateh 2018), digital natives lack the aspects of critical thinking and the ability to validate information. Bencsik et al. (2016) also noted that this generation lacks consequential thinking process which means that they might cross-verify the source of information due to the availability of the internet but are unable to think substantially.

5. **Accustomed to Immediate feedback**: The new generation has always been connected socially in the virtual world. Born into the world of 'likes', Generation Z is keen to get approval and feedback from people in their circle. Be it asking about which trip to take during the Christmas holidays or more straightforward questions like choosing between long hair and short hair, Generation Z appreciates opinions and takes actions accordingly. Therefore, organisations have to adapt to provide immediate feedback while choosing to work with this generation. For instance, rejecting an interviewee without giving proper feedback is a common practice amongst human resource managers which might not be sufficient for this generation.

6. **Entrepreneurial Spirit:** Digital natives are creative because of exposure to media. With this creativity, various studies have found that people from this generation have an entrepreneurial spirit and mindset (Bencsik et al. 2016; Bako 2018). Digital natives are curious to learn skills related to business development, analytics, and communication skills (Montana and Petit 2011). Organisations should

comprehend their entrepreneurial spirit and develop them through training so that they contribute towards the company along with the personal growth of their skills.

7. **Virtual Teamwork and Superficial Relationships:** Due to exposure to media, digital natives feel comfortable in creating virtual experiences and relationships (Bencsik et al. 2016). While the last generation was using technology and social media in particular for work, Generation Z stepped ahead and fell in love with virtual reality. The usage of smartphones was rapidly increased after the year 2000. For Generation Z, the creation, usage, and up-gradation of smartphones came as blessings whereby they can write and edit documents, create and post pictures and video within few seconds and thus, these social media networks became a place of comfort and pleasure for them (Williams 2015).

Emergence of Influencers

With the upsurge of technology and social media platforms, a new concept, namely 'Influencers', has recently emerged in the twenty-first century. As the term suggests, influencers are people or individuals that can influence the purchasing decisions of others. Generally, identified by the number of followers they have, influencers are known for their talent, knowledge, or position. Long before the word influencer was introduced, young entrepreneurs and individuals played a social role by creating trends. Ever since the new generation, i.e. Generation Z, has come up with creative content, growth in the use of this term is evident on social media platforms and the internet. Due to greater exposure to social media, internet, and mobiles, digital natives are hyper-creative and comfortable in gathering and cross-referencing various sources of information. Young people, and especially the members of Generation Z, have a tremendous potent influence on people of all incomes, genders, and ages. With an increase in global connectivity and growth in the number of influencers, consumption of services is likely to follow a pattern, and socio-economic differences would reduce further. The term 'travel influencers' has come into use recently, although there has been no academic definition of the concept. A few similar terms like fashion influencer, health influencer, social influencers have also been used on the majority of social platforms offline and online. According to various internet sources, a travel influencer is an individual or group of individuals responsible for generating content and promoting destinations, services, and niche travel products by posting it on websites through their leverage on social media platforms. A travel influencer is not necessarily a person with a high number of followers or a celebrity figure, but a person who can relate with a broader public and audience through his/her creative and quality content. Digital natives have played a key role in contributing to useful and compelling content to draw the attention of people around the globe.

In the present era of constant change and innovation, influencers play an essential role in not only influencing a larger audience but also assuming social responsibility by representing what people like and dislike. Being an influencer is indeed a challenging task because it requires an individual or a team to post fresh content frequently. Therefore, travel influencers help in assisting a travel organisation or a hotel in increasing its brand profile by posting videos and photographs of their products and services. Their content is generally related to travelling, showcasing the culture and unique character of the destination travelled, monuments, nature, people, food, property or local houses in which they stay, etc. Usually partnering with travel agencies, destination management organisations, hotels, and travel agencies, travel influencers use blogs and social media to express their physical experience at the destination travelled. Business organisations can also collaborate with travel influencers to promote their products amongst the broader public at a reasonable cost. The primary purpose of these influencers is to influence and inspire the people to take up trips to those destinations and indulge in experiential travelling by participating in tourism-related activities. As per a report on travel influencers (Life as a Butterfly 2018), it is found that women are more likely to be influencers than men. However, male travel influencers earn six times more than female influencers. The report also revealed that people carry out this activity as a part-time hobby primarily because they enjoy doing it.

Therefore, it is suggested that organisations must recognise the growing trends of travel influencers and provide an opportunity for digital natives to work from different locations. A similar concept of digital nomadism could prove helpful for companies in retaining the employees of Generation Z for the long term.

Generation Z Leaders

As studied by Arsenault et al. (2008), different generational cohorts have their unique preferences for leaders and their leadership styles. For instance, Millennials preferred leaders who are 'change-agents' and have the ability to challenge the system and status quo. Conversely, Generation X or Baby boomers have a higher preference for leaders who are compassionate, honest, and care for society. A study conducted by Jim Link of Randstad of North America proposed that Generation Z is better than its predecessors, possesses entrepreneurial attributes, and is less likely to be motivated by the financial aspects of a profession (Schawbel 2014). The technological environment in which they are brought up makes them innovative, more educated, creative, and optimistic that everything is possible. This upbringing gradually develops their ability to cope up in different situations (Corbisiero and Ruspini 2018). In the context of tourism, Generation Z tourists are often budget conscious and without setting a specific destination in their mind (Robinson and Schänzel 2019). Digital natives are likely to bring transformation in the tourism industry. With the individualistic characteristic, the era of mass tourism would end, and young tourists would consider independent trips in the coming years (Stănciulescu et al. 2011). In the Indian context, a few leaders amongst Generation Z have started making an impact.

Akshay Makar Managing Director, Climatenza is a Generation Z innovator and climate entrepreneur. He was also involved in creating sustainable livelihoods through handicrafts during his teenage years. He worked with an India-based e-commerce platform, Handcart.com, wherein several local artisans and rural people sell their handicrafts. Through this, the person, along with the company, can outreach a community and help them sustain a livelihood by selling the authentic crafts to a broader public. While working with the platform, local artisans can eradicate the issue of poverty and gender inequality, which were significant problems faced by the communities at large.

Nilay Kulkarni—Co-founder and Chief Technical Officer at Ashioto Analytics is an 18-year old teenager who is a self-taught programmer. He is presently the Chief Technical Officer of one of the firms involved in monitoring crowd flow and analysis of the risk involved therein at any event. He has utilised his skills and knowledge to find solutions to preclude human stampedes in some of the world's largest gatherings such as the Kumbha Festival in India. Kumbha is one of the largest gatherings of pilgrims (i.e. attended by millions of people from all over the world) and is a symbol of Indian culture from an historical point of view. Many people that travel as religious tourists in the respective festivals lost their lives in stampede. At an early age, this leader realised his social responsibility, which is a missing element from the large multinational corporations in the tourism and hospitality industry. He used his technical expertise and invented an electrical mat, which counts the footfalls of people that step on the mat during a specific period to ensure control over the gatherings if reached over a tipping point. The electric mat transmits the footfalls data to local authorities, which allows them to intervene when required. This is a glaring example highlighting the ideals of Generation Z.

Moziah Mo Bridges, Founder of Mo's Bows, is a regular teenager who took a passionate interest in bows and ties at a young age and is now leading his own company by the name Mo's Bows. The company offers an extensive collection of colorful, trendy handmade ties and men's accessories. Mo's Bows has opened up retail stores across the world, and includes partnerships with Neiman Marcus and Bloomingdale. Moah, who is currently 18 years old and started making his bow ties with his Granny, is now serving as the President and Creative Director of an internationally recognised bow tie brand.

Bella Tipping, Founder of KidzcationZ, is a 17-year-old. Bella started her company KidzcationZ when she was just 13 years old. KidzcationZ is a travel review website, which is primarily focused on kids. The website allows kids to give a rating to hotels, restaurants, and attractions at a destination based on their experience and how well these tourism components served and supported their requirements. The tagline of the website reads "Travel advice from kids... to everyone". While giving an interview, Bella mentioned her desire to work in non-profit organisations in future. She further emphasised that she would want to contribute towards social change by making the society inclusive for everyone.

In contemporary times, Generation Z is playing a leading role and standing up together against any discrimination in society, or moral injustice such as the Black lives matter movement in the year 2020 (Ahlquist 2020), and even climate change concerns raised by Greta Thunderberg in the year 2019. Therefore, it is suggested that a different working environment will have to be designed for this young generation to help them bring their creativity and multi-tasking abilities into the workplace.

Challenges Faced by Organisations

When organisations employ people from different generations, differences in age groups, behavior, thinking process, attitude towards work and workplace, flexibility, cultures, technical knowledge are frequently observed. These differences lead to conflicts amongst employees and subsequently pose a challenge for the organisation in the long run (Bencsik et al. 2016). As rightly said by Ryder (1985), though birth cohorts pose a risk to stability, they do offer an opportunity for societal transformation. Thus, these challenges provide opportunities for leaders to take initiatives and demonstrate leadership skills to ensure stability and negotiation amongst employees in conflict situations. Successful leadership demands appropriate management practices for dealing with different individuals or generational cohorts.

Conversely, the organisations which are 'generationally ignorant' attempt to homogenise working procedure which fails in organisational development and effective leadership for the long term. Another critical challenge in organisations is the lack of flexibility in leadership styles adopted by them. It is suggested that organisations should, therefore, evolve their working styles for hiring the new generation, which will join the workforce in the coming years. Companies should consider creating and maintaining an environment of confidence, thriving collaboration and knowledge sharing aspects as crucial for its success and the development of its employees. Moreover, incentive plans, rewards, social events, official trips, employee development sessions, and encouraging leisure activities at the workplace could be some measures towards satisfaction and retention of the future workforce.

Creating a Value System and Leadership Style

Even though Gen Zs are self-learners, they are equally good at idealising and making role models. These role models are an inspiration with whom they feel connected even if the bond is created through virtual platforms. In consideration of this personality trait, corporate leaders may enhance the required skills so that the 'bond' is created easily with the youngest employees in the organisation. This calls for a transition in the traditional leadership styles at the workplaces. Conversely, adopting a carrot and stick approach or the old school leadership style, popularly known as reinforcement leadership, would not be effective to lead employees emerging from Gen Z. It is suggested that a transformational leadership style could be effective for managing and leading the digital native workforce as the style is closely associated with the characteristics of leaders that Gen Z would admire.

Transformational leaders focus on both individual's growth and organisational development. They appreciate the self-development of the team and also promote the achievement factor inside the organisation. The critical feature of transformational leaders is to increase awareness amongst individuals working as a team regarding the most vital issues of the organisation. These types of leaders believe in creating bonds and keep the team together as a bundle. They lead them as a team and, at the same time, boost the morale and confidence of the team members. The ultimate role of transformational leaders is to take care of the achievements, growth, and development of the teammates, which ultimately reflects in the organisational development. To understand the ideal connection between Generation Z and Transformational leadership and the reasons which make transformational leadership best suitable for

Generation Z, we need to focus on the four 'I's' of the present in the transformational leadership style. These four 'I's' are inspirational motivation, idealised influence/charisma, individualised consideration, and intellectual consideration (Bass and Avolio 1990). Earlier research in the field of leadership has proved that transformational leadership is better in terms of effectiveness in comparison to transactional or other forms of leadership.

Amongst the four factors, the first "I", inspirational motivation, is the need of our time. Generation Z leaders at the initial stages of their career embody the quality of inspiring others and at the same time, this is something they seek from their leaders as well. Inspiring talks, and morale-boosting sessions from the existing chain of command influence the digital natives as they believe in role models and trust in inspiring people around them. Leaders with influencing power, imbibe values, and channel their vision which triggers the energy in the employees leading them to accomplish high levels of performance and development.

The second 'I', idealised influence, also known as Charisma, is regarded as the strongest 'I' of transformational leadership. Generation Z is blessed with the quality of confidence. The go-getter attitude of Generation Z suits them for the requirement of becoming a transformational leader. Similarly, existing corporate leadership, demonstrating the visionary leadership, straightforward mission statement earns a lot of respect and trust by this young generation. The existing leadership command which can gain recognition and respect from the young brigade will have a welcoming approach suiting the requirements of Generation Z. These kinds of organisations can be seen demonstrating the optimal utilisation of resources and sustained growth and development because of the high-level performance that they achieve by creating bonds and binding force amongst the teammates. Charisma is the pull factor of such teams, and this may act as a magnet to Generation Z as they believe in idealising people and prefer to be a good follower given the leadership is rational.

Individualised consideration is the third 'I' of the transformational leadership. Leaders with the potential to value every single individual working for the organisation are the most recognised and appreciated ones. These people usually keep a check on every individual's needs and desires and, at the same time, they do listen to their problems and routine issues. This feature of being heard and understood by your seniors and leadership develops a factor of belongingness amongst the youth (Generation Z). The ability to attend to every individual working for the organisation enables them to have trust and faith in the organisation. This further increases their loyalty to the organisation and then they act as followers and devote themselves, rendering the best of their services for the organisation's growth and development. In the long term, these followers turn out to be self-governed people and enforce themselves to achieve the targets or accomplish the goals on their own.

Further, they take their responsibility for self-development and personal growth without losing the bond with the organisation. However, all this will only be possible if there is a presence of transformational leadership inside the organisation. Otherwise, the old school leadership may result in a high labour turnover. Careful integration and prospects of growth and development have emerged as one of the significant concerns of Generation Z, and this, if catered for, will bring improved results to the organisation.

The fourth 'I' of transformational leadership is intellectually stimulating. Generation Z is experimental and believes in the power of creativity. If the existing leadership can display the ability to see old and traditional methods and bring in new approaches blended with creative solutions, then these methods become more acceptable for the new generation. Traditional practices when presented with a twist before Generation Z have a better chance of acceptance as well as better performance from the team, particularly from the new generation. Further, this 'I' of leadership propagates and imbibes the spirit of solving the problems individually. This leadership quality will empower the new young force to come up with new and creative ways of tackling problems and providing unique and improved solutions to them. An intellectually stimulating leader develops his/her followers in more similar ways; in fact, this may prove better in the case of Generation Z.

Conclusion

Generation Z, being creative, virtually connected, strong-headed, ambitious, emotionally stable, inspiration seekers, is one of the most distinct generations, which occupies 20% of the workforce worldwide. The focus of existing leadership and existing leadership commands in every organisation should focus on the strategic utilisation of employees from different generations' skills, technical understanding, and passion towards work. This deployment will enable the organisations to be flexible with individuals belonging to different generations without compromising their vision and ethos. As said by Ryder (1985), every generational cohort is heterogeneous for different variables, and organisations need to understand the requirements and characteristics of their employees belonging to Generation Z. This understanding will ensure better productivity and overall growth of personnel and organisations in the tourism and hospitality industry. If an organisation effectively utilises generational strengths, it can reduce the turnover ratio and increase profits and sales (Kohnen 2002). It is suggested that regular leadership development sessions should be conducted in organisations with particular emphasis on leadership education, generational differences, promotion of flexibility, avoiding presumptions and perceptions for people from different social backgrounds, and work towards an environment wherein managers and leaders promote conversations with employees. Transformational leadership is the need of our time, as it suits Generation Z and every other generation living in the present business scenario. The four "I"s of the transformational leadership will act as a torch in an ambiguous environment whereby, every business industry including the tourism and hospitality industry is standing at the crossroads of managing Generation Z, especially Generation Z along with other generations present in the workforce. As mentioned by Montana and Petit (2011) in their study 'getting along with one another' at the workplace has been considered a crucial hybrid motivating factor for Generation Y and is likely to apply to Gen Z as well. It is also recommended that leadership development programmes should emphasise leadership education, avoiding judging others' perceptions, having generational conversations, offering choice, and promoting flexibility.

The authors suggest that more empirical research is required on the topics of digital nomadism and Generation Z, perspectives of Generation Z on the tourism and hospitality industry, tourism education and Generation Z, and their idea of a suitable organisation. This study suggests that a transformative leadership style is suitable to meet the contemporary trends and characteristics of Generation Z. Further, human resource management must comprehend the requirements of the digital natives and shape their skills in the right direction. It is also advised that organisations in the tourism and hospitality industry need to improve their remuneration structure, training, and development sessions and working environment to retain the youth for the long term. For instance, a training period for six to eight months might not be applicable in the current scenario, wherein the youth is well-versed with technical and informative aspects of a job. Therefore, a more engaging approach is much-needed for the companies.

References

Ahlquist, S. 2020. *Youth Led Group Gen Z: We Want to Live Plans Protest for Sunday in Providence*, June 12. Retrieved June 2020, from Upriseri.com. https://upriseri.com/2020-06-12-gen-z-we-want-to-live/.

Al-Asfour, Ahmed, and Larry Lettau. 2014. "Strategies for Leadership Styles for Multi-Generational Workforce." *Journal of Leadership, Accountability and Ethics* 11 (2): 58.

Arsenault, Paul M., Keith Macky, Dianne Gardner, Stewart Forsyth, Keith Macky, Dianne Gardner, Stewart Forsyth, et al. 2008. "Validating Generational Differences A Legitimate Diversity and Leadership Issue." *Leadership & Organization Development Journal* 25 (2): 124–41. https://doi.org/10.1108/01437730410521813.

Bako, Merve. 2018. "Different Leadership Style Choices,Different Generations." *Prizren Social Science Journal* 2 (2): 127–43.

Bass, Bernard M., and Bruce J Avolio. 1990. "Developing Transformational Leadership: 1992 and Beyond." *Journal of European Industrial Training* 21–27.

Bateh, Dena. 2018. "Leadership from Millennials to Generation Z Transformed." *Journal of Advanced Management Science* 7 (1): 11–14. https://doi.org/10.18178/joams.7.1.11-14.

Bencsik, Andrea, Tímea Juhász, and Gabriella Horváth-Csikós. 2016. "Y and Z Generations at Workplaces." *Journal of Competitiveness* 6 (3): 90–106. https://doi.org/10.7441/joc.2016.03.06.

Berenda, Carlton W., and Karl Mannheim. 1953. "Essays on the Sociology of Knowledge." *Books Abroad*. https://doi.org/10.2307/40092271.

Berkup, Sezin Baysal. 2014. "Working with Generations X and Y In Generation Z Period: Management of Different Generations in Business Life." *Mediterranean Journal of Social Sciences* 5 (19): 218–29. https://doi.org/10.5901/mjss.2014.v5n19p218.

Betz, Cecily L. 2019. "What Generations X, Y and Z Want From Leadership." *INSEAD*. https://doi.org/10.1016/j.pedn.2018.12.013.

Cogin, Julie. 2012. "Are Generational Differences in Work Values Fact or Fiction? Multi-Country Evidence and Implications." *International Journal of Human Resource Management* 23 (11): 2268–94. https://doi.org/10.1080/09585192.2011.610967.

Corbisiero, F., and E. Ruspini. 2018. "Millennials and Generation Z: challenges and future perspectives for international tourism." *Journal of Tourism Futures* 4 (1): 253–55.

Deloitte. 2017. *Deloitte Millenial Survey*. Deloitte Ltd.

Dimock, Michael. 2019. "Defining Generations: Where Millennials End and Generation Z Begins." *Pew Research Center*, 1–7. http://www.pewresearch.org/fact-tank/2019/01/17/where%0Ahttp://www.pewresearch.org/fact-tank/2019/01/17/where-millennials-end-and-generation-z-begins/.

Gardner, Howard, and Katie Davis. 2013. *The App Generation: How Today's Youth Navigate Identity, Intimacy, and Imagination in a Digital World*. The App Generation: How Today's Youth Navigate Identity, Intimacy, and Imagination in a Digital World. https://doi.org/10.1177/146144481560 9591c.

Goh, Edmund, and Cindy Lee. 2018. "A Workforce to Be Reckoned With: The Emerging Pivotal Generation Z Hospitality Workforce." *International Journal of Hospitality Management* 73 (January): 20–28. https://doi.org/10.1016/j.ijhm.2018.01.016.

Hamed, Hend M. 2017. "Marketing Destinations to Millennials: Examining the Compatibility Between the Destination Marketing Organization Website and the Millennial Tourist Prospects." *Journal of Tourism and Recreation* 3 (1): 1–20. https://doi.org/10.12735/jotr.v3n1p01.

Hung, Kineta H., Flora Fang Gu, and Chi Kin Yim. 2008. "A Social Institutional Approach to Identifying Generation Cohorts in China with a comparison of American Consumers." *Journal of International Business Studies* 836–853.

Kohnen, Patricia M. 2002. "When Generations Collide: Who They Are. Why They Clash. How to Solve the Generational Puzzle at Work." *Quality Management Journal*. https://doi.org/10.1080/10686967.2002.11919040.

Levine, A., and D.R Dean. 2012. *Generation on a Tightrope: A Portrait of Today's College Student.* San Francisco: Jossey-Bass.

Life as a Butterfly. 2018. "The Travel Influencer: Who, What Why and When The Research."

Montana, Patrick J., and Francis Petit. 2011. "Motivating And Managing Generation X And Y On The Job While Preparing For Z: A Market Oriented Approach." *Journal of Business & Economics Research (JBER)* 6 (8): 35–40. https://doi.org/10.19030/jber.v6i8.2459.

Murphy, Edward F., John D Gordon, and Thomas L Anderson. 2004. "Cross-Cultural, Cross-Cultural Age and Cross-Cultural Generational ..." *Journal of Applied Management and Entrepreneurship.*

Ozkan, Mustafa, and Betul Solmaz. 2015. "The Changing Face of the Employees – Generation Z and Their Perceptions of Work (A Study Applied to University Students)." *Procedia Economics and Finance.* https://doi.org/10.1016/s2212-5671(15)00876-x.

Parry, Emma, and Peter Urwin. 2011. "Generational Differences in Work Values: A Review of Theory and Evidence." *International Journal of Management Reviews.* https://doi.org/10.1111/j.1468-2370.2010.00285.x.

Petsko, Emily. 2018. *Generation Z Is Coming-and They'll Outnumber the World's Millenial's within a Year.* 20 August. https://www.mentalfloss.com/article/555109/generation-z-will-outnumber-millennials-within-one-year.

Randstad. 2017. "Gen Z and Millennials Collide at Work."

Riad Shams, S.M., and Zhanna Belyaeva. 2019. "Quality Assurance Driving Factors as Antecedents of Knowledge Management: A Stakeholder-Focussed Perspective in Higher Education." *Journal of the Knowledge Economy* 10 (2): 423–36. https://doi.org/10.1007/s13132-017-0472-2.

Robinson, V.M., and H.A. Schänzel. 2019. "A Tourism Inflex: Generation Z travel experiences." *Journal of Tourism Futures* 5 (2): 127–41.

Ryder, Norman B. 1985. "The Cohort as a Concept in the Study of Social Change." In *Cohort Analysis in Social Research*, 9–44. https://doi.org/10.1007/978-1-4613-8536-3_2.

Schawbel, Dan. 2014. *Gen Z Employees: The 5 Attributes You Need to Know.* September 2. Accessed November 2019. https://www.entrepreneur.com/article/236560.

Shatto, Bobbi, and Kelly Erwin. 2016. "Moving on From Millennials: Preparing for Generation Z." *Journal of Continuing Education in Nursing* 47 (6): 253–54. https://doi.org/10.3928/00220124-20160518-05.

Stănciulescu, G., E. Molnar, and M. Bunghez. 2011. "Tourism's Changing Face: New Age Tourism Versus Old Tourism." *Annals of the University of Oradea, Economic Science Series* 245–49.

Strauss, W., and Neil Howe. 1991. "Generations: The History of America's Future." *The History of America's Future, 1584 to 2069.*

Tulgan, Bruce. 2013. *Meet Generation Z.* New Haven: Rainmaker Thinking.

Twenge, Jean M., Stacy M. Campbell, Brian J. Hoffman, and Charles E. Lance. 2010. "Generational Differences in Work Values: Leisure and Extrinsic Values Increasing, Social and Intrinsic Values Decreasing." *Journal of Management.* https://doi.org/10.1177/0149206309352246.

Williams, Alex. 2015. "Move Over, Millenials, Here Comes Generation Z." *The Newyork Times,* 20 September: ST 1.

WTTC. 2019. "WTTC Economic Impact Report."

Zemke, Ron, Claire Raines, and Bob Filipczak. 2000. "Generations at Work: Managing the Clash of Veterans, Boomers, Xers. and Nexters in Your Workplace Chapter 6: Where Mixed Generations Work Well Together." *AMACOM. (C).*

2

Generation Z and Managing Multiple Generational Cohorts Simultaneously in Tourism and Hospitality

Cynthia Mejia and João Pinto

Introduction

According to the World Travel & Tourism Council's 2018 global economic and employment impact of travel and tourism, this leading sector contributed 10.4% of the global GDP and 319 million jobs worldwide, which was 10% of the total employment (WTTC 2019). At the time of this writing, one in ten jobs in the world were related to tourism, and given the widely accepted common knowledge about turnover in the sector, the massive Baby Boomer exodus, followed by

---

C. Mejia (✉)
Rosen College of Hospitality Management, University of Central Florida, Orlando, FL, USA
e-mail: cynthia.mejia@ucf.edu

J. Pinto
ISCTE Business School, Lisbon, Portugal
e-mail: jddrp@iscte-iul.pt

© The Author(s), under exclusive license to Springer Nature
Switzerland AG 2021
N. Stylos et al. (eds.), *Generation Z Marketing and Management in Tourism and Hospitality,*
https://doi.org/10.1007/978-3-030-70695-1_2

a smaller and aging Gen X cohort, creates what has been dubbed "the perfect storm", leaving the tourism and hospitality industries with a talent crisis (Solnet et al. 2016). Prior research on generational differences in the hospitality and tourism industry has revealed a diversity of work values and occupational behaviors; however, common threads remain. Comfort and security, professional growth and working environment, and uniqueness intrinsic to work in the sector, emerged in previous years as collective needs across generations (Chen and Choi 2008). As new generations enter into the workforce, and as economic stressors fluctuate throughout time, the hospitality and tourism industry ebbs and flows with various generational demographics, requiring continuous re-examination of the dynamics between cohorts. In an effort to better understand the dynamics across a multi-generational workforce, it is important to first recognize the distinctions and contributions of each generation independently.

Generational cohort theory asserts that traits vary across generations due to significant historical events and social changes in a society, consequently affecting the values, attitudes, beliefs, and inclinations of its generational cohort members. It is posited that persons born during a particular time period are therefore influenced by identical historical events during periods of human development, central to their lives and producing effects consistent among these individuals over time. One alternative to this widely accepted theory is that an individual's values, attitudes, and beliefs are a direct consequence of age and maturity, rather than attributed to the lived experiences of an entire generation (Jones et al. 2018).

The categorization of generational cohorts evolved from a Western perspective under an assumption that the majority of individuals within the same cohort experience and understand life and important events in a similar way. Given the global nature of the tourism and hospitality sector, and if we are to widely acknowledge generational cohort theory, it has become increasingly important to understand not only the unique characteristics of each generational cohort, but also similarities and differences of each cohort across cultures. It should be of note that the same generation will have different experiences depending on geographical region, and consequently, exhibit different characteristics than their Western counterparts (Jones et al. 2018). The following is a presentation of each of the five cohorts existing in the current global workforce, including strategies for intergenerational management.

Traditionalists and Baby Boomers

The members of the generational cohort who grew out of the Great Depression and World War II are identified as Traditionalists, or those born approximately between 1927 and 1946. Influenced by economic adversity, Traditionalists exhibit values of dedication and sacrifice, a strong work ethic, and prioritize responsibility over self-gratification. They value loyalty and dependability, both from themselves and within the organizations they are members. Traditionalists demonstrate a preference for working independently, rather than in teams, and value obedience over individualism among their colleagues. They prefer a clearly defined management structure in the workplace, and have exhibited high commitment to work, yet are able to delineate work from their personal life. In general, Traditionalists prefer a formal and respectful communication style as it pertains to professional correspondence and interactions (Jones et al. 2018).

Following Traditionalists, are the Baby Boomer generation, or those born between 1946 and 1964. They were raised in prosperous economic times and have a more optimistic perspective on work and life, compared with their predecessors. Baby Boomers envision their work life and careers as an extension of their self-interests or as a means to finance a more abundant lifestyle, motivated extrinsically through monetary rewards (Jones et al. 2018; Costin 2019). In search of a secure retirement, large numbers of Baby Boomers entered into the workforce (Fry 2019; Neal 2019). Baby Boomers place high value on forming relationships, recognizing the importance of networking. They seek to be validated for their knowledge and efforts, and enjoy personal attention. They value creativity and spontaneity, and exhibit strong tendencies for personal growth, gratification, involvement, and self-actualization (Jones et al. 2018; Christfort and Monahan 2019). In the latter stages of their professional life, they prefer flexible and less demanding work arrangements, and tend to work part-time or work from home in exchange for high hourly wages or salaries (Costin 2019; Folz 2019). Both Baby Boomers and Traditionalists in the hospitality and tourism job context are less concerned with individualistic values than the younger generational workforce (Ann and Blum 2020; Papavasileiou et al. 2017).

Baby Boomers have high expectations of themselves and others, and seek to make the world a better place. They have a need to make a long-lasting and valuable contribution to their workplace and communities (Glass 2007) and are intrinsically motivated to bring projects to fruition (Costin 2019). Unlike Traditionalists, Baby Boomers prefer working in teams, valuing collegial workplace relationships with supervisors and colleagues and prefer more informal types of communication. They enjoy connecting with coworkers on a personal level (Jones et al. 2018).

Baby Boomers characterize themselves as being open-minded to change and new technologies, as long as they can understand the value it brings (Glass 2007). Due to the many years in the workplace, they can possess a tremendous amount of organizational knowledge and intellectual capital, with years of experience in the workplace that can benefit the next generational cohorts (Costin 2019); however, when working under a younger person, for example a millennial (who likes detail-oriented communication), Baby Boomers may feel insulted by specific instructions (Glass 2007). Regardless, Baby Boomers are known for their contributions toward improving the work ethic of Generation Xers and Millennials, even if their help is not sought after (Costin 2019).

Generation X

Generation X, or those born approximately between 1965 and 1981, is often described as materialistic, competitive, and individualistic (Francis and Hoefel 2018). Divorce rates increased during the childhood of Gen Xers, and subsequently this cohort learned self-reliance at an early age, dubbed the "latch key" generation who let themselves into their own homes after school, prepared their own dinners, and managed their own homework. The Gen X cohort is highly independent, yet more skeptical

2 Generation Z and Managing Multiple Generational Cohorts ... 29

and less loyal than the Baby Boomer generation (Costin 2019; Christfort and Monahan 2019).

Generation X values a work-life balance, and seeks out organizations that promote skills development and self-improvement (Jones et al. 2018; Neal 2019). They believe that work can be done anytime and anywhere, as they are outcome focused. Gen X does not adhere to the notion of a lifelong job, but rather this generational cohort will leave a job for more meaningful and challenging work, or a higher salary with more benefits (Jones et al. 2018). They are very protective of their personal and family time. For example, during work hours, Gen X will provide 100% of their time and concentration, but the moment they conclude their work, they consider themselves to be "off the clock", thus shifting to 100% attention to personal time (Neal 2019). Research in the hospitality and tourism context has dispelled the notion that Gen X is motivated more so by financial gains than Baby Boomers, yet Gen X is less attached psychologically to a hospitality organization than Millennials (Eyoun et al. 2020).

Gen X can be perceived as apathetic and cynical (Costin 2019), yet they are as confident as the Millennial generation with the ever-changing digital technological landscape. They prefer informal work environments and have been characterized as distrusting of authority (Jones et al. 2018). This generational cohort excels in traditional leadership skills, similar to those of Baby Boomers. Gen X is very capable at problem-solving, tending toward practical solutions, with a good command of technical competence, appreciation for diversity, comfort with change management, and an ability to harness multi-tasking (Neal 2019). Despite these capabilities, they are often overlooked for promotions more often than other generations, perhaps due to a large number of Baby Boomers remaining longer in the workforce. It is notable that the Gen X promotion rate is 20–30% slower than that of the Millennials (Neal 2019), potentially resulting in impatience and consequently affecting their people skills (Jones et al. 2018).

Given the identical position or level of job responsibility, Gen X leaders manage an average of seven direct reports, compared with five direct reports of their Millennial counterparts. Gen X managers are loyal to their employers, and play a critical role in organizational knowledge and intellectual capital retention within companies (Neal 2019). As managers, Gen X exhibits risk-taking behaviors with a focus on results. Promoting independence in the workplace, Gen X managers are "hands-off", with low amounts of face-to-face communications. Gen X managers tend to be critically honest, justifying this approach as caring about an issue. They are direct in communications, often taking opposing stances to test and advance ideas when they want the team to achieve success (Costin 2019; Jones et al. 2018).

Millennials (Generation Y)

Millennials or Generation Y are those born between 1981 and 1996, and have been labelled the "me generation" due to a generalized perception that they are idealistic, overzealous, confrontational, and less willing to accept different points of view when compared with other generational cohorts (Christfort and Monahan 2019; Francis and Hoefel 2018). Despite this negative perception, they are also recognized as respectful and open to new ideas, seeking work opportunities, which afford life-long learning in their professional careers (Ozkan and Solmaz 2015). Within the central tendencies of this cohort, Millennials are commonly portrayed as valuing passion over performance and fulfillment over hard work (Christfort and Monahan 2019).

According to Christfort and Monahan (2019), Millennials are considered methodical, risk-averse, and practical, yet when compared with previous generational cohorts, Millennials are less focused on people, networking, and spontaneity. They are considered to possess in general, higher levels of stress than Generation X and Baby Boomers. Conversely, Millennials who take risks often report lower levels of stress, and perform more effectively under conditions with moderate to high stress levels. These cohort characteristics can be attributed to increased global conflict, economic recessions, and terrorism which became more prevalent in the media and other communications channels in Millennials' younger years (Christfort and Monahan 2019).

2 Generation Z and Managing Multiple Generational Cohorts ... 31

Valuing the contributions of diverse individuals, Millennials propel a sense of optimism, civic duty, confidence, entrepreneurship, and achievement. Similar to Gen X, Millennials distrust centralized authority (Jones et al. 2018). Millennials place much value on work-life balance and career development, prioritizing family and leisure time. This generational cohort holds in high regard the intrinsic aspects of work and career, for example, mentoring, succession planning, and development opportunities (Jones et al. 2018). Millennials enjoy competition and promote healthy rivalry within their work environments (Ozkan and Solmaz 2015). They show a preference for working independently, inclusive of technology use (Schawbel 2014). In corporate environments, Millennials are more partial to flexible work schedules with opportunities to achieve progressively higher levels of individual responsibility (Christfort and Monahan 2019).

Due to the events experienced as children (e.g., September 11), Millennials tend to be more socially minded (Glass 2007), yet demanding in nature. This cohort has a need for constant performance feedback in the workplace, and seeks out new challenges and additional responsibilities. Millennials value connectivity, communication, and collaboration, with high expectations for being heard, and opinions valued (Solnet and Kralj 2011). They are a confident generational cohort, and in general, are not afraid to try new things, often deemed "early adapters" (Glass 2007). They have great attention to detail and a strong ability to follow a structural, methodical approach (Christfort and Monahan 2019). Conversely, Millennials are often associated with parental dependency for career success, thus the term "helicopter parent" was coined due to this phenomenon. Millennials are commonly criticized for an overreliance on digital communication channels, stunting their ability to form personal relationships with others in the work environment (Glass 2007).

Millennials learn best in an ongoing consultation style, seeking real-time feedback for self-correction. They are less likely than other generational cohorts to seek out and employ anti-stress strategies, which could be an opportunity for older generational cohorts to coach Millennials these strategies, resulting in more productive team members (Christfort and Monahan 2019). Millennials are more likely to aspire to be top performers or experts, but not necessarily leaders within their organizations, allowing for greater mobility and flexibility throughout their careers; however, they are known to advocate for a good social environment in the workplace than previous generations (Ozkan and Solmaz 2015). Millennials are attracted to companies where there is collaborative decision-making, rapid career progression, and where their contributions are validated. They hold in high regard corporate philanthropy and social awareness, extending to the need for meaning in the workplace (Glass 2007). In the hospitality and tourism context, well-planned organizational career management has been shown to be a positive predictor of career expectation and career satisfaction among Millennials (Kong et al. 2020).

Millennials expect the same level of digital and technological connectivity in the workplace as they experience in their personal lives, attracted to organizations with the most forward-thinking use of technology (Rossi 2019). They prefer clear and concise forms of communication, mostly in the digital format, favoring text messaging and emails over face-to-face or telephone conversations (Green 2019).

Generation Z

Generation Z, or Gen Z, the most recent demographic cohort beginning in the mid 1990s, are true digital natives as the only cohort constantly exposed to the Internet, social media, and mobile systems since birth (Francis and Hoefel 2018; Ozkan and Solmaz 2015). They are the most diverse and inclusive generational cohort to date, with high expectations in the workplace to mirror their lived experiences. Gen Z is pragmatic, challenging traditional social structures due to inherent curiosities (Ozkan and Solmaz 2015; Francis and Hoefel 2018; Stahl 2018; Trabold 2019; Development 2018). They appear to be more interested in social activities and ethical matters than prior generations (Francis and Hoefel 2018; Ozkan and Solmaz 2015), showing a preference for companies who fight against poverty, support green policies, and advocate for human rights (Costa 2019).

2 Generation Z and Managing Multiple Generational Cohorts ... 33

Gen Z is more concerned with job security than Millennials because they were raised with the 2008 recession and took note of the difficulties of previous generations. Although they exhibit this proclivity toward job security, if they are unhappy in their work environment, they have no loyalty and will quit (Ozkan and Solmaz 2015; Francis and Hoefel 2018; Stahl 2018, 2019a; Development 2018). They are motivated by job benefits, which can enhance their lives, such as health insurance, competitive salaries, and bosses they respect, for example (Trabold 2019). They seek a strong work-life balance, which mandates that employers offer flexible hours, paid vacation time, and paid sick time (Kronos 2019). Gen Z values lifelong learning, training, and development, with a specific focus on negotiation, networking, public speaking, and conflict resolution (Ceniza-Levine 2019; Development 2018; Kronos 2019). They are attracted to collaborative and team-based environments, with positive collegial relationships extending beyond work and social media (Francis and Hoefel 2018; Ozkan and Solmaz 2015; Stahl 2018, 2019b). The hospitality industry is attractive to Gen Z as a career choice because it is seen as a "people's industry" with opportunities for lifelong travel and learning (Goh and Lee 2018).

Gen Z exhibits competitive and independent behaviors, yet they also value team membership, therefore it is important that managers and supervisors strike the right social-solitary balance in the workplace (Arruda 2018). As Gen Z prefers working with technology, they also crave a personalized corporate environment and want others to listen to, value, and respect their ideas (Schawbel 2014). Due to the preponderance of mass shootings, rising suicide rates, climate change, separation and deportation of immigrant families, and reports of sexual harassment in the media, Gen Z is one of the most stressed generations in recent history, compared with their predecessors (Development 2018).

Gen Z is able to organize and process multiple sources of information, interweaving online and offline data (Francis and Hoefel 2018). Compared with Millennials, Gen Z will work harder and remain longer at work if their compensation is commensurate with their responsibilities. While they are technologically savvy, Gen Z is also growth-minded, and values relationships toward achieving their career goals (Stahl 2019a). In general, they are committed to be on time for work, engage as a team, meeting project deadlines and working with customers (Kronos 2019). To leverage these generational characteristics, companies will need to encourage an environment where technology is used, but not as a replacement for human connection (McInnis-Day et al. 2019). Compared with previous generations, Gen Z might need more training and education with building critical thinking, and older generations can contribute to these efforts, helping to expose Gen Z to other ideas and perspectives not found in social media (McInnis-Day et al. 2019).

Gen Z exhibits optimism about their future in general, but also is anxious about their capabilities to be successful in the workplace. They perceive their lack of motivation and low self-esteem to be barriers to their success in the workforce and feel their education did not prepare them well enough for interpersonal skills such as negotiations, networking, public speaking, the reality of long working hours, and conflict resolution (Kronos 2019). As Gen Z tends to possess a low attention span compared with older generations, they prefer short meetings (Stahl 2019a; Green 2019; He 2019). A large contingent of Gen Z envisions that they should receive a promotion within their first year of work in a new job, yet they also experience a lack of confidence, demonstrated in feeling not good enough, or making mistakes on the job (Development 2018; Ceniza-Levine 2019). They are motivated to accept a job opportunity which could lead to multiple roles within one organization, yet are reserved in asking for help to achieve career development (Development 2018; Stahl 2019a).

Gen Z is a relatively independent generational cohort, and like Gen X before them, does not like authority (Ozkan and Solmaz 2015). While they are not as concerned with climbing a corporate ladder toward success, they are interested in being a part of a team that improves the organization's mission and goals. They seek to be involved with projects from beginning to end, enjoying collaboration and opportunities to be creative (Stahl 2019a). If given a supportive and communicative manager as a mentor, members of the Gen Z cohort will work harder and stay longer on the job (Ceniza-Levine 2019; Development 2018; Kronos 2019). Yet, they can readily disengage from work where they are not directly connected to the outcomes (Development 2018). They have a

2 Generation Z and Managing Multiple Generational Cohorts ...

need to be an essential part of the organization, otherwise, they may feel excluded, and ultimately leave (Trabold 2019).

Like the Millennial generation, Gen Z expects the same technological access and experience on the job as they do in their personal lives and do not tolerate outdated workplace technologies (Kronos 2019). Extending this preference, they want access to information on their mobile devices, particularly training and learning modules delivered in video format (McInnis-Day et al. 2019; Baron 2019; Francis and Hoefel 2018). They prefer real-time synchronous communication, whether in video or in person, and when working remotely, they prefer video calls or voice-to-text rather than phone calls (McInnis-Day et al. 2019; Stahl 2019a; Ceniza-Levine 2019; Green 2019; Kronos 2019). Members of the Gen Z workforce want to participate in regular meetings so they feel heard and also are attracted to a personable work culture with human connection as part of a larger team. Conversely, they are conflict averse, and prefer to conduct difficult or uncomfortable conversations via texting rather than in person (Stahl 2019a).

Gen Z seeks constant validation and works best with regularly scheduled performance reviews. As digital natives with access to search engines, they grew up in an information-seeking environment, accustomed to asking questions and receiving answers immediately, thus this penchant for knowledge acquisition has led to a need for frequent and constant feedback and communication (Development 2018; Stahl 2019a; Green 2019; Ceniza-Levine 2019). In addition, Gen Z workers expect feedback that is measurable, trackable, and specific (Stahl 2019b). In their quest for authentic communication, members of this cohort are often skeptical of information, and want to contribute to the knowledge base, seeking opportunities to share knowledge in the work environment (Green 2019).

Intergenerational Misconceptions and Mutual Understanding

Intergenerational misconceptions exist based on cross-generational assumptions and stereotypes. In the highly competitive work environment, with potentially five generations working side by side or throughout the organization's hierarchy, negative stereotypes only serve to polarize the members between generations. Intergenerational stereotypes are harmful to a tourism and hospitality business and the consumers they serve, as these negative stereotypes adversely impact organizational performance, workers' commitment, and job satisfaction (Weeks 2017; Zopiatis et al. 2012). As an example, Millennials account for 15% of the global labor force and 35% of the U.S. workforce, and are estimated to comprise 75% of the global workforce by 2025 (Catalyst 2019; Fry 2018), thus attracting much of the negative criticisms and stereotyping in the current workforce climate. They are perceived to be less loyal than members of previous generational cohorts, which can be attributed to the adverse economic conditions they endured while growing up (Buckley et al. 2015). Millennials are anecdotally described as lacking loyalty, regardless that the true rate of job turnover is not significantly different from that of previous generations. This observation can be explained by a misinterpretation of aging, where high turnover is common among the young workforce, compared with older workers. In addition, Millennials in general are marrying and forming households much later than those members of prior generational cohorts (Buckley et al. 2015).

Generation Z has recently begun to enter the workforce, a generation larger than Gen X and 60% of the size of the Baby Boomers. Consulting firms have suggested that Gen Z requires different and more involved marketing efforts, attracting their attention through positive daily work experiences, but keeping in mind that they have not yet quite optimized their capabilities for social interactions. The inclusion of Gen Z in the workforce substantially widens the generational gaps, giving organizations unique challenges, both within a business and at the customer interface (Morris 2018).

Generational diversity can be subject to the formation of out-groups, especially as it pertains to communication and coordination in the workplace, inviting conflict. Age discrimination in the work environment has been shown to reduce the commitment of all workers in a business, thus impinging upon an organization's financial performance (Boehm and Kunze 2015). Given that the similarity-attraction paradigm explains the behaviors of like-minded or similar individuals, members from the same generation gravitate to one another, thus enhancing in-group communication and coordination. Intensified generational diversity introduces wide variances in the perception of career norms and traditional job roles (Boehm and Kunze 2015). Highly educated younger workers might suffer, for example, when promoted ahead of older workers without similar education status, initiating perceptions of age discrimination (Boehm and Kunze 2015).

In these instances, communication is critical for ensuring transparency and intergenerational understanding in the workplace (Ceruto 2019; Glass 2007). Strategies such as active listening, mindful analyses, and forming transparent processes allow for a window of appreciation for the other generational members' perspectives on an issue, toward conflict resolution (Mehta 2019). Additional strategies for creating a more inclusive intergenerational work environment include revisiting corporate human resource policies, budgeting for internal age diversity training programs, creating collaborative decision-making platforms, and forming procedures for fair conflict management policy (Glass 2007).

Strategies for Intergenerational Management

Age diversity in the workplace is of tremendous benefit to all stakeholders, yet from a managerial perspective, potentially challenging to operationalize. Anecdotal evidence in this area suggests that communication style, adapting to change, and technical skills are the three greatest differences among generations in the workplace (Lipman 2017). The following overarching strategies aim to ameliorate these challenges, while providing potential solutions for successful knowledge transfer and

Reverse Mentoring and Group Mentoring

The traditional notion of mentorship emanates from a top-down approach; however, in a learning economy, all members of an organization or society have the knowledge to share (Hirsch 2019). Historically, mentoring has been viewed as an effective practice among organizations, resulting in mostly positive experiences for the mentor and mentee. In recent years, due to the retirement of Baby Boomers and the associated decrease in intellectual capital, organizations have adopted "reverse mentoring" as a way to engage older and younger workers, while transferring important knowledge and updating skills (Half 2015). Reverse mentoring is described as the pairing of a junior employee from a younger generational cohort, who shares his or her knowledge and expertise with a senior colleague, who acts as the mentee (Marcinkus Murphy 2012). For example, older workers who have been identified as being highly competent in managing relationships can be paired with employees from the younger generations, who tend to be more adept with the latest technological trends. Reverse mentoring as an initiative has proven to be useful in cultivating working relationships between Baby Boomers and Millennials, for example, while engaging and retaining younger workers (Hirsch 2019).

As with the intention of traditional mentoring, reverse mentoring can boost morale, while reducing the knowledge gap between employees within different generational cohorts of an organization. Managers in reverse mentoring relationships also stand to benefit from these exchanges through building relationships with their employees. In turn, younger workers in a reverse mentoring relationship can identify organizational and external challenges and opportunities from an emergent point of view, thus opening new avenues to explore and develop. Reverse mentoring relationships have the ability to transfer a sense of purpose to new generations of workers, in addition to giving them access to influential members of the organization. Well-established older workers afford

Table 2.1 Generational cohort comparisons and integrated managerial strategies[a]

Cohort	Values	Leadership style	Teaching/learning and training preferences	Intergenerational managerial strategy
Traditionalists *Born between 1927 and 1946*	Dedication; Sacrifice; Strong work ethic; Responsibility	Clearly defined management structure; Independence	Formal and respectful; In person	Job sharing; Collaborative workspace design
Baby Boomers *Born between 1946 and 1964*	Relationships; Networking; Collegial	High expectations; Working in teams	Personal attention; Personal growth; Informal communications	Reverse and group mentoring with Gen Y and Z; Job sharing; Collaborative workspace design
Generation X (Gen X) *Born between 1965 and 1981*	Competitive; Individualistic; Relationships	Work-life balance; Informal work environments; Traditional leadership skills	Self-development; Self-improvement; Low face-to-face interactions	Knowledge chunking; Job sharing; Collaborative workspace design
Millennials (Gen Y) *Born between 1981 and 1996*	Open to new ideas; Idealistic; Passionate; Family time; Mobility; Connectivity and technology	Values diversity; Work-life balance; Independence; Flexible work schedules; Collaborative decision-making	Prefers constant and real-time feedback; Expects to be heard; Methodical approach to learning	Reverse and group mentoring with Baby Boomers; Knowledge chunking; Gamification; Collaborative workspace design

(continued)

Table 2.1 (continued)

Cohort	Values	Leadership style	Teaching/learning and training preferences	Intergenerational managerial strategy
Generation Z (Gen Z) *Born in mid-1990s*	Social justice; Job security; Work-life balance; Flexible working hours; Relationships; Technology	Team collaboration; Personalized corporate environment	Lifelong learning preferences; Collaborative team-based learning; Transparent succession planning; Technological access; Regularly scheduled feedback mechanisms	Reverse and group mentoring with Baby Boomers; Knowledge chunking; Gamification; Collaborative workspace design

[a]Bouncken and Reuschl (2016), Christfort and Monahan (2019), Costin (2019), Francis and Hoefel (2018), Frost (2017), Half (2015), Jones et al. (2018), Leclercq-Vandelannoitte and Isaac (2016), Meister and Willyerd (2010), Negruşa et al. (2015), Ozkan and Solmaz (2015), and Uhereczky (2019)

many opportunities for younger workers in sharing historical perspectives and decision-making, along with operational, financial, and human capital leadership strategies (Half 2015).

In a similar vein, reciprocal mentoring can be activated, where anyone can participate regardless of age, position, or gender, as the partners take turns in the mentor role, sharing expertise and fresh perspectives on procedures, for example. Group mentoring is another style of transferring knowledge, where three-four executives might mentor three-four younger workers using a social media platform. This method has been found to reduce training costs, while boosting engagement (Meister and Willyerd 2010). Finally, anonymous mentoring has shown some promise in the workplace, as the anonymity protects the identities of both the mentor and the mentee, permitting the benefits of free-flowing information transfer without the burden of a job title, or lack of one (Meister and Willyerd 2010). Non-traditional forms of mentoring have the ability to transform organizations, particularly with regard to the hierarchical structures, moving a company culture to a collaborative and more inclusive workplace where all members' views are heard, valued, and considered for implementation (Hirsch 2019).

Knowledge Transfer and Chunking

Chunking information is a process for transferring knowledge in a short, simple, and memorable way, designed so that individuals can readily store more information (Frost 2017). In situations when rapid knowledge transfer is expected (i.e., in a new job), or among cognitively diverse generations, chunking enables individuals to absorb smaller bits of complex information. The use of chunking for transferring knowledge across generations in the workforce appeals to Millennials and Gen Z, who prefer short bursts of learning. Learning chunks are designed to limit cognitive load and can be organized to build upon other chunks of information, allowing an individual to recall previous learnings through repetition and connection (Frost 2017). Implementing a chunking system for knowledge transfer may require allocated resources for established processes in a formalized environment, or can also be implemented more affordably through the use of technology (i.e., 60–90 second videos produced on mobile devices) (Cancialosi 2017). *The Millennials in Motion* leadership mentoring program at The Breakers Palm Beach in Florida, USA utilizes chunking strategies, or "burst learning" to meet the training and development needs of their employees "where they are", enabling learning any time and any place (for more information about the *Millennials in Motion* leadership mentoring program at The Breakers Palm Beach Florida, USA, see p. 12 in https://issuu.com/thebreakersp almbeach/docs/sir_report_2016) (Warech 2017).

Gamification

Similar to a chunking strategy for knowledge transfer, gamification uses games for training and education, which is appealing to all generations. Gamification boosts employee engagement and encourages a teamwork culture, building in social elements which instill a sense of community (Negruşa et al. 2015). Gamification in the workplace entices employee's natural curiosity over a variety of topics, built on their own intrinsic motivation to learn and succeed as they compete with their colleagues, building competency, and receiving recognition for these efforts (Negruşa et al. 2015). There are many technologies, which support gamification including personal mobile devices and other mobile technologies, Web 2.0, and augmented reality devices. By 2030, nearly half of the world's population will be online and connected via mobile technology, thus moving toward gamification as a learning and training channel will be central to retaining employees, particularly in the tourism and hospitality industries which are subject to high turnover rates (Negruşa et al. 2015).

Costa Cruise Line in partnership with Hydra-New Media organized a gamification strategy to teach travel agents, retailers, and sales staff about cruise ship packages, destinations, and special offers. In this company, previous attempts at e-Learning were not successful in training the staff due to the lack of interaction, feedback, and competition. Instead, three cruise ship-themed games were created, each targeting different levels of learning. The organizations who participated in the gamification initiatives reported significant increases in time spent by the employees on the platform, who visited the learning modules several times each, and most answered the questions correctly (Negruşa et al. 2015).

Another example of successful gamification can be seen in Marriott International's recruitment and hiring process, launching the online game, "My Marriott Hotel" in June 2011. This game was developed for social media platforms in multiple languages to recruit Millennials outside the U.S. Analyses of the traffic on the game observed users from 120 different countries simultaneously engaged in the game successfully executing tasks. One-third of those gamers clicked the "try it for real" button which redirected them to Marriott's career website to begin the application process (Negruşa et al. 2015).

Job Sharing

Job sharing is a full-time job split between two individuals, and a good solution for workers who seek to achieve better work-life balance, reduce working hours, and remain in a position, which meets their level of qualifications (Uhereczky 2019). Technological advancements such as virtual conferencing, corporate communications channels, texting applications, etc. have allowed for increased working capabilities both synchronously and asynchronously. Due to the talent shortage in the tourism and hospitality industries, job sharing might offer the scheduling flexibility craved by both the younger generations and the older generations seeking to phase out of the workplace toward retirement (Uhereczky 2019). Job sharing might also be attractive to members of the Gen Z cohort, as it allows for time away from work for training and educational pursuits, perhaps even advanced degrees.

The main benefit of job sharing is flexibility, and organizations who wish to retain qualified employees, particularly those who have worked for a number of years and possess the intellectual capital of a business, benefit from the arrangement. Passing on tacit corporate knowledge to younger generations can be seamless, as long as there is effective and consistent communication between those who are sharing the job. Regular meetings should be scheduled, along with consistent daily communications over message boards between the job sharers in order to clarify gray areas and responsibilities (Driver 2017).

Shared Collaborative Workspaces

Another strategy for combining intergenerational workers and their capabilities is to create collaborative workspaces in the physical or virtual business design. Collaborative workspaces are related to the trends as a result of the sharing economy in two important dimensions: shared physical assets and shared social interactions (Bouncken and Reuschl 2016). Collaborative workspaces have been shown to boost creativity and employee innovation, offering permanent or temporary use affording both flexibility and autonomy. These social spaces encourage interpersonal interactions among coworkers who benefit from the social, educational, cultural, and business-related objectives of an organization (Bouncken and Reuschl 2016).

Employees in collaborative workspaces build on their own autonomy, choosing when to interact with others, provide and receive feedback, and establish relationships. These unstructured interactions allow for experimentation of thought and creativity, and combined with directed organizational tasks, workers with a variety of levels of expertise have the opportunity to shape a more diverse culture. Unstructured interactions within a collaborative culture allow for diverse opinions, capabilities, and concepts of life, which is known to improve job satisfaction, trust, and social integration (Bouncken and Reuschl 2016; Leclercq-Vandelannoitte and Isaac 2016).

The sense of community arising out of a collaborative workspace diminishes a sense of isolation (Leclercq-Vandelannoitte and Isaac 2016). Increasingly, hotels are adopting communal working spaces through modern design, connecting traveling professionals, entrepreneurs, and local residents for networking and inspiration. Among many others, Accor Hotels and Jin Jiang have heavily invested in building collaborative workspaces both inside and outside their hotel facilities (Wich 2019).

Following this trend for consumers, tourism and hospitality companies can adopt this paradigm for its own workers. Companies have observed that creating opportunities for increased interactions across employees from different departments, and even with other stakeholders (e.g. suppliers, customers) can lead to increased productivity, efficiency, and creativity (Leclercq-Vandelannoitte and Isaac 2016). Collaborative workspace design may be a means for retaining older generations of workers, while recruiting younger generations, thus leveraging existing knowledge capital while allowing for the co-creation of new ideas and business strategies. Given the high growth rate of the collaborative workspace design in the hotel sector for consumers, tourism and hospitality companies should translate this model inward, with a focus on attracting younger generations of workers.

Conclusion

According to a recent study, the Gen Z workforce possesses a more favorable view of the tourism and hospitality sector than did past generational cohorts. Not motivated strictly by salary, Gen Z workers envision the industry as exciting and fulfilling (Goh and Lee 2018). Also motivated by career growth opportunities, jobs in tourism and hospitality are appealing to Gen Z workers, as this sector affords many opportunities for climbing up the ladder due to high levels of turnover. Due to this potentially rapid rate of ascension, Gen Z workers have an opportunity in the current workforce representative of five-generational cohorts, to interact and work within the diversity of generations. The strategies for management and succession planning offered in this chapter shed light on new perspectives for intergenerational management as it pertains to the thriving and growing tourism and hospitality global sector.

References

Ann, S., & Blum, S. C. (2020). Motivating Senior Employees in the Hospitality Industry. *International Journal of Contemporary Hospitality Management, 32*(1), 324–346.

Arruda, W. (2018, November 13). How To Make Your Workplace Ready For Gen Z. *Forbes [Online]*. Retrieved September 27, 2019, from https://www.forbes.com/sites/williamarruda/2018/11/13/how-to-make-your-workplace-ready-for-gen-z/#4b0732a54d30.

Baron, J. (2019, July 3). The Key To Gen Z Is Video Content. *Forbes [Online]*. Retrieved from https://www.forbes.com/sites/jessicabaron/2019/07/03/the-key-to-gen-z-is-video-content/#c92c3fd34848.

Boehm, S. A., & Kunze, F. (2015). Age Diversity and Age Climate in the Workplace. In: Bal, P., Kooij, D., Rousseau, D. (eds) *Aging Workers and the Employee-Employer Relationship*. Springer.

Bouncken, R. B., & Reuschl, A. J. (2016). Coworking-Spaces: How a Phenomenon of the Sharing Economy Builds a Novel Trend for the Workplace and for Entrepreneurship. *Review of Managerial Science, 12(*1), 317–334. https://doi.org/10.1007/s11846-016-0215-y.

Buckley, P., Viechnicki, P., & Barua, A. (2015, October 17). A new Understanding of Millennials: Generational Differences Reexamined. *Deloitte [Online]*. Retrieved October 8, 2019, from https://www2.deloitte.com/us/en/insights/economy/issues-by-the-numbers/understanding-millennials-generational-differences.html.

Cancialosi, C. (2017, January 18). 6 Key Steps to Influencing Effective Knowledge Transfer in Your Business. *Forbes [Online]*. Retrieved October 3, 2019, from https://www.forbes.com/sites/chriscancialosi/2014/12/08/6-key-steps-to-influencing-effective-knowledge-transfer-in-your-business/#4ca121895fe6.

Catalyst. (2019). Generations-Demographic Trends in Population and Workforce: Quick Take. *Catalyst [Online]*. Retrieved November 29, 2019 from https://www.catalyst.org/research/generations-demographic-trends-in-population-and-workforce/.

Ceniza-Levine, C. (2019, June 6). Gen-Z Survey Reveals How To Get The Most From This New Workforce. *Forbes [Online]*. Retrieved September 27, 2019, from https://www.forbes.com/sites/carolinecenizalevine/2019/06/06/gen-z-survey-reveals-how-to-get-the-most-from-this-new-workforce/#1ffa09a1fac8.

Ceruto, D. S. (2019, August 28). The Basics Of Intraoffice Conflict Management For Effective Executives And Managers. *Forbes [Online]*. Retrieved October 9, 2019, from https://www.forbes.com/sites/forbescoachescouncil/2019/08/28/the-basics-of-intraoffice-conflict-management-for-effective-executives-and-managers/#6afe7644254b.

Chen, P. J., & Choi, Y. (2008). Generational Differences in Work Values: A Study of Hospitality Management. *International Journal of Contemporary Hospitality Management, 20*(6), 595–615.

Christfort, K., & Monahan, K. (2019, May 16). The Millennial Mix: What Leaders Should Know. *Deloitte US. [Online]*. Retrieved September 17, 2019, from https://www2.deloitte.com/us/en/pages/finance/articles/cfo-insights-the-millennial-mix-what-leaders-should-know.html.

Costa, G. (2019, June 13). Corporate Social Responsibility, Purpose Brands And Gen-Z. *Forbes [Online]*. Retrieved September 27, 2019, from https://www.forbes.com/sites/esade/2019/03/13/csr-purpose-brands-and-gen-z/#1e8a2d215849.

Costin, G. (2019, August 7). A Day in the Life of a Working Baby Boomer and Gen Xer. *Forbes [Online]*. Retrieved from https://www.forbes.com/sites/forbesbooksauthors/2019/08/07/a-day-in-the-life-of-a-working-baby-boomer-and-gen-xer/#34746eb06e76.

Development, I. O. (2018, November 10). The Ultimate Guide to Generation Z in the Workplace. *Resources [Online]*. Retrieved October 1, 2019, from https://resources.insideoutdev.com/generations/gen-z.

Driver, S. (2017, December 12). What Is Job Sharing? *Business News Daily [Online]*. Retrieved October 6, 2019, from https://www.businessnewsdaily.com/10439-job-sharing-pros-cons.html.

Eyoun, K., Chen, H., Ayoun, B., & Khliefat, A. (2020). The Relationship Between Purpose of Performance Appraisal and Psychological Contract: Generational Differences as a Moderator. *International Journal of Hospitality Management, 86*.

Folz, C. (2019, August 16). Four Myths About the Multigenerational Workplace. *SHRM [Online]*. Retrieved September 30, 2019, from https://www.shrm.org/resourcesandtools/hr-topics/behavioral-competencies/global-and-cultural-effectiveness/pages/four-myths-about-the-multigenerational-workplace.aspx.

Francis, T., & Hoefel, F. (2018). 'True Gen': Generation Z and Its Implications for Companies: The Influence of Gen Z – The First Generation of True Digital Natives – Is Expanding. *McKinsey & Company [Online]*. Retrieved from https://www.mckinsey.com/industries/consumer-packaged-goods/our-insights/true-gen-generation-z-and-its-implications-for-companies.

Frost, R. (2017, November 8). What Makes Chunking Such An Effective Way To Learn? *Forbes [Online]*. Retrieved October 3, 2019, from https://www.forbes.com/sites/quora/2017/11/08/what-makes-chunking-such-an-effective-way-to-learn/#4e71ceb860a9.

Fry, R. (2018, April 11). Millennials Are the Largest Generation in the U.S. Labor Force. *Pew Research [Online]*. Retrieved October 6, 2019, from https://www.pewresearch.org/fact-tank/2018/04/11/millennials-largest-generation-us-labor-force/.

Fry, R. (2019). Baby Boomers Are Staying in the Labor Force at Rates Not Seen in Generations for People Their Age. *Pew Research [Online]*. Retrieved from https://www.pewresearch.org/fact-tank/2019/07/24/baby-boomers-us-labor-force/.

Glass, A. (2007). Understanding Generational Differences for Competitive Success. *Industrial and Commercial Training, 39*(2), 98–103. https://doi.org/10.1108/00197850710732424.

Goh, E., & Lee, C. (2018). A Workforce to Be Reckoned With: The Emerging Pivotal Generation Z Hospitality Workforce. *International Journal of Hospitality Management, 73*, 20–28.

Green, S. (2019, April 9). How To Set Up Millennial Managers To Successfully Lead Gen Z Workers. *Forbes [Online]*. Retrieved September 27, 2019, from https://www.forbes.com/sites/forbescoachescouncil/2019/04/09/how-to-set-up-millennial-managers-to-successfully-lead-gen-z-workers/#2d716c733d17.

Half, R. (2015, April 7). Reverse Mentoring: Turning Tables on Tradition. Retrieved October 9, 2019, from https://www.roberthalf.com/blog/management-tips/reverse-mentoring-turning-tables-on-tradition.

He, E. (2019, February 25). Gearing Up For Gen-Z: What Employers Should Know About Today's Young Workers. *Forbes [Online]*. Retrieved September 27, 2019, from https://www.forbes.com/sites/emilyhe/2019/02/25/gearing-up-for-gen-z-what-employers-should-know-about-todays-young-workers/#3fd0ab3d1bee.

Hirsch, A. S. (2019, August 16). Knowledge Is Best Shared. *SHRM [Online]*. Retrieved October 6, 2019, from https://www.shrm.org/hr-today/news/all-things-work/pages/knowledge-is-best-shared.aspx.

Jones, J. S., Murray, S. R., & Tapp, S. R. (2018). Generational Differences in the Workplace. *Journal of Business Diversity, 18*(2).

Kong, H., Okumus, F., & Bu, N. (2020). Linking Organizational Career Management with Generation Y Employees' Organizational Identity: The Mediating Effect of Meeting Career Expectations. *Journal of Hospitality Marketing & Management*, *29*(2), 164–181.

Kronos, W. I. (2019, June). Meet Gen Z. The Next Generation Is Here: Hopeful, Anxious, Hardworking, and Searching for Inspiration. *Workforce Institute [Online]*. Retrieved from https://workforceinstitute.org/workforce-institute-ressources-assets/.

Leclercq-Vandelannoitte, A., & Isaac, H. (2016). The New Office: How Coworking Changes the Work Concept. *Journal of Business Strategy*, *37*(6), 3–9. https://doi.org/10.1108/jbs-10-2015-0105.

Lipman, V. (2017). Hot to Manage Generational Differences in the Workplace. *Forbes [Online]*. Retrieved November 29, 2019 from https://hbr.org/2010/05/mentoring-millennials.

Marcinkus Murphy, W. (2012). Reverse Mentoring at Work: Fostering Cross-Generational Learning and Developing Millennial Leaders. *Human Resource Management*, *51*(4), 549–573.

McInnis-Day, B., COO, & SuccessFactors, SAP. (2019, June 20). The Gen-Z Workforce: A Balance of High-Tech and High-Touch. *Forbes [Online]*. Retrieved September 27, 2019, from https://www.forbes.com/sites/sap/2019/06/03/the-gen-z-workforce-a-balance-of-high-tech-and-high-touch/#138d71164b95.

Mehta, K. (2019, February 25). A Better Way To Manage Conflicts In The Workplace. *Forbes [Online]*. Retrieved October 9, 2019, from https://www.forbes.com/sites/iese/2019/02/25/a-better-way-to-manage-conflicts-in-the-workplace/#c3e8f1e47df9.

Meister, J. C., & Willyerd, K. (2010). Mentoring Millennials. *Harvard Business Review [Online]*. Retrieved November 29, 2019 from https://hbr.org/2010/05/mentoring-millennials.

Morris, C. (2018). 61 Million Gen Zers Are About to Enter the US Workforce and Radically Change If Forever. *CNBC@work [Online]*. Retrieved November 30, 2019 from https://www.cnbc.com/2018/05/01/61-million-gen-zers-about-to-enter-us-workforce-and-change-it.html.

Neal, S. (2019, July 29). Are Companies About to Have a Gen X Retention Problem? *Harvard Business Review [Online]*. Retrieved September 20, 2019, from https://hbr.org/2019/07/are-companies-about-to-have-a-gen-x-retention-problem.

Negruşa, A., Toader, V., Sofică, A., Tutunea, M., & Rus, R. (2015). Exploring Gamification Techniques and Applications for Sustainable Tourism. *Sustainability, 7*(8), 11160–11189.

Ozkan, M., & Solmaz, B. (2015). The Changing Face of the Employees–Generation Z and Their Perceptions of Work (A Study Applied to University Students). *Procedia Economics and Finance, 26*, 476–483.

Papavasileiou, E., Lyons, S., Shaw, G., & Georgiou, A. (2017). Work Values in Tourism: Past, Present and Future. *Annals of Tourism Research, 64*, 150–162.

Rossi, R. (2019, July 3). Understanding Millennials' and Technology's Role In The Workforce, Part One. *Forbes [Online]*. Retrieved September 30, 2019, from https://www.forbes.com/sites/forbesbusinessdevelopmentco uncil/2019/07/03/understanding-millennials-and-technologys-role-in-the-workforce-part-one/#59fc2d0b2034.

Schawbel, D. (2014, September 2). Millennials and Gen Z Global Workplace Expectations Study. *Millennial Branding [Online]*. Retrieved on September 13, 2019, from http://millennialbranding.com/2014/geny-genz-global-wor kplace-expectations-study/.

Solnet, D., Baum, T., Robinson, R. N., & Lockstone-Binney, L. (2016). What About the Workers? Roles and Skills for Employees in Hotels of the Future. *Journal of Vacation Marketing, 22*(3), 212–226.

Solnet, D., & Kralj, A. (2011). Generational Differences in Work Attitudes: Evidence from the Hospitality Industry. *FIU Hospitality Review, 29*(2), 37–54.

Stahl, A. (2019a, August 21). How To Manage Generation Z Employees. *Forbes [Online]*. Retrieved from https://www.forbes.com/sites/ashleystahl/2019/09/26/how-to-manage-generation-z-employees/#18e7ae69681e.

Stahl, A. (2019b, September 10). How Generation-Z Will Revolutionize the Workplace. *Forbes [Online]*. Retrieved September 27, 2019, from https://www.forbes.com/sites/ashleystahl/2019/09/10/how-generation-z-will-revolutionize-the-workplace/#68112a104f53.

Stahl, A. (2018, September 26). Gen Z: What to Expect from the New Workforce. *Forbes [Online]*. Retrieved from https://www.forbes.com/sites/ashleystahl/2018/09/26/gen-z-what-to-expect-from-the-new-work-force/#67f6489663e0.

Trabold, E. (2019, January 9). How Tech Companies Can Attract And Motivate Gen Z. *Forbes [Online]*. Retrieved September 30, 2019, from https://www.forbes.com/sites/forbestechcouncil/2019/01/09/how-tech-companies-can-attract-and-motivate-gen-z/#367b69ac1150.

Uhereczky, A. (2019). Are You Missing Out on the Latest Workplace Revolution?: The Untapped Potential of Job Sharing. *Forbes [Online]*. Retrieved November 30, 2019 from https://www.forbes.com/sites/agnesuhereczky/2019/07/02/are-you-missing-out-on-the-latest-workplace-revolution-the-untapped-potential-of-job-sharing/#558ca52e3403.

Warech, M. A. (2017). How the Hospitality Industry Is Rethinking Development for Its Next Generation of Leaders. *Hotel Business Review [Online]*. Retrieved November 30, 2019, from Cornell University, SHA School site: https://scholarship.sha.cornell.edu/cihlerfom/4.

Weeks, K. P. (2017, July 31). Every Generation Wants Meaningful Work - But Thinks Other Age Groups Are in It for the Money. *Harvard Business Review [Online]*. Retrieved October 4, 2019, from https://hbr.org/2017/07/every-generation-wants-meaningful-work-but-thinks-other-age-groups-are-in-it-for-the-money.

Wich, S. (2019). Coworking Spaces in Hotels – A Match Made in Heaven? *Hospitalitynet [Online]*. Retrieved November 30, 2019 from https://www.hospitalitynet.org/opinion/4092975.html.

WTTC. (2019). World Travel & Tourism Council: Travel & Tourism Economic Impact 2019: World. *WTTC [Online]*. Retrieved November 30, 2019 from https://www.wttc.org/economic-impact/country-analysis/region-data/.

Zopiatis, A., Krambia-Kapardis, M., & Varnavas, A. (2012). Y-ers, X-ers and Boomers: Investigating the Multigenerational (mis) Perceptions in the Hospitality Workplace. *Tourism and Hospitality Research, 12*(2), 101–121.

3

Generation Z and Tourism Entrepreneurship: Generation Z's Career Path in the Tourism Industry

Senem Yazici and Reyhan Arslan Ayazlar

Introduction

Tourism is the fastest growing industry that creates jobs and affects the global economy tremendously. According to WTO statistics, the tourism industry grew by 4% in 2019 (World Tourism Organization 2019). It is important to indicate that the current population of the world is 7.6 billion (World Population Prospects Report 2019) while international tourist arrivals worldwide reached 1.5 billion in 2019 (UNWTO 2020). Therefore, tourism has shown strong growth and is helping in the economic development of countries. The most common definition of tourism is 'the activities of persons travelling to and staying in places outside their usual environment for not more than one consecutive year for leisure, business and other purposes not related to the exercise of an

---

S. Yazici (✉) · R. Arslan Ayazlar
Department of Tourism Management, Faculty of Tourism, Mugla Sıtkı Kocman University, Mugla, Turkey
e-mail: senemyazici@mu.edu.tr

© The Author(s), under exclusive license to Springer Nature Switzerland AG 2021
N. Stylos et al. (eds.), *Generation Z Marketing and Management in Tourism and Hospitality*,
https://doi.org/10.1007/978-3-030-70695-1_3

activity remunerated from within the place visited' (TSA: RMF 2008; Page 2007: 12). The tourism industry is a huge business ecosystem that includes accommodation (hotels, motels, resorts, camping, hostels, bungalows), food and beverages (hotel restaurants, local restaurants, catering), transportation (railway, road, water, air), associated sectors (gift shops, craft shops, local shops), recreation and entertainment, travel services and tour operation businesses (Quattrociocchi et al. 2017). UNWTO (2008: 2) expressed the ecosystem of tourism as 'the activities that typically produce tourism characteristics products'. The development of mass tourism has changed small villages into massive tourist destinations (Ransley 2012). Mass tourism has increased the demand for new products and activities for tourist consumption, although the demand for tourism activities has expanded to increase entrepreneurial activities.

Humanity is in a new era, called the digital era (Kesici and Tunç 2018). The aspect of this era that is having most impact on technology development and its effects on human life. Technological devices have become widely used, both at home and at work (Hoque 2018). This era will also have new employees, from Generation Z. That means that different generations will be involved in business life. Organizations have a more multigenerational structure than ever before. Directors have to manage employees from different generations, adapt their workplaces to this diversity, and attract new talents to the organization—in other words have a good talent management. According to a CNBC article, the oldest 'Gen Zers' have graduated from college and are about to enter the workforce. They have entered the business world after the baby boomers' retirement, but Gen Z is still developing and maturing (Agarwal and Vaghela 2018). Managers of organizations and human resource managers should consider the differences among the generations. They should separately evaluate the generational differences (Barclays 2013). Are managers ready to understand Gen Z's needs and expectations? Do they know enough about how their features might be useful for their businesses? Are they ready to manage this generation? Thus, it is important to understand Generation Z's characteristics, needs, expectations and preferences in business life.

This chapter aims to discuss and highlight Generation Z's (or Gen Z for short) career choices in tourism entrepreneurship. The three main concepts of this chapter are tourism entrepreneurs, intrapreneurs and Gen Z, which are examined by using an extensive literature review. The first part of the chapter highlights the definition of tourism entrepreneurship, types of tourism entrepreneurs and the role of intrapreneurs in tourism enterprises. The second part of the chapter will focus on the characteristics of Gen Z, Gen Z's lifestyle, business choices and the future of Gen Z's tourism entrepreneurial career choices. The final part of this chapter will discuss Gen Z's career choices in the tourism industry.

Tourism and Entrepreneurship

Entrepreneurship has been studied extensively, from as early as the 1950s (Lant and Mezias 1990). Many entrepreneurial theories have been developed and examined empirically by researchers (Nielsen et al. 2017). Two scholars who developed 'classical' theories of entrepreneurship were Schumpeter (1934) and Kirzner (1973) (Shockley and Frank 2011; Isık et al. 2019). Schumpeter (1934) made it clear that entrepreneurship requires innovation, while Krizner (1973) pointed out that alertness is the key to entrepreneurship (Shockley and Frank 2011). Ahmad and Seymour (2008: 9) explained the concepts of entrepreneurship as 'Entrepreneurs are those persons (business owners) who seek to generate value, through the creation or expansion of economic activity, by identifying and exploiting new products, processes or markets. Entrepreneurial activity is enterprising human action in pursuit of the generation of value, through the creation or expansion of economic activity, by identifying and exploiting new products, processes or markets. Entrepreneurship is a phenomenon associated with entrepreneurial activity". Hessels and Naudé (2019: 399) supported that "entrepreneurship is needed for economic development and that medium-sized enterprises (SMEs) are vehicles for such entrepreneurship'.

There are many ways to start a business under the tourism umbrella. The tourism ecosystem includes many tourism enterprises like travel agencies, tour operators, hotels, restaurants and cruises (Farrell and

Twining-Ward 2004). The entrepreneur who can notice opportunities has the key to real success. The tourism industry is full of entrepreneurial opportunities for small and medium-sized enterprises (SMEs). Therefore, the industry is dominated by SMEs (Khoshkhoo and Nadalipour 2016). Tourism SMEs play an important role in a country's economic and cultural development (Chang 2011). Tourism entrepreneurship's rapid developments can create jobs, income and profits, therefore, Koh and Hatten (2002: 30) defined a tourism entrepreneur as 'a creator of a touristic enterprise; there are two commonly practised routes to tourism entrepreneurship: starting from scratch, and acquiring a franchise. The starting from scratch route involves opportunity identification, opportunity assessment and opportunity pursuit. The franchise route is the acquisition of someone else's success formula'.

Tourism entrepreneurship has become more important not only because it creates economic benefits but because it also gives a competitive advantage among tourism destinations (Ireland and Webb 2007). Competition has been an important issue of international tourism (Gursoy et al. 2015). All tourism entrepreneurs must adapt to the highly competitive and international business environment. Cecilia et al. (2011: 246) stressed that tourists' needs, and demands have changed over the years and require more attention to detail from tourism entrepreneurs, which they explained as:

> The new tourists are more experienced, more educated, more 'green', more flexible, more independent, more quality-conscious and 'harder to please' than ever before. Furthermore, they are well-read and know what they want and where they want to go. The different approach of the new tourists creates a demand for new products. The small, medium and micro-entrepreneurs within the tourism industry are dependent on major tourism developments. It is an essential role of these small entrepreneurs to be increased to deal with the changing demands of the new tourists.

Tourism entrepreneurs must react quickly that tourist needs are changing quickly. Otherwise, it will be too late to catch the demand in time. Tourism is so sensible that is affected in many ways. It is not like other industries, it has unique characteristics that means that tourism entrepreneurship differs from others (Solvoll et al. 2015; Tresna and Nirmalasari 2018). The tourism characteristics are:

- 'Intangibility: Services are viewed as performances or actions rather than objects' (Koh and Hatten 2002: 31).
- 'Inseparability: The simultaneous production and consumption of a service. Goods are produced first, then sold and consumed, whereas most services are sold first and then produced and consumed simultaneously' (Bowen 2002: 5).
- 'Heterogeneity: The vagaries of human interaction between and among service contact employees and consumers' (Bowen 2002: 5).
- 'Perishability: The service production characteristic of fixed time and space. Services cannot be saved, stored, resold, or returned' (Bowen 2002: 5).
- 'Seasonality: The concentration of tourism flows at a certain time in a destination country' (Karamustafa and Ulama 2010: 5).
- 'Service management skills: Understanding, developing and deploying service management skills' (Koh and Hatten 2002: 31).

Tourism entrepreneurship differs from general entrepreneurship because of its characteristics. General entrepreneurship literature would be beneficial to learn and apply in a tourism context. However, many issues have not been fully understood yet. Tourism entrepreneurship has not been fully covered, describe the growth of tourism entrepreneur. Recent studies suggested that tourism entrepreneurs are motivated by living styles and conditions known as lifestyles and that they are not profit-oriented (Solvoll et al. 2015; Pırnar 2015). Tourism entrepreneurs require more effective social, public relations, marketing and communication, business development, and service management skills (Sima et al. 2015). Consequently, tourism entrepreneurs who have unique skills like innovative and managerial skills would have a more competitive advantage than others (Pırnar 2015).

Generally, entrepreneurship literature divides entrepreneurs into many different types, such as lifestyle and serial (Schwienbacher 2007), internet entrepreneurs (Serarols-Tarrés et al. 2006), nascent entrepreneurs (Davidsson 2006) and social entrepreneurs (Saebi et al. 2019). Types of tourism entrepreneurs are classified mainly based on the type of journey or service offered by the entrepreneur (Koh and Hatten 2002). The type of entrepreneur is also important because this affects the full journey of entrepreneurship (Rodriguez-Sanchez et al. 2019). There are many arguments about the types of tourism entrepreneurs (Fu et al. 2019), which will be examined in the next section.

Types of Tourism Entrepreneurs

It is essential to examine more details about types of tourism entrepreneurs to understand the nature of tourism entrepreneurship. The typology of tourism has not been studied extensively (Koh and Hatten 2002; McGehee and Kline 2008; Fu et al. 2019). Koh and Hatten (2002) suggested the typology of tourism entrepreneurs as being two categories—product-based or having a behaviour- or motivation-based typology, which is shown in Table 3.1. McGehee and Kline (2008) redefined Koh and Hatten's typologies with an example, which helped to understand their ideas more clearly. Product-based typology includes inventive, innovative and imitative tourism entrepreneurs. Motivation-based includes social, lifestyle, marginal, closet, nascent and serial tourism entrepreneurs. Product-based typology simply refers to the tourism product, whether such a product already exists or whether it could be created. Behavioural-based is related to the entrepreneur's desire, characteristics, skills and abilities.

Product-Based Tourism Entrepreneurs

Product-based tourism entrepreneurs are focused on inventing, creating or applying an existing product into their entrepreneurial venture. It is quite problematic to do that in tourism because of the definition of tourism products. Tresna and Nirmalasari (2018: 39) articulated the definition of tourism products as 'all kinds of products, both goods and services, which are tourism commodities'. Tourism entrepreneurs must be aware of the elements of tourism products that cannot be separated

Table 3.1 Tourism entrepreneurs' typologies and definitions

	Koh and Haten's (2002)	McGehee and Kline (2008)
Product-based typology		
Inventive tourism entrepreneur	Whose offer is entirely new to the industry, for example, when Thomas Cook launched his tour agency	One who has commercialized product is truly new to the tourism industry Example: American Express travellers' cheque
Innovative tourism entrepreneur	Whose offers something entirely new, for instance, casino hotels or the creation of Disneyland	One who has commercialized products is not new but is an adaptation of an existing product or the discovery of a previously untapped market Example: Orbitz.com
Imitative tourism entrepreneur	Where the enterprise offer holds little difference against the established offer, as in the case of franchisees, or differentiated motels, restaurants, cafes etc.	One who is a product is not significantly different from existing products Example: A franchise hotel or restaurant that is not new to the marketplace but may be new to the community
Behaviour-based typology		
Social tourism entrepreneur	Whose founds not-for-profit enterprises such as museums, galleries and community initiatives	One who starts a non-profit tourism enterprise Example: A regional tourism industry association

(continued)

while organizing the package. Tour packages mainly include transportation, accommodation, food, transfer, entertainment and other services (Lis-Gutiérrez et al. 2018). Therefore, there are many ways of being an entrepreneur in tourism.

60　S. Yazici and R. A. Ayazlar

Table 3.1 (continued)

	Koh and Haten's (2002)	McGehee and Kline (2008)
Lifestyle tourism entrepreneur	Whose as the name suggests launches enterprises support their desired lifestyle, hobby or interests with little intention of growing the venture	One who starts an enterprise to support a desired lifestyle; generally, these types of tourism entrepreneurs have no desire to 'grow' the business beyond a certain size Example: BandB owner and avid kayaker who specializes in guided kayak adventures
Marginal tourism entrepreneur	Whose operate businesses in the informal economy and are tolerated but unregulated or unregistered by government. These might include street traders, hawkers and unlicensed tour guides	One who starts and operates a tourism enterprise within the informal and peripheral sector of the tourism industry Example: Unlicensed roadside farmer's market
Closet tourism entrepreneur	Whose moonlights and operate enterprises alongside a full-time job	One who operates a tourism enterprise while maintaining a full-time job as an employee elsewhere Example: A high school teacher who offers guide services during the summer
Nascent tourism entrepreneur	Whose venture is in the creation or early stages of being established as a touristic enterprise	One who is in the process of developing a tourism enterprise Example: An individual developing a business plan or in the process of attracting capital investment

(continued)

Table 3.1 (continued)

	Koh and Haten's (2002)	McGehee and Kline (2008)
Serial tourism entrepreneur	To include those who have founded more than one touristic organization including those whose initial enterprise(s) may have failed	One who has founded a succession of tourism enterprises, either due to failure of the previous enterprise or evolution of one enterprise into another form Example: Tourism enterprise A becomes a corporation, whereupon the serial entrepreneur sells the business and starts tourism enterprise B Note

Source Adapted from Koh and Hatten (2002), McGehee and Kline (2008), and Phelan (2014)

One could become an entrepreneur by creating an unusual package tours, opening different type of accommodations or offering interesting transportations. The inventive tourism entrepreneur invents tourism products or services from scratch. Unfortunately, there are not many inventive tourism entrepreneurs in the world. Good examples of inventive tourism entrepreneurs are Hilton, Marriot, lastminute.com and trivago.com (Ateljevic and Li 2017). On the other hand, innovative entrepreneurs create a new way of doing things or services. A good example would be all-inclusive hotels, themed amusement parks and hotels (Goldsby and Mathews 2018). The differences between innovation and inventive tourism entrepreneurs are risk levels, business idea processes and market competition (Koh and Hatten 2002). The last classification of the product-based typology is imitative tourism entrepreneurs. Imitative tourism entrepreneurs prefer to do similar services to others or franchise a famous brand. This type of entrepreneur does not want to take high risks and is more careful about the needs of the community.

Behaviour-Based Tourism Entrepreneurs

Behaviour- or motivation-based tourism entrepreneurs are linked with entrepreneurs' perceptions, characteristics and skills (Koh and Hatten 2002; McGehee and Kline 2008). Koh and Hatten (2002) suggested six behaviour-based tourism entrepreneurs' characteristics as 'social, closet, nascent, serial, lifestyle, marginal and growth-oriented'. All six behaviour-based tourism entrepreneurs are having different characteristics, motivations and reasons to start a new business. Social, closet, nascent and serial tourism entrepreneurs are recently getting more attention. Social tourism entrepreneurs are founders of non-profit tourism organizations. Reindrawati (2018) defined social tourism entrepreneurs as 'those who conduct tourism business activities that inspire and encourage local communities to participate to carry out business activities travel'. Social tourism entrepreneurs prefer to establish tourism locations for the benefit of other people. Some gardens, museums, aquariums, art galleries and non-profit tourism organizations (the American Hotel and Motel Association, the Travel Industry Association of America, Travel and Tourism Research Association, the International Council of Hotel, Restaurant, and Institutional Education, and the International Society of Travel and Tourism Educators) are good examples of social tourism entrepreneurial ventures (Koh and Hatten 2002; Reindrawati 2018).

The closet tourism entrepreneur, who lives and works in places where tourism occurs, practises tourism-related activities in addition to their full-time duties. The closet tourism entrepreneur has an income from a daily job, while extra earnings come from part-time tourism services that they offer (Koh and Hatten 2002). The nascent tourism entrepreneurs are at the beginning of their tourism venture (Karatas-Ozkan and Chell 2010; Douglas 2017). McGehee and Kline (2008) suggested that nascent tourism entrepreneurs develop a business plan, process financial help, attract investors and actively seek business opportunities. The serial tourism entrepreneurs, who already have tourism-related establishments and continue to find other—related or unrelated—tourism establishments (Koh and Hatten 2002). They have more opportunities than many other types of entrepreneur. Serial tourism entrepreneurs know about running a successful venture. They are well-regarded in terms of getting financial help because they have already received capital for previous enterprises (Nahata 2019). Conversely, marginal, lifestyle entrepreneurs and growth-oriented entrepreneurs have been the subject of the tourism literature.

Marginal Tourism Entrepreneurs

The most attention from scholars has been on marginal tourism entrepreneurs (Dahles 1998; Dahles and Bras 1999; Koh and Hatten 2002; Bird and Mitsuhashi 2003; Ndabeni and Rogerson 2005; Rogerson 2008; King 2009; Berdychevsky 2016; Karunaratne 2017) and lifestyle tourism entrepreneurs (Ateljevic and Doorne 2000; Koh and Hatten 2002; Shaw and Williams 2004; Ollenburg and Buckley 2007; Lashley and Rowson 2010; Dawson et al. 2011; Casado-Díaz et al. 2014; Bredvold and Skålén 2016; Xu et al. 2017; Cunha et al. 2018). Marginal tourism entrepreneurs were known as 'romantic entrepreneurs' (Dahles and Bras 1999), these being one of the most interesting types of tourism entrepreneurs. Berdychevsky (2016) described romantic entrepreneurs by stating: 'local men romancing female tourists can be conceptualized as romantic entrepreneurs since many of them perceive tourist girlfriends as an economic strategy to make a living and secure their future'. King (2009: 231) claimed: 'the concept of 'romantic entrepreneur' adequately describes (young) men putting much effort into the establishment of romantic relationships with female tourists, intending to be supported by these women or of acquiring a ticket to follow them to their home country'.

All studies related to romantic entrepreneurs were conducted in South Asia or undeveloped territories. This type of tourism entrepreneurship could be related to low income, unskilled workers, education levels and economic problems (King 2009). On the other hand, Bird and Mitsuhashi (2003) and Karunaratne (2017) emphasized that the term 'romantic entrepreneur' has a different meaning to entrepreneurship in the Japanese context. Hirschmeier (1964) was one of the scholars who defined Japanese entrepreneurs as 'romantic entrepreneurs'. He explained their style as 'start a new business, often change their industry, type of business or management styles and establish many businesses to achieve maximum wealth' (Hirschmeier 1964, cited in Karunaratne 2017). However, romantic entrepreneurs can also be local boys who exchange their service (as an unofficial tourist guide) or friendship for money with tourists in tourism contexts (Dahles 1998; Dahles and Bras 1999). Afterwards, Dahles and Bras (1999) offered the view that these types of tourism entrepreneurs can be labelled as 'marginal tourism entrepreneurs'. Koh and Hatten (2002) explained that 'marginal tourism entrepreneurs are those who operate their enterprises in the informal and peripheral sector (i.e., the part of an economy where businesses are unregistered but tolerated by the government) of the travel/tourism industry, such as street vendors, hawkers and unlicensed tour guides. They are certainly not employees but are independent business owners'. Marginal tourism entrepreneurs are also portrayed as survivalist (Ndabeni and Rogerson 2005; Rogerson 2008).

Lifestyle Tourism Entrepreneurs

The lifestyle tourism entrepreneur is another type of behavioural-based tourism entrepreneur. Koh and Hatten (2002: 36) described lifestyle tourism entrepreneurs as 'those who launch touristic enterprises to support their desired lifestyles and/or hobbies/interests with no/little intention of growing their enterprises'. Similarly, Fu et al. (2019: 5) described lifestyle entrepreneurs as 'focus more on improving their quality of life by living in a place that they desire, building social networks, and being part of a community, rather than maximizing profits'. For many years, retired people have been the key players of lifestyle tourism entrepreneurs (Casado-Díaz et al. 2014). They often harbour a desire to live in a seaside or rural area, with a slow and natural life (Ollenburg and Buckley 2007). Some people establish a small restaurant because of the enjoyment of cooking and meeting new people (Koh and Hatten 2002).

Lifestyle tourism entrepreneurs start a business because they need to satisfy different interests with low risks and low skills required. Some of the lifestyle entrepreneurs are retired people who have travelled to a place just for the opportunity to run a tourism business venture. Some people pursue a destination to have a different lifestyle. If a tourism entrepreneur knows a specific area like organic food, they may create innovative services and products within their new desired destination, mainly in a rural area (Cunha et al. 2018). Masurel and Snellenberg (2017) emphasized that lifestyle entrepreneurs' competencies are not different than other entrepreneurs. However, Sun et al. (2019) found that lifestyle entrepreneurs' work and personal lives are not separable. This may create some problems in the entrepreneur's life when their circumstances change.

Lifestyle tourism entrepreneurs have always had a relationship with the retirement plan (Prince 2017). Many lifestyle entrepreneurs open 'Bed and Breakfast' (B&B) guest houses or hotels so they can spend their retirement in sunny and small villages (Crawford and Naar 2016b). Crawford and Naar (2016a) found that most of the B&B owners in the USA are lifestyle entrepreneurs. However, some entrepreneurs become lifestyle entrepreneurs because they like the living conditions, personal freedom, more time, financial independence and daily job routine (Peters et al. 2009; Crawford and Naar 2016a, b; Balachandran and Sakthivelan 2013). Many lifestyle tourism entrepreneurs were not wishing to grow because it is risky and may result in failure (Shmailan 2016). The entrepreneur's motivation will influence the company's growth strategy. They may wish to grow or not to grow. Lifestyle entrepreneurs do not want to change anything to earn more money or to have more customers (Kosenius et al. 2020). Lifestyle tourism entrepreneurs may prefer to keep their business as usual.

Growth-Oriented Tourism Entrepreneurs

Another type of tourism entrepreneurs, who are known as growth-oriented entrepreneurs (Getz and Petersen 2005; Mason and Brown 2014; Volery et al. 2015; Kuschel and Lepeley 2016; Lecuna et al. 2017; Kallmuenzer and Peters 2018; Day and Mody 2017; Ali 2018; Fu et al. 2019), became more popular because of economic and other impacts. Growth-oriented entrepreneurs are widely studied in general entrepreneurship literature (Bager et al. 2015; Gutterman 2016, 2018; Masurel and Snellenberg 2017; Lecuna et al. 2017). Growth-oriented entrepreneurs want to create jobs, experience internationalization, explore new markets, enhance innovation, achieve sustainable growth and fuel their strong desire to make money (Getz and Petersen 2004, 2005; Macke 2016; Gutterman 2018).

Growth-oriented entrepreneurs always take risks, with their desire coming from an income-oriented approach (Getz and Petersen 2005). Growth-oriented entrepreneurs want to grow to create jobs and economic benefits. In the tourism industry, there are few growth-oriented tourism entrepreneurs because the tourism industry is dominated by small and medium-sized enterprises (SMEs) (Peters et al. 2019). Entrepreneurs who own tourism SMEs are mainly lifestyle entrepreneurs (Hall and Rusher 2013) rather than growth-oriented entrepreneurs (Getz and Petersen 2005). Getz and Peterson (2005) found that hospitality entrepreneurs' characteristics to be autonomy-oriented, money-centred, with their business being under family ownership and the main motivation to start-up business being 'lifestyle'.

The characteristics of successful entrepreneurs (Shmailan 2016; Lecuna et al. 2017; Hmieleski and Sheppard 2019; Sadeghi et al. 2019) and the abilities of entrepreneurs (Chou et al. 2016; Darnihamedani and Hessels 2016) have been examined extensively in general and tourism literature. Bird (2015: 151) described the successful entrepreneur's characteristics as 'flexibility, field independence, cognitive complexity, openness to experience, visionary and vigilance, as well as his or her ability to form network relationships outside the venture'. Rasca and Deaconu (2018) discussed that entrepreneurial abilities and attitudes can be learnable through entrepreneurial education. An entrepreneur can learn critical thinking, lateral thinking, applying heuristics, and systematic searching (Rasca and Deaconu 2018).

Elsworth et al. (2008) further added that the successful entrepreneur can teach others who wish to be an entrepreneur. In this way, potential entrepreneurs can develop more entrepreneurial abilities and learn from other successful entrepreneurs (Bird 2019). Elsworth et al. (2008) found that entrepreneurial thought and behaviour play a crucial role in being a successful entrepreneur or intrapreneur. They believe that the entrepreneur and the intrapreneur both share similar characteristics and behaviour. However, some of the characteristics of entrepreneurs/intrapreneurs are inherent, while some of them can be learnt through training and education over time.

Tourism Intrapreneurs

Tourism entrepreneurs do not always open and run their own company. There is another way to act like entrepreneurs within an organization, and that is known as 'an intrapreneur'. Along with, companies are no longer looking for ordinary personnel to recruit (Harrison and Delaney 2014). Firms want to hire employees who can 'think like an owner', demonstrate entrepreneurial attitude and skills, think on their feet and possess good problem-solving abilities (West 2013; Kaplan 2015). In today's business world, large companies encourage internal entrepreneurship or cooperate entrepreneurship (Mottiar and Boluk 2017). Intrapreneurship and corporate entrepreneurship are terms used interchangeably and both mean any activities that can create innovative solutions by using an organisation's resources and increasing business growth (Parker 2011). Intrapreneurs act differently to normal employees, pushing boundaries and being more innovative. Therefore, an intrapreneur can be defined as a person who shows entrepreneurial behaviour within an existing organization (Pinchot 1985; Antoncic and Hisrich 2003).

Parker (2011) stressed that the entrepreneur and the intrapreneur may have similar abilities, approaches, mentality and tactics as regards business opportunities. Moriano et al. (2014) argued that intrapreneurs may achieve rewards, access existing resources, and enjoy freedom in different types and sizes of organizations. On the other hand, Bosma et al. (2011) found that certain characteristic traits—risk, creativity, opportunity and analytical thinking—do not differentiate between entrepreneurs and intrapreneurs. Intrapreneurs do have some specific characteristics, like 'networking skills, thinking out of the box, enterprise, being a controller, champion, risk-taker, innovator, creator, success-oriented, challengeable, and a quick learner' (Mohedano-Suanes and Benítez 2018: 111). This may indicate that intrapreneurs may lead to change in terms of creativity and pioneer developments inside the company.

The differences between entrepreneurship and intrapreneurship are shown in Table 3.2. There are different arguments about who is an intrapreneur and who is not (Koh and Hatten 2002; Jyotirmay 2007; Mottiar and Boluk 2017; Antoncic and Antoncic 2018). However, some people who have entrepreneurial skills will start a company and some of them work in a company and use their entrepreneurial skills within the company. If the firm is entrepreneurial and provides working conditions and support for intrapreneurs, the firm will have many intrapreneurs. Intrapreneurship cannot be based on the person's characteristics, skills and abilities. Intrapreneurship, like entrepreneurship, mainly depends on the firm's environment and entrepreneurial eco-systems.

A person's desires and wants may not be enough on their own to help them to pursue intrapreneurship. Companies must support intrapreneurship activity within the organization (Antoncic and Hisrich 2003). Intrapreneurship can only be presented when top management shows support and encouragement (Pinchot 1985). Therefore, management has a key role in executing and enhancing intrapreneurship (Altınay 2004). Management must show tolerance to fail (Alpkan et al. 2010). Some organizations use this as an opportunity and create support systems, reward systems and flexible working systems, with more free time and choice (Bosma et al. 2011). Essentially, intrapreneurship supports management styles to change the old and clichéd job routines to a more proactive and dynamic style (Gawke et al. 2017). Hence, intrapreneurship plays an important role in developing and transforming an organisation's management and a better way of doing business.

Intrapreneurs may show their skills and traits when they see opportunities. Kraleva (2011: 79) pointed out that 'Intrapreneurship, like organizational learning, enforces employees' participation in the decision-making process and their active involvement in achieving the organizational objectives'. Antoncic and Antoncic (2018) found a strong link between intrapreneurship and a firm's growth in tourism. An intrapreneur can be a growth-oriented entrepreneur who holds similar characteristics and attitudes. Mottiar and Boluk (2017: 130) believe

3 Generation Z and Tourism Entrepreneurship ...   69

Table 3.2 Entrepreneurship vs Intrapreneurship

	Entrepreneur	Intrapreneur
Authority	An entrepreneur is an ultimate decision-maker. He works independently and holds the complete authority to whether/not execute a plan	An intrapreneur is just an idea generator. The decision to execute/realize the idea lies with the entrepreneur/owner of the organization
Work environment	An entrepreneur sets the work culture and the environment for his employees	Being an associate at the organization, an intrapreneur has no option but to accustom himself by the pre-existing organizational culture
Finance	The entrepreneur raises funds required to execute/run the enterprise	An intrapreneur plays within an organization. Thus the company raises funds required to deploy an idea
Independence	Wholly independence in the creation and governance of their entrepreneurial project	Relatively independent in the creation and governance of their intrapreneurial project
The constraints	Considerable pressure to demonstrate success quickly	Comparatively less pressure to develop and optimize their project towards successful completion
Risk	The entrepreneur assumes all business risks	The intrapreneur assumes some risk related to their project
Added value	The entrepreneur must demonstrate added value to all stakeholders	The family business' presence offers additional guarantees to stakeholders
Resources	The entrepreneur must find all necessary resources	The intrapreneur has access to core business resources, but they must leverage them to their benefit
Decision making	The entrepreneur is involved in all relevant strategic decision-making	The intrapreneur shares decision-making power

Source Adopted from Kelton Tech (2015) and Laurin (2016)

that the young generations are energetic, visionary, opportunist and like to change the status quo by becoming intrapreneurs in the tourism industry. Tourism businesses owners also aware that companies need new generations to be more creative and innovative (Jyotirmay 2007).

Generation Z

The digital era has really only just started, and three generations are currently in the workforce (Li 2017). The most different generation would be Gen Z, compared to other generations (Mahadi 2018). Gen Z, who number approximately 69 million people in the USA, has already overtaken Gen Y by three million (NDP Group 2017). This generation is also strongly represented in other countries. For example, Gen Z represents 17% of the Turkish population (Mercan 2016). They are considered as the future (NDP Group 2017).

Currently, Gen Z workers tend to enter business life as trainees. They will graduate from colleges in the following year and be part of the workforce or internship programmes. They will form a large part of the changeover in the workforce, accounting for 27% of the workforce by 2025. It is predicted that they will change jobs 18 times and careers six times in their working life (Taş et al. 2017; Agarwal and Vaghela 2018; McCrindle 2019a). The following section outlines the extant literature on Gen Z characteristics, lifestyles and business choices.

Who Is Generation Z?

There are different views about Generation Zers' age range in literature. Most commonly, they are people who have been born after 1996. The NDP Group divides Gen Z into two groups (NDP Group 2017). One group is composed of people who were born between 1997 and 2005. The other group is defined as people born in 2006 and after. The first group is mentioned as 'the first connected kids' whereas the latter is explained as 'the technology inherent' (NDP Group 2017). In general, both groups of Gen Z don't know any time without the internet and social media (*Business Insider* 2019).

Gen Z is defined differently by various sources. Before the current definition, there were different names for this generation, such as 'children of the internet', 'digital natives', the 'media generation', the '.com generation', 'IGen', 'instant online' (Levickaite 2010), the 'homeland generation' and 'post-millennials' (NDP Group 2017). The term of generation is defined as 'a group of people or cohorts who share birth years and experiences as they move through time together, influencing and being influenced by a variety of critical factors' (Kupperschmidt 2000: 66). Every generation has their unique and common backgrounds and life experiences. For example, Gen Y is the generation that has experienced the dissolution of the Soviet Union, the death of Princess Diana, September 11, and war in the Middle East. In contrast, the mortgage crisis in the USA, the world of global terrorism and economic threats can be expressed as the common backgrounds of Gen Z (Arar and Yüksel 2015; Agarwal and Vaghela 2018). They have grown up with economic depression and will begin their business life under economic pressure (Taş et al. 2017). To this can be added pandemics all around the world. According to *Washington Post* news (2020):

> The pandemic has been a relentless destroyer of brick-and-mortar businesses as public health officials warn against in-person interactions. But the coronavirus is boosting almost anything that can be done online or with minimal human contact - grocery deliveries, online learning, takeout food, streaming video, even real estate closings done with online notaries… The reality of office employees logging in from home also could reshape the workplace… A Microsoft executive, said in an online news briefing. 'We're never going to go back to working the way that we did'… Kate Lister, president of consulting firm Global Workplace Analytics, said she expects more than 25% of employees will continue working from home multiple days a week after the crisis fades.

The fast growth of technology is, as a matter of course, the highest priority in Gen Zers' life experiences (Arar and Yüksel 2015). The advanced products of the Apple company, Facebook, Twitter, used by millions of people, and other social media such as Instagram, Pinterest and Foursquare, have become part of Gen Z's daily lives (Berkup 2014). Even a 2-year-old child knows how to use a smartphone or a tablet computer. That's why this generation loves and is addicted to speed in any part of their lives (Arar and Yüksel 2015). These explanations mean that Generation Z will be the fastest adapting group to this mandatorily changing world.

Lifestyles of Generation Z

Lifestyles are the living, spending and working patterns of people using the internet and digital devices (Yu 2011). Any technological device has direct and/or indirect effects on people's lifestyles (Hoque 2018). Gen Zers are true digital natives, connecting more than ten hours in a day (Vision Critical 2019). Their basic characteristics are confidence, independence, individualism, addiction to technology and speed. They have big differences from their parents, who are Generation X. Because they haven't matured yet, researchers don't know which issues will impact most on Gen Z (Alp et al. 2019). However, there is various research comparing Generation Z with Generation Y, which is the nearest generation. Gen Yers are also called 'millennials', 'generation next', 'nexters', 'echo boomers', 'trophy kids', 'generation www', 'net generation', or 'Gen N' (Jain and Pant 2012). They weren't born into the same level of technology as Gen Z, but they live with technology. They have a high level of education, mostly up to postgraduate level. They are experienced with technology and innovation, and they have confidence. They don't like to wait and don't know how to be patient. They want speed. A satisfactory and balanced life is their motivation (Suleman and Nelson 2011; Berkup 2014).

Gen Z, in contrast, is the generation that was born into the internet. Social networking is a part of their daily lives and they embrace this, connecting in informal, individual and straight ways. They are the 'Do-It-Yourself' generation. They are impatient, instant-minded, individualistic, self-directed, and are the most demanding, acquisitive, materialistic and entitled generation so far (Agarwal and Vaghela 2018). Getting contact with any person in any location of the world is possible in seconds. They can also access any kind of information at any time. They are thought to have the highest motor skill synchronization for hand, eye and ear in the history of humanity. They consume rapidly and are interactive, efficient, dissatisfied and result-oriented as they socialize through the internet (Berkup 2014). They want things faster, easier and cheaper (Erickson 2012) (Table 3.3).

Gen Z is evaluated as the best-connected generation. Thus, technology is not an innovation, convenience or necessity, just a part of normal life for Gen Zers. They have been equipped with technological devices since they were babies. Gen Z is the children of PC, GSM and the internet (Berkup 2014). They were exposed to the digital world at a very early ages. Their brain has become rewired in order to react to digital stimulation. Thus, they absorb visual images more than straight text (Hoque 2018). However, they prefer text to speaking, computers to reading books. They don't spend much time outside, communicate

Table 3.3 The rate of stereotypes of the other generations

Top 5 stereotypes of Gen Z	As reported by Gen Z	%		As reported by Gen Y	%
1	Creative	57	1	Lazy	45
2	Open-minded	54	2	Open-minded	41
3	New perspectives/ideas	52	3	Creative	38
4	Intelligent	44	4	Self-centred	37
5	Cutting-edge thinking, lazy	41	5	Lack of focus, easily distracted	35
Top 5 stereotypes of Gen Z	As reported by Gen Z	%		As reported by Gen Y	%
1	Open-minded	56	1	Creative, open-minded	50
2	New perspectives/ideas	55	2	New perspectives/ideas, intelligent	46
3	Creative	54	3	Cutting-edge thinking	38
4	Intelligent	53	4	Entrepreneurial	29
5	Cutting-edge thinking	40	5	Responsible	27

Source Workplace Intelligence (2014)

online, and they can't imagine a life without computers and telephones (Taş et al. 2017). They are interested in many subjects at the same time. They will be expected to have a long life, better life conditions and become wealthier with advanced technology (Berkup 2014). Gen Z prefers Snapchat and Instagram rather than Facebook. They are mobile first. They use the mobile web as a window on the world and a tool for managing daily tasks. They want to do their tasks in just a few clicks. They need fast responses. Therefore, organizations need to develop fast response solutions—such as instant help services—for them. They also tend to use artificial intelligence and robots in order to respond automatically on instant messaging platforms (BNP Paribas 2017).

Gen Z has lived exclusively within an ultra-connected world. They are often called digital natives, but also 'linksters', as no previous generation has spent more time on the internet. Gen Z, the technologically sophisticated generation, are always connected for everything they do: meeting people, creating relationships, education, training, news and shopping (BNP Paribas 2017). Technology is very functional for Gen Z's education process. Almost all of Gen Z uses technology as a part of their formal education and has technology literacy. Education is crucial in order to prepare them for their future career (Delltechnologies 2018), but learning is not limited to the classroom, it is expanded by Youtube videos or free learning sites. They can also find any answers to their questions by searching on Google. Contrary to popular belief, it is interesting to learn that the majority of Gen Z prefers to interact with people face-to-face rather than just on social media (Moore et al. 2017), because they need an advisor to teach them how to learn. According to Purcell, et al.'s (2012) study, 76% of teachers reported that students expect information from their teachers instead of searching by themselves (Table 3.4).

Business Motivation and Expectations of Generation Z

In a changing world, the new workforce—which includes Generation Z—is considering a new style of employment that gives opportunities to learn new things, to work in an innovative work place, and to allow

Table 3.4 Generation Y vs. Generation Z

	Generation Y	Generation Z
Iconic technology	Internet, e-mail, SMS, DVD, playstation, Xbox, iPod	MacBook, iPad, Google, Facebook, Twitter, Wii, PS3, Android
Popular culture	Baseball caps, men's cosmetics, Havaianas	Skinny jeans, V-necks, RipSticks
Influencers	Experiential, peers	User-generated, forums
Training focus	Emotional, stories, participative	Multi-modal, e-learning, interactive
Learning format	Multi-sensory, visual	Student-centric, kinesthetic
Learning environment	Cafe-style, music and multi-modal	Lounge room style, multi-stimulus
Purchase influences	No brand loyalty, friends	Brand evangelism, trends
Finanial values	Short-term wants, credit dependent, lifestyle dept	Impulse purchases, e-stores, life-long debt
Ideal leaders	Empowering, collaborators	Inspiring, co-creators

Source McCrindle (2019b)

Generation Zers to take calculated risks (Schulman 2007). Scholars have widely researched Generation Y's expectations of work compared with Generation X. Studies comparing Generation Y and Z's work needs and expectations have also increased. According to research, Gen Y has had work experience while they were going to school (Alp et al. 2019). They are well-educated, so they expect their salary to be in direct proportion to their education level. In other words, they want a fair effort-reward balance from the organization (Maxwell et al. 2010). However, Gen Y want a work-life balance in their life. Their motto is 'First live, then work'. They are able to keep pace with changes and they can easily access information and solve problems at work. They are able to compile and filter information from different sources and use the appropriate one in order to solve problems. They use social media not only for entertainment and communication but also for information for their business. They can adapt themselves to different cultures and diversities in an organization (Berkup 2014) and they do not suffer when adapting to a new job, as their characters are open to new ideas. They are always active in their organization and want their managers caring about their ideas, and they need feedback about their job performance from their managers.

They want to be a part of critical decisions and innovative work of the organization, as well as having ambitions to get swiftly promoted in their career. If they don't get promoted, their attitude is that they can give up their job and look for a new one (Schawbel 2012).

Generation Zers, on the other hand, have different motivations in terms of business. They have more advantages, so these advantages make them capable of multi-tasking. By means of this, they can quickly move from one task to another (Levickaite 2010). For example, they are able to manage e-mails and messages, view their favourite programme and look up items relevant for their tasks at the same time through digital devices (Hoque 2018). Generation Z's preferences are transparency, self-reliance, flexibility and personal freedom. If this does not happen, frustration among peers, low morale and productivity, and a lack of engagement with the work occurs (Bascha 2011). They need enough independence to prove themselves (Agarwal and Vaghela 2018). Unlike Erickson's (2012) idea, which asserts that Generation Z avoids face-to-face communication with society, Schawbel (2014) states their face-to-face communication preferences, which contrast with their technology addiction. On one hand, according to Bridges (2015), they have a good education, but they believe that this education doesn't meet the required skills needed for real-life problems. On the other hand, they also want their managers to listen to them and value their ideas. Opinions are more important than age for them (Schawbel 2014).

The common points of Generation Y and Z are working with technology in order to reach their aims. They both prefer to be working on hands-on projects (Millennial Branding 2014). They both want to work in an organization integrated with technology, which matches their entrepreneurial and innovative soul, but there are some differences between the two generations in the perspective of work. For example, extrinsic rewards such as salary payments and organizational politics are more important for Generation Y. Innovation (inner motivation) is more important than money (extrinsic motivation) for Generation Z. Having a meaningful job is a crucial motivational factor for them. They care about liking and interiorizing their job more than extrinsic rewards. If Generation Z doesn't like their job, they can easily change it for a more satisfactory job (Alp et al. 2019). Generation Z is more trustworthy, tolerant and less motivated by money compared with Generation Y (Schawbel 2014). Generation Z is described as a cautious generation (NDP Group 2017). Recent research by CivicScience (2017) shows that Generation Z has a more negative outlook on their financial future compared to Generation Y. This generation has a circumspect reputation. Thus, Generation Z wants to have guarantees for their future as well as happiness in their workplaces (Özkan and Solmaz 2015) (Table 3.5).

The level of expectations of Generation Z is also an important subject for their managers. Scholars have studied their expectations for a business workplace, working hours and management. Generation Z wants a flexible and connected workplace, without hierarchy (Micoleta 2012). Because individualism is important for them, they prefer to work alone (Peterson 2014). They also want to reach meaningful and tangible aims,

Table 3.5 The features and thoughts of Gen Y and Gen Z about business

Job specification	Gen Y	Gen Z
Business ethics	Enthusiastic	More realist
Thought about business	I do business to make a difference	I do business with enthusiasm and energy
Personal characteristics	Have a political consciousness, high expectation, make a team, sympathizer to differences, self-confident, open to challenge	Tech-savvy, early matured, spoiled, amplified, against risk, protege
Features about business	– Want to know reasons – Want to be publicly praised – Like an entertaining workplace – Think the importance of work-life balance – Want small targets – Trust their skills – Don't want long term relationship with an organization	– Be creative and cooperative – Have to solve hard environmental, social and economical problems – Have self-leadership – Very speed data processing – More clever

Source Cetin and Karalar (2016)

and they don't attach importance to the place of work. They prefer free and flexible working models and places more. In other words, they don't want traditional offices and office conditions that can be an obstacle to their productivity (Alp et al. 2019). While Generation Y prefers traditional offices, Generation Z may select corporate office space. Generation Z has greater interest in personalizing their own workplaces than Generation Y. However, their second office preferences are identical, in that they both prefer second offices to be a co-working space (Millennial Branding 2014). Telecommuting, in other words home offices, is also suitable for Generation Z (Arar 2016). They prefer teamwork and knowledge sharing at the virtual level (Bencsik et al. 2012), and they want technological equipment and multiple technology solutions in their workplace, as they have been brought up with them (Convene 2019). They also prefer a friendly workplace that encourages their entrepreneurial skills (Bridges 2015).

Generation Z is more aware of their personal needs. Therefore, they want flexible working hours in order to develop themselves and make a better career plan (Mitchell 2008). Long working hours, for example the standard 40 hours for a week, is not interesting for this generation. They see themselves as permanent freelancers. Generation Z has also some expectations from management. Generation Zers who have a liberal nature want to work in a place that has knowledge sharing. Therefore, they want an organic organization structure where there is less emphasis on authority and rules (Arar 2016). They know their own mind, they can express themselves well, they have a spirit of entrepreneurship, and they want a colourful business life, supporting distinctness and less hierarchy (Taş et al. 2017). Having their managers listen to their ideas is crucial for Generation Z (Millennial Branding 2014). Feedback is essential for all generations, including Generation Z, but the frequency of feedback is particularly more important for Generation Z (Prossack 2019). Arar (2016) also explains the expectations of Generation Z from business in general:

– Flexibility in working hours and the workplace, specially mobility
– Work-life balance
– Organic organizations rather than hierarchy

- Both vertical and horizontal career planning
- Duties without monotony, integrated with creativity and technology
- Meaningful duties
- Job evaluation with performance, not time
- Both material and non-material satisfactory opportunities and gains
- Personal office rooms
- Technological devices dedicated to themselves.

Organizations should modify their workplaces and working models according to Generation Zers' different motivations and expectations. For example, organizations should use mobile applications for better management of Generation Z in their workplace. Generation Z wants to have fun in their busy schedule. Organizations need to create more entertaining workplaces. Managers need to be aware that Gen Zers want there to be more screens, less papers and procedures, more flexible working hours and models, and new tasks occurring in their organizations (Taş et al. 2017). When this generation's lines between work and life are blurred, they start to strive for work to be integrated into their lives. They need flexible office times: for example, 08:00 a.m. to 4:00 p.m. instead of 9:00 a.m. to 5:00 p.m. Thus, employees who have enough time to finish work in their lives will be more productive (Prossack 2019). They don't want to be a cubicle worker, working 40 hours in a week (Renfro 2012). Generation Z prefers 'office workspace that is easy to orient within, understand and use'. Therefore, organizations should organize offices with clear functionality in a more flexible environment. Managers also need to provide private phones and rooms, rather than rooms suitable for group meetings (Convene 2019). Feedback is very important for this generation. When feedback comes rarely, it becomes meaningless for them. Therefore, Prossack (2019) proposes that managers deliver feedback more than twice a year. The author has two more pieces of advice for organizations. First, managers may give career opportunities to their employees who want rapid achievement. The second advice is implementing formal, online or app-based learning domains for their employees, because learning and development is this generation's priority and mentoring will be very productive for them.

Generation Z Careers: An Entrepreneur or an Intrapreneur

Bruce (2013) stated that it is difficult to manage Generation Y and Z because of their attitudinal differences. Ghura (2017) confirms that attitude of Generation Z, that providing quality at work and employee retention are three challenges of managers who are faced with working with this generation. Thus, organizations that desire to be entrepreneurial have to learn how to manage this new generation. The organizations have to learn Generation Zers' motivations, then they have to engage, inspire and then rethink and reorganize their existing structure (Grafton 2011).

According to the researchers, Generation Z is more entrepreneurial than Generation Y, because they have a mindset that is not restricted by geopolitical borders. Therefore, they can capture niche areas in the greater 'noise' that will help them to survive in the global area and digital era (Schawbel 2014; Singh 2014; Hoque et al. 2018). Research conducted by BNP Paribas and the Boson Project in France, among 3,200 French people aged between 15 and 20, showed that Generation Z has different views about business life and the business climate. According to this French Generation Z, working in an organization can be 'very hard', 'very complex', 'boring', 'pitiless', 'a wild forest', and 36 out of 100 young people evaluate organizations as stressful. Networking is the key success for 40% of participants (Taş et al. 2017). A study by the Northeastern University demonstrates that 42% of teenagers want to work for themselves (Gayeski 2015). According to another item of research, 50% of Generation Z participants want to start their own company one day (Convene 2019). This rate goes up 72% for high school students, who want to have their individual business, with 76% of them wanting to convert their hobbies into a professional, full-time job (Ghura 2017). However, they are more risk averse (Erlam et al. 2018) and less trusting (Trzesniewski and Donnellan 2010). Generation Z, which has a need for achievement, has higher intentions of engaging in their own business (Frunzaru and Cismaru 2018). A need for achievement is one of the indicators of being an entrepreneur, and is explained as 'the capacity to set high personal, though obtainable goals, the concern for personal achievement rather than the rewards for success and the desire for job-relevant feedback ("how well am I doing?") rather than for attitudinal feedback ("how well do you like me?")' (European Commission 2012: 48). Generation Zers, who have self-efficacy and tend to have at least one parental entrepreneur, also have a tendency to start their own business (Frunzaru and Cismaru 2018). Self-efficacy, which is one of the crucial personal attributes of entrepreneurship, plays an important role in the ability to perform tasks successfully (European Commission 2012).

Most Generation Zers prefer to demonstrate their entrepreneurial skill through social media branding (Spencer 2019). Generation Z is evaluated as being more ambitious, while Generation Y are generally more entrepreneurial. Their adaptable mentality makes them valuable entrepreneurs. They have been mini-CEOs from a very early age and need to follow their own visions. They are willing to solve innovation challenges (Robertson 2019). Schawbel (2014) gives five reasons why Generation Z are more entrepreneurial than Generation Y:

- More opportunity to access resources;
- More opportunity to access programmes;
- More pressure from their parents about their careers;
- More opportunity to communicate with mentors;
- Organizations are engaging high school students.

Millennial Branding (2014) reveals that high school students are more entrepreneurial than college students. According to the report, Generation Zers' parents push them to gain a professional career during high school, and don't seem to need help to do this. High school students are more willing to volunteer in order to acquire work experience, compared with college students. Their top three reasons in looking for an internship are to gain new skills, work experience and mentorship/networking. In a similar vein, Cho et al. (2018) record that career and learning motivations are stronger incentives than value and self-esteem motives in Generation Z's attitudes towards volunteering.

Generation Z is more concerned about environmental issues and has a high responsibility towards the conservation of natural resources

(Agarwal and Vaghela 2018). This situation shows Generation Z's sensitivity. According to the researchers, younger employees are more likely to behave ethically in their workplaces (Lee and Tsang 2013; Goh and Kong 2018). For example, Lee and Tsang (2013) revealed that workplace ethics are very important for tourism and hotel management students. The authors studied subdegree, bachelor's and master's degree students. All degree students reported the importance of ethics in hotels. In addition, subdegree students who are 1st-year students or newcomers to university support strong moral and civic concepts being embedded in their workplaces. Another piece of research conducted by Goh and Jie (2019) found that Generation Z hospitality employees had a tendency to reduce food wastage but they were attached to management directives such as a no take-away policy for unfinished food. In addition, Generation Z hospitality employees seek a reference group in order to approve such things as their food wastage behaviour, such as friends and colleagues, who are the strongest group. Their family, hotel management and teachers form this reference group, respectively. The majority of Generation Zers, who have family as a reference group, have to behave differently at work. They have to engage in food wastage because of workplace pressure. As a result, Generation Z feels guilty and accepts the consequences of wasting food. While they see alternative ways of food wastage in their family, their friends and colleagues as a reference group push them towards waste reduction behaviour at work. Therefore, this situation prompts them to behave differently in the workplace.

Tourism is now one of the biggest industries, all over the world. It is also a multidimensional and multigenerational industry, with the general working age decreasing. This means that the tourism industry will be dominated by younger employees in the future, as they replace older workers. Accordingly, the hospitality workforce has been expanding and 123,000 new employees are needed by 2020. With the majority of younger employees about to graduate and enter the industry, Generation Z will start to generate 20% of total jobs, as Generation Z is more adapted to business life. This trend has been defined as a 'perfect storm' by some academics (Deloitte 2015; Solnet et al. 2016; Goh and Lee 2018). These demographic and generational changes will continue in the tourism industry (Goh and Lee 2018). The question is: Will Generation Z prefer to be an entrepreneur or an intrapreneur in the tourism industry?

Generation Z will work in a business world that is continuously and rapidly changing. Thus, they always have to think about the next idea and/or next opportunity, which makes them perfect for entrepreneurship (Grafton 2011). They also search for jobs that give them new opportunities, such as learning new things, working in innovative ways and allowing them to take calculated risks (Schulman 2007). However, the study results show that Generation Z has low self-efficacy, therefore they need more self-confidence in order to develop their entrepreneurship abilities (Frunzaru and Cismaru 2018). These explanations reinforce the argument that Generation Z is the best-suited generation to be intrapreneurs in the workforce, especially in the tourism industry.

According to research results conducted by Goh and Lee (2018), Generation Z has some positive attitudes, such as searching for fulfilment and seeking travel opportunities, stable careers and opportunities to work in different aspects of the tourism industry. These results show the intrapreneurship characteristics of Generation Z, such as innovativeness, diversity, and searching for new opportunities. However, there can be some negative attitudes of Generation Zers working in the tourism industry, with some of them seeing the industry as having long working hours, being exhausting, rigid and having low pay. Pressure to perform is also an interesting finding of Generation Zers' perceived difficulties of working in the tourism industry. That means that Generation Z has a fear of working with a team. This fear also shows that Generation Z is concerned about their ability to live up to customers' expectations in a live environment. However, human resource managers in tourism should give importance to career counselling in order to engage with Generation Z, such as graduated management traineeship programmes and professional advancement programmes (Goh and Okumuş 2020), because Generation Zers who work in the tourism industry are impatient to climb their career ladder, and are more likely to quit their job if they're not promoted within six months (Smith et al. 2018).

There are only a small number of studies about Generation Z, because this generation is currently maturing. Most of the studies about

Generation Z involve studies comparing the three generations, X, Y and Z. Therefore, more research is needed about Generation Z, their entrepreneurship intentions and behaviours, and their situation in the tourism industry. Taking into consideration that leaving a job is easy for Generation Z, and that there is a high workforce turnover in the tourism industry, managers have to think how to deal with this generation in their organizations. Managers in the tourism industry have to rectify the lack of career planning and progression opportunities and dispense with the attitude of treating young employees as cheap labour (Casado-Diaz and Simon 2016).

Conclusion

This chapter has discussed the meaning of tourism entrepreneurship and tourism intrapreneurship for Generation Z. It has presented the main concepts, features and characteristics of tourism entrepreneurs, intrapreneurs and Gen Z. The first part of the chapter was focused on the typology of tourism entrepreneurs. Different types of tourism entrepreneurs were discussed in detail. Then, intrapreneurship was carefully examined. This chapter searched for the answer to Gen Z's careers as tourism entrepreneurs. In short, the main idea of this chapter was to highlight how generations' career choices and business perspectives will change tourism entrepreneurship or vice versa.

Consequently, this chapter intended to find the link between tourism entrepreneurship and Gen Z future careers. Despite a growing interest in future jobs like being a Youtuber and/or blogger in tourism, tourism entrepreneurs or intrapreneurs will continue to play a vital role. They may decide to be an entrepreneur but in their own way. If the tourism companies have an entrepreneurial ecosystem, this generation will work as an intrapreneur. Gen Z will have many different options in the tourism world. These generations have all alternatives to choose to be any type of tourism entrepreneurs. Moreover, they may create a new typology of tourism entrepreneurs.

In conclusion, Gen Z may choose to be one or a combination of two types of tourism entrepreneurs. Some Gen Zers will be more interested in being social tourism entrepreneurs because it suits better their characteristics. Some of them will prefer to be nascent because it is more interesting for them. Gen Z will have a strong link with growth-oriented tourism entrepreneurs. Some of them may be interested in being marginal tourism entrepreneurs. However, Gen Z likes to be free and do things their own way. Intrapreneurship may be more suitable for them in the future. Therefore, tourism companies and management must change their style to suit new intrapreneurs who will be working with them very soon. As a result, Gen Z may count as a unique generation where people fit many types of entrepreneurial styles. Gen Z is the future of the workforce who may be an intrapreneur in the early stage of their career will be highly likely to be an entrepreneur in their later career.

References

Agarwal, H., and Vaghela, P. S. (2018). *Work values of Gen Z: Bridging the gap to the next generation.* National Conference on Innovative Business Management Practices in 21st Century, Faculty of Management Studies, Parul University, Gujarat, India, 21–22 December.

Ahmad, N., and Seymour R. (2008). *Defining Entrepreneurial activity: Definitions supporting frameworks for data collection.* OECD Statistics Working Papers, No. 2008/01, OECD Publishing, Paris. https://www.oecd-ilibrary. org/economics/defining-entrepreneurial-activity_243164686763. Accessed Date: 18 October 2019.

Ali, R. S. (2018). Determinants of female entrepreneurs growth intentions: A case of female-owned small businesses in Ghana's tourism sector. *Journal of Small Business and Enterprise Development, 25*(3), 387–404.

Alp, G. T., Tuncer, A. D., Sulaiman, S. A. B., and Güngör, A. (2019). *Çalışma hayatında Y ve Z kuşağının motivasyonel farklılıkları.* Proceedings on 2nd International Conference on Technology and Science, November 14–16.

Altınay, L. (2004). Implementing international franchising: The role of intrapreneurship. *International Journal of Service Industry Management, 15*(5), 426–443.

Alpkan, L., Bulut, C., Gunday, G., Ulusoy, G., and Kilic, K. (2010). Organizational support for intrapreneurship and its interaction with human capital to enhance innovative performance. *Management Decision*, *48*(5), 732–755.

Antoncic, B., and Hisrich, R. D. (2003). Clarifying the intrapreneurship concept. *Journal of Small Business and Enterprise Development*, *10*(1), 7–24.

Antoncic, J. A., and Antoncic, B. (2018). Need for achievement of the entrepreneur, intrapreneurship, and the growth of companies in tourism and trade. *Modern Management Tools and Economy of Tourism Sector in Present Era*, 259–265.

Arar, T., and Yüksel, I. (2015). How to manage generation Z in business life. *Journal of Global Economic, Management and Business Research*, *4*(4), 195–202

Arar, T. (2016). *Z kuşağında kariyer geliştirmede yetenek yönetimi*. Kırıkkale Üniversitesi Sosyal Bilimler Enstitüsü Yönetim ve Organizasyon Anabilim Dalı, Yayınlanmamış Yüksek Lisans Tezi.

Ateljevic, I., and Doorne, S. (2000). 'Staying within the fence': Lifestyle entrepreneurship in tourism. *Journal of Sustainable Tourism*, *8*(5), 378–392.

Ateljevic, J., and Li, L. (2017). Tourism entrepreneurship—Concepts and issues. In *Tourism and entrepreneurship* (pp. 30–53). Routledge.

Bager, T. E., Jensen, K. W., Nielsen, P. S., and Larsen, T. A. (2015). Enrollment of SME managers to growth-oriented training programs. *International Journal of Entrepreneurial Behavior and Research*, *21*(4), 578–599.

Balachandran, V., and Sakthivelan, M. S. (2013). Impact of information technology on entrepreneurship (e-entrepreneurship). *Journal of Business Management and Social Sciences Research*, *2*(2), 51–56.

Barclays. (2013). *Talking about my generation: Exploring the benefits engagement challenge*. https://www.mas.org.uk/uploads/artlib/talking-about-my-generation-exploring-the-benefits-engagement-challenge.pdf Accessed Date: 10 April 2020.

Bascha. (2011). *Z. The open-source generation*. https://opensource.com/business/11/9/z-open-source-generation. Accessed Date: 6 April 2020.

Bencsik, A., Horvath-Csikos, G., and Juhasz, T. (2012). Y and Z generations at workplaces. *Journal of Competitiveness*, *8*(3), 90–106.

Berdychevsky, L. (2016). Romance tourism. In J. Jafari and H. Xiao (Eds.), *Encyclopedia of tourism*. Cham: Springer.

Berkup, S. B. (2014). Working with generations X and Y in generation Z period: Management of different generations in business life. *Mediterranean Journal of Social Sciences*, *5*(19), 218–229.

Bird, A., and Mitsuhashi, H. (2003). Entrepreneurs and entrepreneurial processes: Historical and theoretical perspectives on entrepreneurship in the Japanese contexts. *Asian Perspective, 125–175.*

Bird, B. (2015). Entrepreneurial intentions research: A review and outlook. *International Review of Entrepreneurship, 13*(3), 143–168.

Bird, B. (2019). Toward a theory of entrepreneurial competency. In *Seminal ideas for the next twenty-five years of advances* (pp. 115–131). Emerald Publishing Limited.

BNP PARIBAS. (2017). *New banking uses for a new generation?* https://group.bnpparibas/en/news/banking-generation. Accessed Date: 30 March 2020.

Bruce, T. (2013). How to bring out the best in today's talent. *Professional Safety, 58*(10), 38–40

Bredvold, R., and Skålén, P. (2016). Lifestyle entrepreneurs and their identity construction: A study of the tourism industry. *Tourism Management, 56*, 96–105.

Bridges, T. (2015). 5 ways the workplace needs to change to get the most out of Generation Z. https://www.fastcompany.com/3049848/5-ways-the-wor kplace-needs-to-change-to-get-the-most-out-of-generation-z. Accessed Date: 13 April 2020.

Bosma, N. S., Stam, E., and Wennekers, S. (2011). Intrapreneurship versus independent entrepreneurship: A cross-national analysis of individual entrepreneurial behaviour. *Discussion Paper Series/Tjalling C. Koopmans Research Institute, 11*(4).

Bowen, D. (2002). Research through participant observation in tourism: A creative solution to the measurement of consumer satisfaction/dissatisfaction (CS/D) among tourists. *Journal of Travel Research, 41*(1), 4–14.

Business Insider. (2019). Gen Z is leading an evaluation in shopping that could kill brands as we know them. https://www.businessinsider.com/gen-z-sho pping-habits-kill-brands-2019-7. Accessed Date: 24 October 2019.

Casado-Díaz, M. A., Casado-Díaz, A. B., and Casado-Díaz, J. M. (2014). Linking tourism, retirement migration and social capital. *Tourism Geographies, 16*(1), 124–140.

Casado-Diaz, J. M., and Simon, H. (2016). Wage differences in the hospitality sector. *Tourism Management, 52*, 96–109.

Cecilia, S. G., Elisabeta, M., and Magdalena, B. (2011). Tourism's changing face: New age tourism versus old tourism. *Annals of the University of Oradea, Economic Science Series.*

Chang, J. (2011). Introduction: Entrepreneurship in tourism and hospitality: The role of SMEs. *Asia Pacific Journal of Tourism Research, 16*(5), 467–469.

Cho, M., Bonn, M. A., and Han, S. J. (2018). Generation Z's sustainable volunteering: Motivations, attitudes and job performance. *Sustainability, 10*, 1–16.

Chou, C. M., Shen, C. H., and Hsiao, H. C. (2016). Tertiary students' entrepreneurial ability of entrepreneurship-embedded internship program in education service industry. *International Journal of Psychology and Educational Studies, 3*(3), 1–8.

CivicScience. (2017). *When it comes to banking, Gen Z will make Millenials look old school*. https://civicscience.com/banking-gen-z-millennials-look-old-school/. Accessed Date: 24 October 2019.

Convene. (2019). *What Gen Z wants from their workplace*. https://convene.com/catalyst/gen-z-wants-workplace/. Accessed Date: 30 March 2020.

Crawford, A., and Naar, J. (2016a). Exit planning of lifestyle and profit-oriented entrepreneurs in bed and breakfasts. *International Journal of Hospitality and Tourism Administration, 17*(3), 260–285.

Crawford, A., and Naar, J. (2016b). A profile of American bed and breakfast entrepreneurs: Bridging the gap to retirement. *Journal of Human Resources in Hospitality and Tourism, 15*(1), 103–117.

Cunha, C., Kastenholz, E., and Carneiro, M. J. (2018). Lifestyle entrepreneurs: The case of rural tourism. In *Entrepreneurship and structural change in dynamic territories* (pp. 175–188). Cham: Springer.

Cetin, C., and Karalar, S. (2016). X, Y ve Z kuşağı öğrencilerin çok yönlü ve sınırsız kariyer algıları üzerine bir araştırma. *Yönetim Bilimleri Dergisi* (*Journal of Administrative Sciences*), *14*(28), 157.

Dahles, H. (1998). Tourism, government policy, and petty entrepreneurs in Indonesia. *South-East Asia Research, 6*(1), 73–98.

Dahles, H., and Bras, K. (1999). Entrepreneurs in romance. Tourism in Indonesia. *Annals of Tourism Research, 26*(2), 267–293.

Darnihamedani, P., and Hessels, J. (2016). Human capital as a driver of innovation among necessity-based entrepreneurs. *International Review of Entrepreneurship, 14*(1).

Davidsson, P. (2006). Nascent entrepreneurship: Empirical studies and developments. *Foundations and Trends® in Entrepreneurship, 2*(1), 1–76.

Dawson, D., Fountain, J., and Cohen, D. A. (2011). Seasonality and the lifestyle "conundrum": an analysis of lifestyle entrepreneurship in wine tourism regions. *Asia Pacific Journal of Tourism Research, 16*(5), 551–572.

Day, J., and Mody, M. (2017). Social entrepreneurship typologies and tourism: Conceptual frameworks. In *Social entrepreneurship and tourism* (pp. 57–80). Cham: Springer.

Delltechnologies. (2018). *Gen Z is here. Are you ready?* https://www.delltechnologies.com/en-us/perspectives/gen-z.htm. Accessed Date: 31 October 2019.

Deloitte. (2015). *Australian tourism labour force report: 2015–2020 for the Australian Trade Commission.* AUSTRADE. https://www.tra.gov.au/ArticleDocuments/185/Australian_Tourism_Labour_Force_FINAL.PDF.aspx?Embed=Y. Accessed Date: 4 November 2019.

Douglas, E. (2017). Perceptions revisited: Continuing to look at the world through entrepreneurial lenses. In *Revisiting the entrepreneurial mind* (pp. 61–67). Cham: Springer.

Elsworth, J. D., Beck, J. A., and Cichy, R. F. (2008). Think like an owner: Identifying the characteristics that are important for ownership-like thought in the hospitality industry. *FIU Hospitality Review, 26*(2).

Erickson, T. (2012). *How mobile technologies are shaping a new generation.* https://hbr.org/2012/04/the-mobile-re-generation. Accessed Date: 10 April 2020.

Erlam, G., Smythe, L., and Wright-St Clair, V. (2018). Action research and millennial: Improving pedagogical approaches to encourage critical thinking. *Nurse Education Today, 61,* 140–145.

European Commission. (2012). *Effects and impact of entrepreneurship programmes in higher education.* https://ec.europa.eu/growth/content/effects-and-impact-entrepreneurship-programmes-higher-education-0_en. Accessed Date: 10 April 2020.

Farrell, B. H., and Twining-Ward, L. (2004). Reconceptualizing tourism. *Annals of Tourism Research, 31*(2), 274–295.

Frunzaru, V., and Cismaru, D.-M. (2018). *The impact of individual entrepreneurial orientation and education on generation Z's intention towards entrepreneurship.* Kybernetes. https://doi.org/10.1108/K-05-2018-0272.

Fu, H., Okumus, F., Wu, K., and Koseoglu, M. A. (2019). The entrepreneurship research in hospitality and tourism. *International Journal of Hospitality Management, 78,* 1–12.

Gawke, J. C., Gorgievski, M. J., and Bakker, A. B. (2017). Employee intrapreneurship and work engagement: A latent change score approach. *Journal of Vocational Behavior, 100,* 88–100.

Gayeski, D. (2015). Will gen Z even care about HR technology. *Workforce Solutions Review,* 9–11.

Getz, D., and Petersen, T. (2004). The importance of profit and growth-oriented entrepreneurs in destination competitiveness and change. *Reinventing a Tourism Destination: Facing the Challenge*, 135–146.

Getz, D., and Petersen, T. (2005). Growth and profit-oriented entrepreneurship among family business owners in the tourism and hospitality industry. *International Journal of Hospitality Management*, *24*(2), 219–242.

Ghura, A. S. (2017). A qualitative exploration of the challenges organizations face while working with generation Z intrapreneurs. *Journal of Entrepreneurship and Innovation in Emerging Economies*, *3*(2), 105–114.

Goh, E., and Jie, F. (2019). To waste or not to waste: Exploring motivational factors of Generation Z hospitality employees towards food wastage in the hospitality industry. *International Journal of Hospitality Management*, *80*, 126–135.

Goh, E., and Kong, S. (2018). Theft in the hotel workplace: Exploring frontline employees' perceptions towards hotel employee theft. *Tourism Hospitality and Research*, *18*(4), 442–455.

Goh, E., and Lee, C. (2018). A workforce to be reckoned with: The emerging pivotal generation Z hospitality workforce. *International Journal of Hospitality Management*, *73*, 20–28.

Goh, E., and Okumuş, F. (2020). Avoiding the hospitality workforce bubble: Strategies to attract and retain Generation Z talent in the hospitality workforce. *Tourism Management Perspectives*, *33*, 1–7.

Goldsby, M. G., and Mathews, R. (2018). *Entrepreneurship the Disney way*. Routledge.

Grafton, M. (2011). Growing a business and becoming more entrepreneurial: The five traits of success. *Strategic Decision*, *27*(6), 4–7.

Gursoy, D., Saayman, M., and Sotiriadis, M. (Eds.). (2015). *Collaboration in tourism businesses and destinations: A handbook*. Emerald Group Publishing.

Gutterman, A. S. (2016). *Cross-cultural studies: A library of resources for growth-oriented entrepreneurs*. International Center for Growth-Oriented Entrepreneurship. Retrieved from https://alangutterman.typepad.com/files/ccs---cultural-dimensions.pdf.

Gutterman, A. S. (2018). *Growth-orientedd entrepreneurship* (S. Shane, Ed.). Business Expert Press.

Hall, C. M., and Rusher, K. (2013). Risky lifestyles? Entrepreneurial characteristics of the New Zealand bed and breakfast sector. In *Small firms in tourism* (pp. 93–108). Routledge.

Harrison, J., and Delaney, K. (2014). Innovate and transform: Keeping up with the needs of a 21st-century workforce. *Australia's Paydirt*, *1*(217), 12.

Hessels, J., and Naudé, W. (2019). The intersection of the fields of entrepreneurship and development economics: A review towards a new view. *Journal of Economic Surveys*, *33*(2), 389–403.

Hirschmeier, J. (1964). *The Origins of Entrepreneurship in Meiji Japan.* Cambridge, Mass: Harvard University Press.

Hmieleski, K. M., and Sheppard, L. D. (2019). The Yin and Yang of entrepreneurship: Gender differences in the importance of communal and agentic characteristics for entrepreneurs' subjective well-being and performance. *Journal of Business Venturing*, *34*(4), 709–730.

Hoque, A. S. M. M. (2018). Digital device addiction effect on the lifestyle of Generation Z in Bangladesh. *Asian People Journal*, *1*(2), 21–44.

Hoque, A. S. M. M., Awang, Z. B., and Siddiqui, B. A. (2018). Upshot of generation 'Z' entrepreneurs' e-lifestyle on Bangladesh SME performance in the digital era.

Ireland, R. D., and Webb, J. W. (2007). Strategic entrepreneurship: Creating competitive advantage through streams of innovation. *Business Horizons*, *50*(1), 49–59.

Isık, C., Kucukkaltan, E. G., Celebi, S. K., Calkın, O., Enser, I., and Celik, A. (2019). Tourism and entrepreneurship: A literature review. *Journal of Ekonomi*, *1*(1), 1–27.

Jain, V., and Pant, S. (2012). Navigating generation Y for effective mobile marketing in India: A conceptual framework. *Mobile Marketing Association IJMM*, *7*(3), Winter 2002.

Jyotirmay, G. (2007). Intrapreneurship Approach For Tourism Management. *Atna-Journal of Tourism Studies*, *2*(1), 116–123.

Kallmuenzer, A., and Peters, M. (2018). Entrepreneurial behaviour, firm size and financial performance: The case of rural tourism family firms. *Tourism Recreation Research*, *43*(1), 2–14.

Karamustafa, K., and Ulama, S. (2010). Measuring the seasonality in tourism with the comparison of different methods. *EuroMed Journal of Business*, *5*(2), 191–214.

Karatas-Ozkan, M., and Chell, E. (2010). *Nascent Entrepreneurship and Learning.* Cheltenham: Edward Elgar.

Karunaratne, H. D. (2017). In search of silver line from immigrant entrepreneurs in Japan. *Journal of Economics and Development Studies*, *5*(2), 1–12.

Kaplan, R. S. (2015). *What you really need to lead: The power of thinking and acting like an owner*s Harvard Business Press.

Kelton Tech. (2015). *Entrepreneur and intrapreneur: Where does the difference lie?* Retrieved from https://www.kelltontech.com/kellton-tech-blog/entrepreneur-and-intrapreneur-where-does-difference-lie.

Kesici, A., and Tunç, N. F. (2018). Investigating the digital addiction level of the university students according to their purposes for using digital tools. *University Journal of Educational Research, 6*(2), 235–241.

King, V. T. (2009). Anthropology and tourism in Southeast Asia: Comparative studies, cultural differentiation and agency. In Michael Hitchcock, Victor T. King, and Michael Parnwell (Ed.), *Tourism in Southeast Asia: Challenges and new directions* (pp. 43–68).

Kirzner, I. M. (1973). *Competition and entrepreneurship*. Chicago: University of Chicago Press.

Khoshkhoo, M. H. I., and Nadalipour, Z. (2016). Tourism SMEs and organizational learning in a competitive environment. *The Learning Organization*.

Kraleva, N. (2011). Learning organizations: Prerequisite for successful tourism organizations. *UTMS Journal of Economics, 2*(1), 77–82.

Koh, K. Y., and Hatten, T. S. (2002). The tourism entrepreneur: The overlooked player in tourism development studies. *International Journal of Hospitality and Tourism Administration, 3*(1), 21–48.

Kosenius, A. K., Juutinen, A., and Tyrvainen, L. (2020). The role of state-owned commercial forests and firm features in nature-based tourism business performance. *Silva Fennica, 54*(1), 1–23.

Kupperschmidt, B. (2000). Multigenerational employees: Strategies for effective management. *Health Care Management, 19*(1), 65–76.

Kuschel, K., and Lepeley, M. T. (2016). Copreneurial women in start-ups: Growth-oriented or lifestyle? An aid for technology industry investors. *Academia Revista Latinoamericana de Administración, 29*(2), 181–197.

Lant, T. K., and Mezias, S. J. (1990). Managing discontinuous change: A simulation study of organizational learning and entrepreneurship. *Strategic Management Journal*, 147–179.

Laurin, S. (2016). *Entrepreneurship vs Intrapreneurship*. Retrieved from https://intrapreneurialinitiative.org/entrepreneur-vs-intrapreneur/.

Lashley, C., and Rowson, B. (2010). Lifestyle businesses: Insights into Blackpool's hotel sector. *International Journal of Hospitality Management, 29*(3), 511–519.

Lee, S., and Tsang, K. (2013). Perceptions of tourism and hotel management students on ethics in the workplace. *Journal of Teaching in Travel and Tourism, 13*(3), 228–250.

Lecuna, A., Cohen, B., and Chavez, R. (2017). Characteristics of high-growth entrepreneurs in Latin America. *International Entrepreneurship and Management Journal, 13*(1), 141–159.

Levickaite, R. (2010). Generations X, Y, Z: How social networks form the concept of the World without borders (The case of Lithuania). *LIMES, 3*(2), 170–183.

Li, L. (2017). *Collaborative me. Explorative study to create a desirable collaborative experience for Generation Z in the coming workplace.* Retrieved from https://www.politesi.polimi.it/bitstream/10589/132824/1/2017_04_Li.pdf.

Lis-Gutiérrez, J. P., Segura, J. P. M., Gaitán-Angulo, M., Henao, L. C., Viloria, A., Malagón, L. E., and Aguilera-Hernández, D. (2018, June). Dynamics of the air passenger transportation market in Colombia (2016). In *International conference on data mining and big data* (pp. 179–187). Cham: Springer.

Macke, D. (2016). *Growth entrepreneurs profiled.* Center for Rural Entrepreneurship. Retrieved from https://energizingentrepreneursorg.presencehost.net/file_download/inline/f9aeb5bf-ae2f-4f3e-bfca-8a5369c6c229.

Mahadi, S. R. S. (2018). Cyber addiction and the impact towards Gen Zers attitude in learning. *International Journal of Academic Research in Business and Social Sciences, 8*(12).

Mason, C., and Brown, R. (2014). Entrepreneurial ecosystems and growth oriented entrepreneurship. *Final Report to OECD, Paris, 30*(1), 77–102.

Masurel, E., and Snellenberg, R. (2017). Does the lifestyle entrepreneur exist? An analysis of lifestyle entrepreneurs compared with other entrepreneurs on the basis of the development of entrepreneurial competences. *Research Memorandum, 1*, 1–14.

Maxwell, G. A., Ogden, S. M., and Broadbridge, A. (2010). Generation Y's career expectations and aspirations: Engagement in the hospitality industry. *Journal of Hospitality and Tourism Management, 17*, 53–61.

McGehee, N. G., and Kline, C. S. (2008). *Building community capacity for tourism development* (G. Moscardo, Ed.). Oxfordshire, UK: CABI International.

McCrindle (2019a). Gen Z and Gen Alpha infographic update. https://mccrindle.com.au/insights/blogarchive/gen-z-and-gen-alpha-infographic-update/. Accessed Date: 30 March 2020.

McCrindle. (2019b). Generations defined: 50 years of change over 5 generations. https://mccrindle.com.au/insights/blog/generations-defined-50-years-change-5-generations-resource/. Accessed Date: 30 March 2020.

Mercan, N. (2016). X, Y ve Z kuşağı kadınların farklı tüketim alışkanlıklarının modern dünyada inşa edilmesi. *Kadın Araştırmaları Dergisi, 2*(1), 59–70.

Micoleta, J. (2012). *Generation Z teens stereotyped as 'lazy and unaware'.* https://www.huffpost.com/entry/apathetic-teens-generatio_n_1323577. Accessed Date: April 2020.

Millennial Branding. (2014). *Gen Y and Gen Z global workplace expectations study.* https://workplaceintelligence.com/geny-genz-global-workplace-expectations-study/. Accessed Date: 6 April 2020.

Mitchell, D. A. (2008). Generation Z: Striking the balance: Healthy doctors for a healthy community. *Australian Family Physician, 37*(8), 665–672.

Mohedano-Suanes, A., and Benítez, D. G. (2018). Intrapreneurs: Characteristics and behavior. In *Inside the mind of the entrepreneur* (pp. 109–119). Cham: Springer.

Moore, K., Jones, C., and Frazier, R. S. (2017). Engineering education for generation Z. *American Journal of Engineering Education, 8*(2), 111–126.

Moriano, J. A., Molero, F., Topa, G., and Mangin, J. P. L. (2014). The influence of transformational leadership and organizational identification on intrapreneurship. *International Entrepreneurship and Management Journal, 10*(1), 103–119.

Mottiar, Z., and Boluk, K. (2017). Understanding how social entrepreneurs fit into the tourism discourse. In *Social entrepreneurship and tourism* (pp. 117–132). Cham: Springer.

Nahata, R. (2019). Success is good but failure is not so bad either: Serial entrepreneurs and venture capital contracting. *Journal of Corporate Finance, 58*, 624–649.

Ndabeni, L., and Rogerson, C. M. (2005). Entrepreneurship in rural tourism: The challenges of South Africa's Wild Coast. *Africa Insight, 35*(4), 130–141.

NDP Group. (2017). *Guide to Gen Z: Debunking the myths of our youngest generation.* https://www.npd.com/wps/portal/npd/us/news/tips-trends-takeaways/guide-to-gen-z-debunking-the-myths-of-our-youngest-generation/. Accessed Date: 24 October 2019.

Nielsen, S. L., Klyver, K., Evald, M. R., and Bager, T. (2017). *Entrepreneurship in theory and practice: paradoxes in play.* Edward Elgar.

Ollenburg, C., and Buckley, R. (2007). Stated economic and social motivations of farm tourism operators. *Journal of Travel Research, 45*(4), 444–452.

Özkan, M., and Solmaz, B. (2015). The changing face of the employees-Generation Z and their perceptions of work (a study applied to university students). 4th World Conference on Business, Economics and Management-WCBEM, Procedia Economics and Finance, 26, 476–483.

Page, S. J. (2007). *Tourism management: Managing for change* (2nd ed.). London: Butterworth-Heinemann.

Parker, S. C. (2011). Intrapreneurship or entrepreneurship? *Journal of Business Venturing, 26*(1), 19–34.

Peters, M., Frehse, J., and Buhalis, D. (2009). The importance of lifestyle entrepreneurship: A conceptual study of the tourism industry. *Pasos, 7*(2), 393–405.

Peters, M., Kallmuenzer, A., and Buhalis, D. (2019). Hospitality entrepreneurs managing quality of life and business growth. *Current Issues in Tourism, 22*(16), 2014–2033.

Peterson, H. (2014). *Millennials are old news-here's everything you should know about Generation Z.* https://www.businessinsider.com.au/millennials-are-old-news-heres-everything-you-should-know-about-generation-z-2014-6. Accessed Date: 13 April 2020.

Phelan, C. J. (2014). Understanding the farmer: An analysis of the entrepreneurial competencies required for diversification to farm tourism (Doctoral dissertation, University of Central Lancashire).

Pinchot, G. (1985). *Intrapreneuring.* New York, NY: Harper and Row.

Pırnar, I. (2015). The specific characteristics of entrepreneurship process in tourism industry [Turizm Sektöründe Girisimcilik Süreci ve Sektöre Özgü Özellikler]. *Selçuk Üniversitesi Sosyal Bilimler Enstitüsü Dergisi* (34), 75.

Prince, S. (2017). Craft-art in the Danish countryside: Reconciling a lifestyle, livelihood and artistic career through rural tourism. *Journal of Tourism and Cultural Change, 15*(4), 339–358.

Prossack, A. (2019). *Struggling to retain millennials and Gen Z? Here are 4 reasons.* https://www.forbes.com/sites/ashiraprossack1/2019/09/30/retain-millennials-genz/#15b854de220f. Accessed Date: 18 November 2019.

Purcell, K., Rainie, L., Heaps, A., Buchanan, J., Friedrich, L., Jacklin, A., and Zickuhr, K. (2012). *How teens do research in the digital world.* Pew Internet and American Life Project.

Quattrociocchi, Bernardino, Mercuri, Francesco, Mirko, Perano, and Calabrese, Mario. (2017). Tourism supply chain management and strategic partnerships for managing the complexity in tourism industry. *Enlightening Tourism, 7.*

Ransley, M. (2012). *Sustainable tourism practices*. Retrieved from https://www.academia.edu/4820716/Sustainable_Tourism_Practices. Accessed Date: 28 October 19.

Rasca, L., and Deaconu, A. (2018, May). Entrepreneurial motivators and competencies—Main drivers of entrepreneurial success. In *Proceedings of the International Conference on Business Excellence* (Vol. 12, No. 1, pp. 864–874). Sciendo.

Reindrawati, D. Y. (2018). Social entrepreneurship in tourism: A way to involve locals in tourism development *KnE Social Sciences*, 173–185.

Renfro, A. (2012). *Meet Generation Z, Getting Smart*. https://www.gettingsmart.com/2012/12/MEET-GENERATION-Z/. Accessed Date: 28 November 2019.

Robertson, S. (2019). *Gen Z teams are magic for startup leaders who overcome this challenge*. https://www.entrepreneur.com/article/336266. Accessed Date: 10 April 2020.

Rodriguez-Sanchez, I., Williams, A. M., and Brotons, M. (2019). The innovation journey of new-to-tourism entrepreneurs. *Current Issues in Tourism, 22*(8), 877–904.

Rogerson, C. M. (2008). Developing small tourism businesses in Southern Africa. *Botswana Notes and Records, 39*, 23–34.

Sadeghi, V. J., Biancone, P. P., Anderson, R. B., and Nkongolo-Bakenda, J. M. (2019). International entrepreneurship by particular people'on their own terms': A study on the universal characteristics of entrepreneurs in evolving economies. *International Journal of Entrepreneurship and Small Business, 37*(2), 288–308.

Saebi, T., Foss, N. J., and Linder, S. (2019). Social entrepreneurship research: Past achievements and future promises. *Journal of Management, 45*(1), 70–95.

Schawbel, D. (2012). *Millennials vs. baby boomers: Who would you rather hire?* https://business.time.com/2012/03/29/millennials-vs-baby-boomers-who-would-you-rather-hire/. Accessed Dated: 10 April 2020.

Schawbel, D. (2014). *Why 'Gen Z' may be more entrepreneurial than 'Gen Y'.* https://www.entrepreneur.com/article/231048. Accessed Date: 23 October 2019.

Schulman, S. (2007). Crossing the generational divide: Engaging 'young' employees in your organization. *Development and Learning in Organizations: An International Journal, 21*(2), 7–9.

Schumpeter, J. A. (1934). Entrepreneurship as innovation. In R Swedberg (Ed.), *Entrepreneurship: The social science view* (pp. 51–75). Oxford, UK: Oxford University Press.

Schwienbacher, A. (2007). A theoretical analysis of optimal financing strategies for different types of capital-constrained entrepreneurs. *Journal of Business Venturing, 22*(6), 753–781.

Serarols-Tarrés, C., Padilla-Meléndez, A., and del Aguila-Obra, A. R. (2006). The influence of entrepreneur characteristics on the success of pure dot. com firms. *International Journal of Technology Management, 33*(4), 373–388.

Shaw, G., and Williams, A. (2004). *From lifestyle consumption to lifestyle production: Changing patterns of tourism entrepreneurship. small firms in tourism* (pp. 99–113). Oxford: Elsevier.

Shmailan, A. B. (2016). Compare the characteristics of male and female entrepreneurs as explorative study. *Journal of Entrepreneurship and Organization Management, 5*(4), 1–7.

Shockley, G. E., and Frank, P. M. (2011). Schumpeter, Kirzner, and the field of social entrepreneurship. *Journal of Social Entrepreneurship, 2*(1), 6–26.

Sima, E., Bordânc, F., and Sima, C. (2015). Entrepreneurship role in promoting rural tourism. *Agricultural Economics and Rural Development, 12*(1), 71–80.

Singh, A. (2014). Challenges and issues of Generation Z. *IOSR Journal of Business and Management (IOSR-JBM), 16*(7), 59–63.

Solnet, D., Baum, T., Robinson, R., and Lockstone-Binney, L. (2016). What about the workers? Roles and skills for employees in hotels of the future. *Journal of Vacation Marketing, 22*(3), 212–226.

Smith, W., Clement, J., and Pitts, R. (2018). Oh the places they will go: Examining the early career path of hospitality alumni. *Journal of Teaching in Travel and Tourism, 18*(2), 109–122.

Solvoll, S., Agnete Alsos, G., and Bulanova, O. (2015). Tourism entrepreneurship—Review and future directions. *Scandinavian Journal of Hospitality and Tourism, 15*(1), 120–137.

Spencer, J. (2019). *5 simple, science-backed ways entrepreneurs can connect with Gen Z.* https://www.entrepreneur.com/article/328083 Accessed Date: 8 April 2020.

Suleman, R,. and Nelson, B. (2011). Motivating the millenials: Tapping into the potential of the youngest generation. *Leader to Leader, 62*, 39–44.

Sun, X., Xu, H., Köseoglu, M. A., and Okumus, F. (2019). How do lifestyle hospitality and tourism entrepreneurs manage their work-life balance? *International Journal of Hospitality Management*, 102359.

Taş, H. Y., Demirdöğmez, M., and Küçükoğlu, M. (2017). Geleceğimiz olan Z kuşağının çalışma hayatına muhtemel etkileri. *Uluslararası Toplum Araştırmaları Dergisi*-OPUS, *7*(3), 1033–1048.

Tresna, P. W., and Nirmalasari, H. (2018). Sustainable competitive advantage strategies of tourism products in Pangandaran district. *Review of Integrative Business and Economics Research*, *7*, 34–47.

Trzesniewski, K. H., and Donnellan, M. B. (2010). Rethinking 'generation me': A study of cohort effects from 1976–2006. *Perspectives on Psychological Science*, *5*(1), 58–75.

TSA: RMF. (2008). *Tourism satellite account: Recommended methodological framework by united nations, statistical office of the European communities Eurostat, world tourism organization.* Organization for Economic Co-operation and Development. Luxembourg: United Nations.

UNWTO. (2008). *Understanding tourism: Basic glossary.* https://cf.cdn.unwto.org/sites/all/files/docpdf/glossaryenrev.pdf. Accessed Date: 28 October 2019.

UNWTO. (2020). *World tourism barometer 2020.* https://webunwto.s3.eu-west-1.amazonaws.com/s3fs-public/2020-01/UNWTO_Barom20_01_January_excerpt.pdf. Accessed 17 April 2020.

Vision Critical. (2019). *Generation Z characteristics.* https://www.visioncritical.com/blog/generation-z-infographics. Accessed Date: 6 November 2019.

Volery, T., Mueller, S., and von Siemens, B. (2015). Entrepreneur ambidexterity: A study of entrepreneur behaviours and competencies in growth-oriented small and medium-sized enterprises. *International Small Business Journal*, *33*(2), 109–129.

Washington Post. (2020). The new coronavirus economy: A gigantic experiment reshaping how we work and live. https://www.washingtonpost.com/business/2020/03/21/economy-change-lifestyle-coronavirus/. Accessed Date: 10 April 2020.

West, S. A. (2013). Think like an OWNER!. *Strategic Finance*, *95*(6), 30–34. Retrieved from https://sfmagazine.com/wp-content/uploads/sfarchive/2013/12/Think-Like-an-Owner.pdf.

World Tourism Organization. (2019). International tourism highlights (2019 ed.). Madrid: UNWTO. https://doi.org/10.18111/9789284421152. Accessed Date: 28 October 2019.

World Population Prospects Report. (2019). *The 2019 revision of world population prospects.* Retrieved from https://population.un.org/wpp/.

Workplace Intelligence. (2014). Gen Y and Gen Z Global Workplace Expectations Study. http://workplaceintelligence.com/geny-genz-global-workplace-expectations-study/. Accessed Date: 8 April 2021.

Xu, H., Ma, S., and Jiang, L. (2017). Social interactions of lifestyle tourism entrepreneurial migrants. *Tourism Tribune, 32*(7), 69–76.

Yu, C. S. (2011). Construction and validation of an e-lifestyle instrument. *Internet Research, 21*(3), 214–235.

4

Generation Z and Their Perceptions of Well-Being in Tourism

Eric D. Olson and Heejung Ro

Introduction

The need for wellness products and services has increased significantly in the past few years for the hospitality and tourism industries; further, wellness tourism had grown into a $639 billion market by 2017 and is expected to increase to $919 billion by 2022 (Global Wellness Institute, 2018). According to the Wellness Tourism Association, wellness tourism is defined as "a specific division of the global tourism industry defined by the common goal of marketing natural assets primarily focused on

---

E. D. Olson (✉)
Department of Apparel, Events, and Hospitality Management, College of Human Sciences, Iowa State University, Ames, IA, USA
e-mail: olsoned@iastate.edu

H. Ro
Rosen College of Hospitality Management, University of Central Florida, Orlando, FL, USA
e-mail: Heejung.Ro@ucf.edu

© The Author(s), under exclusive license to Springer Nature Switzerland AG 2021
N. Stylos et al. (eds.), *Generation Z Marketing and Management in Tourism and Hospitality*,
https://doi.org/10.1007/978-3-030-70695-1_4

serving the wellness-minded consumer and those who want to be" (2019, para 1). Research has suggested that tourism experiences are associated with tourists' evaluation of well-being (Hwang & Lyu, 2015; Naidoo & Sharpley, 2016), as tourism experiences typically increase positive emotions (Morgan, Pritchard, & Sedgley, 2015; Smith & Diekmann, 2017). While tourism activities are expected to be varied among different generations (Li, Li, & Hudson, 2013), Generation Z tourists are known to be more interested in unique experiences, are concerned about the sustainable impacts of tourism, are expected to travel more frequently, and use technology more for convenience (Whitmore, 2019).

Generation Z, an age cohort born between 1997–2012 (Dimock, 2019), is on track to become the most racially or ethnic-diverse generation in the country (Pew Research Center, 2018). This generation grew up with mobile devices and the Internet, along with social media and constant connectivity and communication (Dimock, 2019, para. 12). Additionally, Generation Z tourists are known to support hospitality organizations that are "doing good" in their local communities, enhancing sustainability/natural environments and creating cultural identity. Furthermore, they are considered to be the "ultimate wellness consumers" who take a broad view of wellness, which includes physical fitness, healthy eating, and mental well-being (Vennare, n.d., para. 6). While Generation Z is generally described with an emphasis on physical fitness, mental health, social issues, technology, and environment, the implications of each area for the hospitality and tourism industry have not been discussed in a holistic manner.

This chapter discusses Generation Z tourists and their perceptions of well-being within the context of hospitality and tourism experiences. We divide Generation Z's well-being perceptions into five areas: (1) physical, (2) mental health/wellness, (2) social, (4) technological/digital, and (5) environmental. Throughout the chapter, examples and implications are provided for hospitality and tourism practitioners who are navigating the complexities of an emerging cohort of tourists.

Physical Well-Being

Physical well-being "includes lifestyle behaviors choices to ensure health, avoid preventable diseases and conditions, and to live in a balanced state of body, mind, and spirit" (American Association of Nurse Anesthetists, 2020, para. 1). In this section, we discuss the well-being aspects of sleep, eating well, and physical activity.

Academic research and the popular press has recently focused on the implications of sleep as a function of daily life. Sleep has been examined in the tourism context as part of an active and willful tourist (Valtonen & Veijola, 2011). According to the National Sleep Foundation, 61% of Generation Z get less than the recommended hours of sleep (2011). The increased use of smart phones has become a distraction against getting a restful night of sleep; as a result, the hospitality industry has embarked on enhancing guests' sleep quality. For example, the hotel industry has responded with a variety of sleep and bed products, including pillow options and sleep menus, enhanced mattresses, blackout shades, and aromatherapy options to enhance guests' quality of sleep.

Physical activity and well-being have become fundamental for Generation Z, as evidenced by increased use of wearable technologies, adventure-based and obstacle races, and enhanced awareness of obesity rates. Generation Z will continue to challenge the notion of physical well-being for the hospitality and tourism industry. According to the Physical Activity Council (2019), Generation Z is the most active age cohort engaged in high-calorie activities, with 18% remaining inactive.

As a result, hospitality providers are responding to new products and services to incorporate physical well-being aspects into their brands. For example, Marriott International provides fitness centers with customized workout programs on video wall displays, wellness retreats, and fitness centers. Hilton hotels promote wellness by including fitness elements into guestrooms, such as a fitness kiosk that includes strength, suspension, and yoga tools (https://fivefeettofitness.hilton.com/). Hotels have also introduced other elements of physical wellness, such as running concierges that provide local running maps and organized runs.

Another example of Generation Z's physical well-being is now occurring at meetings, conventions, and events. For example, many national meetings and conventions have "spa and wellness" rooms, where event attendees can take a break from the main meeting and convention and spend time in a room devoted to relaxation and recharging. Many rooms have yoga and stretching classes, enhanced mood music, massages, and wellness food and drink. Additionally, many conventions and meetings are including 5 K run/walks, and brief stretching activities embedded in their meeting programming.

According to the popular press, Generation Z is also changing the food landscape of restaurants. For example, Generation Z is currently embracing plant-based alternatives, as Generation Z is thought to be the catalyst behind a $5 billion market for plant-based alternatives (Robinson, 2017). Plant-based alternatives have increasingly become available at quick-service restaurants such as Burger King and Subway. In recent years, there has been an increase in the number of food and beverage events and festivals, including beer festivals, wine events, and gastronomic tours, providing Generation Z attendees with a variety of food-related experiences. Generation Z entrepreneurs are creating many of these food and beverage events.

Hospitality managers must remain aware of Generation Z's physical well-being. Generation Z is thought to be active/proactive participants of health and wellness products, influenced by the obesity epidemic and the use of technology in exercises. For instance, managers will want to know how elements can continue to be used in the creation of physical servicescapes and spatial layout of the customer experience through a hospitality organization to enhance physical well-being. The inclusion of physical wellness products, such as gyms, spas, and programming, will remain important for Generation Z. To this end, hospitality managers should continue to recognize the importance of Generation Z's physical well-being.

Mental Health/Wellness Well-Being

Mental health/wellness will continue to be an important dimension of well-being for Generation Z tourists. Mental health is defined as "a state of well-being in which every individual realizes his or her own potential, can cope with the normal stresses of life, can work productively and fruitfully, and is able to make a contribution to her or his community" (World Health Organization, 2012, p. 1). According to the National Institute of Mental Health, almost one in five U.S. adults live with a mental illness, which can vary among degrees of severity and various conditions (National Institute of Mental Health, 2020). Generation Z is significantly more likely (27%) than Millennials (15%) and Generation X (13%) to report their mental health as being fair or poor (Bethune, 2019). Furthermore, 35% of Generation Z has received treatment or therapy from a mental health professional (Bethune, 2019).

According to a report by The American Psychological Association, for Generation Z Americans, the most common stressors for Generation Z are high-profile issues such as sexual harassment and gun violence (2018), as 75% of Generation Z youth report mass shootings and school shootings as significant sources of stress (American Psychological Association, 2018). Generation Z has been nicked named the "Homeland Generation" and is often defined by living in a post-9/11 era, where its worldview has been impacted by safety and security measures, the creation of Department of Homeland Security, and the War on Terror. Academic researchers are beginning to examine safety in the context of physical servicescapes, the environment in which a customer obtains a service. For example, Siguaw, Mai, and Wanger (2019) found that safety is a primary concern of consumers that influence approach-avoidance behavior in a service setting.

Studies in tourism have also examined the role of mental health effects of tourists. Holland, Thomsen, Powell, and Monz (2018), for example, presented a thorough review of studies that have examined the impact of wildland settings (e.g., national parks, national forests) on human health. Frumkin (2001) found evidence of the relationship between natural settings and human health. Chen and Petrick (2013) conducted a literature review of health and wellness travel experiences and found positive benefits of travel experiences on perceived health and wellness of tourists.

The role of mental health/wellness will continue to be a concern and opportunity for hospitality employers with Generation Z employees, i.e., firms that have incorporated psychologically health-related environments into the workplaces have lower turnover, less stress, and higher employee satisfaction (American Psychological Association, 2012). Recently, firms have been writing mental health policies, thus providing information about mental health, increasing awareness, and offering training for managers (Kohll, 2018). Hospitality firms, such as Marriott, provide employees with access to LifeWorks, which is an employee-assistance program (LifeWorks, 2017).

A study by Cigna Health Service revealed that Generation Z and Y youths are lonelier than were youths in other generations (Nemececk, 2018); as such, hospitality firms will need to consider the role of mental health/wellness in the creation of hospitality and tourism products and services. In addition to the increase of tourism products that provide an opportunity to enhance mental wellness, such as medical tourism (Connell, 2006), spa tourism (Han, Kiatkawsin, Jung, & Kim, 2018), and meditation tourism (Jiang, Ryan, & Zhang, 2018), firms are beginning to consider the impact of physical environments on mental health through design, lighting, and the guest experience. Strategies employed will include open spaces where tourist can gather, e.g., enhanced and brightened areas, gardens, and calm and relaxing spaces Hospitality firms should continue to consider mental health/wellness as a dimension of well-being for Generation Z tourists.

Social Well-Being

Reza, Subramaniam, and Islam (2019) summarized social well-being as "an individual's appraisal of their social relationships, how others react to them, and how they interact with social institutions and community" (p. 1250). The World Health Organization also includes social well-being in its definition of health (2019). Keyes (1998) suggested five dimensions of social well-being: social integration, social contribution, social coherence, social actualization, and social acceptance. Inclusive workforces and organizations continue to promote connection with others since Generation Z is expected to be the most racially and ethnically diverse age cohort (Fry & Parker, 2018). Sixty-two percent of Generation Z states that increasing racial/ethnic diversity is good for society, similar to 61% of Generation Y, 52% for Generation X, 48% of Baby Boomers, and 42% of the Silent Generation (Parker, Graf, & Igienik, 2019), although Generation Z is thought to be the most diverse generation yet (Fry & Parker, 2018) and is concerned about issues of diversity and inclusion.

Generation Z grew up in a time of great social awareness and acceptance toward the lesbian/gay/bisexual/transgender plus (LGBT+) community, especially in Western societies; further, recent marriage equality laws have been granted in Taiwan. Although U.S. adults greatly overestimate that about one in four (23.6%) adults are gay or lesbian (McCarthy, 2019), it is estimated that about 4.5% of Americans currently identify as LGBT+ (Newport, 2018). Several hospitality firms have created marketing efforts to support and attract the LGBT+ community. For example, Expedia has a micro-search engine devoted to hotels and flights devoted to the LGBT+ community. Further, professional associations, such as LGBT Meeting Professionals Association, connect LGBT+ meeting and event organizers and planners.

The recent years have also witnessed greater acceptance and recognition among the greater diversity of genders. About one-third of Generation Z knows someone who uses gender-neutral pronouns, 59% of Generation Z says online forms or profiles should include options other than "man" or "woman" (Parker et al., 2019) to greater reflect the diversity of genders. This will impact identification processes, such as meeting/event registrations, hotel/airline reservations, spa/wellness treatments, and travel across various jurisdictions.

One in four Americans has a disability (Centers for Disease Control and Prevention, 2019). Fisk et al. (2018) argue for the fair and accessible treatment of all customers in the context of providing services. Types of disabilities include physical (e.g., paraplegia); intellectual or learning (e.g., learning disability); psychiatric (e.g., schizophrenia); visual (e.g., visually impairment); heating impairment (e.g., hearing loss); and neurological. The United Nations promotes accessible tourism for all, including persons with disabilities, their spouses, and caregivers (2019).

Generation Z is also expected to be more entrepreneurial than previous generations, as 41% of Generation Z expects to start their own business and half belief they will create a product that changes the world

(Entrepreneur, 2019). For example, many Generation Z entrepreneurs have started businesses that are expected to have a positive impact on the greater good of society. Additionally, organizations have been charged with serving the needs of underserved consumers (Fisk, 2009).

Generation Z expects hospitality firms to be welcoming, inclusive, and accessible; further, hospitality firms will need to continue to signal their social well-being programs and diversity efforts to Generation Z tourists and employees. This will result in hospitality and tourism providers becoming leaders in diversity and inclusion. Generation Z will continue to seek out those hospitality organizers that align with this cohort's values.

Technological/Digital Well-Being

Technology/digital well-being refers to an idea that, "when humans interact with technology, the experience should support mental and/or physical health in a measurable way" (TechTarget, n.d., para. 1). Generation Z consumers are described as focusing on innovation, insisting on convenience, emphasizing security, and looking for escapism (Wood, 2013). Known as the first generation of true digital natives (Francis & Hoefel, 2018), Generation Z consumers are accustomed to interacting and communicating in a world that is digitally connected at all times. In addition, as the most ethnically diverse generation in history, Generation Z sees itself both locally and globally. A survey revealed that 42% of Generation Z (age ranged from 14 to 18 years) say they need to travel in order to feel complete (Ting, 2016). Young consumers seek intimacy and connection through authentic tourism experience facilitated by information technologies (Bialski, 2012); further, this trend contributes to the emergence of a sharing economy or collaborative consumption in various tourism and hospitality areas, such as food, transportation, and accommodation (Decrop, Del Chiappa, Mallargé, & Zidda, 2018).

For example, Airbnb.com is one of the more well-known platforms in which travelers seek peer-to-peer short-term rentals mainly to satisfy their quest for authenticity, memorability, and personal transformation (Guttentag, Smith, Potwarka, & Havitz, 2018). While Airbnb is popular among a broad age range of travelers, Couchsurfing appeals to Generation Z travelers. Couchsurfing.com is an online hospitality network that offers global noncommercial accommodation opportunities globally. It has a community of over 15 million travelers and 400,000 hosts; further, the online hub helps budget travelers and backpackers to find hosts who offer free accommodations all over the world (Rodgers, 2019). Participants form a group of like-minded people who encourage the creation of social links and a sense of belonging; in addition, this feeling of connectedness, trust, and friendship is reinforced through the sharing of space and time (Belk, 2014; Molz, 2012). Couchsurfing is considered to be an alternative tourism (Molz, 2013) and transformative tourism (Decrop et al., 2018) that belongs to Generation Z tourists who choose this way to travel principally to learn about themselves through travel (Pera & Viglia, 2015), wanting to live culturally enriching experiences to discover the world, escaping daily routines, and traveling differently from so-called traditional traveling generally focusing on discovery, encounters, and looking for souvenirs or entertainment (Decrop et al., 2018).

In a qualitative study of Generation Z consumers, Prioporas, Stylos, and Fotiadis (2017) revealed that Generation Z expects new devices and electronic processes to be widely available in retail locations, which will give Generation Z more autonomy to make more efficient decisions and faster transactions. Basically, Generation Z expects to handle all transactions (e.g., airline check-ins, accommodation reservations) via mobile and use their phones to serve as a tour guide to find more authentic and local experiences. They also want to be able to ask questions online and receive immediate answers (Vision Critical, n.d.). For example, Marriott Hotels recently launched a new hotel concept called M Beta, which eliminates traditional front desks and uses personal greeters for check-in. Furthermore, M Beta is bringing local chefs to create food and beverage menus that incorporate local ingredients. The hotels also have enhanced social hubs in lobbies and gyms to allow guests to gather and interact, thus creating a sense of community for the guests (Herrera-Davila, 2016). M Beta is further utilizing technology by placing buttons throughout the hotel for guests to send feedback directly to digital boards.

The goal of improving technology/digital well-being is to design technology in such a way that it promotes healthy use and proactively assists the user to maintain a healthy lifestyle. Peters, Calvo, and Ryan (2018) discussed how technology can be designed to support well-being that encompasses more than just an immediate hedonic experience but also its longer *eudaimonia* or true human flourishing and, further, suggested three psychological needs (autonomy, competence, and relatedness) as key factors for well-being-supportive technology design. Also, Pera and Viglia (2015) demonstrated a positive relationship between customers' ability to co-create new products/services and their subjective well-being, thus revealing that empowered customers who are able to create and customize novel products/services are more creative, skilled, passionate, and independent than customers who lack those abilities to do so. Such ability, combined with a sense of community, can lead customers to experience personal happiness and improved well-being.

Environmental Well-Being

Environmental subjective well-being is an integrative concept that links pro-environmental behaviors and subjective well-being (Kerrett, Orkibi, & Ronen, 2014). Young individuals learn pro-environmental behaviors such as frugality in product consumption, protection of nature, and recycling; further, resource conservation contributes to increasing subjective well-being, which includes a cognitive component of life satisfaction and affective components of positive and negative effects (Kerret et al., 2014). Pro-environmental behavior has been found to be positively correlated with subjective well-being (Brown & Kasser, 2005; Corral-Verdugo, Mireles-Acosta, Tapia-Fonllem, & Fraijo-Sing, 2011). Consumers who reported green purchase intention and behavior had higher scores in life satisfaction compared with other consumers after controlling for demographics (Xiao & Li, 2011). Pro-environmental behavior can enhance not only present subjective well-being but expectations of future subjective well-being (Kaida & Kaida, 2016).

Compared with older generations, Generation Z is considered to be the most environmentally friendly group (Williams & Page, 2011), and 77% of Generation Z are willing to pay more for environmentally friendly products, compared with only 51% of Baby Boomers and 66% of the overall population (Levy, 2019). According to Green Match's findings, 72% of Gen Z would spend more money on a service if it were sustainably produced. Generation Z has a strong preference toward switching to brands that take sustainable initiatives, the values of which are more important to Gen Z than cost. Furthermore, Green Match's findings show that Generation Z is more willing to boycott companies that do not meet their values (Turk, 2018).

Understanding sustainability in terms of Generation Z's well-being might be rather complicated than is generally assumed. Although Generation Z is often presented as an environmentally friendly cohort, researchers found that sustainable tourism is not a key concept for Generation Z (Haddouche & Salomone, 2018). Also, Generation Z is generally favorable toward hotels' green practice programs yet express distrust for large hotel corporations' use of green practices as a marketing tool to appeal to customers for cost-saving purposes (Lemy, 2016). Environmental concerns also lead to an increased propensity to volunteer, and such volunteering is positively associated with well-being, but only for those who are concerned about the environment (Binder & Blankenberg, 2016).

Noting Generation Z's attitudes toward food consumption and experiences, some researchers propose food tourism as a force to change and as a catalyst for global food justice and sustainability (Bertella & Vidmar, 2019). Instead of commodifying food in terms of "gastronomic theaters in which chefs play with food to entertain guests," food tourism for Generation Z should be more as a remake of the Grand Tour, where personal growth and transformation were sought through education (Bertella & Vidmar, 2019, p. 173).

Generation Z expects companies to embrace sustainable values and remain environmentally conscious. This generation is willing to be involved in issues that they care about, including environmental and social justice causes. If hospitality companies want to succeed in the rapidly changing demographic landscape, they must signal to Generation Z that they, too, are committed to environmental and social causes. Failure to do so would have significant negative effects on brand awareness and organizational success (Patel, 2017).

Conclusion

Generation Z represents a tremendous opportunity for hospitality and tourism firms: they are diverse, highly educated, embrace technology, and are well-connected. It is recommended that hospitality providers examine their offerings, experiences, and process through the lens of well-being and examine how their services impact the well-being of individuals, employees, and the communities they operate. This chapter has deepened the understanding how well-being is related to physical, mental health, social, technological/digital, and environmental aspects of well-being of Generation Z. Hospitality and tourism providers must continue to utilize these dimensions when creating products, services, and experiences for Generation Z in the tourism sector. Generation Z is expected to be the most racially diverse cohort and tends to be more socially aware of the underserved and minorities, hospitality and tourism organizations that embrace diversity and inclusion efforts of its customers and employees will be supported by Generation Z.

References

American Association of Nurse Anesthetists. (2020, June 16). *Physical well-being*. Retrieved from https://www.aana.com/practice/health-and-wellness-peer-assistance/about-health-wellness/physical-well-being#:~:text=Physical%20Well%2DBeing,body%2C%20mind%2C%20and%20spirit.

American Psychological Association. (2012). *Psychologically healthy workplaces have lower turnover, less stress and higher satisfaction*. Retrieved from https://www.apa.org/news/press/releases/phwa/satisfaction-chart.pdf.

American Psychosocial Association. (2018). *Stress in America Generation Z*. Retrieved from https://www.apa.org/news/press/releases/stress/2018/stress-gen-z.pdf.

Belk, R. (2014). Sharing versus pseudo-sharing in Web 2.0. *The Anthropologist,* *18*(1), 7–23. https://doi.org/10.1080/09720073.2014.11891518.

Bertella, G., & Vidmar, B. (2019). Learning to face global food challenges through tourism experiences. *Journal of Tourism Futures, 5*(2), 168–178. https://doi.org/10.1108/jtf-01-2019-0004.

Bethune, S. (2019). *Gen Z more likely to report mental health concerns.* Retrieved from https://www.apa.org/monitor/2019/01/gen-z.

Bialski, P. (2012). Technologies of hospitality: How planned encounters develop between strangers. *Hospitality & Society, 1*(3), 245–260. https://doi.org/10.1386/hosp.1.3.245_1.

Binder, M., & Blankenberg, A. K. (2016). Environmental concerns, volunteering and subjective well-being: Antecedents and outcomes of environmental activism in Germany. *Ecological Economics, 124,* 1–16. https://doi.org/10.1016/j.ecolecon.2016.01.009.

Brown, K. W., & Kasser, T. (2005). Are psychological and ecological well-being compatible? The role of values, mindfulness, and lifestyle. *Social Indicators Research, 74*(2), 349–368. https://doi.org/10.1007/s11205-004-8207-8.

Centers for Disease Control and Prevention. (2019). *Disability impacts all of us.* Retrieved from https://www.cdc.gov/ncbddd/disabilityandhealth/infographic-disability-impacts-all.html.

Chen, C. C., & Petrick, J. F. (2013). Health and wellness benefits of travel experiences: A literature review. *Journal of Travel Research, 52*(6), 709–719. https://doi.org/10.1177/0047287513496477.

Connell, J. (2006). Medical tourism: Sea, sun, sand and … surgery. *Tourism Management, 27,* 1093–1100. https://doi.org/10.1016/j.tourman.2005.11.005.

Corral-Verdugo, V., Mireles-Acosta, J., Tapia-Fonllem, C., & Fraijo-Sing, B. (2011). Happiness as correlate of sustainable behavior: A study of pro-ecological, frugal, equitable and altruistic actions that promote subjective wellbeing. *Research in Human Ecology, 18*(2), 95–104. https://www.jstor.org/stable/24707465.

Decrop, A., Del Chiappa, G., Mallargé, J., & Zidda, P. (2018). "Couchsurfing has made me a better person and the world a better place": The transformative power of collaborative tourism experiences. *Journal of Travel & Tourism Marketing, 35*(1), 57–72. https://doi.org/10.1080/10548408.2017.1307159.

Dimock, M. (2019). *Defining generations: Where Millennials end and Generation Z begins.* Pew Research Center. Retrieved from https://tony-silva.com/eslefl/miscstudent/downloadpagearticles/defgenerations-pew.pdf.

Entrepreneur. (2019, January 15). *41 percent of Gen Z-ers plan to become entrepreneurs*. Retrieved from https://www.entrepreneur.com/article/326354.

Fisk, R. (2009). A customer liberation manifesto. *Service. Science, 1*(3), 135–141. https://doi.org/10.1287/serv.1.3.135.

Fisk, R. P., Dean, A. M., Alkire, L., Joubert, A., Previte, J., Robertson, N., & Rosenbaum, M. S. (2018). Design for service inclusion: Creating inclusive service systems by 2050. *Journal of Service Management, 29*(5), 834–858. https://doi.org/10.1108/JOSM-05-2018-0121.

Francis, T., & Hoefel, F. (2018). The influence of Gen Z-the first generation of true digital natives-is expanding. *The official site of McKinsey & Company*. Available at: https://www.mckinsey.com/industries/consumer%20packaged%20goods/our%20insights/true%20gen%20generation%20z%20and%20its%20implications%20for%20companies. Accessed 29 May 2019.

Fry, R., & Parker, K. (2018, November 15). *Early benchmarks show 'Post-Millennials' on track to be most diverse, best-educated generation yet*. Pew Research Center. Retrieved from https://www.pewsocialtrends.org/2018/11/15/early-benchmarks-show-post-millennials-on-track-to-be-most-diverse-best-educated-generation-yet/.

Frumkin, H. (2001). Beyond toxicity: Human health and the natural environment. *American Journal of Preventive Medicine, 20*(3), 234–240. https://doi.org/10.1016/S0749-3797(00)00317-2.

Global Wellness Institute. (2018). *Global wellness tourism economy*. Retrieved from https://globalwellnessinstitute.org/industry-research/global-wellness-tourism-economy/

Guttentag, D., Smith, S., Potwarka, L., & Havitz, M. (2018). Why tourists choose Airbnb: A motivation-based segmentation study. *Journal of Travel Research, 57*(3), 342–359. https://doi.org/10.1177/0047287517696980.

Haddouche, H., & Salomone, C. (2018). Generation Z and the tourist experience: Tourist stories and use of social networks. *Journal of Tourism Futures, 4*(1), 69–79. https://doi.org/10.1108/JTF-12-2017-0059.

Han, H., Kiatkawsin, K., Jung, H., & Kim, W. (2018). The role of wellness spa tourism performance in building destination loyalty: The case of Thailand. *Journal of Travel & Tourism Marketing, 35*(5), 595–610. https://doi.org/10.1080/10548408.2017.1376031.

Herrera-Davila, N. (2016, October 11). *Marriott hotels introduces world's first hotel innovation incubator—M Beta at Charlotte Marriott City Center*. Marriot International. Retrieved from https://news.marriott.com/2016/10/

marriott-hotels-introduces-worlds-first-hotel-innovation-incubator-m-beta-charlotte-marriott-city-center/.

Holland, W. H., Powell, R. B., Thomsen, J. M., & Monz, C. A. (2018). A systematic review of the psychological, social, and educational outcomes associated with participation in wildland recreational activities. *Journal of Outdoor Recreation, Education, and Leadership, 19*(3), 197–225. https://doi.org/10.18666/JOREL-2018-V10-I3-8382.

Hwang, J., & Lyu, S. O. (2015). The antecedents and consequences of well-being perception: An application of the experience economy to golf tournament tourists. *Journal of Destination Marketing & Management, 4*(4), 248–257. https://doi.org/10.1016/j.jdmm.2015.09.002.

Jiang, T., Ryan, C., & Zhang, C. (2018). The spiritual or secular tourist? The experience of Zen mediation in Chinese temples. *Tourism Management, 65,* 187–199. https://doi.org/10.1016/j.tourman.2017.10.008.

Kaida, N., & Kaida, K. (2016). Pro-environmental behavior correlates with present and future subjective well-being. *Environment, Development and Sustainability, 18*(1), 111–127.

Kerret, D., Orkibi, H., & Ronen, T. (2014). Green perspective for a hopeful future: Explaining green schools' contribution to environmental subjective well-being. *Review of General Psychology, 18*(2), 82–88. https://doi.org/10.1007/s10668-015-9629-y.

Keyes, C. L. M. (1998). Social well-being. *Social Psychology Quarterly,* 121–140. https://doi.org/10.2307/2787065.

Kohll, A. (2018, November 27). *How to create a workplace that supports mental health.* Forbes. Retrieved from https://www.forbes.com/sites/alankohll/2018/11/27/how-to-create-a-workplace-that-supports-mental-health/#371ecae8dda7.

Lemy, D. M. (2016). *The effect of green hotel practices on service quality: The Gen Z perspective* (pp. 9–13). Heritage: Culture and Society.

Levy, J. (2019). *Want to win Gen Z's respect? Show some respect for the environment.* Retrieved from https://www.genzinsights.com/to-win-gen-z-show-some-respect-for-the-environment..

Li, X., Li, X. R., & Hudson, S. (2013). The application of generational theory to tourism consumer behavior: An American perspective. *Tourism Management, 37,* 147–164. https://doi.org/10.1016/j.tourman.2013.01.015.

LifeWorks. (2017, November 1). *Marriott International with LifeWorks.* Retrieved from https://www.lifeworks.com/resource/marriott-international-lifeworks/.

McCarthy, J. (2019, June 27). *Americans still greatly overestimate U.S. gay population.* Gallup. Retrieved from https://news.gallup.com/poll/259571/americans-greatly-overestimate-gay-population.aspx.

Morgan, N., Pritchard, A., & Sedgley, D. (2015). Social tourism and well-being in later life. *Annals of Tourism Research, 52,* 1–15. https://doi.org/10.1016/j.annals.2015.02.015.

National Institute of Mental Health. (2020). *Mental illness.* Retrieved from https://www.nimh.nih.gov/health/statistics/mental-illness.shtml.

National Sleep Foundation. (2011). *2011 Sleep in America® Poll.* Retrieved from https://www.sleepfoundation.org/sites/default/files/inline-files/SIAP_2011_Summary_of_Findings.pdf.

Nemececk, D. (2018). *Cigna U.S. loneliness index.* Cigna. Retrieved from https://www.multivu.com/players/English/8294451-cigna-us-loneliness-survey/docs/IndexReport_1524069371598-173525450.pdf.

Newport, F. (2018, May 22). *In U.S., estimate of LGBT population rises to 4.5%.* Gallup. Retrieved from https://news.gallup.com/poll/234863/estimate-lgbt-population-rises.aspx?g_source=link_NEWSV9&g_medium=TOPIC&g_campaign=item_&g_content=In%2520U.S.%2c%2520Estimate%2520of%2520LGBT%2520Population%2520Rises%2520to%25204.5%2525.

Molz, J. G. (2012). Couch surfing and network hospitality: 'It's not just about the furniture' . *Hospitality & Society, 1*(3), 215–225. https://doi.org/10.1386/hosp.1.3.215_2.

Molz, J. G. (2013). Social networking technologies and the moral economy of alternative tourism: The case of couchsurfing.org. *Annals of Tourism Research, 43,* 210–230. https://doi.org/10.1016/j.annals.2013.08.001.

Naidoo, P., & Sharpley, R. (2016). Local perceptions of the relative contributions of enclave tourism and agritourism to community well-being: The case of Mauritius. *Journal of Destination Marketing & Management, 5*(1), 16–25. https://doi.org/10.1016/j.jdmm.2015.11.002.

Parker, K., Graf, N., & Igielnik, R. (2019, January 17). *Generation Z looks a lot like Millennials on key social and political issues.* Pew Research Center. Retrieved from https://www.pewsocialtrends.org/2019/01/17/generation-z-looks-a-lot-like-millennials-on-key-social-and-political-issues/.

Patel, D. (2017). *11 environmental causes Gen Z is passionate about.* Retrieved from https://www.forbes.com/sites/deeppatel/2017/10/04/11-environmental-causes-gen-z-is-passionate-about/#356099401849.

Pera, R., & Viglia, G. (2015). Turning ideas into products: Subjective well-being in co-creation. *The Service Industries Journal, 35*(7–8), 388–402. https://doi.org/10.1080/02642069.2015.1015521.

Peters, D., Calvo, R. A., & Ryan, R. M. (2018). Designing for motivation, engagement and wellbeing in digital experience. *Frontiers in Psychology, 9,* 797. https://doi.org/10.3389/fpsyg.2018.00797.

Pew Research Center. (2018). *Nearly half of post-Millennials are racial or ethnic minorities.* Retrieved from https://www.pewsocialtrends.org/2018/11/15/early-benchmarks-show-post-millennials-on-track-to-be-most-diverse-best-educated-generation-yet/psdt-11-15-18_postmillennials-00-00/.

Physical Activity Council. (2019). *2019 physical activity council's overview report on U.S. participation.* Retrieved from https://www.physicalactivitycouncil.com/pdfs/current.pdf.

Priporas, C. V., Stylos, N., & Fotiadis, A. K. (2017). Generation Z consumers' expectations of interactions in smart retailing: A future agenda. *Computers in Human Behavior, 77,* 374–381. https://doi.org/10.1016/j.chb.2017.01.058.

Reza, M. M., Subramaniam, T., & Islam, M. R. (2019). Economic and social well-being of Asian labour migrants: A literature review. *Social Indicators Research, 141*(3), 1245–1264. https://doi.org/10.1007/s11205-018-1876-5.

Robinson, M. (2017, November 1). *Generation Z is creating a $5 billion market for fake meat and seafood.* Business Insider. Retrieved from https://www.businessinsider.com/generation-z-is-eating-fake-meat-2017-10.

Rodgers, G. (2019). *What is Couchsurfing? How to use Couchsurfing for free accommodation.* Retrieved from https://www.tripsavvy.com/what-is-couchsurfing-1458737.

Siguaw, J. A., Mai, E., & Wagner, J. A. (2019). Expanding servicescape dimensions with safety: An exploratory study. *Services Marketing Quarterly, 40*(2), 123–140. https://doi.org/10.1080/15332969.2019.1592860.

Smith, M., & Diekmann, A. (2017). Tourism and wellbeing. *Annals of Tourism Research, 66,* 1–13. https://doi.org/10.1016/j.annals.2017.05.006.

TechTarget. (n.d.). *Digital wellbeing.* Retrieved from https://whatis.techtarget.com/definition/digital-wellbeing.

Ting, D. (2016). *Smart hotel brands are already thinking about Generation Z.* Retrieved from https://skift.com/2016/03/14/why-hotel-brands-are-already-thinking-about-generation-z/.

Turk, R. (2018). *New study shows that Gen Z will strengthen sustainability trend.* Retrieved from https://fashionunited.uk/news/fashion/new-study-shows-that-gen-z-will-strengthen-sustainability-trend/2018092139068.

United Nations, Department of Economic and Social Affairs. (2019). *Promoting accessible tourism for all*. Retrieved from https://www.un.org/dev elopment/desa/disabilities/issues/promoting-accessible-tourism-for-all.html.

Valtonen, A., & Veijola, S. (2011). Sleep in tourism. *Annals of Tourism Research, 38*(1), 175–192. https://doi.org/10.1016/j.annals.2010.07.016.

Vennare, J. (n.d). *Gen Z: The ultimate wellness consumer*. Retrieved from https://insider.fitt.co/gen-z-wellness/.

Vision critical. (n.d). *The everything guide to Generation Z*. Retrieved from https://cdn2.hubspot.net/hubfs/4976390/E-books/English%20e-books/The%20everything%20guide%20to%20gen%20z/the-everything-guide-to-gen-z.pdf.

Williams, K. C., & Page, R. A. (2011). Marketing to the generations. *Journal of Behavioral Studies in Business, 3*(1), 37–53.

Wellness Tourism Association. (2019). *Our glossary of industry tourism*. Retrieved from https://www.wellnesstourismassociation.org/glossary-wel lness-tourism-industry-terms/.

Whitmore, G. (2019, September 13). *How Generation Z is changing travel for older generations*. Forbes. Retrieved from https://www.forbes.com/sites/geo ffwhitmore/2019/09/13/how-generation-z-is-changing-travel-for-older-gen erations/#77f3626f78f7.

World Health Organization. (2012). *Who urges more investments, services for mental health*. Retrieved from https://www.who.int/mental_health/who_ urges_investment/en/#:~:text=Mental%20health%20is%20defined%20a s,to%20her%20or%20his%20community.

World Health Organization. (2019). *Mental health: A state of well-being*. Retrieved from https://www.who.int/features/factfiles/mental_health/en/.

Wood, S. (2013). Generation Z as consumers: Trends and innovation. *Institute for Emerging Issues: NC State University*, 1–3.

Xiao, J. J., & Li, H. (2011). Sustainable consumption and life satisfaction. *Social Indicators Research, 104*(2), 323–329. https://doi.org/10.1007/s11 205-010-9746-9.

Part II
Marketing Section

5

New Sheriff in Town? Discovering Generation Z as Tourists

Irene (Eirini) Kamenidou, Aikaterini Vassilikopoulou, and Constantinos-Vasilios Priporas

Introduction

The generation theory is based on the assumption that individuals born in the same time period have certain common characteristics, beliefs, attitudes and values (Inglehart 1977; Toth-Kaszas 2018). The generation cohort is a group of individuals that are in the same age and life stage

---

I. (Eirini) Kamenidou
Department of Management Science and Technology, School of Business and Economics, International Hellenic University, Kavala, Greece

A. Vassilikopoulou
Department of Business Administration, University of West Attica, Athens, Greece

C.-V. Priporas (✉)
Department of Marketing Branding and Tourism, Business School, Middlesex University, London, UK
e-mail: c.priporas@mdx.ac.uk

© The Author(s), under exclusive license to Springer Nature Switzerland AG 2021
N. Stylos et al. (eds.), *Generation Z Marketing and Management in Tourism and Hospitality*,
https://doi.org/10.1007/978-3-030-70695-1_5

(McCrindle and Wolfinger 2009). Mannheim's (1952 [1927/1928]) theory suggests that generation cohorts share the same experiences worthy of mention (Laufer and Bengtson 1974) that contribute to the formation of similar behaviour and value creation (Kupperschmidt 2000).

However, it is quite difficult to define the age limits for each generational cohort. As Styvén and Foster (2018) conclude, there are no overall accepted age boundaries for each generation. Academics often disagree on the age limits and given names of each generation, particularly after Baby Boomers (McCrindle and Wolfinger 2009).

During the past decades, the tourism market has understood the need to implement differentiated strategies by targeting particular groups of tourists rather than regard the entire market as homogenous (Pennington-Gray et al. 2003). The theory of generation cohorts has been widely applied to the tourism industry. There are several studies which have shown differences, e.g. in selecting destination or vacation activities preferred among certain generation cohorts (e.g. Lehto et al. 2008; Opperman 1995; Pennington-Grey et al. 2003). Pennington-Grey et al. (2003), for example, add that as tourists get older there are less interested in national parks, while they mostly prefer first-class accommodation compared to younger generations. On the other hand, shopping is highly rated as a tourism activity by younger generations. Thus, it may be concluded that destination preferences, activities and tourism behaviour in general, may differ across age groups. For this reason, it is quite important for tourism professionals to examine the unique traits of each generation cohort they wish to target so as to design and implement more efficient strategies.

Based on existing marketing and tourism literature, this chapter highlights and discusses the generation Z cohort as an emerging market in the tourism system (Robinson and Schänzel 2019). Gen Zers are of extreme importance to the tourism industry (Robinson and Schänzel 2019), considering they have the propensity to travel (Wee 2019) and will become the most active consumers in tourism (Monaco 2018). Furthermore, there is a dearth of studies on Generation Z as tourists (Dimitriou and AbouElgheit 2019; Slivar et al. 2019). Although there is a great stream of research on Generation Y, studies on Generation Z are limited (Southgate 2017). As Cavagnaro et al. (2018) add, this is quite surprising since approximately one in four tourists in 2015 were aged between 16 and 29. Against this background the aim of this work is to present an overview on this new tourism market and its unique characteristics which makes this work pertinent and well-timed and contributes to the ongoing literature of Generation Z cohort in the tourism context.

The chapter will begin with a discussion on Generation Z characteristics by reviewing the recent literature. It will then examine this generational cohort both as independent and family tourists based on a comprehensive literature review. The chapter will conclude by suggesting ways for tourism practitioners to accommodate Generation Z tourism needs. It should be noted that the chapter offers a fresh perspective as well as challenges for academics, practitioners and policymakers, since this generation will impact the tourism industry socially and economically.

Generation Z

Generation Z follows Generation Y. Generation Z is a larger group than the Millennials, but they do share common characteristics (Rodriguez et al. 2019). According to Dawson (2018), Gen Zers represent 27% of the American population. Generation Z incorporates individuals born from 1995 to the late 2000s (Bassiouni and Hackley 2014; Kamenidou et al. 2019a, b; Priporas et al. 2017, 2019) or between 1995 and 2010 (Tanaid and Wraight 2019). Nevertheless, there are other scholars who claim that Generation Z has different age boundaries. For example, Dimock (2018) believes that Generation Z is anyone born between 1994 and 2000 (Dimock 2018). According to Toth-Kaszas (2018) members of Generation Z were born in 1995–2005. Monaco (2018) argues that this age cohort includes people born in the 1996–2010 period. Nagy (2017) states that Generation Z consists of children of the digital age, born between 1995 and 2012, while Kapusy and Lógó (2017) agree that Gen Z includes individuals born from 1995 to early 2010s. The main difference between Gen Y and Gen Z is that Gen Z was born in a diverse environment, needs immediate access to the Internet and social media, smartphones are perceived as a status symbol and believes that online connection is an essential tool which promote competitiveness (Nagy 2017).

This digital generation is realistic and persistent (Kapusy and Lógó 2017). They are familiar with web search engines and use online sources to gain knowledge as they truly believe in the accuracy of online information (Kapusy and Lógó 2017). Furthermore, they are internet content creators, are interested in multimedia and visual materials, can perform multiple tasks and have the ability to openly express their emotions (Berk 2009; Çetin and Halisdemir 2019). Gen Z has grown up, in general, with fewer siblings than previous generations. The reduction in family size has resulted in greater attention to the children and more pocket money as well as increased levels of individualism and egocentrism (Çetin and Halisdemir 2019). However, according to Seemiller and Grace (2015), Generation Z is concerned with education and equality and is willing to help others. Although this generation has never faced severe financial crisis, they are money conscious, placing emphasis on value (Dawson 2018). They do not care much about prices compared to other generations and are less likely to be loyal to retailers and brands (Kapusy and Lógó 2017). Seeking uniqueness is one of their priorities, which is mainly expressed through their brand patronage (Kapusy and Lógó 2017). Moreover, they are more likely to stay with their parents longer than other generation cohorts (Dawson 2018), are traditional, responsible (Williams and Page 2011) and seek pleasure and memorable experiences (Törőcsik et al. 2014).

Although some Zers are still too young to make independent buying decisions, it must be noted that teenagers nowadays do have spending power. Organics and non-GMOs are important for Zers with buying power (Dawson 2018). They also look for products that match their personal brand, which is connected to their dominant presence in social networks, e.g. Facebook, MySpace, Twitter, Flickr, Skype, etc. (Çetin and Halisdemir 2019). e-WOM is an important source of information for Generation Z (Dawson 2018). Singh (2014) adds that Gen Zers are unconventional; they would go abroad to study and like to work without a strict schedule.

Their dominant trait is their digital footprint; they are familiar with new technologies since early childhood (Combi 2015). Scholz and

Vyugina (2019) assert that Gen Zers are self-actualised based on Maslow's hierarchy of needs since they want "to know, to be able, to understand, to explore" (p. 278).

Generation Z as Independent Tourists

This age cohort, which includes individuals born in the 1996–2010 period, along with Generation Y constitute the "travellers of the future" (Monaco 2018) or "future of tourism" (Cavagnaro and Staffieri 2015). The tourism industry recognises the importance of young travellers and tourism operators try to target directly or indirectly this younger age cohort (Carr 2011). As Preko et al. (2019, p. 6) point out, youth is one of the "most important target markets that will feed global tourism". Moisă (2010) adds that focusing on youth travel could contribute to the development of the whole tourism industry. Preko et al. (2019) conclude that young people should be the target group of tourism products and services as they are the ones who will become active decision-makers, and transfer tourism values to their families and peers. Furthermore, young tourists are energetic and highly exposed to media and, as a result, are easy to be targeted (Linh 2015).

Gen Zers may travel for different reasons. According to some scholars (e.g. Demeter and Bratucu 2014; Moisă 2010) there are six main types of youth tourism (youth defined as 15–25-years old), namely: Educational tourism (youngsters are involved in a learning experience), volunteering (combine holidays with working for a worthy cause), work and travel (young individuals are hired by a foreign company abroad and young workers have the opportunity to blend in with locals, learn a foreign language, etc.), cultural exchange (exchange of young individuals among different countries), sports and adventure tourism (participate in a sports event while travelling) and leisure tourism (travel mainly for entertainment purposes). Eusébio and Carneiro (2015) segmented the student travel market and extracted the following groups: (a) culture lovers, (b) fun lovers (this is the larger cluster), (c) sun and beach lovers and (d) nature lovers. There are notable differences among these groups regarding their motivations and interactions. For example, nature lovers are mostly motivated by escape activities and prefer to be in a tranquil environment or be closely connected to nature. On the other hand, culture lovers like to gain new knowledge and focus on novelty. As Linh (2015) notes, their trip duration is usually short (i.e. less than five days for first-year students). Some authors believe that Gen Z tourists are active during their vacations and try various activities (Xu et al. 2009), such as sunbathing, sightseeing (Frändberg 2010) and shopping (Xu et al. 2009). Shopping is also mentioned by Lin and Huang (2018) as being an important motive for young tourists from China.

For Zers, there are various motivations to travel. Their tourism patterns may be connected to hedonic behaviour, i.e. travelling embraces socialisation and empowerment. These traits are often translated into searching for promotion and low-cost opportunities as well as last-minute travel decisions. WOM (i.e. being influenced by reviews) is also important (Haddouche and Salomone 2018). A tourism experience allows the young generation to escape from the everyday routine, while getting unique experience is also a perceived synonym of travelling. The financial constraints that some Zers face may have an impact on the destination selection. Travelling abroad, for example, could be unaffordable for certain groups or cultures. However, they almost all often participate in recreational or school trips. Travelling is related to relaxing, taking a break and having fun (Haddouche and Salomone 2018). Moreover, they have an interest in discovering culture (e.g. cultural events, festivals, monuments, sites, blending in with locals). Cavagnaro and Staffieri (2015) agree that relaxation and escape from everyday routine are key components that describe travelling as perceived by students. They add that socialisation, growth and development and sustainability are also important. Eusébio and Carneiro (2015) revealed that students' most important travel motivations are being in a different environment, learning new things and exposure to different activities. Setiawan et al. (2018) add that young tourists are highly interested in discovering new destinations.

Since Zers widely use social media as part of their identity, they also spread e-WOM and generally share details on their trip. The need to share travel experiences mainly stems from self-centred motivations (Munar and Jacobsen 2014). Skinner et al. (2018) argue that Generation

Z seeks adventure and focuses on experiential destinations. Zers should be surprised so they can share their differentiated experience with their friends (e.g. through social media). Young travellers want to be innovative and become the first ones to try something (n.a. 2018a). Finally, King and Gardiner (2015) found that education is also a key motivation for travelling. Thus, students decide to move to another country to study. Some organisations facilitate youth mobility within the European Union (Moisă 2010).

Hajiyeva (2018), who examined youth tourism in Azerbaijan and collected questionnaires from 16–25-year-old travellers, found that the main reasons for travelling are entertainment and relaxation, while approximately 63% of the respondents prefer to travel abroad. The results of the study also revealed that more than half of the participants travel with their families, 38.9% with friends and just 14.1% travel alone.

Linh (2015), used undergraduate students in Vietnam as a sample to investigate, among others, young tourists' motivations. The author concludes that entertainment is the key factor for travelling, while gaining new experiences and an escape from daily life are also important. Young travellers also state that they are mostly informed about tourism from friends and relatives and the Internet. In addition, they are mostly influenced by the safety level and the climate when choosing a tourist destination. They select a tourism package mostly based on the prestige of the operator and the accommodation (Linh 2015). Members of Generation Z prefer staying in a hotel (Dimitriou and AbouElgheit 2019) and they do not pay attention to the hotel brand (local or international) as long as they find value in it for them (Wiastuti et al. 2020). Also, the findings by Stavrianea et al. (2020) confirm the appreciation of Gen Zers of the value they receive for the money spent. However, different Gen Z demographic characteristics lead to different hotel attribute preferences and satisfaction level (Stavrianea et al. 2020; Wiastuti et al. 2020).

A research conducted by "Cox and Kings", a well-known Indian travel agent, found that approximately 72% of Indian young travellers would prefer to explore Europe by bike, bus or train. They would also use the Internet to select a place to eat, primarily looking for local food (n.a.,

2018b). Their study also concludes that it is important for 89% of the sample to choose a hotel that respects the physical environment (e.g. solar power usage, waste facilities, etc.).

A report held by the World Youth Student and Educational Travel Confederation in the Netherlands states that international young travellers' trips are sponsored by their families. As a result, they have the time to travel longer and spend more, compared to other tourists, while 60% of their budget is spent at the destination (Hughes 2015). Hajiyeva (2018), who used young people from Azerbaijan as a sample, found that approximately 24% of the respondents would be willing to spend $1,501–$2,000 for an international trip, and 19% from $1001 to $1500. Furthermore, it is worth mentioning that more than half of young travellers return to destinations that they had visited when they were younger (Hughes 2015). Richards (2011) concludes that young travellers spend $2,600 on an average, which is far above the spending of the average tourist.

Styvén and Foster (2018) found that it is very important for Zers that the selected destinations reflect their discernment and uniqueness. They aim at creating a favourable impression to others through the selection of a tourist destination. The highly perceived importance of their social image also makes them place emphasis on influencing other individuals' tourism-related selections. Moreover, the more they perceive their chosen destination as unique, the more they share their travel experience with their peers in social media. According to Hughes (2015), teenagers appreciate beach areas as well as relevant programmes offered by hotels. For example, the Resort at Pelican Hill offers among other things mobile phone scavenger hunts, movie nights and beach sports (Hughes 2015).

It is important, however, to note that the independent travelling of Zers may be influenced by culture. As Preko et al. (2019) argue, in Africa, independent youth travel is rare or even unwelcome as African culture promotes communality rather than individuality. Moreover, parents in Africa would not let their children travel alone (e.g. due to safety reasons), and finally, financial constraints are a key obstacle against independent youth tourism. Finally, Chinese (i.e. collectivistic culture-loneliness avoidance), young backpackers prefer to travel (particularly in Europe) in small groups, while they do not hesitate to search for travel companion online (Cai 2018). While Western young travellers are driven by inner needs (e.g. psychological fulfilment) to travel, Chinese youth is motivated by the need to feel temporarily free from societal restrictions (Huang 2008).

Haddouche and Salomone (2018) found that Generation Zers do not often make independent decisions but are mostly guided by their family's desires when travelling with adults. On the other hand, getting involved in the preparation experience is conspicuous only when Zers travel alone or with friends. Regarding their decision-making processes, Gen Zers are more guided by influencers on social media and travel site reviews (Dimitriou and AbouElgheit 2019).

Niemczyk et al. (2019) provide a synopsis of the Zers profile as tourists with the following characteristics: (1) they were born in an era of technological advancement (internet, smartphones) thus, many times there is not a clear boundary between real life and the virtual world. Accordingly, tourism can be an opportunity that allows them to break away from the online reality and open to new experiences and social values which are only present in real life; (2) as the geographical barriers are disappearing mainly with the use of internet, generation Z is one of the most open generations in terms of tourist travel. Zers travel an average of 29 days per year; (3) they usually know foreign languages and are at ease in a multicultural environment, making it easy to establish global relations. These, in turn, lead to trips aimed at visiting friends; (4) their motto is YOLO (You Only Live Once), so they like to travel and are not put off by the thought of leaving home; (5) Zers are not afraid of distance and hence when they have the opportunity, many of them decide to pursue a journey abroad in order to learn about the world. Furthermore, Setiawan et al. (2018) based on their findings categorised Generation Z members as explorers according to Cohen's (1972) typologies since they plan their own trips, use facilities of an adequate standard, and have a high level of interaction with locals.

In conclusion, Slivar et al. (2019) point out that their characteristics influence their travel habits, making their tourist behaviour distinct. The shift towards placing the value on experiences, rather than material things is noticeable.

Generation Z as Family Tourists

Studies in the past mostly focus on parents in family decision-making as these are the ones who actually make the final decision (Blichfeldt et al. 2010). However, children nowadays have much more power than they used to have as they are more active members of their families. On top of that, parents are more likely to listen to their children's needs and wants (Carr 2011). The level of influence that teenagers have on their parents is increasing with age. Teenagers have a more dominant role in the family holiday decision-making process (Shavanddasht and Schanzel 2019). Shavanddasht and Schanzel (2019) found that children of authoritative parents express higher levels of satisfaction during holidays compared to children with authoritarian parents. Authoritative parental style permits children to be more independent.

Generation Z has become an attractive tourist market because of their growing consumption. However, some tourism professionals show interest in Zers as they increasingly influence their parents (Gaumer and Arnone 2010). Gen Z plays a key role in the family decision-making process. In particular, Ting (2016) points out that Gen Zers become influential in family travel decisions. In the same vein, Dimitriou and AbouElgheit (2019) highlight that Cen Zers play an important role in the decision-making process of their parents when booking a holiday. Pickard (2017) argues that 93% of parents claim that their purchases are influenced by their children. Young individuals, for example, may choose where the next destination for their families could be (n.a. 2018a). Parents are willing to spend more time with their children and wish to have a family vacation, particularly when children grow into adolescence. As a result, children are actually given more decision power, to ensure that the entire family will have quality time together during holidays (Carr 2011). However, Wiastuti et al. (2020) suggest that Gen Zers travel mainly with their parents because they are still living with them, although spending time with family was not the main purpose for travelling.

Conclusions

To understand the future, we have to decipher young people and their needs, wants and desires since it is up to them to shape the future. The future growth of tourism depends to a certain degree on how well the industry senses the social and demographic trends influencing traveller behaviour (Moscardo et al. 2010). As Moisă (2010) notes, designing a tourism product targeting young tourists is not easy, as their needs are unique, they have different interests (Carr 1998), and overall present several differences compared to other groups of tourists.

Generation Z form an increasing group of future travellers with unique qualities. It's essential for tourism professionals to have a deep understanding of their attitudes and behaviour so as to design effective tourism management strategies (Styvén and Foster 2018). According to certain authors, Generation Z is the most socially empowered cohort in history (Desai and Lele 2017). Young travellers present unique consumer preferences and different ideas and behaviours (Puiu 2016). Thus, according to Chen et al. (2018), the analysis of the Generation Z traits is crucial.

Generation Z seeks something unique; they wish to live a memorable experience while travelling and share their most highlighted moments with their peers on social media. As Hajiyeva (2018) proposes, personnel in hotels or other tourist destinations should be trained to serve young tourists. Moreover, hotels could create youth clubs, sports events and tourist agents should promote the recreational potential of each destination. The importance of sports and other physical activities in the youth market has contributed to the fast growth of the sports and adventures tourism industry (Schlegelmilch and Ollenburg 2013). Adventure tourism also includes the increase of fun as well as other more extreme emotions such as fear, danger and adrenaline rush (Khoo-Lattimore and Yang 2018).

Cultural and sports events could be "unusual" to inspire Gen Zers who will feel the urge to post photos and videos in their social networking while travelling alone, with friends or parents. Travel agencies should promote their products and services innovatively and make them look appealing (Ray and Wakelin-Theron 2018). Targeting the entire family for younger Zers would be an excellent tourism market opportunity. As modern families love to have holidays together, keeping the children happy through special activities and services designed particularly for young tourists or the whole family is important. Families, nowadays, face numerous challenges and their quick rhythm of living does not give them the spare time needed to make a thorough search for hotels, restaurants, museums, etc. Thus, travel agents could offer holiday packages that would fulfil all families' needs and personal preferences. Certain hotels have already approached young family members as a profitable target market, providing special kids menu, entertainment for children, etc. For example, Amathus Hotel in Cyprus offers slippers and bathrobes for children, while its entertainment activities include, among others, bubble and magic shows, jugglers and clowns, disco parties as well as a great variety of sports activities (e.g. table tennis, water ski, scuba diving, canoeing, etc. (www.amathuslimassol.com). Leading family hotels and resorts (www.leadingfamilyhotels.com/) have water slides, children's spa, private swimming lesson, while their kids club operates up to twelve hours per day.

Gen Zers also want to relax and escape from everyday routine (Cavagnaro and Staffieri 2015). Hotels targeting independent Gen Z tourists should ensure that their guests have the opportunity to feel comfortable, safe and to forget their everyday problems. This could be achieved with discreet presence of personnel, opportunity to select room areas, pools and cafes where no young children or large groups are allowed, have chilled music in most hotel's public areas, and an all-inclusive choice (so as not to worry about money and several payments).

For young travellers interested in culture, tourism professionals could organise trips that incorporate cultural activities (Eusébio and Carneiro 2015) and provide the opportunity to blend in with locals.

Minciu and Moisă (2009) argue that young tourists are highly informed about visited places, which is especially true for Gen Zers (Dimitriou and AbouElgheit 2019; Lin and Huang (2018). As friends and the Internet seem to be the key sources of information (Dimitriou and AbouElgheit 2019; Linh 2015), tourism practitioners could primarily invest in web advertisement and e-WOM control (e.g. respond to negative reviews, promote positive ones, etc.). Furthermore, as Gen Zers are primarily concerned about safety (Teitler-Regev et al. 2015) and environment (Linh 2015), these two characteristics of the destination should be properly promoted and emphasised if exceeding the desirable standards. Safety should also be a primary concern in all leisure areas, as according to Biber et al. (2013) Gen Zers may be reluctant to perform some sports activities due to their fear of getting injured.

Educational tourism is quite popular and still increases (Demeter and Bratucu 2014). Tourism professionals could further invest in this form of youth tourism and develop tourism products and services related to education (e.g. short-term education programmes locally or abroad for younger and older students, low-cost hostels or BB services for foreign students, etc.).

Although some aspects of the future are unpredictable and we have started to become acquainted with Generation Z, it seems that this generation will be the new sheriff (tourists) in town (tourist market) as is evident from the current analysis. Generation Z challenges us to move our thinking forward despite the fact each generation makes its own stride and leaves its footprint in tourism and other industries, since there are notable differences between generations. Therefore, it is worthy and expected to be the epicentre of future inquiries, which is a necessity and marketing challenge considering that greater knowledge is needed on how this generation will position itself not only as tourists, but also as consumers and citizens in a continuously changing world.

References

Bassiouni, Dina, and Chris Hackley. 2014. "Generation Z' Children's Adaptation to Digital Consumer Culture: A Critical Literature Review." *Journal of Customer Behaviour* 13(2): 113–133.

Berk, Ronald Alan. 2009. "Teaching Strategies for the Net Generation." *Transformative Dialogues: Teaching & Learning Journal* 3: 1–24.

Biber, David D., Daniel R. Czech, Brandonn S. Harris, and Bridget F. Melton. 2013. "Attraction to Physical Activity of Generation Z: A Mixed Methodological Approach." *Open Journal of Preventive Medicine* 3: 310–319.

Blichfeldt, Bodil Stilling, Bettina Pederson, Anders Johansen and Line Hansen. 2010. "Tween Tourists: Children and Decision-Making." *Journal of Tourism Consumption and Practice* 2(1): 1–24.

Cai, Wenjie. 2018. "Donkey Friends in Europe: A Mobile Ethnographic Study in Group Orientation of Chinese Outbound Backpackers." In *Asian Youth Travellers. Insights and Implications*, edited by Catheryn Khoo-Lattimore, Elaine Chiao, Ling Yang, 79–96. Singapore: Springer.

Carr, Neil. 1998. "The Young Tourist: A Case of Neglected Research." *Progress in Tourism and Hospitality Research* 4(4): 307–318.

Carr, Neil. 2011. *Children's and Families' Holiday Experiences*. London, UK: Routledge.

Cavagnaro, Elena, and Simona Staffieri. 2015. "A Study of Students' Travellers Values and Needs in Order to Establish Futures Patterns and Insights." *Journal of Tourism Futures* 1(2): 94–107.

Cavagnaro, Elena, Simona Staffieri, and Albert Postma. 2018. "Understanding Millennials' Tourism Experience: Values and Meaning to Travel as a Key for Identifying Target Clusters for Youth (Sustainable) Tourism." *Journal of Tourism Futures* 4(1): 31–42.

Çetin, Münevver, and Meral Halisdemir. 2019. "School Administrators and Generation Z Students' Perspectives for a Better Educational Setting." *Journal of Education and Training Studies* 7(2): 84–97.

Chen, Mei-Hua, Bryan H. Chen, and Christina Geng-qing Chi. 2018. "Socially Responsible Investment by Generation Z: A Cross-Cultural Study of Taiwanese and American Investors." *Journal of Hospitality Marketing & Management* 28(3): 334–350.

Cohen, Erik. 1972. "Towards a Sociology of International Tourism." *Social Research* 39(1): 164–182.

Combi, Chloe. 2015. *Generation Z: Their Voices, Their Lives*. London: Windmill Books.

Dawson, Gloria. 2018. "Don't Ignore Generation Z." *Restaurant Hospitality*, January 25. https://restaurant-hospitality.com. Accessed on 5 July 2019.

Demeter, Timea, and Gabriel Bratucu. 2014. "Typologies of Youth Tourism." *Bulletin of the Transilvania University of Braşov*. Series V: Economic Sciences 7(56): 115–122.

Dimitriou, Christina K., and Emad AbouElgheit. 2019. "Understanding generation Z's travel social decision-making." *Tourism and Hospitality Management* 25(2): 311–334.

Desai, Supriya Pavan, and Vishwanath Lele. 2017. "Correlating Internet, Social Networks and Workplace—A Case of Generation Z Students." *Journal of Commerce & Management Thought* 8(4): 802–815.

Dimock, Michael. 2018. "Where Millennials end and Post-Millennials begin." Pew Research Center. https://www.pewresearch.org/fact-tank/2018/03/01/defining-generations-where-millennials-end-and-post-millennials-begin/. Accessed on 3 August 2019.

Eusébio, Celeste, and Maria João Carneiro. 2015. "How Diverse is the Youth Tourism Market? An Activity-Based Segmentation Study." *Tourism* 63(3): 295–316.

Frändberg, Lotta. 2010. "Activities and Activity Patterns Involving Travel Abroad While Growing Up: The Case of Young Swedes." *Tourism Geographies* 12(1): 100–117.

Gaumer, Carol J., and Carol Arnone. 2010. "Grocery Store Observation: Parent-Child Interaction in Family Purchases." *Journal of Food Production Marketing* 16(1): 1–18.

Hajiyeva, Leyla. 2018. "The Study of Consumer Preferences of young Tourists." *ЕКОНОМИКА* 63(3): 37–46.

Kapusy, Kata, and Emma Lógó. 2017. "Values Derived from Virtual Reality Shopping Experience Among Generation Z." 8th IEEE International Conference on Cognitive Infocommunications.

Haddouche, Hamed, and Christine Salomone. 2018. "Generation Z and the Tourist Experience: Tourist Stories and Use of Social Networks." *Journal of Tourism Futures* 4(1): 69–79.

Huang, Feng Yi. 2008. "Western and Asian Backpackers in Taiwan: Behaviour, Motivation and Cultural Diversity." In *Asian Tourism: Growth and Change*, edited by Janet Cochrane, 171–182. Oxford: Elsevier.

Hughes, Paul. 2015. "Next Big Tourism Thing: Millennial' Little Siblings?" *Orange County Business Journal*. May: 26–28.

Inglehart, Ronald. 1977. *The Silent Revolution: Changing Values and Political Styles among Western Publics*. Princeton, NJ: Princeton University Press.

Kamenidou, Irene C., Spyridon A. Mamalis, Stavros Pavlidis, and Evangelia-Zoi G. Bara. 2019a. "Segmenting the Generation Z Cohort University Students Based on Sustainable Food Consumption Behavior: A Preliminary Study." *Sustainability* 11(3): 837.

Kamenidou, Irene, Spyridon A. Mamalis, Stavros Pavlidis, and Evangelia-Zoi G. Bara. 2019b. "Developing Attracting Destinations for Generation Z Based on Desired Destination Components." Proceedings of the 12th Annual Conference of the EuroMed Academy of Business, Thessaloniki, 2019, 457–467. EuroMed Press.

King, Brian, and Sarah Gardiner. 2015. "Chinese International Students. An Avant-Garde of Independent Travellers?" *International Journal of Tourism Research* 17(2): 130–139.

Kupperschmidt, Betty R. 2000. "Multigeneration Employees: Strategies for Effective Management." *The Health Care Manager* 19(1): 65–76.

Laufer, Robert S., and Vern L. Bengtson. 1974. "Generations, Aging, and Social Stratification: On the Development of Generational Units." *Journal of Social Issues* 30(3): 181–205.

Khoo-Lattimore, Catheryn, and Elaine Chiao Ling Yang. 2018. "Asian Youth Tourism: Contemporary Trends, Cases and Issues." In *Asian Youth Travellers. Insights and Implications*, edited by Catheryn Khoo-Lattimor Elaine Chiao Ling Yang, 1–14. Singapore: Springer.

Lehto, Xinran Y., SooCheong (Shawn) Jang, Francis T. Achana, and Joseph T. O'Leary. 2008. "Exploring Tourism Experience Sought: A Cohort Comparison of Baby Boomers and the Silent Generation." *Journal of Vacation Marketing* 14(3): 237–252.

Lin, Li-Pi, and Shu-Chun Huang. 2018. "Modeling Chinese Post-90's Tourism Loyalty to the Ex-Rival State Using the Perceived Value Approach." *Tourism and Hospitality Management* 24(1): 23–40.

Linh, Nguyen Thi Khanh. 2015. "Student and Youth Tourism: A Case Study from Vietnam." *The Journal of Developing Areas* 49(5): 293–307.

Mannheim, Karl. 1952 [1927/1928]. "The Problem of Generations." In *Karl Mannheim: Essays*, edited by Paul Kecskemeti, 276–322. New York: Routledge.

McCrindle, Mark, and Emily Wolfinger. 2009. *The ABC of XYZ: Understanding the Global Generations*. Sydney: UNSW Press.

Minciu, Rodica, and Claudia Olimpia Moisă. 2009. "Fundamental Aspects Regarding Youth and Their Decision to Practice Tourism." *Annales Universitatis Apulensis Series Oeconomica* 11(2): 1009–1018.

Moisă, Claudia Olimpia. 2010. "Aspects of Youth Travel Demand." *Annales Universtatis Aplensis Series Oeconomica* 12(2): 575–582.

Monaco, Salvatore. 2018. "Tourism and the New Generations: Emerging Trends and Social Implications in Italy." *Journal of Tourism Futures* 4(1): 7–15.

Moscardo, Gianna, Laurie Murphy, and Pierre Beckendorff. 2010., "Generation Y and Travel Futures." In *Tourism and Demography*, edited by Ian Yeoman, Cathy H.C. Hsu, Karen Smith, and Sandra Watson, 87–100. Oxford: Goodfellow Publishers.

Munar, Ana María, and Jens Kr. Steen Jacobsen. 2014. "Motivations for Sharing Tourism Experiences through Social Media." *Tourism Management* 43: 46–54.

n.a. 2018a. "Tourism for Millennials and Generation Z: Bets and Challenge." ForeignAffairs.co.nz. September 27. https://foreignaffairs.co.nz/ Accessed on 3 July 2019.

n.a. 2018b. "74% of Indian Youth Avoids Destinations Reeling Under Mass Tourism: Cox & Kings Study." Travel Biz Monitor. June. https://www.travelbizmonitor.com/. Accessed on 14 July 2019.

Nagy, Szabolcs. 2017. "The Impact of Country of Origin in Mobile Phone Choice of Generation Y and Z." *Journal of Management and Training for Industries* 4(2): 16–29.

Niemczyk, Agata, Renata Seweryn, and Agnieszka Smalec. 2019. "Z Generation in the International Tourism Market." In Proceedings of the 38th International Scientific Conference on Economic and Social Development, Rabat, Morocco, 21–22 March 2019, 123–132.

Opperman, Martin. 1995. "Family Life Cycle and Cohort Effects: A Study of Travel Patterns of German Residents." *Journal of Travel & Tourism Marketing* 4(1): 23–45.

Pennington-Gray, Lori, Joseph D. Fridgen, and Daniel Stynes. 2003. "Cohort Segmentation: An Application to Tourism." *Leisure Sciences* 25(4): 341–361.

Pickard, Katherine. 2017. "Generation Z and Its 3 Most Important Consumer Behaviors." https://www.precisiondialogue.com/generation-z-consumer-behaviors/. Accessed on 4 July 2019.

Preko, Alexander, Frederick Doe, and Samuel Ato Dadzie. 2019. "The Future of Youth Tourism in Ghana: Motives, Satisfaction and Behavioural Intentions." *Journal of Tourism Futures* 5(1): 5–21.

Priporas, Constantinos-Vasilios, Nikolaos Stylos, and Irene (Eirini) Kamenidou. 2019. "City Image, City Brand Personality and Generation Z Residents' Life Satisfaction Under Economic Crisis: Predictors of City-Related Social Media Engagement." *Journal of Business Research*, May. https://doi.org/10.1016/j.jbusres.

Priporas, Constantinos-Vasilios, Nikolaos Stylos, and Anestis K. Fotiadis. "Generation Z Consumers' Expectations of Interactions in Smart Retailing: A Future Agenda." *Computers in Human Behavior* 77: 374–381.

Puiu, Silvia. 2016. "Generation Z—A New Type of Consumers." *Young Economists Journal* 13(27): 67–78.

Ray, Genevieve, and Nicola Wakelin-Theron. 2018. "Understanding a Tourism Culture Amongst Students to Advance Domestic Tourism in South Africa." *African Journal of Hospitality, Tourism and Leisure* 7(4): 1–13.

Richards, G. 2011. "An Economic Contribution that Matters." In *The Power of Youth Travel*, edited by Fitzgerald, Deborah, Peter Jordan, and Laura Egido. Madrid : United Nation World Tourism Organization and World Youth Student & Educational Travel Confederation (UNWTO and WYSE Travel Confederation).

Robinson, Victor Mueke, and Heike A. Schänzel. 2019. "A Tourism Inflex: Generation Z Travel Experiences." *Journal of Tourism Futures* 5(2): 127–141.

Rodriguez, Michael, Stefanie Boyer, David Fleming, and Scott Cohen. 2019. "Managing the Next Generation of Sales, Gen Z/Millennial Cusp: An Exploration of Grit, Entrepreneurship, and Loyalty." *Journal of Business-to-Business Marketing* 26(1): 43–55.

Schlegelmilch, Fabian, and Claudia Ollenburg. 2013. "Marketing the Adventure: Utilizing the Aspects of Risk/Fear/Thrill to Target the Youth Traveller Segment." *Tourism Review* 68(3): 44–54.

Seemiller, Corey, and Meghan Grace. 2015. *Generation Z Goes to College*. San Francisco, CA: Jossey-Bass.

Shavanddasht, Mercede, and Heike Schanzel. 2019. "Measuring Adolescents' Tourism Satisfaction: The Role of Mood and Perceived Parental Style." *Tourism and Hospitality Research* 19(3): 308–320.

Scholz, Tobias M., and Daria Vyugina. 2019. "Looking into the Future: What We Are Expecting from Generation Z." In *Generations Z in Europe. The Changing Context of Managing People*, edited by Christian Scholz and Anne Rennig, 277–284. Emerald Publishing Limited.

Setiawan, Budi, Ni Luh Putu Trisdyani, Putu Pramania Adnyana, I. Nyoman Adnyana, Kadek Wiweka, and Hesti Retno Wulandani. 2018. "The Profile and Behaviour of 'Digital Tourists' when Making Decisions Concerning Travelling Case Study: Generation Z in South Jakarta." *Advances in Research* 17(2): 1–13.

Singh, Anjali. 2014. "Challenges of Issues of Generation Z." *IOSR Journal of Business and Management* 16(7): 59–63.

Skinner, Heather, David Sarpong, and Gareth R.T. White. 2018. "Meeting the Needs of the Millennials and Generation Z: Gamification in Tourism Through Geocaching." *Journal of Tourism Futures* 4(1): 93–104.

Slivar, Iva, Dražen Aleric, and Sanja Dolenec. 2019. "Leisure Travel Behavior of Generation Y & Z at the Destination and Post-Purchase." *E-Journal of Tourism* 6(2): 147–159.

Southgate, Duncan. 2017. "The Emergence of Generation Z and its Impact in Advertising: Long-Term Implications for Media Planning and Creative Development." *Journal of Advertising Research* 57(2): 227–235.

Stavrianea, Aikaterini, Irene Kamenidou, and Evangelia Zoi Bara. 2020. "Gender Differences in Satisfaction from Hotel Room Attributes and Characteristics: Insights from Generation Z." In *Strategic Innovative Marketing and Tourism*, edited by Androniki Kavoura, Efstathios Kefallonitis, and Prokopios Theodoridis, 139–147. Cham: Springer.

Styvén, Maria, and Tim Foster. 2018. "Who Am I if You Can't See Me? The "Self" of Young Travellers as Driver of eWOM in Social Media." *Journal of Tourism Futures* 4(1): 80–92.

Tanaid, Kayla L., and Kevin L. Wright. 2019. "The Intersection between Chickering's Theory and Generation Z Student of Color Activism." *Vermont Connection* 40(1): 105–114.

Teitler-Regev, Sharon, Helena Desivilya-Syna, and Shosh Shahrabani. 2015. "Decision-Making Patterns of Young Tourists Regarding Risky Destinations." *African Journal of Hospitality, Tourism and Leisure* 4(1): 1–15.

Ting, D. 2016. Smart Hotel Brands Are Already Thinking About Generation Z. [Online] Available at: https://skift.com/2016/03/14/why-hotel-brands-are-already-thinking-aboutgeneration-z/

Törőcsik, Mária, Krisztián Szűcs, and Dániel Kehl. 2014. "How Generations Think: Research on Generation Z." *ACTA Universitatis Sapientiae, Communicatio* 1(1): 23–45.

Toth-Kaszas, Nikoletta. 2018. "Is a Mid-Sized Town Enough for the Generation Z? What Is Needed to Keep the Young People in Their (Home) Town?" *Management* 13(1): 33–48.

Wee, Desmond. 2019. "Generation Z Talking: Transformative Experience in Educational Travel." *Journal of Tourism Futures* 5(2): 157–167.

Wiastuti, R. D., N S. Lestari, Bejo Mulyadi Ngatemin, and Anwari Masatip. 2020. "The Generation Z Characteristics and Hotel Choices." *African Journal of Hospitality, Tourism and Leisure* 9(1): 1–14.

Williams, Kaylene C., and Robert A. Page. 2011. "Marketing to the Generations." *Journal of Behavioral Studies in Business* 3(1): 1–17.

www.amathuslimassol.com.

www.leadingfamilyhotels.com.

Xu, Feifei, Michael Morgan, and Ping Song. 2009. "Students' Travel Behaviour: A Cross-cultural Comparison of UK and China." *International Journal of Tourism Research* 11: 255–268.

6

Gen Z Tourists and Smart Devices

Serap Ozdemir-Guzel and Yonca Nilay Bas

Digital Era and Gen Z

Developing technology causes young generations to be constantly exposed to social and technological changes and this situation requires new skills and investments in acquiring, sharing, and creating information that requires access to information systems and networking. These developments have changed the use of traditional media. In this information society, everything is present and nothing can be erased. Many businesses have experienced what the power of the Internet can do to

---

S. Ozdemir-Guzel (✉)
Istanbul University-Cerrahpasa Tourism and Hotel Management Program,
Istanbul, Turkey
e-mail: serap.guzel@istanbul.edu.tr

Y. N. Bas
Istanbul University-Cerrahpasa Business Management Program, Istanbul,
Turkey

© The Author(s), under exclusive license to Springer Nature
Switzerland AG 2021
N. Stylos et al. (eds.), *Generation Z Marketing and Management
in Tourism and Hospitality*,
https://doi.org/10.1007/978-3-030-70695-1_6

its image. This change in media usage and continuous flow of information has led to the demand for transparency from businesses (Wirokarto 2013).

Generation Z refers to the young generation born from the mid-1990s to the end of 2010, who had never lived before the internet era (Roblek et al. 2019). No other generation has ever lived in an age when technology was so easily accessible at such a young age (Prensky 2001). For this generation, new digital technologies—computers, mobile phones—are the primary mediators of human-to-human connections. Thanks to technological advances in multimedia such as tablets, smartphones, social media and flat-screen TVs, Generation Z youth have always become accustomed to interacting and communicating in a world where they connect with others (Turner 2015). According to Toronto (2009), the Internet has become a defining feature of the global community. Since the wave of technological progress that began in the 1990s, the Internet has played a prominent role in the lives of generation Z youth. This is not only about the number of devices and how often they interact with digital technologies, but also about how technology shapes thoughts, facilitates communication, redefines the concept of community, becomes the essence of their learning, and is almost an extraordinary companion. Generation Z is a generation of globally connected, socially connected, technologically best-known information in history. It is also the most educated generation, who will consume more, travel more, create more and do more work in their lives than their predecessors (Madden 2017).

Generation Z uses different technologies to keep in touch with communication, learning, and social practices. Because Gen Z is digitally capable, social and mobile, information and communication technologies are a critical component in accessing services and opening up to the outside World (Robinson and Schänzel 2019). Technology allows them to join different networks at the same time, which makes them different from previous generations. They prefer to use the Internet and smartphones are an important part of their lives. However, smartphones are not only sufficient as a device, but members of the Z generation are using social media applications to express themselves (e.g., Instagram, Facebook, Snapchat, YouTube, WhatsApp). This generation is education-oriented (especially for lifelong learning), fully integrated into the Internet environment professionally and having a lot of knowledge about new technologies (Roblek et al. 2019).

Wood (2013) emphasized that generation Z has four distinct characteristics:

(1) Focus on innovation: Being up-to-date in technological and design-based innovation is an area where this generation wants to spend its money. This generation is not surprised by product aging and has a high expectation for the "more, smaller, better" versions of technological products to emerge quickly.
(2) Insist on convenience: The lack of exposure to "from scratch" consumption and the increasing pressure for today's youth to succeed at a young age, has led to an increase in commitment to such elements; product features (for example, time-saving devices or mobile devices), product delivery (for example, retail channels that increase ease of purchase), product experience (e.g., easy to cook, consume, install, etc.) and product messaging (for example, "just-in-time" mobile or abbreviated ads). It is clear that most of the e-commerce features that cause uncertainty or concern for Baby Boomers or Generation X (e.g., delivery fees, consumer tracking, lack of offline stores) will not have the same concern for Generation Z.
(3) An underlying desire for security: Generation Z is more pragmatic and scarce. Generation Z may feel more careful and discriminatory where they spend their money. Similar to Generation X, this can lead to consumers who are very brand sensitive but not brand loyal.
(4) Tendency to escape: Generation Z can be a powerful market for escape-seeking products. The desire to escape this opportunity is likely to be facilitated by technological advances; (1) to make entertainment products such as video games more realistic and attractive, (2) offering 24/7 more access to social networks, and (3) escape devices (e.g., mobile phones with media and internet availability) offer greater mobility.

Generation Z members are influenced by a brand's online communication, are more likely to buy from a brand they follow on a social network, and tend to learn more about the brands they see online (Wirokarto 2013).

Generation Z tends to prefer online social sites to communicate with and interact with people they know, they are happy to provide active feedback and comments on the brands/services/products they use, and they value the opinions of others (PrakashYadav and Rai 2017). This generation is a strong participant, a high-level consumer of online content; they have a strong attraction for online communication, where they prefer to interact and stay connected with the technology available at their fingertips.

The Internet allows Z generation to grow in a customized environment as a prerequisite for developing various experiences. This also affects what this generation expects from the market, and therefore focuses more on customized services and products to meet their personal needs. This also has an impact on how marketing is applied to Generation Z. Functionality and easy-to-use products can be successful because they fit the multitasking lifestyle embraced by people of this generation. Moreover, given that individuals in this generation are almost highly dependent on technology, a business must be online to attract the attention of these generations (Haglind and Jonsson 2012).

Gen Z Tourist

The Z generation is the first generation of the twenty-first century, born into technology and adapted from birth to the digital world. Gen Z is called also smart tourist in tourism. Smart tourist "is a very comfortable generation and accustomed to virtual world" (Kusmayadi et al. 2017: 1). In brief, Gen Z tourist is a technological era tourist and has grown up with digital technology and uses smart devices. Generation Z, one of Europe's most budget-sensitive generations, starts the research and planning process without considering a specific destination and conducts research through smartphones while searching for travel inspiration (Southan 2017).

Gen Z, which is different from the previous X and Y generations, is an important target group in predicting future travel trends. It is predicted that Gen Z will be a target group that will drive travel movements as a population and which tourism enterprises and authorities will focus on carefully. Traveling purposes of this generation (Schiopu et al. 2016);

- To obtain new experiences,
- Recognition and integration of different cultures,
- Work,
- Study,
- Visiting family and friends,
- To learn language,
- To participate in events and others.

It is important for the tourism industry to determine the characteristics of Gen Z which will guide the tourism and to understand it well. Gen Z tourist characteristics can be listed as follows (Schiopu et al. 2016; Kusmayadi et al. 2017; Hamed 2017; Starĉević and Konjikušić 2018);

- They balanced their budget (promotions, cheap flight, peer-to-peer accommodation last minute offers),
- They care about a new and unusual, unique experience,
- They have an approach away from traditional holiday,
- They are not tourist explorer,
- They are comfortable generations,
- They prefer city breaks, weekend,
- They are longer travelers with visiting numerous locations,
- They are the most international traveling generations,
- They prefer right than luxury,
- They desire to visit authentic locations,
- They enjoy socializing with both locals and other tourists,
- They mostly travel with their friends or family,
- They communicate more online,
- When they are deciding on traveling, they rely on opinions, information, and recommendations of various social groups,
- They use numerous online information sources throughout their travel planning,

- They are most engaged in social media, where they find inspiration for traveling in most cases.

Gen Z is a generation that is interlocking with tourist technology. This generation use smartphones and spend a long time with it. For this reason, they often use social media and other smart applications. Communicates with family and friends through social networks. They rely on social media to make travel decisions. Technological developments provide easy access to information, opportunities, and places. So the behavior and experiences of the Z generation in a destination are influenced by developments in information and communication technologies (Robinson and Schänzel 2019). Kusmayadi et al. (2017) concluded that Gen Z mostly uses smartphones and majority of the users prefer Instagram applications in the social media usage. The most preferred applications after Instagram is Facebook, Youtube, Path, Twitter, etc. When the activities of this group with smart devices and applications are examined, it is seen that the time spent on social media is high, 45.3% of them are planning holiday trips and 40.6% looking for food references.

Gen Z tourist acquires information pre-travel and plans to travel according to the information acquired. Budget is an important element in their travel decisions. Besides, price, quality, positive comments, discounts, and product variety are effective in travel decisions. They make their reservations through online channels. They prefer to make their reservation with smartphones. They provide feedback after the trip. Feedbacks; wom, e-wom (recommending posts, rating, Instagram and Facebook) (Kusmayadi et al. 2017).

Generation Z also has a major impact on the family's holiday decisions at the pre-travel stage because family members prefer to consult them before traveling. Furthermore, since generation Z prefers to experience rather than possess, it tends to travel more in search of fun experiences. For individuals of this generation, travel is also a time of pleasure, socialization and empowerment (Robinson and Schänzel 2019).

Smart Devices in Tourism Industry

The development of information and communication technologies and the transition to industrial 4.0 made it necessary for the tourism sector to adapt to these changes. accommodation, transportation, travel, food and beverage industry and destination marketing organizations have started to use smart technologies. Using smart devices can help businesses survive, as well as cost, service quality, accessibility, marketing, management, strategic management, and managing the target group. They need to adapt to this change in order to address the generation of technology.

Gen Z, using technology at every moment of their lives, often prefers smart devices for touristic trips. They use various applications and the Internet to meet communication, information, changes, reservations, purchase of air tickets, maps usage, social interaction, social media sharing, etc., needs pre-, onsite, and post-travel. Various applications are used under the internet on things (IoT). That are ICT, smartwatches, QR codes, NFC tags, Apps, Augmented Reality (AR), smartphones, are frequently used by tourists in their travel. Some definitions about smart tools in tourism are;

- *Augmented Reality (AR)*: "is a real-time device mediated perception of a real-world environment that is closely or seamlessly integrated with computer-generated sensory objects" (Geroimenko 2012: 447).
- *Application (Appls)*: "application is a small piece of software that enables a specific goal to be achieved through the exchange of information" (Put-van Beemt and Smith 2016: 5). Applications can set many activities such as making reservations, finding directions, translation, guidance, and access to information.
- *Near Field Communication (NFC)*: "is short range wireless radio communication protocol that can function between a tag/ chip that transmits data stored on it to electrical device that read/receive the data" (Put-van Beemt and Smith 2016: 7). The application provides touchless communication. It is frequently used in museums and attractions. It is used for information, translation, payment, and navigation services.

- *Quick Response (QR)*: "is a matrix code developed and released primarily to be a symbol that is easily interpreted by scanner equipment" (Rouillard 2008: 52).
- *Wearable devices*: is an electronic device such as smartwatches, glasses, bracelets.

Smart Devices in the Hospitality Industry

The use of smart devices is preferred for value-added purposes both business and consumer. The smart device applications that add value to the consumer and differentiate their experiences in the hospitality sector, are as follows;

- **Reservation Apps**: It allows to easily book and follow the reservations.
- **Smart Reserved Parking**: It is an intelligent system that allows customers to park their vehicles. It is used with hotel applications and sensor relationships. Park place is assigned before guest check-in.
- **Remote Check-In/Check-Out**: is an application that can perform quickly check-in and check-out with mobile devices.
- **Mobile room keys**: Guests can access their rooms with mobile application. Guests access their rooms via their smartphone app. With this application, room temperature, opening the curtains, such features are provided with this application. Guests can be in the control room via smartphone apps.
- **Smart Roomservice**: It is the application that sends the room service menu as a vibration to the guests' phones. Through beacon technology, the location of the guest is determined and a message is sent to the location.
- **Voice-controlled services**: it can allow customers to request room service, book a table at the hotel restaurant, or book spa sessions by simply speaking to a device in their room (revfine.com 2019).
- **Augmented Reality (AR)**: it provides an opportunity to experience such as online 360-degree hotel tour, room experience, etc., especially before traveling.

- **VR (Virtual Reality)**: Accommodation businesses can make promotion and marketing with wearable tools. Guests can be seeing or getting experience about hotel facilities with wearable device.

Smart Devices in Smart Tourism Destinations

Smart tourism destinations "is to focus on tourists' need, combining the ICT with casual culture" (Huang et al. 2012: 445). Smart cities and smart tourism destinations are enhanced tourist experienced. According to Buhalis and Amaranggana (2015) enhanced experienced differs from amenities (sustainability, efficient consumption) accessibility (real-time information and location of vehicles), attractions (VR and AR), available packages (Guidance, tour packages, translation of languages), and ancillary services (quick feedback).

One of the most needed systems for tourists in smart destinations is transportation information. In this context, tourists can access the transportation networks with QR codes and NFC tags and learn how to get from one point to another quickly. It also provides information on the vehicles and their duration of the stop. In addition, people can easily find directions through the features in the smart devices such as bluetooth, GPS, and beacon technology.

Another smart application used in the destination is VR and AR applications. People can experience the city, museum, etc., quickly with wearable devices. VR offers virtual reality. It is an attractive element for tourists who with limited time. Also, smart destination apps are often used. Smart destinations offer all the information that will facilitate the travel of visitors in one application. For instance, in Barcelona, which stands out in terms of international visitors, various applications meet tourists through apple and play store in order to meet their needs to discover the city. One of these applications is "Visit Barcelona," which is the official guide to Barcelona on your smartphone and provide interactive tourist information. Tourists can easily access general information about Barcelona, Top20 attractions, World heritage sites, and places near Barcelona with this app. There is information about the guided routes,

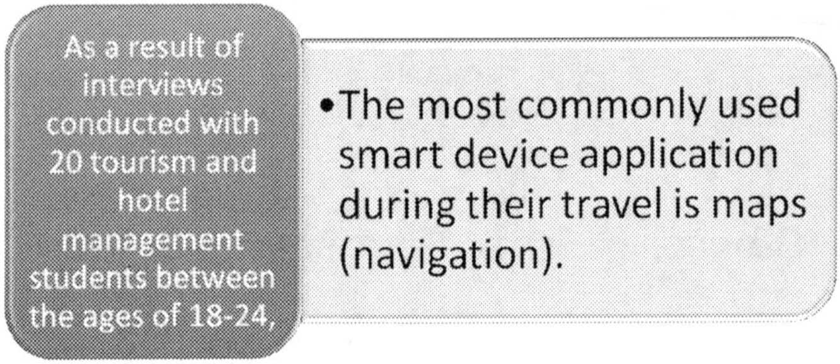

150   S. Ozdemir-Guzel and Y. N. Bas

As a result of interviews conducted with 20 tourism and hotel management students between the ages of 18-24,

• The most commonly used smart device application during their travel is maps (navigation).

Fig. 6.1 Gen Z tourists' most used application

museums, architecture, art, leisure, restaurants, cafes and bars, shopping, and accommodation topics. The application is also included in the regions of Barcelona and Barcelona photos. The maps section is a must for a tourist. This expectation is also met by the application. The application also allows them to tap the favorite places. The application is designed for use in different languages (Barcelonaturisme.com 2020).

As a result of interviews conducted by the authors of this chapter with 20 tourism and hotel management students between the ages of 18–24, it was determined that the most common application that students use with their smart devices during their travels is the maps application. This finding reveals the importance of the direction of travel for tourists (Fig. 6.1).

Various smart applications provide information about the destination and the attractions. This information allows tourists to spend their time better and more effective. For example, what time does a museum open and close? Also which activities are in the museum? etc. Intelligent guidance services are also in smart destination applications. In particular, requests that tourists may need such as translation, guidance services, tour packages, etc., are digitalized.

Smart Devices in Food and Beverage Industry

Smart devices, which have an important function in improving the service quality of restaurant businesses, also affect customer experiences significantly. The most complained issues in restaurants are not being able to communicate with the waiters. In this context, this problem can be solved with smart applications and devices and a faster, more efficient, and quality service is achieved with IoT. Applications for smart devices in restaurant establishments are as follows:

- **Mobile payment**: It is IoT, which allows customers to pay with a tablet or mobile application from their seat. NFC tags and QR codes are used.
- **Smart Menu**: They give an order instantly from a smart device at the table.
- **Loyalty App.**: It is an application that allows loyal customers to place orders in advance in other ways preordering services. That is to provide customers skip the line.

Smart Devices in Museums

Museums began to change shape and digitize with the development of technology, and start to use 4D systems and to use experience-oriented technological applications. Some applications for smart devices in museums are as follows:

- **Near Field Communication (NFC)**: It is an intelligent system that provides wireless communication. With this application, payment, sharing information, purchase product, banking transactions such as various transactions can be made.
- **Museum App.**: With the museum applications, tourists can find directions by navigating within the museum and listen to the information about the exhibition works. They also use translation services.
- **QR codes/NFC tags**: QR codes and NFC tags provide easy access to information. The tourist can scan the QR code and wants to listen to the relevant work in any foreign language.
- **Augmented Reality (AR)**: "offer a natural view of real scenes enriched with virtual objects" (Wojciechowski et al. 2004). Tourists can get

experience about museums, pre-travel, and on-site seeing with wearable device.

* **VR (Virtual Reality)**: Reality is a simulation in virtual reality. Everything is virtual. Museums are experienced with virtual tours. For instance, you can visit the Metropolitan Museum of Art with a VR tour. Visitors should download the app and can get experiences through VR. Also can get 360 virtual tours offline.

Smart Devices in Airline Industry

Tourists prefer the airline from their transport network during their travels. There are areas where people can use smart devices in the process from arrival to departure. There are park, c-in, checking bag, security, airport activities, boarding, departure, inflight entertainment, arrival, customs, baggage claim, and leaving airport (Mariani et al. 2019).

A message is sent to the mobile phone on which point the baggage will be taken. Various information can be provided by QR codes. They use operations for intelligent applications such as c-in from mobile application, opening boarding pass by message or opening from application, providing pass-through QR code, bagging with smart devices, or making other entry operations. In addition, the smart glasses can access information such as translation, information. Smart watches and bracelets warn tourists about any changes and information about their flights at airports.

Smart Devices in Tours

The most used smart devices during travel are applications that facilitate travel. Especially in international travels, the language problem comes to the forefront. In this context, this need is met with QR codes and audio guides in destinations. Recently mobile tour and apps. has been used frequently. Some applications for smart devices in tours are as follows:

* **QR codes and NFC tags**: They can help with information, translation, and payment during travel.

- **Audio guide**: It allows tour without guide. Guidance service is taken with smart devices and applications.
- **Mobile tour and apps**.: Virtual tours are provided to the tourists on their mobile phones as well as touch screens installed at various locations (Lee et al. 2011).

Smart Device Experiences in Pre-travel, On-site, and Post-travel

The concept of "smart" has become a widely used term in marketing for everything developed with technology, this concept has become important not only for communication channels but also in terms of booking procedures and information search in tourism communication. Smartness is often closely related to increasing the usability of certain products through the application of technologies. In this context, information and communication technology and the Internet of Things, which express both the use of the Internet and the combination of product and service provision, should be considered (Nabben et al. 2016). Recent developments such as the use of cloud computing, sensors and GPS, virtual and augmented reality, full adoption of social media and mobile technologies have led to the emergence of smart concept in tourism (Femenia-Serra et al. 2019). It is known that especially tourists use the internet before, during and after travel. Wireless, smart devices such as smartphones, watches, tablets, etc., have had a major impact on tourist behavior (Atembe and Abdalla 2015).

Intelligent technologies in tourism serve for energy monitoring in hotels, consumers use it through the implementation of QR codes; sensors, tags, RFID, and cloud computing in smart city establishments are examples of smart technologies in tourism. However, in addition to the latest developments in the field of technology, "smart" technologies appear to be wearable. Wearable technology is a term used to describe many different forms of body-mounted technology (Atembe 2016).

Tools such as QR codes or NFC tags add value to the tourist experience by providing connections between the physical and digital world. They increase tourist access to information about nearby interests. A smart tourism tool with augmented reality allows visitors to have experience at a different location and at a different time, enabling travel guides to be implemented in real-time locations (Nabben et al. 2016). The development of a new flow of wearable devices, including head-mounted displays (HMDs), smart watches, wristbands, and body-worn cameras, has become one of the main drivers of the transformation of tourist behavior and tourism experiences. In this context, the latest generation of VR devices such as Oculus Rift and Samsung Gear represent the most advanced tools for target marketing efforts, allowing the creation of highly immersive and realistic virtual experiences. These advanced devices are expected to have a revolutionary impact on tourism experiences, including the pre-travel stage, where awareness, interest, and expectation can be created in the mind of the tourist. New technologies have also changed the way tourism providers create and present tourism experiences and how tourists perceive and experience targets. New technologies, especially mobile technologies, enable tourists to participate in both real and virtual experiences at the same time. In short, advances in technology (internet, social media, and smartphones) have strengthened internet-based travel services, it has changed traveler expectations and the resulting travel experiences (Robinson and Schänzel 2019). This takes place in all three stages of the travel process, before, during, and after the travel (Marasco et al. 2018). Overall, these tools have the basic benefit of enhancing the tourist experience. In this process, information and communication technologies support tourists through various activities such as preliminary information search, comparison, decision-making, travel planning, communication, information acquisition, and sharing of experiences. Based on the above, a conceptual framework has been developed on the smart devices usage in the three stages of the travel process, as illlustrated in Fig. 6.2.

Pre-travel Stage

The pre-travel stage represents a very important moment in the general experience process, since at this stage tourists develop their expectations of the visit and activate their decision-making processes. At this stage, new technologies play an important role as tourism providers and target organizations are able to promote their products and locations in an innovative and more effective way (Marasco et al. 2018). In the smart tourism system, tourists can experience new smart services related to brand, food, accommodation, tour, shopping, entertainment, and other elements. Electronic wallet, WeChat Pay, Alipay, and other online payment methods can be used for online booking, travel plan, and other services prior to travel (Wu 2017).

Websites and social media are the most commonly used technological tools to promote destinations and tourism products. These technologies are used to gather information and improve social interactions with other users interested in tourist attractions. Tourism organizations can take advantage of augmented reality (AR) to attract new visitor streams and improve tourists' experiences at their destination. In parallel, VR has emerged as a powerful tool for the target market. VR can assist target marketers in creating unforgettable experiences that integrate with their communication strategies and assist tourists in their search for information and decision-making processes (Marasco et al. 2018).

According to Gretzel and Jamal (2009), the pre-travel phase is defined as an actively involved and socially intensive phase. With the advent of the Internet, social media and virtual worlds enable tourists to experience and evaluate a destination before their physical journey. Social media sites, such as Facebook, YouTube, or TripAdvisor, allow individuals to explore the destination and live experiences of other consumers, using both their own social environment and unknown partner consumers. What's more, Second Life, the most popular among virtual environments, has become an attractive platform for businesses to represent their products and services in a three-dimensional online world. The arrangement through avatars allows tourists to experience their destination before or after their holiday (Neuhofer et al. 2012). In addition to these technologies, smart watches are used in destinations for status updates, comments, photo tags, check-ins, etc. (Atembe 2016).

Marketers need to use immersive virtual reality technology to integrate sensory experiences into communication strategies, and use experience-based internet marketing to support tourist information-seeking and decision-making (Huang et al. 2013).

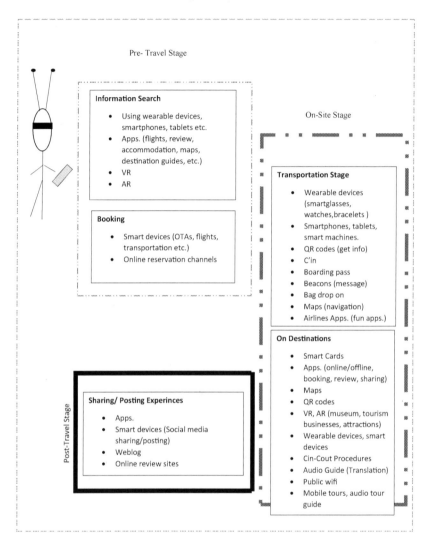

Fig. 6.2 Smart devices usage in pre-travel, on-site, and post-travel

On-site Stage

Different technologies are used when tourists are on the move, traveling, or at their destination. Increased mobility has been key tools of mobile technologies because they provide information retrieval anywhere and anytime. Mobile technologies, such as location-based services, provide instant access to information, videos, or referral sites about the current location. This provides opportunities for destinations to contact and assist tourists (Neuhofer et al. 2012). In the process of traveling, modern technologies such as the Internet of Things can effectively transmit information instantly and provide smart guided tours to tourists (Wu 2017: 168).

Many tourism products actually use VR or VR-type technologies to attract tourists. For example, there are many hotels and destinations that offer "virtual tours" on the internet. In addition, various multimedia information can be embedded in a VR so that access to various useful information can be provided through a single application. The educational potential of VRs can be used in museums, heritage sites, and other tourist sites (Guttentag 2010). Tuscany is the official augmented reality application of Tuscany. This app offers to discover what's around you and get details about location, accommodation, attractions, restaurants, museums, etc. Just click the AR icons. For example, if you are looking for a hotel to stay, it shows you the hotels around you. You can get information by clicking on any AR icons and using map, you can see how to get there from where you are (Tourismintuscany.it 2020).

Bracelets/watches in the accommodation can monitor guests' sleeping patterns and can be used as a clock to awaken with slight vibrations. Wristbands used in accommodation may be the key to the hotel room. With the use of smart glasses in the museums, tourists can use the smart glasses prototype of the museum to see the cultural artifacts in the museum, and at the same time, they can activate digital contents such as videos, games, photos, etc., on the glasses screen through the glasses screen. For instance, international chain brands such as Mariott International offer Iot Guestroom service. In that brands, voice control devices started to be used in guest rooms. Voice-activated devices can be used to communicate with hotel, control the room such as lights, temperature, TVs, etc. (News.marriott.com 2020). In addition, with the use of smart glasses in art galleries, zoos, theme parks, or aquariums, visitors to the art gallery and museum can easily switch between real objects and augmented reality (Atembe 2016).

In sum, while traveling smart devices make valuable the travel experience of tourists especially Gen Z and also guide the planning of their ongoing travels. Especially smartphones (Mang et al. 2016), tablets, smartwatches, glasses, and wristbands are the most used portable smart devices. With these devices, it is faster to explore the destination and capture the moment. Portable smart devices allow them to access everything they need while traveling, using applications such as navigation, translation, communication, maps, access to information, VR, and AR. At the same time, smart devices, especially smartphones, are often used to take photos and connect to social media (Mang et al. 2016). In the destination, tourists use smart devices, particularly when using maps, finding directions, downloading, or using transportation network maps (online/offline).

Food and Beverage and accommodation companies, museums, and other attractions within the scope of the destination also respond to the changing demands of the tourists with smart devices and applications. These smart opportunities provided by businesses facilitate processes such as mobile or apps purchasing, payment, c-in and c-out, reservation, boarding, navigation and finding restaurants and cafes, using smart menus and ordering from these menus they need during their travels.

Post-travel Stage

Tourists share their experiences with others through interactive websites, virtual travel communities, social networking sites, weblogs, videos, commentary sites, mobile apps, etc. People also give positive/negative advice to their close circle via WOM. Following the experiences, tourists make ratings through websites or mobile applications and creates business-related content. Many tourists also contact the business to provide positive/negative feedback and offer suggestions for service development/improvement.

According to Robinson and Schänzel (2019), there are three factors that shape the experiences of generation Z:

– Immediate influences: family, friends, and events in the home country.

- Destination influences: sociopolitical, cultural, physical characteristics.
- Global influences: Climate change, terrorism, financial volatility, geographical policies, and technological developments.

As a result of interviews conducted by the authors of this chapter with 20 tourism and hotel management students between the ages of 18–24 on the use of smart devices and applications in tourism, it was found that the students used primarily smartphones, tablets, wearable devices, AR, and VR in their travels. Their preference when traveling with these devices is shown in Fig. 6.3.

According to Fig. 6.3, it is revealed that Gen Z tourists make the most reservations with smart devices. In addition, payment, information acquisition, feedback, vehicle tracking systems, smart translation services, smart menu applications, and smart guides are preferred. Smart enterprises are also among the reasons for preference.

It was determined that smart devices and applications were used more frequently before and during travel. After traveling, smart devices and applications are preferred more for sharing the travel experience. Before the trip, it was found that various information, reservation transactions were made with smart devices and applications. While the tendency to

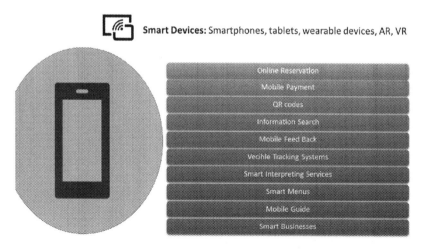

Fig. 6.3 Gen Z tourist and smart device usage

obtain information about Tripadvisor, Instagram accounts, road condition is emerging in the foreground, booking providers such as online booking and booking are used.

Marketing Advices for the Gen Z Tourist

A Gen Z tourist shows a different trend from the usual tourist profiles. This generation of smart tourists, also can be called technology age tourists. Travel trends and preferences differ from other generations. In general, it is a generation that uses smart devices that are valuable in time, looking for a unique experience, authenticity, planning their own budget and their own journey. Gen Z tourist is influenced by attractive images in social media and advertising, therefore, marketers who want to inspire and transform Gen Z travelers should implement a visually appealing and integrated cross-device marketing strategy (Southan 2017).

Gen Z tourists use smart devices from the beginning to the end of the trip. In the context of the Internet of things, many smart devices and applications are preferred. Travels and experiences are different with smart devices. In addition, travel movements, travel planning easier, while experiencing a faster travel process experience. They have the opportunity to access and experience information (AR, VR app. etc.). Smart devices and applications allow you to quickly solve problems while traveling and share all the memories of your trip. Due to all these issues Gen Z prefers to use smart devices.

In the marketing activities for this generation, the tourism sector should pay attention to smart device applications are as follows;

- The use of smart devices and the incorporation of smart applications will enable enterprises to come to the forefront in the market.
- Gen Z tourists represent the technology—age people. Therefore, the use of smart devices and applications by touristic enterprises will increase the demand. The decrease in interest of young people in museums increased with the use of wearable devices in museums (Conyette 2015).

- They prioritize social interaction. Social interaction with wearable devices should be supported (Atembe 2016).
- Gen Z, a generation with low-cost sensitivity, following opportunities, reviewing reviews, therefore, Gen Z-oriented businesses should include opportunity and review tabs in their apps.
- Destination Planning Organizations should ensure that such platforms (couchsurfing, eatwith, blablacar, etc.) are easily accessible with smart applications by showing the necessary sensitivity to the sharing economy in tourism. These platforms, supported by smart applications, will be preferred for Gen Z who want to experience unique experiences, socialize, and recognize different cultures from the local point of view.
- Time is very important for this generation who wants to move fast. Businesses should be able to use their time more effectively with various smart applications.
- Map applications are the most commonly used applications by Gen Z. These applications should be located within all businesses and destinations.
- Guidance applications must be used in destinations.
- The goal of destination marketing organizations should be traveler-centered rather than the promotion of the physical characteristics of destinations (King 2002).
- Smart devices play an active role in creating unique experiences.
- It should be possible to embody the abstract tourist products in the purchasing process and to allow them to experience with wearable devices before the purchase process.
- AR offers a unique experience. Destination stakeholders should focus on AR applications for traveling with unique experience-oriented Gen Z tourist.
- Gen Z tourist wants to use applications on smart devices even without internet. Therefore, businesses should focus on mobile applications that do not require internet.

References

Atembe, R. 2016. "The use of smart technology in tourism: evidence from wearable devices." *Journal of Tourism and Hospitality Management*, 312, 224–234. https://doi.org/10.17265/2328-2169/2015.12.002.

Atembe, R., and Abdalla, F. 2015. "The use of smart technology in tourism: evidence from wearable devices." In *ISCONTOUR 2015-tourism research perspectives: proceedings of the international student conference in tourism research* (Vol. 23). BoD–Books on Demand.

Barcelonaturisme.com. 2020. https://www.barcelonaturisme.com/wv3/en/page/1464/mobile-apps.html. Accessed on May 1, 2020.

Buhalis, D., and Amaranggana, A. 2015. "Smart tourism destinations enhancing tourism experience through personalisation of services." In Tussyadiah, I., and Inversini, A. (eds.), *ENTER 2015 proceedings*, Lugano, Springer-Verlag, Wien. ISBN:9783319143422, pp. 377–390.

Conyette, M. 2015. 21st century travel using websites, mobile and wearable technology devices. Athens: ATINER's conferences Paper Series, No. TOU2015-1475.

Femenia-Serra, F., Perles-Ribes, J. F., and Ivars-Baidal, J. A. 2019). "Smart destinations and tech-savvy millennial tourists: hype versus reality." *Tourism Review*, 74(1), 63–81.

Geroimenko, V. 2012. "Augmented reality technology and art: the analysis and visualization of evolving conceptual models." In Banissi, E. (ed.), *IEEE, 16th international conference on information visualisation (IV)*, Montpellier, France, 11–13th July 2012, IEEE, pp. 445–453.

Gretzel, U., and Jamal, T. 2009. "Conceptualizing the creative tourist class: Technology, mobility, and tourism experiences." *Tourism Analysis*, 14(4), 471–481.

Guttentag, D. A. 2010. "Virtual reality: applications and implications for tourism." *Tourism Management*, 31(5), 637–651.

Haglind, L., and Jonsson, C. 2012. "Understanding perceptions towards, and usage of, social media in the context of relationship building: a generational comparison."

Hamed, H. 2017. "Marketing destinations to millennials: examining the compatibility between the destination marketing organization website and the millennial tourist prospects." *Journal of Tourism and Recreation*, 3(1), 1–20.

Huang, X. K., Yuan, J. Z., and Shi, M. Y. 2012. "Condition and key issues analysis on the smarter tourism construction in China." In *Multimedia and signal processing*. Springer, Berlin, Heidelberg, pp. 444–450.

Huang, Y. C., Backman, S. J., Backman, K. F., and Moore, D. 2013. "Exploring user acceptance of 3D virtual worlds in travel and tourism marketing." *Tourism Management*, 36, 490–501.

King, J. 2002. "Destination marketing organisations—connecting the experience rather than promoting the place." *Journal of Vacation Marketing*, 8(2), 105–108.

Kusmayadi, H., Wiweka, K., Kurniawati, R., and Adnyana, I. N. 2017. "The profile and behavior of "SMART TOURIST' (Generation Z) in making decisions and travelling case study: young tourist in Jabodetabek." In *4th world research summit for tourism and hospitality*, December 8–11. Orlanda, Florida, US.

Lee, C. K., Lee, J., Lo, P. W., Tang, H. L., Hsiao, W. H., Liu, J. Y., and Lin, T. L. 2011. "Taiwan perspective: developing smart living technology." *AUSMT International Journal of Automation and Smart Technology*, 1(1), 93–106.

Madden, C. 2017. *"Hello Gen Z: engaging the generation of post-millennials."* Hello Clarity, p. 310.

Mang, C. F., Piper, L. A., and Brown, N. R. 2016. "The incidence of smartphone usage among tourists." *International Journal of Tourism Research*, 18, 591–601.

Marasco, A., Buonincontri, P., van Niekerk, M., Orlowski, M., and Okumus, F. 2018. "Exploring the role of next-generation virtual technologies in destination marketing." *Journal of Destination Marketing & Management*, 9, 138–148.

Mariani, J., Krimmel, E., Zmud, J., Sen, R., and Miller, M. 2019. "Flying smarter the smart airport and the Internet of Things." https://www2.del oitte.com/us/en/insights/industry/public-sector/iot-in-smart-airports.html. Accessed on November 27, 2019.

Nabben, A., Wetzel, E., Oldani, E., Huyeng, J., Boel, M., and Fan, Z. 2016. "Smart technologies in tourism: case study on the influence of iBeacons on customer experience during the 2015 SAIL Amsterdam event." In *The international tourism student conference*, pp. 1–32.

Neuhofer, B., Buhalis, D., and Ladkin, A. 2012. "Conceptualising technology enhanced destination experiences." *Journal of Destination Marketing & Management*, 1(1–2), 36–46.

News.marriott.com. 2020. https://news.marriott.com/news/2017/11/14/mar riott-international-teams-with-samsung-and-legrand-to-unveil-hospitalityindustrys-iot-hotel-room-of-the-future-enabling-the-company-to-deepen-personalized-guest-experience. Accessed on April 20, 2020.

PrakashYadav, G., and Rai, J. 2017. "The generation Z and their social media usage: a review and a research outline." *Global Journal of Enterprise Information System*, 9(2).

Prensky, M. 2001. "Digital natives, Digital immigrants part 1." *On the Horizon*, 9(5), 1–6. https://doi.org/10.1108/10748120110424816.

Put-van Beemt, W., & Smith, R. 2016. "Smart tourism tools: linking technology to the touristic resources of a city." In *Smart tourism congress*. Barcelona, Spain. 1–12.

Revfine.com. 2019. "How the Internet of Things (IoT) can benefit the hospitality industry." https://www.revfine.com/internet-of-things-hospitality-industry/. Accessed on November 20, 2019.

Robinson, V. M., and Schänzel, H. A. 2019. "A tourism inflex: generation Z travel experiences." *Journal of Tourism Futures*. https://doi.org/10.1108/jtf-01-2019-0014.1-15.

Roblek, V., Mesko, M., Dimovski, V., and Peterlin, J. 2019. "Smart technologies as social innovation and complex social issues of the Z generation." *Kybernetes*, 48(1), 91–107.

Rouillard, José. 2008. "Contextual QR codes." In *The third international multi-conference on conference: computing in the global information technology*. ICCGI '08. 50–55. https://doi.org/10.1109/iccgi.2008.25. Accessed on November 20, 2019.

Schiopu, A. F., Padurean, A. M., Tala, M. L., and Nica, A-M. 2016. "The influence of new technologies on tourism consumption behavior of the millennials." *Amfiteatru Economic*, 18(10), 829–846.

Southan, J. 2017. "From boomers to Gen Z: travel trends across the generations." Globetrender Magazine, May 19. Available at: http://globetrender magazine.com/2017/05/19/travel-trends-across-generations/. Accessed on November 20, 2019.

Starĉević, S., and Konjikušić, S. 2018. "Why millennials as digital travelers transformed marketing strategy in tourism industry." 221–240. https://www.researchgate.net/publication/328791775. Accessed on October 8, 2019.

Tourismintuscany.it. 2020. http://www.tourismintuscany.it/smartphone-apps/. Accessed on April 20, 2020.

Turner, A. 2015. "Generation Z: technology and social interest." *The Journal of Individual Psychology*, 71(2), 103–113.

Wirokarto, D. A. 2013. "Online branding to generation Z" (Doctoral dissertation). ISCTE Business School.

Wojciechowski, R., Walczak, K., White, M., and Cellary, W. 2004. "Building virtual and augmented reality museum exhibitions." In *Web3D symposium proceedings*. 135–144. https://doi.org/10.1145/985040.985060.

Wood, S. 2013. "Generation Z as consumers: trends and innovation." [online] Available at: https://iei.ncsu.edu/wp-content/uploads/2013/01/GenZConsumers.pdf. Accessed on November 20, 2019.

Wu, X. 2017. "Smart tourism based on internet of things." *Revista de la Facultad de Ingeniería U.C.V.*, 32(10), 166–170.

7

Generation Z and Digital Influencers in the Tourism Industry

Danielle Barbe and Larissa Neuburger

Introduction

As Generation Z grows to become the largest consumer market on the planet (Dunkley 2017), digital influencers have equally become an essential marketing tool. With the rise of Generation Z and their entering into the labour market where they will have substantial spending power, several marketing organizations have generated reports that explain the best way to reach this market (e.g. Bradley 2019; Digital Marketing Institute 2019; Fontein 2019; Forbes Communication Council 2018). While

---

D. Barbe (✉)
Department of Marketing, Operations and Systems, Northumbria University, Newcastle upon Tyne, UK
e-mail: danielle.barbe@northumbria.ac.uk

L. Neuburger
Department of Tourism, Hospitality and Event Management, University of Florida, Gainesville, FL, USA
e-mail: l.neuburger@ufl.edu

© The Author(s), under exclusive license to Springer Nature
Switzerland AG 2021
N. Stylos et al. (eds.), *Generation Z Marketing and Management in Tourism and Hospitality*,
https://doi.org/10.1007/978-3-030-70695-1_7

the recommendations in each report vary, one aspect remains the same: Generation Z responds best to digital influencers, even when they know the content from an influencer is sponsored (Dunkley 2017).

According to an article by Affilinet (2015), Generation Z's trust in digital influencers is so high that it falls just behind word-of-mouth (WOM) recommendations from friends and family and is greater than mainstream media and traditional advertising. Similar studies have found that 52% of Generation Z said they trust information from an influencer (Fontein 2019) and 63% prefer to see an influencer in an advertisement than a celebrity (Arthur 2016). Digital influencers have the ability to build an authentic bond with Generation Z in just eight seconds or less (Bradley 2016). Even with an increasing number of influencers taking advantage of their ability to persuade audiences by monetizing their social media efforts and working with brands for promotions and sponsorships (Newman 2014), this does not appear to be affecting Generation Z as they either are unaware of this or simply do not seem to care (Dunkley 2017). This generation trusts 'real people', making digital influencers a vital tool for the promotion of products and services (Newman 2014).

What are digital influencers? A digital influencer is a new type of independent third-party endorser who shapes audience attitudes through blogs, tweets, and the use of other social media (Freberg et al. 2011: 90). Digital influencers are users of social media who have generated a great online following, established credibility, and whose reach and perceived authenticity can impact and persuade their followers (De Veirman et al. 2017). Influencers are opinion leaders; they have the ability to increase the influence of information they receive and transmit that information to others (Magno and Cassia 2018). They have built a reputation for their knowledge and expertise on a particular topic through social media and engage their followers (Ristova and Angelkova Petkova 2019), making them a vital marketing tool for Generation Z (Dunkley 2017).

Digital influencers span across a number of social media platforms, including blogs, Instagram, YouTube, Facebook, Twitter (Solis 2012) and Tik Tok. However, Instagram is the clear-cut favourite with 80% considering it the primary platform for brand collaborations (Chadha 2018). On Instagram, digital influencers can create visual content using photos and videos and post them on the platform with the potential to reach hundreds of thousands, to even millions of viewers.

What allow influencers to be so influential are the perceptions they developed within their followers. Digital influencers are perceived to be experts (Lyons and Henderson 2005; Wagner and Bolloju 2005) and may cover specific subjects, such as travel, food, or fashion, and give advice, useful information, tips, or insightful comments based on their (professional) experiences and observations (Uzunoğlu and Kip 2014). However, even digital influencers without perceived expertise on a specific topic may gain influence solely through the content they post and their dedication to fruitful engagement with their followers (Uzunoğlu and Kip 2014). Regardless of whether they are experts or not, the power of influencers is undeniable, particularly when marketing to Generation Z.

Generation Z has a greater connection with those they perceive as being authentic and trustworthy, which has given the ability for digital influencers to take on celebrity status (Dunkley 2017; Saul 2016). Influencer marketing is effective for this generation because they already have an established connection and engagement with the influencers they follow and therefore trust their opinions. Similarly, Generation Z is known to have a high FOMO (fear of missing out) and thus wants to engage in the same activities as others they see online (Dunkley 2017). In addition, members of Generation Z are not only consumers of influencer-generated content, but also content creators. This generation is technology savvy and therefore knows how to optimize internet-based tools for content creation, enabling even 'ordinary individuals' to elevate themselves to the role of a digital influencer (Dunkley 2017).

While there is an abundance of research on the effects of user-generated content (UGC) on consumer's travel-related attitudes and behaviours, the effects of digital influencers on their followers have been overlooked in the tourism literature (Ge and Gretzel 2018; Magno and Cassia 2018), despite the tremendous presence of digital influencers in the industry. Looking across all tourism sectors, digital influencers have an enormous presence in the marketing of destinations (Oates 2016; Shankman 2014a, b), hotels (Ristova and Angelkova Petkova 2019), food

170 D. Barbe and L. Neuburger

and beverage establishments (Ranteallo and Andilolo 2017), transportation (Media Kix 2016; Zilles 2019), or festivals and events (CPC Strategy 2018).

This book chapter will begin with a review of the general literature on influencers and their rise to prominence by Generation Z. Then the chapter will describe the growth and current state of influencer marketing across the various sectors of the tourism industry, including destination marketing, hospitality marketing (food and beverage, hotels), festival and event marketing, or transportation marketing (airlines, train).

Influencer Marketing

Influencer marketing is a relatively new concept with a limited amount of research (Uzunoğlu and Kip 2014). Influencer marketing can be defined as the promotion of products, services, experiences, or places by social media users, who gained status and popularity by their large network of followers due to the material and content they post online and through their self-marketing efforts (Carter 2016; De Veirman et al. 2017; Khamis et al. 2017). "They reinforce social proof in all they do, even when not paid to do so. What they wear, ride, listen to, where they go, intrigues and inspires communities" (Solis 2016: 1). Being seen as a friend with expertise in a certain area but especially being perceived as 'a person next-door' gives influencers their credibility and trustworthiness (Activate 2018; Solis 2016).

With influencer marketing, digital influencers mediate messages between brand and target audience, allowing messages to be rapidly and easily disseminated with the potential to go viral (Uzunoğlu and Kip 2014). The ability of influencers to persuade their audiences is likely due to their role as opinion leaders. Literature on opinion leadership extends back to the 1950s, where Katz (1957) explained that opinion leaders have three common characteristics and behaviours. First, opinion leaders personify certain values. They have certain traits that allow them to have a greater influence than others. Second, opinion leaders have competence, a level of expertise on certain subjects. Third, they have a strategic location within their social network. The size of their network and number of people who value their leadership allows opinion leaders to influence a large number of audiences. These characteristics of traditional opinion leaders, such as openness to messages, taking the role of the discussant, and influence and value among social contacts are the same as in today's digital influencers (Uzunoğlu and Kip 2014).

The rise of influencers began with the advancement in technology and the Internet, particularly web 2.0 which enabled two-way communication between users and the ability for anyone to create content online. With web 2.0, online reviews gained prominence, where people could share their opinions and experiences with a product or service to a vast audience. Understanding the value that online reviews have on shaping opinions, certain individuals took advantage of this opportunity by devoting time to provide genuine opinions through written blogs, video blogs (called vlogs), and social media platforms, including Facebook, Twitter, and Instagram (Ristova and Angelkova Petkova 2019). Bloggers and vloggers may be considered the first digital influencers, before the term became popularized. Today, while some influencers started their online career with a website where they continue to publish blog articles about various topics, influencers in the year 2019 and beyond are expected to be present in one (if not more) social media channels (Fig. 7.1).

Many organizations are now recognizing and encouraging influencers to promote their products or services, realizing their ability to create trends, and persuade audiences. Influencer marketing is considered the 'next golden goose' of marketing (Newman 2015) and the most important new marketing approach for those at the leading edge of purchase decision-making (Ristova and Angelkova Petkova 2019), particularly for Generation Z.

Digital influencers exist in various forms. Before social media users began influencing lifestyle, fashion or travel trends, it was mostly celebrities who acted as company ambassadors to spread the word about products and services. Organizations continue to spend a significant portion of their marketing budget on celebrity endorsements due to their perceived trustworthiness, expertise, and attractiveness, each of which

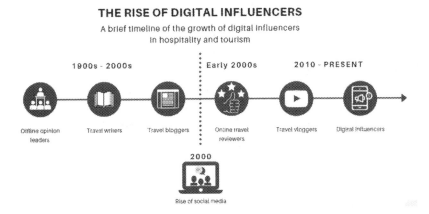

Fig. 7.1 Timeline of digital influencers

have been found to be important dimensions impacting purchase decisions (Ohanian 1990). When a celebrity is introduced into a brand, they bring their own audience with them (Hearn and Schoenhoff 2015). Celebrity endorsers use both traditional media and social media, and when celebrities have large social media followings, the followers are also added to the equation to influence the audience (Hearn and Schoenhoff 2015). Also in the celebrity endorsement literature, self-congruity theory postulates that consumers prefer brands with personalities congruent with their own (Aaker 1995). On social media, users may tend to follow those whom they feel they can identify with or are more similar to themselves, which for Generation Z may not be celebrities but digital influencers. For example, studies focusing on teenagers in the U.S. show that Generation Z is more likely to trust and feel connected to influencers on YouTube than music or movie stars (Del Rowe 2018; Djafarova and Rushworth 2017; Solis 2016). Therefore, when reaching Generation Z, hospitality and tourism marketers may find it more beneficial to work with niche influencers that this generation can relate to and deems credible as opposed to celebrities in the traditional sense (i.e. actors, musicians, athletes).

Influencers can be classified into different categories based on the number of followers (Table 7.1) (Solis 2016).

7 Generation Z and Digital Influencers in the Tourism Industry 173

Table 7.1 Classification of digital influencers

Category	Follower count
Mega-influencer (celebrities)	>500 k followers
Mid-tier influencer	100 k–500 k followers
Micro-influencer	5 k–100 k followers
Nano-influencers	<5 k followers

While most times an influencer is defined as a single person who is managing one or more social media accounts, there are also other trends that should be mentioned. Sometimes one social media account is managed by influencer duos that are mostly siblings, friends, or couples. Pet influencers, where content focuses solely on the pet of a person or CGI influencer accounts that can be described as virtual avatars with content that is produced by artificial intelligence are other upcoming trends of influencer marketing (Activate 2019). In tourism, the Instagram account of the travelling cat 'Sukii' (@sukiicat) with 1.9 million followers shows the impact pet influencer accounts have momentarily. As with all trends on social media, it is difficult to predict what will take over long term or what will remain a niche-trend.

Another important element to distinguish between influencer content is the differentiation between sponsored and non-sponsored posts. In 2017, the Federal Trade Commission published an Endorsement Guide to ensure that influencers clearly disclose relationships they have with brands when they are promoting their services or products on social media (Federal Trade Commission 2017). Since then, influencers have to make sure they clearly state if they were paid to post certain social media content or not. Further, it became common that influencers also state when they were not sponsored or paid to promote a product, service, or destination that they are using/buying/visiting on their own. Despite the need to disclose brand relationships, research has indicated that sponsored posts do not seem to be affecting the impact influencers have on Generation Z as they still regard influencer-generated content as highly credible, authentic, and trustworthy (Dunkley 2017).

When it comes to brand-influencer relationships, engagement is an important factor measuring the success of influencer campaigns, which is often forgotten when focusing too much on the number of followers an influencer has (Shaw 2019). Thereby, micro-influencers are the ones that brands work with most often as they show high engagement rates among their followers (Activate 2019). Another contributing factor to the success of influencer campaigns is that posts by influencers are perceived as electronic Word of Mouth (eWOM), that can be explained as all online informal communication between users but also between suppliers and consumers (Evans et al. 2017; Litvin et al. 2008). Generation Z prefers WOM over any other marketing forms and will trust sponsored posts by an influencer more than direct marketing from the brand. These consumers want to listen to other consumers rather than brands (Pollack 2013). Influencers, therefore, have huge impact on Generation Z's purchase behaviour and decision-making process (Dunkley 2017; Newman 2014; Smart Insights 2015). Generation Z often finds a brand's content unengaging (Reggars 2015). As digital influencers already have established connections with their audience and know what content they want to see, they are invaluable in helping brands create online content that engage Generation Z audiences (Dunkley 2017).

Influencer Marketing in Hospitality and Tourism

Online opinion leaders sharing their travel experiences are not a completely new concept in tourism. Over 10 years ago, blogs were the most popular 'social media site' to share travel experiences (Schonfeld 2008). Travel bloggers had their own websites (=blogs) where they shared their opinions, advice, and experiences with their audience. These travel bloggers were widely used as a marketing tool for hotels and destinations to gain attention, improve the image and promote their services among bloggers' audiences (Glover 2009; Mack et al. 2008). Magno and Cassia (2018) found that a follower's intention to adopt the travel suggestions provided by bloggers depends on the blogger's perceived trustworthiness and the quality of information provided. As tourism marketing is mostly focused on visual content, vlogs, and later social media channels that are

7 Generation Z and Digital Influencers in the Tourism Industry   175

based on visuals have been successfully used to promote hotels, destinations, or experiences especially to inspire and influence travel decisions (Beeton 2004; Xiang and Gretzel 2010).

In order to acknowledge the importance and success of tourism and hospitality influencer marketing among Generation Z, it is crucial to understand that this particular generation is the first to grow up with the Internet from the very beginning. With the oldest Generation Z children being 10 years old at the time the first iPhone came on the market in 2007, they grew up with the popularity of mobile devices. Growing up with ubiquitous technology from the beginning resulted in change of behaviours, attitudes, and lifestyle among Generation Z when compared to older generations that had to adapt and adjust to the growing trend of technology in their stage of development (Dimock 2019).

As a result of growing up in the Internet era, one factor that strengthens the success of influencers among this generation is their ability to provide orientation through the unlimited amount of information available online. In the hospitality and tourism industry, the planning and decision-making process involves sorting through thousands of destinations, accommodations, tour options, airlines, restaurants, and other information that is necessary to plan a trip. Influencers take over the task to sort out the newest trends, products, travel destinations, or hotels and create posts about their choices of relevant ones. People, especially among Generation Z, already adapted their decision-making process to that and often follow the recommendations of selected influencers (Finch 2016). Therefore, getting the attention of Generation Z means to engage and provide them with useful information and rewarding experiences. Combined with their intensified online behaviour it is important for businesses to understand that all communication with Generation Z as their potential target group has to happen as engaging two-way communication instead of one-way messages (Finch 2016).

Another characteristic that can be seen as one of the factors resulting in a very specific niche of influencers is the ethnic diversity of Generation Z, specifically in tourism marketing. A research study by the Pew Research Center shows that nearly half (48%) of Americans between the age 6 and 21 are non-white (Fry and Parker 2018). As this population grows to become the next generation of travellers, this positively opens the door for more diversity and inclusivity in the online world of influencers. Not having reached mainstream yet, many influencers have started to gain popularity who do not conform to the image of a skinny, white female, male, or couple. Instagram accounts such as @latinaswhotravel, @travelingblackwomen, @fatgirlstraveling, @queertravel, or @lgbt_travelgram_represent examples of niche travel influencers that specifically target racial, ethnic, sexual orientation or other underrepresented minority groups. Although popular in the online community, brands, and destinations have not yet discovered the importance and the potential of working with underrepresented minorities in order to promote the diversity aspect of their products, services, or experiences (Lasane 2019; Yeboah 2019).

Another online trend that can be seen on social media platforms is influencers who promote sustainable travel. As Generation Z does not significantly differ from the former Generation Y and X, sustainability and climate change remain important topics for this generation (Parker et al. 2019). This trend is represented by influencers who question traditional ways of travelling and instead promote sustainable ways of transport (e.g. @greensuitcasetravel) or responsible travel focusing on local and indigenous communities (e.g. @I_like_local). Oftentimes it is also the local community itself that uses social media as a counter-narrative of the real life in a destination versus the solely visual 'instagrammable' content influencers show of a destination without referring to the context of a place (e.g. @mimaincuba) (McLaughlin 2019).

Influencer Marketing for Destinations

The potential of influencers when it comes to destination marketing for the tourism industry can be seen in a study by Expedia Group (2018) that shows that two-thirds of Generation Z travellers do not decide on a certain destination before they decide to take a trip. Therefore, they use social media and, in particular, channels of influencers as their source of inspiration to make a decision about their travel destination. Another study about social media influencers in Singapore showed that social media influencers can improve the image of a destination what in further notice can positively influence travel intentions of tourists (Ong and Ito 2019). Previous literature has indicated that destination image is strongly connected to travel intentions (Fakeye and Crompton 1991). Therefore, influencer content that generates positive feelings toward a destination or a positive destination image, may lead to travel intentions to that destination.

Many influencer marketing campaigns for destinations show the impact of these campaigns for the awareness and image of a destination. For example, the influencer campaign around #VisitPhilly featured seven influencers from New York City and generated 2.2 million impressions by sharing and tagging photos that were made at 'instagrammable' places within Philadelphia (Visit Philadelphia 2018). Also, the island of Curaçao gained the attention of nearly 10 million users by hiring influencers (PMYB 2019).

In juxtaposition to successful examples that show the positive impact of influencer marketing on a destination, possible negative consequences have to also be noted. Negative consequences of influencers are mostly connected to overtourism or an overflow of tourists that was provoked by paid and/or unpaid social media coverage. The world's longest and highest glass bridge located in China overseeing the Zhangjiajie Grand Canyon was closed 13 days after the opening in 2016 when an influx of too many tourists aiming for an 'instagrammable' picture sitting on the glass bottom floor of the bridge risked the stability of the structure (Wang and Yu 2016). After renovations and further safety tests, the bridge reopened two months later with a daily visitor limit and a monitoring system (Avakian 2016). The #poppynightmare is another example of negative consequences of influencers on destinations. After influencers posted selfies in the destination on social media, the influx of tourists caused damage and traffic problems in the Californian village, Lake Elsinore (Gammon 2019).

The 'insta-worthiness' or 'instagrammability' of a place describes features that are so aesthetically unique that it makes a place 'worthy' for visual social media channels such as Instagram. The desire to travel to one of these unique places featured on social media to get the same or a better picture may lead to an overflow of tourists to often small villages or places that have to cope with the problem of overcrowding, as seen in examples of the Greek island Santorini, the Trolltunga Fjord in Norway or a small place called Wanaka in New Zealand (Arnold 2018; Hayhurst 2017; Misrahi 2018; Miller 2017). Therefore, influencer marketing for destinations, while effective, should also be done with caution of negative consequences.

Influencer Marketing for the Hospitality Industry

The power of social media as a marketing tool for the hospitality industry is unprecedented (Ristova and Angelkova Petkova 2019). The food and beverage industry was one of the first hospitality sectors to benefit from the power of social media, particularly visual-based tools with photos of food swarming social media pages, and the hashtag #foodporn being one of the top trending hashtags on social media, where people post photos of their restaurant meals, especially while engaging in culinary tourism (Ranteallo and Andilolo 2017). 'Food representations via social media, especially in the form of photos, have created broader awareness of the diverse chain of global food production, distribution and consumption' (Ranteallo and Andilolo 2017: 117). Blogs and social media accounts dedicated to food and food photography are now commonplace.

With the restaurant industry heavily reliant on recommendations and WOM, restaurant or 'foodie' influencers are increasingly gaining prominence, with 35% of Americans indicating they have dined in a restaurant they saw in a post on social media (McLaren 2018). The website www.influence.co that provides a list of digital influencers based on number of followers for multiple categories lists over 2000 'restaurant influencers', with one of the top influencer @forkmeetsfood having 642 k followers on Instagram. However, digital influencers for restaurants are not limited to only those branded as 'restaurant influencers' who focus on this particular category, as many lifestyle, travel, and fashion influencers also frequently post photos of restaurants on their social media accounts (IZEA 2019). For example, lifestyle and travel influencer @tourdelust (306 k followers on Instagram) posted a photo on 5 December 2019 at a café in Paris, France which generated over

5,800 likes and 220 comments. In this post, @tourdelust wrote about her five favourite restaurants in Paris, enabling not only the café in the photo to gain reach and publicity, but also the other cafés and restaurants mentioned in the caption. Due to the popularity of visuals when it comes to marketing food and beverage businesses, Instagram is a popular platform for influencer marketing in this sector.

Hotel organizations have also reaped the benefits of influencer marketing. Platforms like Facebook, Twitter and Instagram have made it easier than ever for hotels to target specific markets based on age, location, gender, and interests (Ristova and Angelkova Petkova 2019). Lanz et al. (2010) recommend that hotels employ a dedicated social media marketer to engage target audiences. As with many hospitality and tourism industries, hotels are also dependent on WOM and with Generation Z, digital influencers are a key tool to spread eWOM to this target audience. For Generation Z, using an influencer to promote a hotel brand and facilities can draw a high level of attention and popularity, resulting in increased revenue and better visibility (Think with Google 2014).

Hotels are increasingly using influencers as the face of their advertisements. Influencers share content and opinions on social media platforms and help spread potentially viral conversations about the hotel brand, changing the way guests are making their accommodation decisions (Ristova and Angelkova Petkova 2019). Hotel guests are more inclined to make accommodation decisions based on what the influencers they follow are posting (Ristova and Angelkova Petkova 2019). For hotels, using digital influencers enables the opportunity to build relationships with the influencer's followers which can build relationships for the hotel brand. In addition, regardless of the size of the influencer's audience, they can enable a reach beyond what the hotel may be able to have on their own (Ristova and Angelkova Petkova 2019). By getting an influencer with a respective niche to share a post, the hotel can get thousands of potential guests viewing the post in a short amount of time.

The hotel industry benefits from using influencers in marketing campaigns, particularly among younger travellers who can be significantly influenced on where they plan their trip based on someone else's vacation posts on social media (Ristova and Angelkova Petkova

2019). Digital influencers are 'the new generation of reviewers' who can provide real-life experiences of the hotel through UGC (Ristova and Angelkova Petkova 2019). By collaborating with digital influencers, the hotel industry can generate engaging content which can drive bookings and accomplish the hotel's marketing goals. According to Ristova and Angelkova Petkova (2019) influencers that infuse their unique perspective into the content they post about a hotel can be as effective as online reviews when it comes to marketing to Generation Z.

As of 2019, the most important platforms for hotels to employ influencers are Instagram (89%), YouTube (70%), Facebook (45%), Blogs (44%), and Twitter (33%) (Bailis 2019). However, the hotel should choose the platform which suits their target audience best. At the same time, Ristova and Angelkova Petkova (2019) explain that even though each platform has its own audience, none of them compare to Instagram. Instagram content is easy to produce, approve, and publish, as a single photo and caption requires less production cost and effort than videos or longer form content, allowing the platform to be an affordable option for hotels to test influencer marketing. In addition, influencers tend to focus on a specific niche which can be aligned with the hotel's target audience. There are several influencers who focus on luxury resorts, for example, @amyseder uses Instagram to post stunning photos and videos of luxury resorts all over the world, from the Venetian Las Vegas to the Shangri-La in Muscat, Oman. With 241 k followers, @amyseder's photo at the Venetian with a paid partnership with @Vegas on 15 December 2019 generated over 2000 likes and 60 comments in under 24 hours.

While chain hotel brands may have the greatest budget for influencer marketing, Zhang et al. (2019) found that influencer marketing generated more positive attitudes towards independent hotel brands and suggests that hospitality managers of these brands consider the benefits of including them in their marketing strategy. As independent hotels are less known, influencer marketing can prove a credible source in communicating information about unfamiliar hotel properties (Zhang et al. 2019). As Generation Z becomes the next, and largest group of consumers of hospitality products, implementing digital influencers into the marketing strategy will prove an efficient way for hospitality brands to reach this target audience.

Influencer Marketing for Events and Festivals

Social media strategies of festivals and events have to include more than event hashtags and live videos. A study about influencer marketing reveals that Generation Z (together with Generation Y) are more attracted to buy tickets to events and festivals that they have seen through an influencer than any other generation (CPC Strategy 2018).

One of the most popular examples of a festival that is connected to influencer marketing is the case of the 2017 Fyre Festival that ended in a disaster. In order to promote the festival, Fyre Festival connected with around 400 Instagram influencers of all levels of popularity (celebrities and non-celebrities). In only 48 hours the festival reached over 300 million people and boosted their ticket sales. Despite the wide reach of users, the campaign is highly criticized for many reasons, including not disclosing paid partnerships between influencers and the festival, and the spread of false information (Shaw 2019).

Another festival that is known for its instagrammability, its density of attending celebrities and influencers, as well as being the festival with the highest growth of income, is the Coachella music festival. With social media as their most important promotion tool, Coachella is catered to millennials and Generation Z. Although most social media users know that posts of (staged) selfies are sponsored, the engagement of so-called 'Coachella-Moments' posts is high and created 4 million uses of Coachella-related hashtags to share and promote the festival in 2018 (Battan 2019; Pometsey 2019).

Hereby, different social media activities can be used by influencers to promote an event or a festival. Oftentimes, events let the respective influencer take over their social media accounts to post their content on the official social media account of the event. With this strategy influencers bring more followers to interact with the official event channels regularly. Live show coverage and 'behind-the-scenes' content can increase the engagement between followers and event with the help of influencers even more (Dahan 2015). Previous studies have found that online engagement with a festival throughout each phase (before, during, after) has led to increased sense of community and loyalty among attendees (Barbe et al. 2020). With the additional broad coverage before, during, and after the event, awareness of the event brand can be additionally improved (Martin 2019) and working with the right influencers, events can reach new and unknown audiences. As with all influencer related topics, congruence between the event and the influencer, who is covering the event, is the most important aspect (Businesswire 2016).

However, similar to destinations, also some festivals experience negative consequences of the influencer trend. The festival 'Burning Man' in the desert of Nevada was founded as an experimental event that targets alternative crowds of artists, musicians, and fans of a 'commerce-free' lifestyle. Since the instagrammability of Burning Man has been discovered by influencers, the festival shifted from offering camping and RV sites to all-inclusive camps with WIFI, air condition, and showers in lodges for $25,000–$100,000 for one week. Moreover, brand sponsorships were established for the first time and together with the spread of social media posts the festival is criticized to have lost its de-commercialization character (Battan 2019). Therefore, festivals and events, such as Burning Man, have to develop a strategy how to find the right influencer and how to benefit from them without losing their original character.

Influencer Marketing for the Transportation Sector

From airlines to trains, influencer marketing is also becoming widely used in the transportation sector. According to an article in The Guardian (Topham 2016), the airline industry was predicted to generate $40 billion (£30 billion) in profits in 2016, indicating prominence of this industry and its likelihood to grow as Generation Z enters the marketplace. Due to the high competition within the airline industry, many airlines are adopting influencer marketing to create content aimed at reaching engaged audiences. For example, the Australian airline Qantas partnered with travel influencer @aggie (815 k followers) in November 2019 where @aggie posted a series of photos in Australia, in a Qantas plane, and outside the Qantas check-in counter at the airport. One of these Instagram posts generated over 23,000 likes and 230 comments, highlighting the tremendous reach that Instagram influencers can have for the airline industry.

Quantas initiated a similar partnership in 2015, where they teamed with one of Australia's most influential influencers, Nicole Warne, to act as the airline's official digital consultant (Qantas 2015). This partnership allowed Qantas to reach Warne's 1.6 million Instagram followers by directing a series of video guides for the airline and posting brand-sponsored content (Qantas 2015). Similar digital influencer marketing efforts have been taken by British Airways and Alaska Airlines (Media Kix 2016).

However, the airline industry is not the only transportation sector to take advantage of influencer marketing. Amtrak launched the #Amtrak-TakeMeThere campaign in the beginning of 2019 where they used social media contests focused on UGC and digital influencers to increase their ridership (Zilles 2019). Instead of focusing on mega influencers, Amtrak's campaign targeted 'relatively unknown' users who are not expecting money from their creation of content for the brand. London North Eastern Railway (LNER) also launched an influencer campaign in the beginning of 2019 where they 'engaged a range of influencers to create authentic and relatable content on their journeys to and from destinations including Edinburgh, Leeds, and York' (Feeley 2019). The campaign used YouTube, Facebook, Instagram and Twitter for posting videos from 6 to 60 seconds in length by micro-influencers who capture their seemingly real-life experiences on their train journeys (Feeley 2019) (Fig. 7.2).

Recommendations for Influencer Marketing in Tourism and Hospitality

As seen in this chapter, influencer marketing is an effective way for reaching and persuading the purchasing behaviours of Generation Z across all sectors of the hospitality and tourism industry. The question remains, however, *how* to best optimize the use of digital influencers to solicit business from this lucrative and upcoming market. Researchers and marketers suggest several strategies. Based on the knowledge and

Influencer Marketing in Hospitality and Tourism			
Destinations	Hospitality	Events & Festivals	Transportation
2/3 of Gen Z decide to take a trip before they decide on the destination. Influencer marketing can... • aid in destination choice • enhance destination image and awareness • negatively impact destinations through overtourism	• Instagram is popular for marketing of food and beverage due to visual emphasis • Influencer marketing can allow hotels to target niche markets that coincide with their brand (luxury, budget, eco-friendly) • Influencers are 'the new generation of reviewers' who provide feedback on hotel experiences through UGC	• Gen Z (and Gen Y) are more attracted to events and festivals that they have seen through an influencer • Festivals such as Fyre Festival and Coachella have gained most of their attention from influencer marketing • Live show coverage and behind-the-scenes posts by influencers can increase online engagement with the event/festival	• Many airlines have adopted influencer marketing to create content aimed at reaching engaged audiences • Train companies (e.g. Amtrak, LNER) have also adopted influencer marketing to try and increase ridership using a variety of platforms, including YouTube, Facebook, Twitter and Instagram

Fig. 7.2 Summary of influencer marketing for each hospitality and tourism sector

behaviours of Generation Z, Swant (2015) recommends that organizations allow influencers to customize, curate, and remix the content to make it their own. Digital influencers know their audience best and therefore allowing them to create personalized content, where they put the brand in the background, may be seen as the best way to engage their followers and thus lead to a better eWOM for the brand. Using the established trust that digital influencers have with their audience to recommend the brand or organization is an effective marketing strategy for Generation Z.

As Generation Z sees digital influencers as celebrities, incorporating influencers in traditional advertisements may be more influential than using celebrities (Uzunoğlu and Kip 2014). In addition, Generation Z suffers from FOMO. By inviting influencers to promote events, festivals, destinations, hotels, and restaurants may entice the FOMO from their audiences and may be an effective strategy for increasing bookings and attendance. Further, because digital influencers need to keep updated and informed, marketers can take advantage of influencers to provide opportunities for launching new products or introducing an existing product to a new market (Uzunoğlu and Kip 2014).

Uzunoğlu and Kip (2014) provide various selection criteria for choosing which influencer to work with. First, there must be a match between the influencer and the brand. As the brand aims to reach the appropriate target audience, the match between this audience and the influencer's followers is essential. Influencer marketing goes beyond attempting to maximize reach. Micro-influencers and non-influencers can have tremendous impact because they have a unique bond with their followers. Second, the tone of voice and style of content must match with the brand's identity and the message they want to disseminate to their potential audiences. Third, the content they post should offer something of value to the brand's target audience. Uzunoğlu and Kip (2014) also suggest that they have a large number of followers and reach, however this may not be as relevant now as research has indicated that engagement with followers may actually decrease as the number of followers increases. Finally, reliability is an important criterion for selecting a digital influencer as recommendations from a reliable influencer bring prestige and credibility to the brand (Uzunoğlu and Kip 2014). Influencers should compliment the brand's marketing strategy but should not be the sole strategy.

This chapter highlights the effectiveness and importance of influencer marketing for Generation Z in the hospitality and tourism industry and provides recommendations for how to best optimize digital influencers to reach this growing market.

References

Aaker, J.L. (1995). Brand Personality: Conceptualization, Measurement and Underlyingpsychological Mechanism (doctoral dissertation). Available from ProQuest Dissertations and Theses database (UMI No. 9602828).

Activate. (2018). Two Sides of the Same Coin: Exploring the Brand and Influencer Relationship in Influencer Marketing. State of Influencer Marketing Study. https://static1.squarespace.com/static/5a9ffc57fcf7fd301e0e9928/t/5adf328c575d1fb25a2dc4c5/1524576915938/2018+State+of+Influencer+Marketing+Study+Report.pdf.

Activate. (2019). Double or Nothing: Betting Big on Influencer Marketing. State of Influencer Marketing Study. https://static1.squarespace.com/static/

5a9ffc57fcf7fd301e0e9928/t/5c7fd9c9f4e1fcc96b896b7e/1551882706715/ ACTIVATE+2019+Influencer+Marketing+Study.pdf.

Affilinet. (2015). Bloggers Trusted More Than Celebrities, Journalists, Brands and Politicians. *Affilinet.* https://www.affili.net/uk/about-affilinet/press-cen tre/2015/bloggers-trusted-more-than-celebrities-journalist.

Anderson, M., & Jiang, J. (2018). Teens, Social Media & Technology 2018. *Pew Research Center, 31,* 1673–1689.

Arnold, A. (2018). Here's How Much Instagram Likes Influence Millennials' Choice of Travel Destinations. https://www.forbes.com/sites/andrewarnold/ 2018/01/24/heres-how-much-instagram-likes-influence-millennials-choice-of-travel-destinations/#403c46f34eba.

Arthur, R. (2016). Generation z: 10 Stats from SXSW You Need to Know. *Forbes.* https://www.forbes.com/sites/rachelarthur/2016/03/16/gen eration-z/#69fbe57b2909.

Avakian, T. (2016). The World's Highest Glass Bridge Is Reopening to Tourists. https://www.travelandleisure.com/attractions/china-highest-glass-bridge-reopening.

Bailis, R. (2019). The State of Influencer Marketing: 10 Influencer Marketing Statistics to Inform Where You Invest. *BigCommerce.* https://www.bigcom merce.com/blog/influencer-marketing-statistics/#key-takeaways-on-influe ncer-marketing-for-2019.

Barbe, D., MacKay, K., Van Winkle, C., & Halpenny, E. (2020). A Clustering Approach to Understanding the Impact of Multi-Phase Social Media Engagement at Festivals. In *Proceedings from the 50th Annual Travel and Tourism Research Association International Conference,* Victoria, Canada.

Battan, C. (2019). Tech Billionaires Haven't Killed Burning Man's Anti-capitalist Spirit—But Influencers Might. https://www.fastcompany.com/ 90378291/tech-billionaires-havent-killed-burning-mans-anti-capitalist-spi rit-but-influencers-might.

Beeton, S. (2004). Rural Tourism in Australia—Has the Gaze Altered? Tracking Rural Images Through Film and Tourism Promotion. *International Journal of Tourism Research, 6*(3), 125–135.

Bradley, D. (2016). The New Influencers. *PR Week.* https://www.prweek.com/ article/1379310/new-influencers.

Bradley, D. (2019). Gen z on Marketing to gen z. *PR Week.* https://www.prw eek.com/article/1663064/gen-z-marketing-gen-z.

Businesswire. (2016). TapInfluence Unveils No. 1 Thing Motivating Social Influencers When Working with Brands, and It's Not Money. https://www.

businesswire.com/news/home/20161110005789/en/TapInfluence-Unveils-No.-1-Thing-Motivating-Social.

Carter, D. (2016). Hustle and Brand: The Sociotechnical Shaping of Influence. *Social Media + Society*, *2*(3), 1–12.

Chadha, R. (2018). For Influencers, Instagram Is the Clear-Cut Favorite. *eMarketer.com*. https://www.emarketer.com/content/for-influencers-instagram-is-close-to-the-only-platform-that-matters.

CPC Strategy. (2018). The 2018 Influencer Marketing Report. https://learn.cpcstrategy.com/rs/006-GWW-889/images/2018%20Influencer%20Marketing%20v3.pdf.

Dahan, E. (2015). 5 Ways Brands Partnered with Influencers During NYFW. https://www.socialmediatoday.com/news/5-ways-brands-partnered-with-influencers-during-nyfw/453548/.

Del Rowe, S. (2018, January–February). Tapping into Social's Sphere of Influence. *Customer Relationship Management*. Issue, 26–30.

De Veirman, M., Cauberghe, V., & Hudders, L. (2017). Marketing Through Instagram Influencers: The Impact of Number of Followers and Product Divergence on Brand Attitude. *International Journal of Advertising*, *36*(5), 798–828.

Digital Marketing Institute. (2019). The Changing Customer: How to Cater to Generation Z. https://digitalmarketinginstitute.com/en-ca/blog/the-changing-customer-how-to-cater-to-gen-z.

Dimock, M. (2019). Defining Generations: Where Millennials End and Generation Z Begins. Pew Research Center. https://www.pewresearch.org/fact-tank/2019/01/17/where-millennials-end-and-generation-z-begins/.

Djafarova, E., & Rushworth, C. (2017). Exploring the Credibility of Online Celebrities' Instagram Profiles in Influencing the Purchase Decisions of Young Female Users. *Computers in Human Behavior*, *68*, 1–7.

Dunkley, L. (2017). Reaching Generation Z: Harnessing the Power of Digital Influencers in Film Publicity. *Journal of Promotional Communications*, *5*(1).

Evans, N.J., Phua, J., Lim, J., & Jun, H. (2017). Disclosing Instagram Influencer Advertising: The Effects of Disclosure Language on Advertising Recognition, Attitudes, and Behavioral Intent. *Journal of Interactive Advertising*, 1–12.

Expedia Group Media Solutions. (2018). A Look Ahead: How Younger Generations are Shaping the Future of Travel. Report. https://info.advertising.expedia.com/hubfs/Content_Docs/Premium_Content/pdf/2018%20-%20Gen%20Z%20Travel%20Trends%20Study.pdf?hsCtaTracking=

a63196b4-62b8-4673-93e2-7d3ad0dc73e3%7Cfd9915c8-dc7f-492d-b123-265614cef08a.

Fakeye, P. C., & Crompton, J. L. (1991). Image Differences Between Prospective, First-Time, and Repeat Visitors to the Lower Rio Grande Valley. *Journal of travel research*, *30*(2), 10–16.

Federal Trade Commission. (2017). FTC Staff Reminds Influencers and Brands to Clearly Disclose Relationship. https://www.ftc.gov/news-events/press-rel eases/2017/04/ftc-staff-reminds-influencers-brands-clearly-disclose.

Feeley, M. (2019). LNER Unveils Influencer-Led Social Media Campaign. *The Drum*. https://www.thedrum.com/news/2019/03/20/lner-unveils-influe ncer-led-social-media-campaign.

Finch, J. (2016). What Is Generation Z, and What Does It Want? Fast Company. https://www.fastcompany.com/3045317/what-is-generation-z-and-what-does-it-want.

Forbes Communication Council. (2018). 12 Ways to Market to Generation Z. *Forbes*. https://www.forbes.com/sites/forbescommunicationscouncil/2018/08/29/12-ways-to-market-to-generation-z/#3a8f2ad35d3b.

Fontein, D. (2019). Everything Social Marketers Need to Know About Generation Z. *Hoot Suite*. https://blog.hootsuite.com/generation-z-statistics-social-marketers/.

Freberg, K., Graham, K., McGaughey, K., & Freberg, L. A. (2011). Who Are the Social Media Influencers? A Study of Public Perceptions of Personality. *Public Relations Review*, *37*(1), 90–92.

Fry, R., & Parker, K. (2018). Early Benchmarks Show 'Post-Millennials' on Track to Be Most Diverse, Best-Educated Generation Yet. Pew Research Center. https://www.pewsocialtrends.org/2018/11/15/early-benchmarks-show-post-millennials-on-track-to-be-most-diverse-best-educated-genera tion-yet/.

Gammon, K. (2019). #Superbloom or #poppynightmare? Selfie Chaos Forces Canyon Closure. https://www.theguardian.com/environment/2019/mar/18/super-bloom-lake-elsinore-poppies-flowers.

Ge, J., & Gretzel, U. (2018). A Taxonomy of Value Co-creation on Weibo—A Communication Perspective. *International Journal of Contemporary Hospitality Management*, *30*(4), 2075–2092.

Glover, P. (2009). Celebrity Endorsement in Tourism Advertising: Effects on Destination Image. *Journal of Hospitality and Tourism Management*, *16*, 16–23.

Hayhurst, L. (2017). Survey Highlights Instagram as Key Factor in Destination Choice Among Millennials. http://www.travolution.com/articles/102216/

survey-highlights-instagram-as-key-factor-in-destination-choice-among-mil lennials.

Hearn, A., & Schoenhoff, S. (2015). From Celebrity to Influencer: Tracing the Diffusion of Celebrity Value Across the Data Stream. *A Companion to Celebrity*, 194–212.

IZEA. (2019). Restaurant Social Media Influencers. https://izea.com/2019/04/26/restaurant-social-media-influencers/.

Katz, E. (1957). The Two-Step Flow of Communication: An Up-to-Date Report on an Hypothesis. *Public Opinion Quarterly*, *21*(1), 61–78.

Khamis, S., Ang, L., & Welling, R. (2017). Self-Branding, 'Micro-Celebrity' and the Rise of Social Media Influencers. *Celebrity Studies*, *8*(2), 191–208.

Lanz, L., Fischhof, B., & Lee, R. (2010). How Are Hotels Embracing Social Media in 2010. Examples of How to Start Engaging. *New York: HVS Sales and Marketing Services.*https://www.hvs.com/staticcontent/library/nyu2010/Journal/articles/SocialMediaIn2010.pdf.

LaSane, A. (2019). A Black Fashion Blogger Shared a Bunch of Pictures That Prove the Influencer World Has a Huge Diversity Problem. Insider. https://www.insider.com/influencer-calling-out-brands-lack-of-diversity-2019-6.

Litvin, S.W., Goldsmith, R.E., & Pan, B. (2008). Electronic Word-of-Mouth in Hospitality and Tourism Management. *Tourism Management*, *29*(3), 458–468.

Lyons, B., & Henderson, K. (2005). Opinion Leadership in a Computer-Mediated Environment. *Journal of Consumer Behaviour*, *4*(5), 319–329.

Mack, R.W., Blose, J.E., & Pan, B. (2008). Believe It or Not: Credibility of Blogs in Tourism. *Journal of Vacation Marketing*, *14*(2), 133–144.

Magno, F., & Cassia, F. (2018). The Impact of Social Media Influencers in Tourism. *Anatolia*, *29*(2), 288–290.

Martin, A. (2019). Why You Should Use Influencer Marketing to Promote Events. https://www.eventbrite.co.uk/blog/use-influencer-marketing-to-promote-events-ds00/.

McLaren, B. (2018). Infographic: Influence in the Restaurant Industry. *Seven Rooms.* https://sevenrooms.com/en/blog/influence-in-the-restaurant-industry/.

McLaughlin, M. (2019). Instagram Ruined Travel. A New Generation Of Influencers Is Trying To Fix It. Refinery29. https://www.refinery29.com/en-us/instagram-social-media-travel-sustainable-influencers.

Media Kix. (2016). How Top Social Influencers Help Airlines Soar. *Media Kix.* https://mediakix.com/blog/top-social-influencers-marketing-airlines/.

Miller, C. (2017). How Instagram Is Changing Travel. https://www.nationalg eographic.com/travel/travel-interests/arts-and-culture/how-instagram-is-cha nging-travel/.

Misrahi, T. (2018). #Travelgoals: Why Instagram Is Key to Understanding Millennial Tourism. https://www.weforum.org/agenda/2018/07/travelgoals-why-instagram-is-the-key-to-millennial-tourism/.

Newman, D. (2014). Why Brands Should Pay Influencers? *Forbes.* http:// www.forbes.com/sites/danielnewman/2014/11/19/why-brands-should-pay-influencers/#63d851b445e6.

Newman, D. (2015). Love It or Hate It: Influencer Marketing Works. *Forbes.* https://www.forbes.com/sites/danielnewman/2015/06/23/love-it-or-hate-itinfluencer-marketing-works/#54bfb854150b.

Oates, G. (2016, January 7). Australia Tourism Turns to USER-Generated GoPro Films for New Year's Eve Bash. *Skift.* https://goo.gl/1YVNXz.

Ohanian, R. (1990). Construction and Validation of a Scale to Measure Celebrity Endorsers' Perceived Expertise, Trustworthiness, and Attractiveness. *Journal of Advertising, 19*(3), 39–52.

Ong, Y.X., & Ito, N. (2019). "I Want to Go There Too!" Evaluating Social Media Influencer Marketing Effectiveness: A Case Study of Hokkaido's DMO. In J. Pesonen & J. Neidhardt (Eds.), *Information and Communication Technologies in Tourism 2019* (pp. 132–144). Springer, Cham.

Parker, K., Graf, N., & Igielnik, R. (2019). Generation Z Looks a Lot Like Millennials on Key Social and Political Issues. Pew Research Center. https://www.pewsocialtrends.org/2019/01/17/generation-z-looks-a-lot-like-millennials-on-key-social-and-political-issues/.

PMYB. (2019). 7 Great Travel Influencer Campaigns That Increased the Sales of Travel Brands! https://pmyb.co.uk/7-great-travel-influencer-campaigns/.

Pollack, S. (2013). Say Hello to the Next Generation: iGen. *PR Week.* http:// www.prweek.com/article/1275669/say-hello-next-generation-igen.

Pometsey, O. (2019). How Sponsorship Swallowed Coachella. https://www.gq-magazine.co.uk/article/coachella-2019-influencers-business.

Qantas. (2015). Qantas Announces Online Influencer, Nicole Warne as Digital Consultant. *Qantas Newsroom [Press Release].* https://www.qantas newsroom.com.au/media-releases/qantas-announces-online-influencer-nic ole-warne-as-digital-consultant/.

Ranteallo, I.C., & Andilolo, I.R. (2017). Food Representation and Media: Experiencing Culinary Tourism Through Foodgasm and Foodporn. In *Balancing Development and Sustainability in Tourism Destinations* (pp. 117–127). Springer, Singapore.

Reggars, N. (2015). Generation Z: The 21st Century's Social Media Managers. *Campaign Live.* http://www.campaignlive.com/article/generation-z-21st-cen turys-social-media-managers/1351541.

Ristova, C., & Angelkova Petkova, T. (2019). How Are Social Media Influencers Changing the Hotel Industry. Can Your Hotel Benefit from It? In *Proceedings from the 18th International Scientific Conference—Contemporary Trends in Tourism and Hospitality "Get ready for iGeneration"* Novi Sad, Serbia.

Saul, H. (2016). Instafamous: Meet the Social Media Influencers Redefining Celebrity. *The Independent.* http://www.independent.co.uk/news/people/ins tagram-model-natasha-oakley-iskra-lawrence-kayla-itsines-kendall-jenner-jor dyn-woods-a6907551.html.

Schonfeld, E. (2008). Top Social Media Sites of 2008 (Facebook Still Rising). https://techcrunch.com/2008/12/31/top-social-media-sites-of-2008-facebook-still-rising/.

Shankman, S. (2014a). The Changing Relationship Between Travel Brands and Instagram Influencers. *Skift.* Retrieved from https://skift.com/2014/10/02/the-changing-relationship-between-travel-brands-and-instagram-influe ncers/.

Shankman, S. (2014b). Instagram Influencers Double the Reach of Los Angeles' Latest Campaign. *Skift.* Retrieved from https://skift.com/2014/07/14/instagram-influencers-double-the-reach-of-los-angeles-latest-campaign/.

Shaw, A. (2019). What Marketers Can Learn from the Fyre Festival's Influencer Marketing Fiasco. https://www.forbes.com/sites/forbescommunicatio nscouncil/2019/04/16/what-marketers-can-learn-from-the-fyre-festivals-inf luencer-marketing-fiasco/#1a70950e1308.

Smart Insights. (2015). From Blogger to Powerhouse Advocate: How Digital Influencers Changed the Fashion World. Smart Insights. http://www.smarti nsights.com/online-pr/influencer-marketing/digital-influencer-strategy/.

Solis, B. (2016) The Influencer Marketing Manifesto: Why the Future of Influencer Marketing Starts with People and Relationships Not Popularity. *Report by Altimeter on Behalf of TapInfluence.* https://cdn2.hubspot.net/hubfs/1882019/TapInfluence/Resources/1020%20%20Influencer_Market ing_Manifesto.pdf.

Solis, B. (2012). The Rise of Digital Influence: A "How-to" Guide for Businesses to Spark Desirable Effects and Outcomes Through Social Media Influence. *Altimeter Group.* https://www.slideshare.net/Altimeter/the-rise-of-digital-influence.

Swant, M. (2015). Millennials Aren't Who You Think They Are, The Economist Says 'They Curate, They Consume and They Create'. *Ad Week*. http://www.adweek.com/news/advertising-branding/millennials-arent-who-you-think-they-are-economist-says-167428.

Think with Google. (2014). The 2014 Traveler's Road to Decision. https://www.thinkwithgoogle.com/consumer-insights/2014-travelers-road-to-decision/.

Topham, G. (2016). Airline Industry Profits Expected to Increase by 12% in 2016. *The Guardian*. https://www.theguardian.com/business/2016/jun/02/airline-industry-profits-expected-to-increase-2016-iata.

Uzunoğlu, E., & Kip, S.M. (2014). Brand Communication Through Digital Influencers: Leveraging Blogger Engagement. *International Journal of Information Management*, *34*(5), 592–602.

Visit Philadelphia. (2018). Key Stories & Stats from the Annual Hospitality Event. https://www.visitphilly.com/media-center/press-releases/visit-philadelphia-reports-a-record-2017-for-leisure-tourism-announces-marketing-plans-for-2018/.

Wagner, C., & Bolloju, N. (2005). Supporting Knowledge Management in Organizations with Conversational Technologies: Discussion Forums, Weblogs, and Wikis. *Journal of Database Management*, *16*(2), i–viii.

Wang, S., & Yu, E. (2016). China's Record-Breaking Glass Bridge Closes. https://www.cnn.com/travel/article/china-zhangjiajie-glass-bridge-closed/index.html.

Xiang, Z., & Gretzel, U. (2010). Role of Social Media in Online Travel Information Search. *Tourism Management*, *31*(2), 179–188.

Yeboah, S. (2019). By Only Using White Influencers, Brands Are Telling Black Women We Don't Belong. Metro. https://metro.co.uk/2019/06/03/by-only-using-white-influencers-brands-are-telling-black-women-we-dont-belong-9744197/.

Zhang, L., Kuo, P.J., & McCall, M. (2019). Microcelebrity: The Impact of Information Source, Hotel Type, and Misleading Photos on Consumers' Responses. *Cornell Hospitality Quarterly*, *60*(4), 285–297.

Zilles, C. (2019). New Way to Think About Social Media Influencers. *Social Media HQ*. https://socialmediahq.com/a-new-way-to-think-about-social-media-influencers/.

8

Generation Z: Young People's Perceptions of Cruising Safety, Security and Related Risks

Truc H. Le and Charles Arcodia

Introduction

The increase in demand for cruising in all markets worldwide signifies that the industry is on an upward trend (Cruise Lines International Association - CLIA 2019), contributing to increasingly sophisticated passenger expectations and a requirement for higher satisfaction levels during cruise trips. Cruising's rapid growth and progressively sophisticated customer demands suggest that competition within the industry is becoming more intense. This competitiveness prompts significant concerns for cruise operators, who must satisfy their current customers in order to increase customer retention and attract new customers (Baker and Stockton 2013). To remain viable with this retention rate, it is vital

T. H. Le (✉) · C. Arcodia
Department of Tourism, Sport and Hotel Management, Griffith University, Brisbane, QLD, Australia
e-mail: truc.le@griffith.edu.au

© The Author(s), under exclusive license to Springer Nature Switzerland AG 2021
N. Stylos et al. (eds.), *Generation Z Marketing and Management in Tourism and Hospitality*,
https://doi.org/10.1007/978-3-030-70695-1_8

for the cruising business to improve cruise experiences and implement effective marketing strategies.

Previous research found that customer satisfaction and cruising constraints are key variables impacting customer cruise retention (Baker and Stockton 2013; Bowen et al. 2014; Le and Arcodia 2018). Moreover, safety and security of cruise passengers play key roles in determining on-board cruise experiences and satisfaction (Bowen et al. 2014), thus influence purchase intentions, and mediate the decision-making processes (Henthorne et al. 2013; Le and Arcodia 2018). As a result, having a thorough understanding of both new and returning passengers, especially their perceptions of risk, safety and security while on a cruise, is a significant success factor for cruise companies who wish to remain competitive.

Characterised by a long period of cohabitation, restricted space and a variety of activities both on-board and at ports of call (Kak), cruise passengers are exposed to a number of risks on-board, which have commonly been reported and reviewed in the cruising literature: infection outbreaks, sexually transmissible diseases, motion sickness, cruise accidents, and terrorism, piracy and crime. Nevertheless, very few studies investigate how people perceive risks, safety and security on cruise ships (i.e. Ahola et al. 2014; Baker and Stockton 2013; Bowen et al. 2014; Henthorne et al. 2013; Le and Arcodia 2017, 2018; Neri et al. 2008). These studies, however, only examine passengers' perceptions of a single risk, so consequently they lack a holistic approach that offers a more comprehensive understanding of risk perceptions from a consumer perspective. This scarcity has posed significant gaps in understanding cruise passengers' behaviour, specifically perceptions of risks, safety and security.

More importantly, the population targeted in the aforementioned studies was cruise passengers in the actual ships, while the investigation among potential cruisers has generally been absent, not to mention the emerging segment of youth markets (Le and Arcodia 2018). A number of recent studies have indicated that cruisers are becoming younger and have been an attractive market segment (CLIA 2019; Le and Arcodia 2017, 2018). Young people regarded in this study are Generation Z/Post-Millennials, who were born from the mid-1990s to the late 2000s

(Montana and Petit 2008; Williams and Page 2011). According to CLIA (2019), Gen Z (Generation Z) is a new category of cruisers that is set to become the largest consumer generation by the year 2020 and set to outpace even the Millennials. This generation like the Millennials, prefers experiences over material items and is seeking travel to multiple destinations and unique experiences, such as for example, music festivals at sea (CLIA 2019). In terms of travel motivation, CLIA (2018) points out that the majority of Millennials and Gen Z cruisers and non-cruisers take cruise vacations to see and do new things and to explore new adventures. In terms of risk-taking behaviour, young people particularly possess different travel motivations and personality traits from the broader population, such as sensation-seeking and a stronger inclination to engage in physical risks (Carr 2001; Lepp and Gibson 2003). Further, they are more prone to the sensation-seeking phenomenon of 'out of space, out of time, and out of mind' (Pritchard and Morgan 2006) that can easily distort their risk perceptions and trigger risk-taking behaviour (Berdychevsky and Gibson 2015). Considering cruisers enjoy travelling in groups (i.e. with friends, companions, spouses and family), and their travel motivation is to have fun and adventure (CLIA 2018) and to search for authentic experiences (Le et al. 2019), it is therefore imperative to understand how the emerging Gen Z market perceives risks and safety on cruise ships.

Following this, the ensuing inquiry is put forward with the aim of gaining a better understanding of this important cruising market segment: how and to what extent Gen Z perceives safety, security and risks associated with cruise ships. In response to this question, the paper utilises the relationship between the two risk components: uncertainty and adverse consequences (Bauer 1960; Le and Arcodia 2018) to approach risk perceptions expressed by Gen Z. Specifically, this study seeks to answer two research questions: (1) to what extent Gen Z feels safe and secure when on a cruise ship; and (2) how Gen Z perceives physical risks on cruise ships. These questions are significant to understand the behaviours of young people and obtain appropriate responses to changes in this market demand.

The next section consists of a brief analytical review of current literature on cruising risk perceptions, and a discussion of risk perception measurement. The methodology used is then explained and the empirical findings are subsequently presented and discussed. Finally, research implications and recommendations for cruise operators are provided.

Literature Review

Defining Perception of Cruise-Related Risks

Defining Risk Perception

Defining risk perception firstly requires the understanding of risk conceptualisation. Risk is defined as the uncertainty of buying a product (Dowling and Staelin 1994), or the unfavourable outcomes of a purchase (Cunningham 1967). Above all, however, Dowling (1986) and the international standard, ISO 31000 (2009) offer a relatively sufficient definition of risk by conceptualising a risk in a combination of the likelihood of occurrence, and the consequences resulting from that event.

The aforementioned risk definition has directed how risk perception is conceptualised in this study. Specifically, this study adopts a similar two-dimensional framework of risk perception proposed by Bauer (1960) including uncertainty and adverse consequences. As risk perception is seen as subjective risk judgements for harmful activities (Slovic et al. 1982), the framework proposed by Bauer (1960) is sufficient to conceptualise this somewhat fuzzy consumer behaviour concept (Dowling 1986). Specifically, Bauer (1960) defines uncertainty as probabilistic beliefs, and adverse consequences as the importance of loss when trying to accomplish a set of buying objectives. Apart from the risk conceptualisation, perceptions of risk can also be defined in terms of multi-faceted types of loss such as social, physical, financial, psychological, and time loss (Dowling 1986). This study focuses on physical risks since it deals with the loss caused by the surrounding physical environment on the ship, specifically, the five types of physical risks on cruise ships which have attracted research interest over the last decades: infections outbreaks; sexually transmitted infections (STIs); motion sickness; cruise accidents; and terrorism, piracy and crime. This typology of physical risks has been proposed in Le and Arcodia's (2018) conceptual framework.

Types of Physical Cruise-Related Risks

Infection outbreaks on cruise ships represent a significant public health issue considering the increasing number of passengers potentially at risk (Mouchtouri et al. 2010). The infectious agents can enter and spread easily through the water and food supply or sanitation systems and result in substantial illness, which is even worse considering the proximity and interactions among passengers and crew members in confined spaces (Bert et al. 2014; Kak 2007).

Sexually transmissible infections (STIs) are the most common sexual health issues, acquired by engaging in unprotected sexual behaviour or having multiple sexual partners (Bellis et al. 2004; Berdychevsky and Gibson 2015). Travellers, especially young people, are most at risk of involving themselves in risky sexual behaviours and acquiring STIs because of the absence of normal strictures during the travel period (Sadovszky 2008); and the higher hedonistic, sensation-seeking and risk-taking behaviour of young people which distorts their risk perceptions and normative inhibitions (Bellis et al. 2004; Berdychevsky and Gibson 2015).

Motion sickness is one of the main reasons why travelling by sea can be regarded as a risky mode of travel and acts as a constraint which demotivates cruising intention (Weeden et al. 2016). There have only been a few studies that have investigated motion sickness as a cruising problem that may affect passengers' experiences negatively. Cooper et al. (1997) revealed 47.8% of all hospital incidents were for motion sickness. Bledsoe et al. (2007) observed patterns of injuries and illnesses among cruise passengers in Antarctica and found that motion sickness was the most common cause for medical visits. Motion sickness was also found to have significant impacts on on-board safety since it reduces the crew members' effectiveness and improvising capability when confronting a hazardous situation (Fernandez 2013).

The incident of collision, equipment failure, explosion, fire or flooding on cruise ships can result in severe damage with catastrophic consequences (Ahola et al. 2014; Ventikos 2013), thus placing ship safety as a key priority for ship design and operation (Spyrou 2010). Existing literature places significant emphasis on determinants and severity of cruise-related on-board accidents, yet how people perceive safety within the cruising context is mostly under-examined.

Terrorism, piracy and crime are major security threats that can cause serious violence to cruise passengers (Bowen et al. 2014; Panko et al. 2009; White and Wydajewski 2002) and even force the shipping companies to end their operation in several geographic areas. While terrorism is increasingly becoming one of the greatest threats to cruise passengers (Bowen et al. 2014; Rubackly 2010), pirate attacks continue to be a serious problem for cruise operators and cruise passengers in certain regions (Nikolić and Missoni 2013). It is argued that although safety and security are considered a signature feature of cruising, cruise ships still experience inherent vulnerabilities from unpredictable terrorist attacks (Bowen et al. 2014; Greenberg et al. 2006), possible threats from piracy (Kraska and Wilson 2009), and assaults, thefts, and other crimes on-board (Dickerson 2014).

Measuring Risk Perception: The Interaction Between Uncertainty and Adverse Consequences

The two-dimensional framework of risk perception proposed by Bauer (1960) further suggests a measurement of risk perceptions by determining the relationship between the two components of risks: uncertainty and adverse consequences (see Table 8.1). This framework has been utilised by many perceived risk scholars since 1976 (e.g. Mitchell and Vassos 1997; Peter and Ryan 1976; Winter and Parker 2007). Table 8.1 presents two approaches to determine the interaction between uncertainty and adverse consequences; however, the multiplicative equation is considered less conceptually approachable than the additive because it poses some limitations from a mathematical standpoint, that if either

Table 8.1 The relationship between uncertainty and adverse consequences (adopted from Le and Arcodia 2018)

Multiplicative version	Perceived risk = Uncertainty × Adverse consequences Overall perceived risk = $\sum_{i=1}^{n}$ Uncertainty × Adverse consequences n = the number of types of loss i
Additive version	Perceived risk = Uncertainty + Adverse consequences Overall perceived risk = $\sum_{i=1}^{n}$ Uncertainty + Adverse consequences n = the number of types of loss i

uncertainty or adverse consequences equals zero, it will result in a perceived risk of zero (Dowling 1986).

Perceptions of Safety, Security and Cruise-Related Risks

Previous cruising literature demonstrates a limited knowledge of risk perceptions and their impacts on cruiser decision-making and behaviour. Henthorne et al. (2013) investigate risk and safety perceptions on cruise ships and suggest that risk and safety perceptions have significant impacts on cruisers' intentions to return to a specific destination. Ahola et al.'s (2014) findings indicate perceptions of the surrounding cruise environment significantly affect cruise behaviour, suggesting that passengers' conduct may put all other passengers' safety at risk if they obtain inadequate safety perceptions. Peter (2017) examines cruise passengers' security perceptions and reports 70% of the participants from all ages considered security to be a serious issue and they take it into consideration when deciding on a cruise holiday. However, the generalisability of this study is questionable since the findings emerged from only 81 questionnaire responses.

Other studies delimit their scope by examining perceptions of specific cruise-related risks. For instance, Neri et al. (2008) examine passengers' hand sanitation beliefs and practices and found that passengers did not perceive the disease's consequences as serious and did not understand the risk factors associated with contracting the disease. Baker and

Stockton (2013) study passengers' perceptions of food safety and indicate that cruise ship's food safety practices were not the major concern for cruise passengers because they are knowledgeable about food safety and highly aware of serious incidents widely reported by media. Bowen et al. (2014) focus on investigating perceptions of terrorist threats in UK and report nearly half of the respondents perceived the possibility of a terrorist attack on a cruise ship to be likely, even though safety and security is seen as a 'hallmark' of cruising. Peter (2016) examines security awareness among cruise passengers and observes that the cruise passengers did not see any visible security which had taken place; however, they were not concerned with the security invisibility and were not willing to experience a high level of 'invasive' security (Peter 2016). However, the subsequent study (Peter 2017) reports cruise consumers were not very concerned about security when planning a cruise holiday. The lack of methodological clarity calls for a more rigorous research approach towards risk perceptions on cruise ships. Specifically, the extant literature has touched only the smallest tip of the iceberg where perceptions have been examined among a single risk, calling for a holistic view of risk perceptions on cruise ships and a systematic methodological approach towards such perceptions.

Risk Perceptions in Youth Travel Behaviour

In the context of consumer behaviour, existing literature places significant emphasis on the effect of risk perceptions on purchase intentions (Henthorne et al. 2013; Le and Arcodia 2017, 2018; Sönmez and Graefe 1998b). Reisinger and Mavondo (2006) further emphasise that risk perceptions create anxiety and fear affecting the purchasing intentions, which place substantial travel constraints, encourage more cautious behaviours and therefore negatively affect tourist experiences and satisfaction. On the other hand, risk perceptions can simulate risk-taking behaviour that, while risk-adverse may always attempt to reduce the perceived risk, risk-taking is inclined to ignore the risk consequences (Le and Arcodia 2018).

However, inadequate research in travel risk perception has been conducted among young travellers, even though this segment represents an increasingly dominant actor in contemporary tourism (Sarman et al. 2016). Previous studies on the topic of young travellers' risk perception are listed as followings (i.e. Adam 2015; Carr 2001; Desivilya et al. 2015; Lepp and Gibson 2003; Lin et al. 2012; Qvarnström and Oscarsson 2014; Pizam et al. 2004; Sarman et al. 2016). Adam's (2015) study on backpackers' risk perceptions found that although backpackers were found to mostly be associated with physical risks due to their risk-taking and sensational-seeking nature (Adam 2015; Carr 2001), they are more concerned with expectation risks (or service failure) than physical risks. Likewise, despite many potential risks imposed when travelling overseas, young tourists are inclined towards adventure tourism which exposes them to novel and sensational experiences (Lin et al. 2012). Young tourists are also akin to 'out of space, out of time, and out of mind' behaviour (Pritchard and Morgan 2006) which easily distorts their risk perceptions (Berdychevsky and Gibson 2015), makes them more vulnerable to STIs and increases risk-taking behaviour with little experience in prevention efforts against HIV/STIs, especially when it comes to travelling abroad (Qvarnström and Oscarsson 2014). This research, however, mentioned young tourists as a generic cohort, which lacks substantial attention on the specific travel behaviour of Gen Z. It is indeed important for tourism researchers to be up-to-date with this emerging market, as well as to understand the market's behaviour in advance in order to accommodate their travel needs and wants.

These issues therefore raise significant awareness of understanding youth risk perceptions in the context of cruise ships, which has been generally overlooked thus far. Moreso, no research has attempted to examine Gen Zers' perceptions of risk on cruise ships. As a result, two questions are explored in this study as follows:

1. To what extent does Gen Z feel safe and secure when travelling on a cruise ship?

This question is posed in order to gain a better understanding of this segment's perceptions of cruise ships concerning with their feelings of safety and security.

2. To what extent does Gen Z perceive physical risks on cruise ships?

This question is posed in order to determine this segment's perceptions of specific physical risks that have been discussed in the literature and are of significance for the cruise industry.

Methodology

This study utilises a quantitative approach to respond to the two research questions and adopts Bauer's (1960) two-dimensional framework of risk perception. The population considered for this study is Gen Z, who were born from the mid-1990s to the late 2000s, following the age range defined by Montana and Petit (2008) and Williams and Page (2011). However, due to ethical concerns regarding research dealing with participants under 18 years old, the focus is on participants who were 18 and above. Following this, a questionnaire was developed as a tool to examine perceptions of cruising safety, security and related risks among Gen Z. The questionnaire used in this study consisted of eight closed-ended questions. Table 8.2 specifies the items and the scales used in each question. The questionnaire was subsequently pre-tested among 10 participants to identify any ambiguity and to test if the research questions and elicited responses were congruent with the aims of the study. The 10 participants were chosen on the basis that they had never cruised before, to ensure that all questions could be understood by potential respondents irrespective of their cruising experience.

The questionnaire was in English and administered via an online survey and targeted young people whose ages ranged from 18 to 25 years (representing the upper age range of Gen Z) and who were members of social media networks. Snowball sampling was chosen for this study to make use of the widespread network generated through social media. Initially 60 participants were identified and approached through the

8 Generation Z: Young People's Perceptions of Cruising Safety ...

Table 8.2 Construct and selection of its measures

Construct measured	Question	Scale	Items
Perceptions of cruise ship safety and security	How safe you would feel when you are: – Participating in pool activities on-board – Participating in alcohol-related scenes (e.g. bars, clubs) on-board – On a ship going through uncomfortable weather – Dining in a restaurant with lots of people on-board – On a ship visiting unstable political regions	Five-point scale (1 = very unsafe; 5 = very safe)	Items related to perceptions of cruising safety in selected situations Items resemble Pinhey and Iverson's (1994), Reisinger and Mavondo's (2005), and Sönmez and Graefe's (1998a) seven-item scale used to measure travellers' perceptions of safety in various tourism and recreation situations (i.e. sightseeing, water sports)

(continued)

researchers' social network and asked to suggest the questionnaire link to other participants who also fit the criteria, which allowed a snowball effect of the sample. Of the total 270 responses received, there were 243 valid responses.

Responses from the questionnaire were tabulated and analysed and the means of these two components and the overall perceived risk scores were calculated to examine the perception of each risk. The perceived risk score was then classified into a five-scale ranking which closely resembles the risk rating matrix (see Table 8.3). In this study, this matrix presents a perceived risk rating that is used during perceived risk assessment to define various levels of perceived risk based on the two components:

204   T. H. Le and C. Arcodia

Table 8.2 (continued)

Construct measured	Question	Scale	Items
Perceptions of cruise-related risks	How likely do you think these risks will happen on cruise ships? How severe do you think the consequences of these risks will be?	Five-point scale (1 = rare; 5 = almost certain) Five-point scale (1 = negligible; 5 = severe)	Five cruise-related risks documented from existing cruising literature: infection outbreaks; sexually transmissible infections; motion sickness; cruise accidents; and terrorism, piracy and crime Scale adapted from Cunningham's (1967) and Mitchell and Vassos's (1997) measurement of perceived risk: Overall perceived risk = Perceived probability + Perceived severity of the consequences

perceived probability and perceived severity (Ruan et al. 2015). This perceived risk rating incorporates the additive version of perceived probability and perceived severity (on a scale of one to five for each element) in representing the perceived risk (the overall perceived risk score ranging from two to ten).

Table 8.3 Perceived risk rating

		Perceived probability				
		1	2	3	4	5
Perceived severity	1	2 Minimum	3 Minimum	4 Low	5 Low	6 Moderate
	2	3 Minimum	4 Low	5 Low	6 Moderate	7 High
	3	4 Low	5 Low	6 Moderate	7 High	8 High
	4	5 Low	6 Moderate	7 High	8 High	9 Extreme
	5	6 Moderate	7 High	8 High	9 Extreme	10 Extreme
		Overall perceived risk score = (2;10)				

Findings and Discussion

Table 8.4 presents the characteristics of the sample respondents in terms of gender, ethnicity, age and past cruise experiences. The majority of respondents was from the 22–25 age range (60.1%), yet only 28% of respondents from this age range had cruised before. A higher proportion emerging from the 18–21 age range had cruised before (33%), which

Table 8.4 Characteristics of respondents

Characteristics	Responses	Percentage	N
Gender			N = 243
Female	132	54.3	
Male	111	45.7	
Ethnicity			
Asia	157	51.5	
North America	75	24.6	
Europe	37	12.1	
Oceania	31	10.2	
Others	5	1.6	
Age			
18–21	97	39.9	
22–25	146	60.1	
Past cruise experiences			
Have cruised	73	30.0	
Have never cruised	170	70.0	

may potentially result from having cruise trips with families. Overall, cruisers (who had cruised before) only accounted for nearly one-third (30%) of the Gen Z sample in this study. Nevertheless, this study does not focus solely on the cruiser's perspective, since the insights emerging from ones that had no cruise experiences will also be particularly useful for implementing marketing strategies to attract new cruise customers. This responds appropriately to the notion that Gen Z is set to become the largest consumer generation by 2020 (CLIA 2019). Also, while the majority of sampled respondents (51.5%) was of Asian ethnicity (yet 35% had cruised before), which may compromise the study's generalisability, this is considered a preliminary effort to target more specifically the Asian cruisers—a strongly potential and loyal market since 95% of Asian ethnicity (the highest among other ethnicities) are very likely to book a cruise for their next vacation (CLIA 2018).

Perceptions of Safety and Security

Feelings of safety may vary depending on the circumstances with which people are involved (Pinhey and Iverson 1994; Sönmez and Graefe 1998a). Table 8.5 depicts the means and standard deviations of respondents' perceived safety and security in relation to selected cruising situations. Specifically, dining in a restaurant with many people ($M = 3.7$) received the highest safety assessments, followed by pool activities and alcohol-related scenes ($M = 3.6$). These perceptions appear to contradict the actual risk measures, that: swimming pools usually experience high

Table 8.5 Perceived safety in selected cruising situations

Cruising situations	Mean	SD
Pool activities	3.6	0.9
Alcohol-related scenes (e.g. bars, clubs)	3.6	0.9
Uncomfortable weather	2.4	1.1
Restaurant with lots of people	3.7	0.9
Unstable political regions	2.2	1.1

Note 1 = Very Unsafe
5 = Very safe

numbers of passengers, who are more inclined to suffer from Legionnaires' disease (Kak 2007), and from other serious diseases that result from close interaction with others and poor sanitation systems (Cramer et al. 2006). Also, a cruise ship setting with high alcohol consumption is argued to potentially lead to crimes; sexual assaults; and even unprotected sexual behaviour, which causes a considerably higher likelihood of acquiring STIs (Berdychevsky and Gibson 2015; Panko et al. 2009). These high perceived ratings can also be explained through the less significant information people (Gen Z) expose to mass media and social media when it comes to risks associated with crowded areas such as swimming pools and restaurants, as well as hedonic activities induced from the high level of alcohol consumption.

On the other hand, respondents reported feeling least safe when visiting unstable political regions ($M = 2.2$). This finding supports the results from Sönmez and Graefe (1998b) that perceived safety is strongly related to avoiding politically unstable regions, and Brun et al. (2011) and Peter's (2016, 2017) studies that tourists were more concerned about their own safety and security especially after major terrorist incidents. For example, in Sönmez and Graefe's (1998b) study, it was reported that people felt safer during cruise travel to North America, Europe, and Africa, whereas they reported feeling more unsafe visiting Asia and South America. Cruise operators also tend to avoid troubled regions and countries (or even terminate the route as in the case of MSC and Costa after the Tunisia attack in 2015) as they would not get the number of passengers required nor the insurance providers who are willing to absorb the associated risks (Peter 2017).

Perception of Physical Risks on Cruise Ships

Perceptions of the five cruise-related risks were ranked in terms of the three perceived risk components: perceived probability, perceived severity and overall perceived risk. Table 8.6 depicts the mean scores and standard deviations for each risk according to the three perceived risk components. It was found that motion sickness ($M = 3.40$) was believed to most likely occur on cruise ships followed by infection outbreaks ($M = 2.60$),

Table 8.6 Means and standard deviations of perceived probability, perceived severity and overall perceived risk

Cruise-related risks	Probability		Severity		Overall risk	
	Mean	SD	Mean	SD	Mean	SD
Infection outbreaks	2.60	0.94	3.27	0.99	5.87	1.56
STIs	2.41	1.09	3.04	1.11	5.45	1.72
Motion sickness	3.40	1.10	2.67	1.04	6.07	1.68
Cruise accidents	2.50	0.98	3.94	1.08	6.44	1.48
Terrorism, piracy & crime	2.35	1.12	3.91	1.27	6.25	1.63

Note 1 = Rare, Not at all
5 = Almost Certainly, Severe.

which corresponds to the actual measured risk that motion sickness and infection outbreaks were the most common on-board illnesses (Bledsoe et al. 2007). Terrorism, piracy, and crime ($M = 2.35$) was perceived as the least likely risk, supporting the argument that the world's oceans have not historically been a major locus of terrorist activity with only 2% of the international incidents in the last 30 years (Greenberg et al. 2006). The finding also aligns with Nikolić and Missoni's (2013) assertion that the probability of being injured or killed on-board by pirates is actually very low in the context of declining piracy on the world's seas.

While motion sickness was believed to most likely occur on cruise ships, it was perceived as resulting in the least severe consequences ($M = 2.67$). In contrast, although terrorism, piracy and crime were regarded as the most unlikely risk, it received the second highest perceived severity level ($M = 3.91$). Cruise accidents ($M = 3.94$) were in fact considered as the most severe risk. Overall, one emerging theme is that the risk with very high probability was regarded as less severe in terms of consequences, and vice versa. This signifies an interesting assumption about Gen Z's perceptions: that they are inclined to believe that risks with high possibility are less harmful than uncommon risks. Overall, cruise accidents ($M = 6.44$) received the highest overall perceived risk assessment, followed by terrorism, piracy and crime ($M = 6.25$). This finding supports the work of Bowen et al. (2014), Panko et al. (2009) and Rubackly (2010) that one of the greatest threats cruise passengers face today is terrorism and crime. This also aligns with Greenberg et al.'s (2006) argument that despite the low incident rate, there has been ongoing concern regarding maritime terrorism since a single strike can lead to disastrous injuries.

Infection Outbreaks

Percentage distributions of the overall perceived risk component of the five cruise-related risks are presented in Fig. 8.1. In general, the respondents were concerned about infection outbreaks on cruise ships. The probability of infection outbreaks was regarded as the second most likely risk to happen ($M = 2.60$), which is aligned with Baker and Stockton's (2013) and Bert et al.'s (2014) suggestion that perceived a higher likelihood of infection diseases on a cruise ship. Also, infection outbreaks received significant concern regarding the severity of consequences ($M = 3.27$), meaning that young people were highly aware of the serious health consequences resulting from infection outbreaks (Bert et al. 2014; Kak

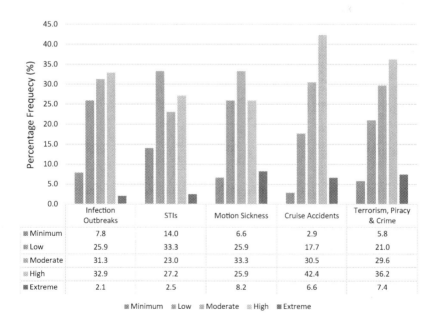

Fig. 8.1 Percentage distributions of overall perceived risk

2007; Mouchtouri et al. 2010). This could be the positive influence of effective media coverage of the escalated number of infection outbreaks on ships in recent years.

Sexually Transmissible Infections (STIs)

Gen Z generally did not place sufficient awareness on STIs and was not very concerned about them (47.3% of respondents viewed STIs as a low or minimum risk). Specifically, the perceived possibility of acquiring STIs on-board was extremely low ($M = 2.41$), indicating that young people participating in this study did not perceive STIs as a common risk while on a cruise. More importantly, the respondents perceived STIs as causing minor to negligible consequences ($M = 3.04$), signifying STIs were overlooked by Gen Z in terms of both probability (ranked as *the most unlikely*) and consequence severity (ranked as *the second least severe*), whereas the issue of acquiring STIs among young people when travelling by cruise ship has been emphasised in the existing literature (López 2013; Ward and Plourde 2006). However, the perceived probability of acquiring STIs is determined by how likely the individual is open to unprotected sexual behaviour or having multiple sexual partners, which are bound by certain cultural orientations (Le and Arcodia 2018). As a result, there are possibilities to explore this matter further by incorporating a cultural lens in examining risk perceptions.

Motion Sickness

In contrast with the initial assumption that motion sickness should be perceived as the least important risk when travelling by cruise ship, the respondents were highly aware of motion sickness on-board, and the majority (67.4%) portrayed moderate and high level of concern. Indeed, motion sickness was considered as the most likely risk to occur on-board ($M = 3.40$), aligning with Cooper et al.'s (1997) and Bledsoe et al.'s (2007) findings that motion sickness accounted for nearly half of all medical encounters during cruise trips. As expected, the respondents did not regard motion sickness as a harmful risk ($M = 2.67$). Efforts should be made to emphasise the potential impacts of motion sickness, which can result in severe consequences for on-board safety and crew members' effectiveness and improvising capability when confronting a hazardous situation (Fernandez 2013).

Cruise Accidents

It was shown that nearly half of the respondents (49%) perceived cruise accidents as a high risk with the second highest overall risk assessment ($M = 6.44$), indicating that Gen Z respondents were highly concerned about cruise-related accidents. This level of concern is essential for people's wellbeing while on a cruise, as Chang and Liao (2008) argue that obtaining an accurate perception of cruise safety will reduce the possibility of placing cruise passengers' and others' lives at risk. Cruise accidents were considered as relatively unlikely ($M = 2.50$) (following terrorism, piracy and crime and STIs); however, cruise accidents received the highest severity assessment ($M = 3.94$). This finding is comparable with Ahola et al.'s (2014), Spyrou's (2010) and Ventikos' (2013) studies which supported the fact that the amount of severe damage and number of lives lost due to cruise accidents has been substantial in recent decades, resulting in catastrophic consequences to the ship, its passengers and the environment.

Terrorism, Piracy and Crime

Figure 8.1 indicates that the majority of Gen Z (73.2%) showed moderate and high level of risk concern about terrorism, piracy and crime with the second highest overall risk assessment ($M = 6.25$). These findings support the claim of Bowen et al. (2014), Panko et al. (2009) and White and Wydajewski (2002) that terrorism, piracy and crime are major security threats that cause serious violence to a large number of cruise passengers, and correspond to Peter's (2017) finding that 70% of cruise passengers stated that terrorism-related security was a major factor determining their cruising intention. While terrorism, piracy and crime were perceived as the least likely risk to occur on-board ($M =$

2.35), the respondents were highly aware of severe consequences caused by terrorism, piracy and crime (resulting in *the second most severe consequences*) ($M = 3.91$). These findings, on one hand, do not align with Bowen et al.'s (2014) study, whose findings revealed that nearly half of 144 respondents considered a terror attack on a cruise ship as probable. This significant difference might also be explained by the high level of security alert that the UK was experiencing at the time Bowen et al. (2014) conducted the study. The perceived probability of such risks therefore is dependent on the geographical areas in consideration, as well as past experiences the individual had with politically unstable regions. This engenders a number of avenues for future research focusing specifically on factors influencing risk perceptions among Gen Z. On the other hand, the low probability of piracy at sea perceived by Gen Z aligns with Nikolić and Missoni's (2013) and White and Wydajewski's (2002) claim that the probability of piracy on-board is actually very low. The finding regarding the perceived severity also supports previous studies of Bowen et al. (2014), Panko et al. (2009) and White and Wydajewski (2002), which reinforce the claim that terrorism, piracy and crime result in serious violence and severe consequences to the cruise industry. The finding suggested Gen Z participants were fully aware of the significance of terrorism, piracy and crime and its impacts on their cruise travel.

Conclusion and Implications

As mentioned earlier in those studies by Brun et al. (2011), Peter (2016, 2017) and Sönmez and Graefe (1998b) regarding perceptions towards different cruising situations, Gen Z felt significantly less safe when the ship passed politically unstable regions or encountered uncomfortable weather. However, in contrast with initial predictions, Gen Z respondents generally perceived fewer risks emerging in restaurants with many people, pool activities, and alcohol-related situations. These findings imply that Gen Z may not be aware of the potential risks associated with these settings, or they may believe they are capable of mitigating or avoiding the risks themselves.

The investigation into perceptions of the five cruise-related risks revealed that motion sickness and infection outbreaks were perceived to be the two most common risks on-board, supporting Bledsoe et al.'s (2007) claim that these two risks accounted for most of the medical interventions on cruise ships. More importantly, respondents were highly aware of the severity of consequences which resulted from cruise accidents and terrorism, piracy and crime, corresponding to the actual ship incidents reported in the extant cruise literature. While terrorism, piracy and crime was viewed as the most unlikely risk to happen (accounted for 2% of international cruise incidents according to Greenberg et al. (2006) and Nikolić and Missoni's (2013) within the last 30 years), yet, received the second highest perceived severity level among Gen Z respondents, supporting the conclusions of Bowen et al. (2014), Panko et al. (2009) and Rubackly (2010) that one of the greatest threats cruise passengers face today is terrorism and crime. Peter (2017) emphasises the need of warranting the security on-board among cruise passengers by stating that 70% of passengers placed security issues as a top priority when travelling by cruise ship. This study also found that STIs were overlooked in terms of both probability and consequence severity, suggesting that young people do not place enough awareness on STIs and do not have significant concern about the severity of STIs on cruise ships. This unanticipated outcome to some extent, has reinforced the finding which emerged from the previous section that young people especially Gen Z lacked significant attention to personal health and safety when participating in alcohol-related situations on-board.

Implications and Recommendations

The findings in this study have generated several implications that are beneficial to academic researchers and cruise operators. Firstly, the measurement model of perceived risk incorporated by the two components (perceived probability and perceived adverse consequences) is believed to offer some possibilities to conduct investigations into perceived risk/risk perception in different contexts where future research of risk perceptions can build upon. This measurement model is believed to facilitate the examination of relationships between risk perception and other constructs (e.g. demographic factors). Secondly, since there have been no empirical studies offering a holistic picture of the extent to which people perceive different types of cruise-related risks, and even no studies targeting the youth market, this study calls for future research attention on the youth market and its behaviour, especially Gen Z, leading to better predictions on cruising intentions which are based on developing decisions involving physical risk assessments.

In terms of managerial implications, firstly, cruise operators should not neglect ship safety and security since there was evidence that the significant variations in Gen Z's perceptions were associated with their past cruise experiences. In addition, cruise operators should implement more specialised marketing campaigns to raise attention among the Gen Z market, thus establishing more clearly the safety and security 'hallmark' of cruising. Secondly, the examination of risk perceptions on cruise ships can aid the development of cruise risk management plans tailoring specifically how passengers are aware of the risks and their responses when the risks occur. For example, cruise operators should be more aware that young people especially Gen Z tends to overlook their personal health and safety in crowded restaurants, alcohol-related contexts, and pool activities, and therefore should generate more appropriate safety and security policies on ships that involve young customers, especially the alcohol-involved settings, to mitigate the possibility of any emerging risks that negatively affect their customers' cruise experiences.

Thirdly, Gen Z respondents were greatly concerned about cruise accidents and terrorism, piracy and crime risk. The cruise ship industry readily understands that due to these considerably high perceptions, any single attack on the vessel would severely damage the cruise operator's reputation and impact revenues, as it would intensify the concern among customers and could potentially result in delayed bookings or trip cancellations (Bowen et al. 2014; Peter 2016, 2017). Taking into account recent terror attacks, cruise operators should carefully consider which routes and destinations they choose for cruise voyages, as well as establish effective cooperation with insurance providers to allay customers' concerns about safety and ease their fears of terrorism.

Finally, the examination of perceptions of each cruise-related risk implies a need for more rigorous communication of health and safety information, specifically tailoring the needs and demands of Gen Z passengers, which is a proactive approach mitigating the likelihood of infection outbreaks and on-board accidents. Customer trust is vital in the risk communication process because it is intrinsically related to market demand (Baker and Stockton 2013). In addition, cruise operators should implement more sophisticated alcohol policies on-board, promote safe sex practices among Gen Z cruise passengers and enhance security measures, especially during high seasons.

Limitations and Suggestions for Future Research

Although the sample size was sufficient, the first limitation of this study relates to the representativeness of the sample due to the snowball sampling technique. Also, bias generated from conducting an online questionnaire only in the context of social media somewhat reduces the findings' generalisability. Furthermore, as shown in Table 8.2, since the majority of participants in the sample was from Asian ethnicity, the findings from this study should be applied and interpreted with caution in other contexts. Risk perceptions of Gen Z sampled in this study therefore may not represent risk perceptions of the whole Gen Z's market. Nevertheless, considering the limited literature on perceptions of cruise-related risks among young people, especially Gen Z, findings from this study act as preliminary results that offer significant insights for future research. More importantly, further research based on risk perceptions among Gen Z cruise passengers or among Gen Z across different geographic areas would make a stronger contribution to the generalisability of risk perceptions on cruise ships.

Also, some significant variations in perceptions of cruise-related risks were observed in this study, which suggest influences of various factors on Gen Z's risk perceptions and call for the specific examination on the cultural factor and nationality in determining risk perceptions. Future research therefore can fulfil this gap by examining the potential factors affecting risk perceptions on cruise ships. Past research also suggests the overarching effect of national cultures on other demographic factors (Le and Arcodia 2018; Reisinger and Mavondo 2005, 2006), consequently, further research is needed to validate this claim in the cruising context.

Considering the severe impacts of COVID-19 on the cruising industry and the extensive media attention on COVID-19 cases on cruise ships (e.g. Ruby Princess outbreak in Australia; Diamond Princess and Grand Princess outbreaks in the US), perception of risks on cruise ships among the public has changed substantially. It is therefore imperative for cruise operators to start investigating risk perceptions more deeply to understand customers' needs as a means to enhance business and industry recovery post-COVID-19. Understanding risk perceptions among cruisers also contributes to the effectiveness of control measures, as long as these are communicated effectively to cruisers. A full investigation into risk perceptions of Gen Z post-COVID-19 and a comparison between pre- and post-COVID-19 pandemic are indeed essential for understanding this segment's cruise behaviour in an attempt to recover cruise businesses.

References

Adam, I. (2015). Backpackers' Risk Perceptions and Risk Reduction Strategies in Ghana. *Tourism Management, 49*, 99–108.

Ahola, M., Murto, P., Kujala, P., & Pitkänen, J. (2014). Perceiving Safety in Passenger Ships—User Studies in an Authentic Environment. *Safety Science, 70*, 222–232.

Baker, D. A., & Stockton, S. (2013). Smooth Sailing! Cruise Passengers Demographics and Health Perceptions While Cruising the Eastern Caribbean. *International Journal of Business and Social Science, 4*(7), 8–17.

Bauer, R. A. (1960). Consumer Behavior as Risk Taking. In S. Robert (Ed.), *Dynamic Marketing for a Changing World* (pp. 389–398). Hancock, Chicago, IL: American Marketing Association.

Bellis, M. A., Hughes, K., Thomson, R., & Bennett, A. (2004). Sexual Behaviour of Young People in International Tourist Resorts. *Sexually Transmitted Infections, 80*(1), 43–47.

Berdychevsky, L., & Gibson, H. (2015). Women's Sexual Sensation Seeking and Risk Taking in Leisure Travel. *Journal of Leisure Research, 47*(5), 621–646.

Bert, F., Scaioli, G., Gualano, M. R., Passi, S., Specchia, M. L., Cadeddu, C., & Siliquini, R. (2014). Norovirus Outbreaks on Commercial Cruise Ships: A Systematic Review and New Targets for the Public Health Agenda. *Food and Environmental Virology, 6*(2), 67–74.

Bledsoe, G. H., Brill, J. D., Zak, D., & Li, G. (2007). Injury and Illness Aboard an Antarctic Cruise Ship. *Wilderness & Environmental Medicine, 18*(1), 36–40.

Bowen, C., Fidgeon, P., & Page, S. (2014). Maritime Tourism and Terrorism: Customer Perceptions of the Potential Terrorist Threat to Cruise Shipping. *Current Issues in Tourism, 17*(7), 610–639.

Brun, W., Wolff, K., & Larsen, S. (2011). Tourists Worries After Terrorist Attacks: Report from a Field Experiment. *Scandinavian Journal of Hospitality and Tourism, 11(3)*, 387–394.

Carr, N. (2001). An Exploratory Study of Gendered Differences in Young Tourists Perceptions of Danger within London. *Tourism Management, 22*(5), 565–570.

Chang, Y., & Liao, M. (2008). Air Passenger Perceptions on Exit Row Seating and Flight Safety Education. *Safety Science, 46*(10), 1459–1468.

Cooper, C., Dunbar, N., & Mira, M. (1997). Sex and Seasickness on the Coral Sea. *The Lancet, 350*(9081), 892.

Cramer, E. H., Blanton, L. H., Blanton, C. J., Vaughan, G. H., Bopp, C. A., & Forney, D. L. (2006). Epidemiology of Gastroenteritis on Cruise Ships, 2001–2004. *American Journal of Preventive Medicine, 30*(3), 252–257.

Cruise Lines International Association (CLIA). (2018). *Cruise Travel Report January 2018.* Retrieved from https://cruising.org/-/media/research-updates/research/consumer-research/2018-clia-travel-report.pdf.

Cruise Lines International Association (CLIA). (2019). *Cruise Trends & Industry Outlook 2019.* Retrieved from https://cruising.org/-/media/research-updates/research/clia-2019-state-of-the-industry-presentation-(1).pdf.

Cunningham, S. M. (1967). The Major Dimensions of Perceived Risk. In D. F. Cox (Ed.), *Risk Taking and Informationhandling in Consumer Behavior* (pp. 82–108). Boston, MA: Harvard University Press.

Desivilya, H., Teitler-Regev, S., & Shahrabani, S. (2015). The Effects of Conflict on Risk Perception and Travelling Intention of Young Tourists. *EuroMed Journal of Business, 10*(1), 118–130.

Dickerson, T. A. (2014). The Cruise Passenger's Rights and Remedies 2014: The Costa Concordia Disaster: One Year Later, Many More Incidents Both on Board Megaships and During Risky Shore Excursions. *Tulane Maritime Law Journal, 38*(2), 515–581.

Dowling, G. R. (1986). Perceived Risk: The Concept and Its Measurement. *Psychology and Marketing, 3*(3), 193–210.

Dowling, G. R., & Staelin, R. (1994). A Model of Perceived Risk and Intended Risk-Handling Activity. *Journal of Consumer Research, 21*(1), 119–134.

Fernandez, R. P. (2013). The Seasickness as Marine Problem-Case Study. *Journal of Marine Science and Application, 12*(1), 58–64.

Greenberg, M. D., Chalk, P., Willis, H. H., Khilko, I., & Ortiz, D. S. (2006). *Maritime Terrorism: Risk and Liability*. Pittsburgh, PA: Rand Corporation.

Henthorne, T. L., George, B. P., & Smith, W. C. (2013). Risk Perceptions and Buying Behavior: An Examination of Some Relationships in the Context of Cruise Tourism in Jamaica. *International Journal of Hospitality and Tourism Administration, 14*(1), 66–86.

ISO 31000. (2009). *Risk Management—Principles and Guidelines*. Retrieved from https://www.iso.org

Kak, V. (2007). Infections in Confined Spaces: Cruise Ships, Military Barracks, and College Dormitories. *Infectious Disease Clinics of North America, 21*(3), 773–784.

Kraska, J., & Wilson, B. (2009). Fighting Pirates: The Pen and the Sword. *World Policy Journal, 25*(4), 41–52.

Le, T. H., & Arcodia, C. (2017). Perceptions of Risks on Cruise Ships Among Young People. Paper Presented at CAUTHE 2017, 6–8 February, University of Otago (pp. 837–840).

Le, T. H., & Arcodia, C. (2018). Risk Perceptions on Cruise Ships Among Young People: Concepts, Approaches and Directions. *International Journal of Hospitality Management, 69*, 102–112.

Le, T. H., Arcodia, C., Abreu Novais, M., & Kralj, A. (2019). What We Know and Do Not Know About Authenticity in Dining Experiences: A Systematic Literature Review. *Tourism Management, 74*, 258–275.

Lepp, A., & Gibson, H. (2003). Tourist Roles, Perceived Risk and International Tourism. *Annals of Tourism Research, 30*(3), 606–624.

Lin, Y., Lee, Y., & Wang, S. (2012). Analysis of Motivation, Travel Risk, and Travel Satisfaction of Taiwan Undergraduates on Work and Travel Overseas Programmes: Developing Measurement Scales. *Tourism Management Perspectives, 1*(2), 35–46.

López, I. E. A. (2013). *Sex on Amazonian Riverboats: A Neglected Public Health Problem That Merits Innovative HIV/STIs Prevention Interventions* (Master Thesis, University of Washington, Seattle, United States). Retrieved from https://digital.lib.washington.edu/researchworks/bitstream/handle/1773/22865/AlvaLopez_washington_0250O_11471.pdf?sequence=1.

Mitchell, V. W., & Vassos, V. (1997). Perceived Risk and Risk Reduction in Holiday Purchases: A Cross-Cultural and Gender Analysis. *Journal of Euro-Marketing, 6*(3), 47–79.

Montana, P. J., & Petit, F. (2008). Motivating Generation X and Y on the Job and Preparing Z. *Global Journal of Business Research, 2*(2), 139–148.

Mouchtouri, V. A., Nichols, G., Rachiotis, G., Kremastinou, J., Arvanitoyannis, I. S., Riemer, T., Jaremin, B., & Hadjichristodoulou, C. (2010). State of the Art: Public Health and Passenger Ships. *International Maritime Health, 61*(2), 49–98.

Neri, A. J., Cramer, E. H., Vaughan, G. H., Vinjé, J., & Mainzer, H. M. (2008). Passenger Behaviors During Norovirus Outbreaks on Cruise Ships. *Journal of Travel Medicine, 15*(3), 172–176.

Nikolić, N., & Missoni, E. (2013). Piracy on the High Seas—Threats to Travelers' Health. *Journal of Travel Medicine, 20*(5), 313–321.

Panko, T. R., George, B. P., & Henthorne, T. L. (2009). Personal Safety and Security on Cruise Ships: A Study of Crimes on Board. *Journal of Hospitality Application & Research, 4*(2), 31–44

Peter, C. (2016). Cruising with Terrorists: Qualitative Study of Consumer Perspectives. *International Journal of Safety and Security in Tourism/Hospitality, 1*(14), 1–12.

Peter, C. (2017). Navigating the High Seas: Can Security Perceptions Be Influenced by Demographic Factors? *Journal of Safety and Security in Tourism/Hospitality,* 1–15

Peter, J. D., & Ryan, M. J. (1976). An Investigation of Perceived Risk at the Brand Level. *Journal of Marketing Research, 13*(2), 184–188.

Pinhey, T. K., & Iverson, T. J. (1994). Safety Concerns of Japanese Visitors to Guam. *Journal of Travel & Tourism Marketing, 3*(2), 87–94.

Pizam, A., Jeong, G.-H., Reichel, A., van Boemmel, H., Lusson, J. M., Steynberg, L., & Montmany, N. (2004). The Relationship Between Risk-Taking, Sensation-Seeking, and the Tourist Behavior of Young Adults: A Cross-Cultural Study. *Journal of Travel Research, 42*(3), 251–260.

Pritchard, A., & Morgan, N.J. (2006). Hotel Babylon? Exploring Hotels as Liminal Sites of Transition and Transgression. *Tourism Management, 27*(5), 762–772.

Qvarnström, A., & Oscarsson, M. G. (2014). Perceptions of HIV/STI Prevention Among Young Adults in Sweden Who Travel Abroad: A Qualitative Study with Focus Group and Individual Interviews. *BMC Public Health, 14*(1), 897.

Reisinger, Y., & Mavondo, F. (2005). Travel Anxiety and Intentions to Travel Internationally: Implications of Travel Risk Perceptions. *Journal of Travel Research, 43*(3), 212–225.

Reisinger, Y., & Mavondo, F. (2006). Cultural Differences in Travel Risk Perceptions. *Journal of Travel & Tourism Marketing, 20*(1), 13–31.

Ruan, X., Yin, Z., & Frangopol, D. M. (2015). Risk Matrix Integrating Risk Attitudes Based on Utility Theory. *Risk Analysis, 35*(8), 1437–1447.

Rubackly, T. (2010). *How Safe Are We at Sea?* Retrieved from https://www.cru isemates.com/articles/consumer/security.cfm#axzz1N0EKJCRH.

Sadovszky, V. (2008). Preventing Women's Sexual Risk Behaviors During Travel. *JOGNN - Journal of Obstetric, Gynecologic, and Neonatal Nursing, 37*(5), 516–524.

Sarman, I., Scagnolari, S., & Maggi, R. (2016). Acceptance of Life-Threatening Hazards Among Young Tourists: A Stated Choice Experiment. *Journal of Travel Research, 55*(8), 979–992.

Slovic, P., Fischhoff, B., & Lichtenstein, S. (1982). Why Study Risk Perceptions? *Risk Analysis, 2*(2), 83–93.

Sönmez, S. F., & Graefe, A. R. (1998a). Determining Future Travel Behaviour from Past Travel Experience and Perceptions of Risk and Safety. *Journal of Travel Research, 37*(2), 171–177.

Sönmez, S. F., & Graefe, A. R. (1998b). Influence of Terrorism Risk on Foreign Tourism Decisions. *Annals of Tourism Research, 25*(1), 112–144.

Spyrou, K. (2010). *Ship Design for Safety and Environmental Protection.* Athens, Greece: NTUA Press.

Ventikos, N. P. (2013). Exploring fire Incidents/Accidents Onboard Cruise and Passenger Ships. *Journal of Economics and Business, 63*(3-4), 146–157.

Ward, B. J., & Plourde, P. (2006). Travel and Sexually Transmitted Infections. *Journal of Travel Medicine, 13*(5), 300–317.

Weeden, C., Lester, J. A., & Jarvis, N. (2016). Lesbians and Gay Men's Vacation Motivations, Perceptions, and Constraints: A Study of Cruise Vacation Choice. *Journal of homosexuality, 63*(8), 1068–1085.

White, B. L., & Wydajewski, K. J. (2002). Commercial Ship Self Defense Against Piracy and Maritime Terrorism. *OCEANS '02 MTS/IEEE, 2,* 1164–1171.

Williams, K. C., & Page, R. A. (2011). Marketing to the Generations. *Journal of Behavioral Studies in Business, 3*(1), 37–53.

Winter, L., & Parker, B. (2007). Current Health and Preferences for Life-Prolonging Treatments: An Application of Prospect Theory to End-of-Life Decision Making. *Social Science and Medicine, 65*, 1695–1707

9

The New Foodie Generation: Gen Z

Burhan Kılıç, Aydan Bekar, and Nisan Yozukmaz

Introduction

Food, with its power and significance, is an indispensable part of our life and existence. Food is something that we all need, want, have or do not have. However, beyond being a fundamental need, connotations of food cover more than nutrition. Food is related to culture, traditions, socialization and personal expression. Though the rise of foodie movement

---

B. Kılıç · A. Bekar
Faculty of Tourism, Mugla Sitki Kocman University, Muğla, Turkey
e-mail: bkilic@mu.edu.tr

A. Bekar
e-mail: abekar@mu.edu.tr

N. Yozukmaz (✉)
Faculty of Tourism, Pamukkale University, Denizli, Turkey
e-mail: nisany@pau.edu.tr

© The Author(s), under exclusive license to Springer Nature
Switzerland AG 2021
N. Stylos et al. (eds.), *Generation Z Marketing and Management in Tourism and Hospitality*,
https://doi.org/10.1007/978-3-030-70695-1_9

around the world has been studied in the field of sociology, it has not been analysed in detail in terms of tourism marketing.

Foodie culture is an intensely aestheticized form of food consumption and foodies are an avant-garde type of marketing society (Ambrozas 2003). Indeed foodie market is conceptualized as a part of Slow Food movement which is the intersection of leisure, recreation, agriculture and social change (Dunlap 2012). The rise of foodie movement brings out some basic questions such as "Who is a foodie?", "Who does this term include?", "Is it a phenomenon varying by cultures?", "Does it involve a sophisticated culinary experience?". Foodie phenomenon blurs the line between exclusive and mainstream foods. Combining food both as a physiological need and as an emotional encounter, foodies are a heterogenous consumer segment which requires deep research (Mohsen 2017).

The second major point of focus of this chapter is Generation Z who has not been studied in detail. Generation Z belongs to a new sociological category feeding on information technologies, Internet and social network (Haddouche and Salomone 2018). This generation is the biggest marketing challenge because it is the generation of technology and innovation. This generation has a great purchase power and generates a quarter of the UK's population and 40% of consumers in the USA (Priporas et al. 2017).

This study combines these two new and different market segments and examines their characteristics and their profiles. Firstly, the unique characteristics of these two groups are explained; then the common grounds where they meet and form one market segment are examined with the exemplary studies in literature. As a result, the foodie behaviours and characteristics of Generation Z are explained in detail and some practical implications are suggested.

Foodies

According to Kline et al. (2015), researchers have theorized some segments of food tourists, have analysed their activities, motivations and outputs. A lot of these segments have been determined by the change in interests within culture, heritage and authenticity through food (Johnston and Baumann 2010). On the other hand, "foodie" research and foodies' activities at home are known as a topic that has not been studied in detail so far (Getz and Robinson 2014a, b).

According to Oxford English Dictionary, the first usage of the term foodie was seen in an article published in New York Times Magazine in 1980. Then the term was used in the article named "Cuisine Poseur" published in Harpers and Queen magazine in 1982 (Barr and Levy 1985). Foodie movement came to another level with the release of The Official Foodie Handbook-Be Modern-Worship Food written by Ann Barr and Paul Levy in 1985. Barr and Levy define foodies simply as people who are very interested in food (1985). In the book, historical events within foodie world are explained chronologically and the relationship between health and food, famous recipes, restaurants, chefs, global foods and foodie community are discussed in an entertaining way.

One of the recent contributions to foodie literature is the book titled Foodies: Democracy and Distinction in the Gourmet Foodscape by Johnston and Baumann (2010) who explain the history of foodism in detail starting from 1940s when French haute cuisine was popular to the day when organic and local foods are popular and the effect of technology on foodie culture. However, except the book of Johnston and Baumann, academic studies on foodies are scarce.

The Definition of Foodie and Foodie Characteristics

According to Watson (2013), in recent years, a group of people has emerged whose need to dine in a specific restaurant is due not to fulfil just a physical need but due to the food and experience (Barr and Levy 1985). These people can travel long distances or book months before in order to eat a meal of an exclusive chef or to eat a meal made with certain ingredients or in a specific location (Ross 2003). These people are called as foodies (Barr and Levy 1985).

Johnston and Baumann (2010) mention about the differences between two discourses of foodie concept. One of these discourses is democracy, the other is related to distinction and money. Some believe that foodies are democratic and they enjoy all kinds of food; they are not snobbish. This belief is related to the global movement of healthy eating, support for local production, local fairs and ecological and organic product preferences. In other words, being a foodie is a part of a trend that everyone can participate in. On the other hand, some think that foodie movement is a snobbish and elitist trend; foodies are privileged, pampered upper-class gourmets within dazzling consumption. These foodies collect cultural capital with food consumption. Or they try to have a lifestyle or a social group talking and informing about food experiences that only the rich and the educated can afford. These two discourses have some merits and foodies can belong to one of them. But behaviour whether it is an elitist consumption in a five-star hotel or a visit to a local market, can not define foodies. Being a foodie is about personal identity or about how they feel about themselves.

According to Ambrozas (2003), whose study is a detailed explanation of foodies' cooking, shopping, eating and reading practices, foodie is a term used by media and foodies themselves halfheartedly. Ambrozas (2003) defines foodies as people whose identities are partly formed by eating good food and who consume various food-related products such as food magazines, Tv programmes and special kitchen utensils.

Johnston and Baumann (2010) define foodies under 4 contexts: (1) education, (2) identity, (3) exploration and (4) evaluation. Regardless of their knowledge level, foodies are just curious people towards learning about food. In terms of identity, foodies consider food as a part of their selves. This can be related to familial traditions that have shaped their childhood or to how they see and perceive the world. Their exploration feature means that foodies always want to try new food, cuisine types and new recipes. Lastly, enjoyment for foodies is the synonym of evaluation of food. They enjoy talking and discussing about food.

Cairns et al. (2010) examine the role of gender within foodie culture. The authors define foodies as people who are not food professionals but have a passion towards eating and learning about food for a long time. Cairns et al. (2010) assert that as being a foodie is a hobby requiring both cultural and economic capital, foodies have specific privileges.

Robinson and Getz (2014) in their study on foodies and their travel experiences define foodies as people who have a passion towards food and a high food-involvement level. According to Bourdain (2012), foodie is an umbrella term describing people who are interested in food, cooking and restaurants, but unfortunately it is associated with being snobbish and fashion enthusiast.

Getz et al. (2014) define the term foodie as a food lover, person integrating food, food preparation process and its enjoyment into his/her lifestyle and also as a person whose personal and social identity includes food quality, cooking, sharing food and food experiences. According to Wilkinson (2016), the term foodie refers to a food lover; a person integrating food quality, cooking, sharing food and food experiences into their personal and social identity; foodies include all aspects of food in their lifestyles and this encourages them to travel for new and authentic food experiences. According to Yozukmaz et al. (2017) and Kline et al. (2018), the term foodie is used to describe people who are passionate about and interested in food and can travel for food or food-related events and activities like festivals or cooking classes. According to Mohsen (2017), these various and imperfect definitions put foodie phenomenon at the phase of immature research subject which requires detailed research on foodies.

Although foodie concept is often mentioned in daily life, it is shaped by actors and other institutions within gourmet world like chefs and food programmes (Cairns et al. 2010). On the other hand, in an article published in The Sunday Times (Atkinson 2013), it is stated that there is a foodie culture growing even within student lifestyle. Although foodies may have higher standards in choosing food, it does not mean that their food needs are expensive or gourmet like which other people often perceive foodies (Johnston and Baumann 2010). Watson et al. (2008) focus on the difference between foodies and gourmets and admit that gourmets are older, upper-class while foodies are young couples from ambitious classes who have grown up as the children of consumption craze and that they criticize about the food they eat in a restaurant and later try to make it at their home, and they collect food experiences like tourists collect souvenirs and they try to visit famous restaurants.

Being a foodie is a free emotional choice including a symbolic consumer behaviour created by products and services offered by a restaurant. These people are skilled amateurs who have knowledge about food

228   B. Kılıç et al.

and its content (Stebbins 1992). They worship food and see food as equal to art. For anyone to call himself/herself a foodie, he/she does not need a membership to anywhere (Barr and Levy 1985). According to Ambrozas (2003), foodies are cultural and social experts considering cultural distinction forms above socioeconomic forms. For example, their consuming exotic or expensive local foods like pomegranate molasses shows their cultural capital. At the same time, their preference to consume local organic foods symbolically proves their resistance towards industrial agriculture and genetically modified product technology. Indeed, core foodies like upper-class chefs criticize both and they are active representatives of organic food and slow food. Foodies use their support for alternative farming practices as an indicator of their culinary capital. She also claims that foodies are more socially aware and know how to use this for differentiating themselves from overall consumers. Johnston and Baumann (2010) state that they care about ecological sustainability and authenticity in their food experiences and most of their choices are based on the desire of curbing industrialization in food production system.

Foodies think that food is a joy for their lives and a tool for entertainment. Also, foodies use their food knowledge and desire to learn continuously in order to collect cultural capital and to differentiate themselves from other food consumers, accordingly to build their own identity. Foodies emphasize that for them food is a great personal investment. They talk about commitment to self-learning and "education of palate". This educational interests can be summarized as learning new cooking techniques, trying new restaurants, participating in food programmes and reading magazines, food books, cuisine history and food blogs. Foodies mention their ever-growing food knowledge as a cultural capital which is some kind of cultural difference separating them from an average food consumer (Cairns et al. 2010).

Foodies collect food experiences just like tourists collect souvenirs or take photos of monuments in a destination (Watson et al. 2008) and they visit famous restaurants (Watson 2013). Foodies can cook with the products they grow in their gardens; visit upscale restaurants; be politically active in changing legal regulations within food production and write on blogs about their adventures related to cooking and eating (Green 2013).

Foodies are aware of being in a special situation belonging to their leisure and lifestyles and they know that being a foodie is about their personal and social identity and travel for food is very important to them. If there are some keywords for foodies, they can be "passion", "love", and "experience". Their purpose is not to replace hedonism, but to add value into their experiences through targeted benefits like training and practical training (Getz et al. 2014). Also, for many foodies online consumer reviews especially food blogs presenting amateur restaurant reviews are an important information source (Zhu and Zhang 2010). Accordingly, food blogging can be an important tool within foodie culture.

In the study of Getz and Robinson (2014b) the most popular food-related activities in which the participants participate are found as visiting farmer markets, ethnic and cultural festivals, wine and food tastings, food-related festivals and visiting expensive restaurants. The study reveals that foodies enjoy food-related activities that require participation. The participants are asked about their mostly preferred food-related experience in Australian destinations; the highest ranked answer is found as authentic culinary experience in local restaurants.

The most important characteristics of foodies are enjoying to cook, learning about food, expressing themselves through these activities, thinking about the quality of food, sharing food, establishing social interactions via social gatherings focused on food, being meticulous in purchasing and preparing food. Despite being important for many foodies, healthy eating is highlighted as a specific characteristic of foodies (Yozukmaz et al. 2017). They are people who are interested in eating quality foods, trying new recipes, cooking with local materials, following the latest trends in nutrition, restaurants, chefs and food and travelling to try new food and beverages (Kline et al. 2018).

As foodies are not a homogenous group (Sloan 2013) they can be differentiated in terms of their identities, interests, involvement levels, travel preferences and food-related activities (Getz et al. 2014). Barr and Levy (1985) offer seven different types of foodies. This is the first attempt in classifying foodies and it is created according to their interests like growing vegetables in garden, trying to cook with local ingredients or ethnic flavours (Green 2013). In 2011, a foodie typology is presented on Huffington Post which divided foodies into segments like

"Made it Myself, Organivore, Europhile, One Upper, Snob, Anti-Snob, Avoider, Blogging Food Pornographer, Bacon Lover, and DIYer (Do-It-Yourself-er)" (Brones 2011). Bourdain, in her book Comfort Me with Offal (2012), examines modern foodies under 85 titles. Some of them are "chefestants, pizzaratti and coffeegeeks" (Green 2013). In 2012, in a research conducted in the USA it is asserted that foodies are not a homogenous group and they are divided into six groups as organic foodies, healthy foodies, fans of foreign/spicy food, gourmet foodies, enthusiastic chefs and restaurant foodies (Sloan 2013). Another attempt to divide foodies into groups is made by Leggett (2013). Some of the typologies of Leggett (2013) are fast food foodies, hipster foodies who want their food to be Instagrammable and Do-It-Yourself foodies growing or making their own food. Although these foodie categories have not been supported empirically and only generated for entertainment, the reason why this typology is given a place here is to the popularity of foodie concept in popular culture.

Foodies' Travel Behaviour

Today many tourists travel due to food and food-related activities with which a segmentation can be made in tourism industry. In this sense, foodies can be a starting point for segmenting food tourism market. However, despite the increase in the research on food tourism and food tourist, the information about foodie behaviour and foodie characteristics is still approached with suspicion (Dunlap 2012). In a few studies, foodies are analysed beyond general foodie concept as a potential food tourism market. The line between food tourist and foodie is not thin. Foodies participate in food-related activities regularly, not just while travelling, and they define themselves as foodies (Green 2013). Getz et al. (2014) define foodie within tourism context as "people who travel for their food passion because of their special interest". Foodies also seek innovation and desire to taste new meals and to gain new experiences. Thus many foodies travel due to these motivations and choose destination in terms of these motivations (Getz et al. 2014). Barr and Levy (1985) claim that as tastes and smells of local food are some things that need to be experienced in person, "foodies love traveling more than other people".

Robinson and Getz (2014) investigate foodies and their travel experiences and approach foodies as tourists seeking food tourism experiences and desiring to participate in these experiences. Most of the participants who describe themselves as foodies have a high food-involvement level. One-third of the participants have a subscription to food magazines; one-fifth of them write online food blogs or food forums; 6% have a food club membership; 11% have a wine club membership. In terms of their travel behaviour, it is observed that one-third of the participants are planning a domestic food-related travel in the ensuing year.

According to Green (2013), tourism industry has also started to adopt the term and send marketing messages to the people identifying themselves as foodies. The purpose of Green's (2013) study is to determine the food-related activities and food habits of travelling and potential foodies. In their study on foodies and food-related events, Getz and Robinson (2014a) posit that some participants have travelled for a food-related experience in the recent year and claim that this is an indicator of the strong connection between foodies and gastro-tourism. In their study, it is also seen that foodies care mostly about authenticity, tradition and local customs. The commonalities related to food-related attractions in destinations are found as wine, local production and food service. In line with this, It is determined that during their travel, foodies seek culturally authentic food experiences, educational experiences related to traditional food and socializing opportunities through food experiences (Getz and Robinson 2014b).

Accordingly, Kline et al. (2018) focused on travel habits and food-related activities, and supported that people describing themselves as foodies enjoy and can be categorized into certain sub-groups. The cluster in which the participants describe themselves as foodies is called "pioneers". The most important activity that these "pioneers" join is experiencing special food and beverage types such as local food, cultural food and local beverages.

Authenticity is a subject that has been studied in detail in food and food-related tourism literature (Beer 2008; Johnston and Baumann 2010). Johnston and Baumann (2010) suggest that authenticity lies in the process and form of food production and in the fact that food unites the eater with the producer, heritage and traditions. Even foodies travelling for experiencing exotic foods search for these foods and help them be defined.

Generation Z

The generation is defined as a community of people connected by an affinity that emerges by sharing events that change the society in which they grow up. These events are often a combination of social, economic, political or technological complexities (Merriman 2015). Therefore, Generation Z is defined as the individuals born in the same temporary period hosting events like 9/11 (Mannheim 2011). Generation Z is defined by many other terms like Gen Z, Zs, Gen Z'ers and because they have grown up in the era of digital technology, they are named as Internet generation—IGen, iGeneration, Net Generation—net gen, and Digital Natives (Renfro 2012; Euromonitor 2011; Singh 2014; Turner 2015; Fister-Gale 2015).

Specifically, with regard to Generation Z, Renfro (2012) claims that the exact starting and ending points are not clear in terms of generational labels related to Gen Z. The birth dates of Generation Z vary by different authors and researchers. But most claim that Gen Z covers those born in 1995 and after (Fister-Gale 2015; Priporas et al. 2017; Su et al. 2019; Devenyns 2019; Maynard 2019; Singh 2014). In this chapter, Generation Z is called as Gen Z, Gen Z'ers and Digital Natives. Their date of birth is accepted as 1995 and after.

Gen Z Characteristics

Although they are from diverse groups in terms of life stage, nationality and ethnicity, the globalization and digitalization of society has enabled Gen Z to share some common features such as a sense of community and technological skills (Euromonitor 2011). These are titled in this chapter as (1) Supporters of Diversity, (2) Community Oriented, (3)

Independent/Individualistic, (4) Self-confident & realistic, (5) Digital Natives.

Gen Z supports diversity: Gen Z is a very mixed group representing many cultures and ethnic origins (Aaron Allen & Associates 2018). They recognize diversities in the population (Renfro 2012) and are more tolerant of different cultures (Singh 2014). Gen Z is less discriminatory and more embracing than previous generations. As they grow up in a politically correct and multicultural society, they have more social adaptability (Euromonitor 2011). As they are an ethnically diverse group, they believe in diversity, equality and poverty alleviation (Vision Critical 2016).

Gen Z is community-oriented: In general, Gen Z'ers are community-oriented young people (Su et al. 2019; Euromonitor 2011). They care about cooperation and relationships. They join online chat groups and multiplayer video games. (Tavares et al. 2018). They expect an equal and respectful co-existence with others regardless of age (Merriman 2015). Although young, Gen Z is more socially and environmentally conscious than previous generations (Renfro 2012). They know the social responsibilities and laws and regulations that we have to assume within the society (Singh 2014). They have a higher sense of social responsibility. Almost 60% of them state that they are interested in changes in sustainable development (Su et al. 2019).

Gen Z is individualistic and independent: Gen Y is said to be group or team-oriented, but today's youth is more individualistic and independent (Euromonitor 2011). They care more about independence rather than authority. They want freedom in everything they do, e.g. freedom to choose or freedom to express (Tavares et al. 2018). They desire to create their own solutions (Merriman 2015). Gen Z is a natural born individualist and believes in expressing and speaking its own opinions on the Internet, at home or at school (Euromonitor 2011). Z'ers do not need to be controlled very much, especially because they can easily find answers of questions about their passions and curiosity (Renfro 2012).

Gen Z is self-confident and more realistic: Gen Z is more realistic, practical and materialistic than other generations (Euromonitor 2011). Generation Z members have grown up under very different circumstances and conditions. They have seen that their parent lost their jobs and sold their houses and all these have changed them (Fister-Gale 2015). The increase in collective self-confidence has infused young people with a desire to succeed, the biggest source of which is the Internet. Under the influence of recession, this generation will be more timid about taking risks, travelling and working abroad (Euromonitor 2011).

Gen Z'ers are Digital Natives: According to Prensky (2001), modern youth is defined as digital natives because they have seen no life without the Internet. Gen Z is the first generation to be born into the digital world (Singh 2014). No other generation has ever experienced a time when technology was so accessible at an early age (Prensky 2001; Euromonitor 2011). With technological advances in the multimedia world, including tablets, smartphones, social media, media players and flat-screen TVs, Generation Z is used to interacting and communicating in a world that is always connected (Turner 2015). They are typically tech-savvy (Singh 2014) and connected with their peers through social media (Renfro 2012).

Gen Z as Tourist

Getting on the stage now, Gen z is a generation with a high purchase power. It is a challenge because their behaviours are different than those of previous generations and these behaviours cause changes in their consumer behaviours too (Schlossberg 2016). According to Forbes, Gen Z'ers cover $ 29 billion to $ 143 billion of direct spending (Devenyns 2019).

Gen Z will bring the mobile revolution into travel and tourism as much as it can (Vision Critical 2016). Gen Z consumers are particularly frequent buyers of customizable applications, and it is therefore important for marketers to understand how consumer behaviour is linked to smart shopping (Priporas et al. 2017). They want to be able to handle all the necessary tasks from their choice of destination to flight, hotel or restaurant reservations with their mobile phones or tablets. They want to ask questions online and get answers while making their decisions. While travelling, they also want to take care of their mobile transactions, such as airline check-ins or tour-guide bookings. They want their phone to serve them like a tour guide, and they want more than ordinary sights or tourist traps. They expect to find more authentic and local experiences. For example, Four Seasons Hotels & Resorts has produced an app with a wide range of recommendations from concierges for more than 100 destinations and allows to discover unique, desirable and different experiences. At the same time, some companies have made applications for the usage of mobile phones as hotel room keys (Vision Critical 2016).

They have higher expectations; do not have brand loyalty and they are more interested in experiences (Schlossberg 2016). They are not provoked by luxury brands. They care more about value and personal style than designer labels (Vision Critical 2016). Gen Z prefers to have control over their own experiences or create their own experiences. Therefore, companies offering mass customization and personalization are more successful in targeting this generation. (Euromonitor 2011).

As Haddouche and Salomone (2018) point out, young tourists representing Gen Z are hard-to-understand and knowledgeable and expect much from their travels. Generally, it draws a travel profile away from traditional tourism with its travel and accommodation preferences and its relations with the environment and local people. In particular, Gen Z is involved in different leisure activities than in older generations. In the UK, for example, young people aged 16–24 rate cultural activities less than other activities, such as visiting exhibitions and museums (Halliday and Astafyeva 2014). For this reason, in order to establish a connection with this age group in terms of leisure activities, it is necessary to target the youth's desire to create social interaction, sharing and experience in a virtual world (Skinner et al. 2018).

Gen Z, the most ethnically diverse generation in history, feels itself at a global village: they come from all over the world and want to be local and global residents. Almost 40% of those aged between 14 and 18 say they need a trip to feel their life is complete. Almost 70% argue that travelling alone without parents is an indicator of adulthood (Vision Critical 2016). According to Haddouche and Salomene (2018), Gen Z, which is projected as a narcissistic generation and wants to emphasize their own selves or personalities (e.g. by sharing selfie), exhibits great humility during tourist experiences, because the community factor as the opposite of individualism is an important feature of this generation.

According to Haddouche and Salomene (2018), young tourists can be both sensitive to environmental protection and extremely open-minded. Young people expect a lot from their travels. The consumption of accommodation becomes a hedonist behaviour: tourism is a moment of empowerment, inference, socialization and entertainment at the same time. While traveling, new friendships are created, interaction with indigenous people is sought and deep meaning is sought for personal life and personal development. All of these needs are evident in specific purchasing behaviour: last-minute decisions, seeking opportunities, resorting to word-of-mouth communication, and the use of low-cost services. This young generation also has the prescription power. In 94% of their families' purchasing decisions, they present their ideas and undoubtedly take part in destination choices. Research shows that they have an increasing sensitivity to solidarity tourism and useful travel (Mignon 2003).

Food-Related Behaviour of Gen Z

As spending power increases, this tech-savvy group will transform the food and beverage industry. They affect 600 billion dollars of family spending (blacksmithapplications.com). Gen Z generates a sustainable food segment with a high potential. Therefore understanding of this consumer group is very important to create an effective approach for sustainable marketing (Su et al. 2019). Gen z is the leader of change in many restaurant trends and therefore has forced operators to review their menus. (McSweeney 2019). Indeed, Gen Z was born into foodie culture and grew up aware of the purpose of food and the role it played in a good life (www.blacksmithapplications.com).

According to Mintel's research, Gen Z is a force that is big enough to shake the food industry and has the potential to change health and well-being expectations, increase the accessibility and culinary creativity of international cuisine (blacksmithapplications.com). Hartman Group said that more than half of Gen Z liked to cook, one-quarter of them cook their own food, and one-third wanted to improve their cooking skills. They mostly cook food such as are eggs, pasta, rice, vegetables, cookies, brownie, pancakes, waffles and French toast. Today's young people prepare their own meals because of their busy family programmes and eat more often alone (Mullen 2019).

Gen Z sees customization of food as an expression of who they are. This may be an extension of maturing with social media in their hands. Because of social media, food should not only be sharable on Instagram, but also a representation of one's mood and feeling that day (Devenyns 2019). Gen Z'ers have always been stereotyped as people staring at the screens of their phones. But this group also values experiences; specially to dining experiences. They consider eating out as a social activity and focus on spending their time with their family and friends (Aaron Allen & Associates 2018).

Their food-related attitudes and behaviours are discussed under their commonalities such as (1) technology, (2) health, (3) authenticity, (4) fast food and snacks.

Technology: For Gen Z, which is growing in the social media era and is expected to change the food and beverage industry, online shopping and online ordering will be the most important food habit (Demeritt 2018). In 2015, a fast service restaurant chain became the first in its field to make a mobile app with which food can be ordered and paid for both in drive-through and dine-in. In doing so, the chain has Gen Z in mind. This application allows confident Gen Z to place orders on its own without interacting with people. Their desire to solve their own problems has been met by the ability to customize each menu item in the traditional menu, but without the obvious additives and extras. Their creativity is driven by the unlimited options offered by the app, and their desire to be connected allows them to share their new menu creation on sites such as HacktheMenu.com (Merriman 2015). Gen Z are frequent users of restaurant applications and online ordering With their growing interest in food, Gen Z tends to order from restaurants at nights when they can't go out. Online ordering has become Gen Z's best friend (McSweeney 2019).

Young people don't go to restaurants without a phone. This shows that their commitment to technology is stronger than previous generations.

Sharing the account, looking at the menu from Facebook, and sharing real-time online reviews are some of the Gen Z behaviours. When it comes to eating out, many Gen Z'ers will look at Facebook and Instagram Pages before going to restaurants (McSweeney 2019). Technology, photography and social media are part of their daily lives and this is the case in their dining experiences too (Blog B2BIO 2019).

Their independence at home and their easy access to information give Gen Z self-confidence in the kitchen. Many are able to cook through YouTube and other social media networks due to their tendency to discover fun and informative food content and their desire to experiment with fast and fun video-based recipes (Mullen 2019). What is different for today's youth is that information, entertainment and instructions about cooking are plentiful and accessible. The abundance of information gives young people the feeling that they can cook whatever they want (Demeritt 2018).

Health: In some ways, Gen Z is healthier than previous generations because they have grown under the bombardment of messages advocating the importance of healthy eating and being fit (Euromonitor 2011). On the other hand, according to Su et al. (2019), Gen Z is more knowledgeable about sustainable life than previous generations because they have access to healthy lifestyle options at an early age. They are environmentally friendly; prioritizing health when making food choices and paying more attention to higher quality of life than other generations.

They prefer fresh ingredients rather than processed food. The words like "natural", "sustainable", or "organic" on products packages or restaurant menus draw their attention (Vision Critical 2016). Even the youngest members of this generation know the responsibilities that must be taken to protect the planet. They do not care about nutritional values as much as Millennials, but their priority is the production of food with natural, organic and sustainable ingredients (Blog B2BIO 2019). According to a Nielsen survey with 30,000 participants, 41% of Gen Z is willing to pay more for the foods they perceive to be healthier (Su et al. 2019). The vast majority of Gen Z seeks food that conforms to their values (McSweeney 2019). And they want a balance of vegetables and protein in their meals (www.bestfoodfacts.org).

They prefer vegetable consumption and they are more open to being vegetarians than millennials for ethical reasons (Maynard 2019). Producing iconic pastas and cheeses since 1937, Kraft Foods added the pasta produced from cauliflower and flaxseed to its product line in 2010 and released its Smart product line. In April 2015, the company changed its original recipe and replaced it with a recipe from natural and organic foods. They expect sophisticated and healthy menus when eating out, as they are more independent in their choice of food, and more enthusiastic for fresh food (Vision Critical 2016). In 2016, PepsiCo released a product range made from cane sugar instead of high fructose corn syrup, as they tend to be vegetarians and prefer cleaner and healthier brands (Devenyns 2019). About 14% of American restaurants offer meat products prepared with vegetable ingredients. An example of this is the Impossible Burger from Burger King's Whopper series (Maynard 2019). Gen Z would like to see fermented foods like Kombucha in the menus. It has entered the radar of Gen Z with remarkable health benefits and high prices (McSweeney 2019).

Authenticity and Diversity: Another powerful feature of Gen Z's eating habits is that they try authenticity and flavours from all over the world. This is because the new generation has different ethnic identities and is following international trends through the Internet. Gen Z is not afraid to try new cuisines and wants to experience authentic experiences by trying dishes from other parts of the world. The key is that this is not just an authentic cooking technique or a search for ingredients, but an authentic experience with that culture (Rewards Network 2019). According to Food Business News, Gen Z seeks bold taste profiles and extreme sensations from more authentic flavour combinations than the Millennials (Devenyns 2019). As Gen Z consumers age, they develop a taste for international foods, local or premium foods and unique and spicy flavours and begin to try different culinary delights, such as Asian and Mexican flavours (Maynard 2019; Demeritt 2018). This group is also open to experimentalism in nutrition. They are constantly experimenting with a new diet; such as keto, paleo, vegetarian or vegan. They are not afraid of new types of food and everywhere they ask if there is plant-based meat product (Weise 2019). Whether they like classic food or not, they look for a slightly more fun version of the classics (Rewards

Network 2019). For this young generation, only different combinations of these classic flavours with more spices and varieties can be made (Gordon Food 2019).

This group wants to try new and adventurous dishes, such as food trucks or street food that taste good and offer a unique dining experience. (www.bestfoodfacts.org). According to Technomic's latest report, 42% of Gen Z wants to see street food in the menus (McSweeney 2019).

Fast food and snacks: Although there is a general trend towards healthy living, young people's fast lifestyles and junk food love make it an important market segment for fast food and snack companies Going to fast food places, coffee shops and 24-h open restaurants is a popular activity among young people (Euromonitor 2011). Hamburger and pizza will continue to be on the trend list. But this time they prefer hamburgers and pizzas made with more organic ingredients or locally produced with quality ingredients (McSweeney 2019; Blog B2BIO 2019). They have an interest in continuous snacks and meal replacement. They sometimes even spend a meal with snacks. According to Food Dive's report, Gen Z is used to consuming snacks during the day, moving away from three-course meals (Mullen 2019).

Discussion and Conclusion

Food has been and will be the topmost priority for people as it is the primary need in our lives. However, there are some people who see food more than just a need. This group of people is called as foodies. According to Barr and Levy (1985), foodie is a person who is very interested in food. Foodies talk about food at almost every gathering. They salivate while talking about restaurants, recipes and even radicchio. They do not think that they talk nonsense. Foodies consider food as an art form at the same level with painting or drama. Their attitudes towards food, behaviours related to food and activities are different than other people. Food is the centre of their lives and this does not require any membership or being rich, etc.

Generation Z is the people born in 1995 and after and it is very different in various ways from its predecessors. Gen Z members are both community-oriented and individualistic. They are independent, open-minded and embracing diversities more easily than other generations. All these are caused by their relationship with Internet and tehcnology. The constant access to Internet gives them self-confidence and makes them knowledgable about many things happening around the world. All these characteristics of Gen Z are reflected in their consumer behaviour and food consumption behaviour.

They are already called as fresh foodies which proves that Gen Z is a foodie generation. Their food preferences and food-related behaviours are parallel to those of foodies. To explain this, we can give the example of foodies' interest in sustainable, organic and locally produced food. Gen Z cares more about green, sustainable, organic and local products, because it is more socially and environmentally aware and wants to protect the planet. Thus they can be categorized as organic foodies.

These young people are also curious about learning about food and thanks to Internet, they can learn whatever they want from Youtube channels or Instagram. They are similar to do-it-yourself foodies in this regard. As they are always connected online, they always want to share their moment to moment experiences and their own opinions on social media sites. With this characteristic, they can be grouped under hipster foodies. Also, it is known that food blogging has been developing within foodie culture.

Also, one of the most important aspects of foodies is their focus on authenticity and authentic experiences. As foodies, Gen Z members are always seeking new flavours such as foreign or spicy food or international cuisines like Asian or Mexican as they are a diverse group of people and come from different ethnicities and nationalities. In a study which is similar to Green (2013), it is found that the members of Gen Z are mostly moderate foodies as a result of their self-reported foodie rating and their most favourite foodie activities are eating street food, trying new restaurants and new recipes (Kılıç et al. 2018).

Another thing is that foodie identity is increasing within a student lifestyle which shows that younger Gen Z'ers may be more foodie than their elders. All these similarities between foodies and Generation Z also indicate that these young people will travel for food, especially for gaining authentic food experiences.

Suggestions and Practical Implications

While tourists want to explore their interests during their travel, their behaviour can change in their daily lives. Research on daily behaviours of foodies is important to the understanding of various foodie types, right marketing strategies for them and their decision processes in participating food tourism. Determining their lifestyle choices related to food, purchasing wine, taking cooking classes, visiting local markets, cooking, gardening, their thoughts on sustainability and other food-related activities is of vital importance for every destination that desire to develop experiences and food products (Kline et al. 2015). For attracting foodies who have a great passion towards food and can travel due to this special passion, their food-involvement levels, travel motivations, travel preferences and their characteristics should be understood. Any research on this kind of a niche market should be based on theory for evaluating this within gastronomy tourism (Wilkinson 2016).

Economists argue that Gen Z will contribute $ 29–143 billion to the US economy and become the largest consumer market in 2020. These statistics necessitate the market segmentation of the factors affecting the purchasing decisions of Gen Z in the sustainable food market and a detailed examination of this segment (Su et al. 2019). According to the way Gen Z sees the world, all brands and companies need to be constantly online like themselves, and even for them, connections must be fast and effective (Vision Critical 2016). The tactics that can be used to increase Gen Z'ers spending power are as follows: (1) A restaurant experience investing in social responsibility. (2) An active social media account. (3) Menu updates. (4) Provide fast and reliable service. (5) Create a comfortable space (Janzer 2019). Also, words such as natural, organic and sustainable on menus affect Gen Z more than other generations. Restaurants can use words like local, authentic, farm-grown, organic and cage-free in their menus to attract Gen Z consumers who are willing to pay more for products that support social responsibility (Gordon Food 2019). Combining traditional food with adventurous elements, chefs—such as fermented garnishes or hot peppers—can please these young people (Aaron Allen & Associates 2018).

Since travelling and taking a vacation are one of the reasons for saving money, this saver generation is a great opportunity for companies that know how to address them and reach them interactively through their preferred mobile channels. Their attention can be drawn via 10-s or shorter ad commercials or videos like Snapchat as their attention spans are shorter (Vision Critical 2016).

In future research, the cultural differences regarding foodie behaviour of Generation Z can be studied. Because cultural variables have an impact upon the generational differences. Also, food tourists among Gen Z can be examined in terms of their food-involvement levels.

References

Aaron Allen & Associates. 2018. https://aaronallen.com/blog/gen-z-food-trends. Accessed on September 12, 2019.

Ambrozas, Diana. 2003. "Serious Feast: Vancouver Foodies in Globalized Consumer Society." PhD diss., School of Communication-Simon Fraser University.

Atkinson, Laura. 2013. "The New Young Foodie Culture". *The Sunday Times*, 30–33.

Barr, Ann, and Paul Levy. 1985. *The Official Foodie Handbook*. New York: Arbor House Publishing Company.

Beer, Sean. 2008. "Authenticity and Food Experience–Commercial and Academic Perspectives." *Journal of Foodservice* 19, no. 3: 153–163.

Blog B2BIO. 2019. https://www.b2bio.bio/en/noticias-productos-ecologicos/the-top-8-food-preferences-of-generation-z. Accessed on September 12, 2019.

Bourdain, Ruth. 2012. *Comfort Me with Offal: Ruth Bourdain's Guide to Gastronomy*. Andrews McMeel Publishing.

Brones, Anna. 2011. "The 10 Types of Foodies". https://www.huffingtonpost.com/anna-brones/the-10-types-of-foodies_b_1170430.html. Accessed on September 12, 2019.

Cairns, Kate, Josée Johnston, and Shyon Baumann. 2010. "Caring About Food: Doing Gender in the Foodie Kitchen." *Gender & Society* 24, no. 5: 591–615.

Demeritt, Laurie. 2018. "Enter Gen Z: The New Disruptors of Food Culture". https://www.smartbrief.com/original/2018/09/enter-gen-z-new-disruptors-food-culture. Accessed on September 12, 2019.

Devenyns, Jessi. 2019. "How to Make Food and Drink Generation Z will Crave." https://www.fooddive.com/news/how-to-make-food-and-drink-generation-z-will-crave/563457/. Accessed on September 12, 2019.

Dunlap, Rudy. 2012. "Recreating Culture: Slow Food as a Leisure Education Movement." *World Leisure Journal* 54, no. 1: 38–47.

Euromonitor. 2011."Make Way for Generation Z: Marketing to Today's Tweens and Teens" *Euromonitor International: Strategy Briefing.* https://oaltabo2012.files.wordpress.com/2012/03/make-way-for-generation-z1.pdf Accessed on September 12, 2019.

Fister-Gale, Sarah. 2015. "Forget Gen Y: Are You Ready for Generation Z?" https://www.chieflearningofficer.com/2015/07/07/forget-gen-y-are-you-ready-for-gen-z/. Accessed on September 12, 2019.

Getz, Donald, and Richard N. S. Robinson. 2014a "Foodies and Food Events." *Scandinavian Journal of Hospitality and Tourism* 14, no. 3: 315–330.

Getz, Donald, and Richard N. S. Robinson. 2014b. ""Foodies" and Their Travel Preferences." *Tourism Analysis* 19, no. 6: 659–672.

Getz, Donald, Richard Robinson, Tommy Andersson, and Sanja Vujicic. 2014. *Foodies and Food Tourism.* Oxford: Goodfellow Publishers.

Gordon Food Service Contributors. 2019. https://www.gfs.com/en-us/ideas/gen-z-food-preferences. Accessed on September 12, 2019.

Green, Erin. 2013. "A Study of Travelers' Foodie Activity Dimensions, Demographic Characteristics, and Trip Behaviors." Unpublished Masters Thesis. East Carolina University, Greenville NC, U.S.A.

Haddouche, Hamed, and Christine Salomone. 2018. "Generation Z and the Tourist Experience: Tourist Stories and Use of Social Networks." *Journal of Tourism Futures* 4, no. 1: 69–79.

Halliday, Sue, and Astafyeva, Alexandra. 2014. "Millennial Cultural Consumers: Co-creating Value Through Brand Communities." *Arts Marketing: An International Journal* 4, no. 1/2: 119–135.

Janzer, Cinnamon. 2019. "Serving Generation Z: How restaurants Can Get Ready." https://www.lightspeedhq.com/blog/serving-generation-z-how-restaurants-can-get-ready/. Accessed on September 12, 2019.

Johnston, Josée, and Shyon Baumann. 2010. *Foodies: Democracy and Distinction in the Gourmet Foodscape.* New York: Routledge.

Kılıç, Burhan, Aydan Bekar, Nisan Yozukmaz, and Ezgi Sayman. 2018. "The Determination of Foodie Activities of Gen Z." In *The Proceedings of 4th International Gastronomic Tourism Congress*, ed. Betül Öztürk and Feray Irigüler, 123–133. İzmir: İzfaş Yayınevi.

Kline, Carol S., Jerusha Greenwood, and Leah Joyner. 2015. "Exploring Foodie Segmentation." *Journal of Tourism Insights* 6, no. 1: 3.

Kline, Carol, Seungwoo John Lee, and Whitney Knollenberg. 2018. "Segmenting Foodies for a Foodie Destination." *Journal of Travel & Tourism Marketing* 35, no. 9: 1234–1245.

Leggett, Tabatha. 2013. "The 7 Differet Types of Foodie." https://www.buzzfeed.com/tabathaleggett/the-different-types-of-foodie. Accessed on September 12, 2019.

Mannheim, Karl. 2011. *Le problème des générations*. Armand Colin.

Maynard, Micheline. 2019. "The Food World's Next Big Question: What Does Generation Z Want to Eat?" https://www.forbes.com/sites/michelinemaynard/2019/06/06/the-food-worlds-next-big-question-what-does-generation-z-want-to-eat/#7a03f9e32684. Accessed on September 12, 2019.

McSweeney, Ryan. 2019. "Generation Z Food Trends and Eating Habits." https://upserve.com/restaurant-insider/generation-z-new-food-trends/. Accessed on September 12, 2019.

Merriman, Marcie. 2015. "What If the Next Big Disruptor Isn'ta What But a Who?" https://www.ey.com/Publication/vwLUAssets/EY-what-if-the-next-big-disruptor-isnt-a-what-but-a-who/$File/EY-what-if-the-next-big-disruptor-isnt-a-what-but-a-who.pdf. Accessed on September 12, 2019.

Mignon, J. M. 2003. "Le tourisme des jeunes. Une valeur sure." *Cahier Espaces* 77.

Mohsen, Marwa Gad. 2017. "Foodies in the UK: A Sense of Self, Connection and Belonging Beyond the Passion?" In *Creating Marketing Magic and Innovative Future Marketing Trends*, 457–467. Springer, Cham.

Mullen, Caitlin. 2019. "Gen Z Changes the Taste of the Food Industry." https://www.bizjournals.com/bizwomen/news/latest-news/2019/05/gen-z-changes-the-taste-of-the-food-industry.html?page=all. Accessed on September 12, 2019.

Prensky, Mark. 2001. "Digital Natives, Digital Immigrants." https://www.marcprensky.com/writing/Prensky%20-%20Digital%20Natives,%20Digital%20Immigrants%20-%20Part1.pdf. Accessed on September 12, 2019.

Priporas, Constantinos-Vasilios, Nikolaos Stylos, and Anestis K. Fotiadis. 2017. "Generation Z Consumers' Expectations of Interactions in Smart Retailing: A Future Agenda." *Computers in Human Behavior* 77: 374–381.

Renfro, Adam. 2012. "Meet Generation Z. Getting Smart." https://gettingsm art.com/2012/12/meet-generation-z/. Accessed on September 12, 2019.

Renfro, Adam. (2015). "Meet Generation Z". http://gettingsmart.com/2015/ 12/meet-generation-z/.

Rewards Network. 2019. "Not So Millennial: Restaurant Food Trends for Generation Z." https://www.rewardsnetwork.com/blog/not-millennial-food-trends-generation-z/. Accessed on September 12, 2019.

Robinson, Richard N. S., and Donald Getz. 2014. "Profiling Potential Food Tourists: An Australian Study." *British Food Journal* 116, no: 4: 690–706.

Ross, Jack. 2003. "Top Restaurant To Home Cooking". *The Scotsman*, https:// www.scotsman.com/news-2-15012/top-restaurant-to-home-cooking-1-602189. Accessed on September 12, 2019.

Schlossberg, Mallory. 2016. "Teen Generation Z is Being Called 'Millennials on Steroids,' and That Could Be Terrifying for Retailers." *Business Insider*.https://www.businessinsider.in/retail/teen-generation-z-is-being-cal led-millennials-on-steroids-and-that-could-be-terrifying-for-retailers/slidel ist/53565468.cms. Accessed on September 12, 2019.

Singh, Anjali. 2014. "Challenges and Issues of Generation Z." *IOSR Journal of Business and Management* 16, no. 7: 59–63.

Skinner, Heather, David Sarpong, and Gareth R. T. White. 2018. "Meeting the Needs of the Millennials and Generation Z: Gamification in Tourism Through Geocaching." *Journal of Tourism Futures* 4, no. 1: 93–104.

Sloan, A. Elizabeth. 2013. "The Foodie Phenomenon." *Food Technology* 67, no. 2: 18.

Stebbins, Robert A. 1992. *Amateurs, Professionals, and Serious Leisure*. McGill-Queen's Press-MQUP.

Su, Ching-Hui Joan, Chin-Hsun Ken Tsai, Ming-Hsiang Chen, and Wan Qing Lv. 2019. "US Sustainable Food Market Generation Z Consumer Segments." *Sustainability* 11, no. 13: 3607.

Tavares, Jean Max, Madhuri Sawant, and Olimpia Ban. 2018. "A Study of the Travel Preferences of Generation Z Located in Belo Horizonte (Minas Gerais–Brazil)." *e-Review of Tourism Research* 15, no. 2/3.

Turner, Anthony. 2015. "Generation Z: Technology and Social Interest." *The Journal of Individual Psychology* 71, no. 2: 103–113.

Vision Critical. 2016. "The Everything Guide to Generation Z." https:// cdn2.hubspot.net/hubfs/4976390/E-books/English%20e-books/The%20e verything%20guide%20to%20gen%20z/the-everything-guide-to-gen-z.pdf. Accessed on September 12, 2019.

Watson, Pamela, Michael Morgan, and Nigel Hemmington. 2008. "Online Communities and the Sharing of Extraordinary Restaurant Experiences." *Journal of Foodservice* 19, no. 6: 289–302.

Watson, Pamela Janet. 2013. "Grab Your Fork: A Netnographic Study of a Foodie Blog and Its Community." PhD diss., Bournemouth University.

Weise, Sarah. (2019). "Gen Z+ Food: What the Food Industry Needs to Know About Marketing to a New Generation". https://bixaresearch.com/blog/2019/7/22/gen-z-food-what-the-food-industry-needs-to-know-about-marketing-to-a-new-generation. Accessed on September 12, 2019.

Wilkinson, Paul F. 2016. "Foodies and Food Tourism." *Annals of Leisure Research* 19, no. 1: 139–141.

Yozukmaz, Nisan, Aydan Bekar, and Burhan Kılıç. 2017. "A Conceptual Review of "Foodies" in Tourism." *Journal of Tourism and Gastronomy Studies* 170–179.

Zhu, Feng, and Xiaoquan Zhang. 2010. "Impact of Online Consumer Reviews on Sales: The Moderating Role of Product and Consumer Characteristics." *Journal of marketing* 74, no. 2: 133–148. Accessed on September 12, 2019.

https://www.bestfoodfacts.org/gen-z-favors-fun-fresh-food/. Accessed on September 12, 2019.

https://blacksmithapplications.com/gen-z-is-shaping-the-future-of-food-and-beverage/. Accessed on September 12, 2019.

10

Perceptions of Gen Z Tourists on Street Food in Hong Kong

Derrick Lee, Tingzhen Chen, and Wilco Chan

Introduction

Street foods refer to ready-to-eat foods and beverages prepared at home or on streets and consumed on the streets without further preparation or with a little preparation (Rane, 2011). Street foods are a source of food that is socially and culturally accepted, low-price, convenient and often tantalizing preparations for both urban and rural populations worldwide (Namugumya and Muyanja 2012). The impact of globalization has led to changes in modern lifestyles and family structures, limited food

---

D. Lee (✉)
Academic Division, Singapore Institute of Management, Clementi, Singapore
e-mail: derricklee@sim.edu.sg

T. Chen
Tourism, James Cook University, Townsville, North QLD, Australia

W. Chan
Institute for Tourism Studies, Macau, China

© The Author(s), under exclusive license to Springer Nature
Switzerland AG 2021
N. Stylos et al. (eds.), *Generation Z Marketing and Management in Tourism and Hospitality*,
https://doi.org/10.1007/978-3-030-70695-1_10

249

preparation time, along with other socio-economic reasons, have led to significant changes in consumers' food selection attributes and consumption patterns. Consumers today are visiting different street food outlets, seeking convenience and value for their money. This provides opportunities for street vendors to sell food and earn income as a means of supporting their families (Acho-Chi 2002).

Researchers suggest that satisfying food tourism experiences can enhance tourists' perceptions of a destination (Smith and Xiao 2008). It is recommended in *The Telegraph* that travellers can consume street food at the world's tastiest culinary capitals in Asia—Bangkok (Thailand), Ho Chi Minh city (Vietnam), Osaka (Japan), Hong Kong (China), Shanghai (China) and Singapore (Hinson 2019). As destinations are promoting street food as a part of tourism attractions, there is growing interest among tourism scholars examining popular street food destinations particularly in Asia such as Bangkok, Fukuoka, Hanoi, Manila, Penang, Phnom Penh, Seoul, Singapore, Taipei and Xi'an (Chavarria and Phakdee-auksorn 2017; Yeap and Ong 2019).

Government views food tourism strategy favourably as an effective means to boost the tourism sector. For example, researchers noted that Hong Kong Tourism Board (HKTB) utilized food tourism strategy effectively and created a competitive advantage in differentiating the city as a gastronomic destination from other competing destinations (Enright and Newton 2005; Okumus et al. 2007). However, the tourism sector suffered a decline in tourist arrivals as the tourist arrivals in 2018 reached 56.5 million compared to 60.8 million in 2014, a decline of 7.6 per cent (HKTB Research 2019). To revive the tourism sector, Hong Kong Tourism Board (HKTB) government added a variety of street food options by introducing the food trucks concept as a means of attracting tourists and creating a new food consumption experience for visitors. The food truck industry is rapidly growing in food tourism chain and expected to have a fourfold increase from 2012 by generating $2.7 billion in revenue in the USA by 2017. It is reported that the food truck industry in the USA will generate US$1.1 billion in 2020 (IBISWorld 2020). Witnessing the potential growth of the food truck industry, HKTB launched a new Food Truck Pilot Scheme (FTPS) in 2017, which was a part of their street food campaign, with the aim of boosting the city's appeal as a food tourism destination offering diverse, high quality and hygienic foods for visitors.

There is a growing trend of researching on younger generations' motivation and behaviour, as tourism providers seek to modify product offerings to match target markets' needs. The younger generations refer to Gen Y (millennials) and Gen Z (post-millennials). According to World Economic Forum, Gen Z will account for 2.47 billion people out of global population of 7.7 billion in 2019—that is 32% and surpasses the 2.43 billion millennials generation. Gen Zers are tech-savvy as they are living in the era of social media platforms and looking for entertaining content to share with their peers (Miller and Lu 2018; Su et al. 2019; Wood 2018). Gen Z, i.e. individuals born between 1996 and 2010, are becoming a growing consumer market in the restaurant industry, and they fuel the industry's overall growth (Yeap and Ong 2019). Yoon and Chung (2018) emphasized that millennial generation are motivated to try new food and experience new food culture, however, there are limited food tourism studies on the emerging Gen Z consumers (Le and Arcodia 2018). Today's food service industry is concerned with Gen Z or foodie generation consumers as they like to dine out and adventurous in trying new foods (Lukovitz 2009; Sung et al. 2013; Wallace 2018). Therefore, Gen Z segment is a good target market in the street food industry that provides exotic, adventuresome, memorable dining experience for consumers (Solomon 2018). This chapter focuses on understanding perception of Gen Z on street food and identifying consumer needs which could be a powerful driver of street food industry success. The current study aims to explain features of Gen Z tourists, and to justify their significance as an attractive segment for tourism and street food businesses (Moreno et al. 2017).

Literature Review

Food Tourism

Researchers suggest that food is becoming a key factor motivating people to travel and choose a destination (Boniface 2017; McKercher et al.

2008). Food tourism has become an indispensable component of the marketing strategy of a destination (Du Rand and Health 2006). With examination of related research literature, it is suggested that the relationship between food and tourism can be assessed from different aspects. Food can be viewed as (a) a reflection of the culture of a destination and its people, (b) a tourist attraction and (c) a way to provide and enhance tourists' destination experience (Boniface 2017; du Rand and Health 2006; McKercher et al. 2008). In essence, food tourism incorporates visitors experiencing a specific food, learning local culture and food features as the key motives for tourists (Chen and Huang 2016).

There are greater research interests on authenticity of dining experiences especially in the areas of tourism, hospitality and leisure since 2002. This emerging trend is consistent with the evolution of conceptualizations of authenticity in the tourism context as previously discussed, notable instigated by Wang's (1999) authenticity in typology. Touristic dining experiences were mostly examined in the setting of ethnic-themed restaurants and ethnic/local cuisine restaurants, suggesting the important role of local culture and authentic cuisine in shaping the attractiveness of a tourist destination (Chang et al. 2011; Cohen and Avieli 2004; Engeset et al. 2015; Wijaya et al. 2013). Other studies also examined authentic cuisines in general restaurant industry (De Vries and Go 2017; O'Connor et al. 2017) and restaurant chain settings (DiPietro 2017; Özdemir and Seyitoğlu 2017). Authenticity is rather a cultural construct closely tied into Western notions (Mkono et al. 2013) shaping non-Western countries into minor ethnicities, and their cuisines into ethnic cuisines. Findings of these Western-centric studies were consistent with literature on tourism, hospitality and events. It is important to promote authentic dining experiences as a tool to promote local and national cuisines and destination competitiveness (Le et al. 2019).

Local food is a core manifestation of a destination's intangible heritage, and through consumption, tourists can gain a truly authentic cultural experience. Local food and food markets represent a destination's intangible heritage as tourists gain in-depth knowledge of local cuisines and its cultural heritage. More importantly, tourists view consumption of local food favourably as it enhances travellers' tourism experience (Bjork and Kauppinen-Raisanen 2016; Hjalager 2004; Kivela and Crotts 2005; Lee and Scott 2015). There is extensive literature on destination marketing, however, there is a lack of empirical evidence on how food is used in tourism marketing (Echtner and Prasad 2003; Hudson and Miller 2005), leaving many unanswered questions related to consumption of local food by tourists and creating opportunities for scholarly attention (Kim et al. 2009).

Food studies in Hong Kong focused on restaurants, hotels and food festivals (McKercher et al. 2008). Earlier food tourism studies in Hong Kong also distinguished the impact of culture on tourists from different nationalities. For example, Mak et al. (2017) distinguished the food consumption motives of Taiwanese tourists compared to UK tourists. Lee et al. (in press) identified eight motivational dimensions of food consumption of Chinese tourists and Western tourists and found that both segments have different emphasis on food consumption in terms of value, variety, prestige and ambience. Academic literature on street food globally focused mainly on hygienic/food safety in California (Vanschaik and Tuttle 2014) and Orlando (Okumus et al. 2019) promoting organic street food in Toronto (Holmes et al. 2018), service quality of street food in USA (Shin et al. 2019), innovation and efficiency performance in Turin (Alfiero et al. 2017). There is a lack of research on analyzing tourists' perceptions of street food industry in Hong Kong despite the increasing demand for street food experience among Gen Z. The current study focuses on examining the Gen Z visitors on their perceptions and key considerations when patronizing street food and consumption of local food in Hong Kong. The study also identified the underlying cultural differences between Chinese and Western Gen Zs' food perceptions. Findings provide useful insights and implications for policymakers and destination marketers in promoting street food as an appealing tourism attraction for visitors in Hong Kong.

Street Food

Street foods refer to ready-to-eat food sold on streets, markets, bazaars and other public places (Kowalczyk and Kubal-Czerwińska 2020; Rane 2011). Street foods are generally considered as cheap, convenient and

254 D. Lee et al.

commonly accepted by diverse cultures (Namugumya and Muyanja, 2012). More importantly, consumers' changing demands and personal food preferences to eat out motivate them to visit different street food outlets, seeking convenience and value for their money.

Street foods are popular with visitors with its variety of choices and have become cultural icons and tourist attractions (Dawson and Canet 1991; Henderson 2000; Timothy and Wall 1997). Tourists are keen to consume local street foods such as pork satay (Bangkok), egg waffle (Hong Kong), banh mi/ baguette (Ho Chi Minh) or bhel puri (Mumbai) (Connelly 2016; Shea 2018). Travellers can also enjoy local foods in food halas (India), night markets (Taiwan and Thailand), street stalls (Korea) or Yatai (Japan) (Gupta et al. 2018). Findings of tourists' perceptions on street food in Delhi (Guptaet al. 2018), Phuket (Chavarria and Phakdee-auksorn 2017) and Yogyakarta (Yusuf 2017) were consistent with literature as street food offers unique cultural experience and the importance of high standards in hygiene practices. Chavarria and Phakdee-auksorn (2017) conclude that local authorities can introduce training programme to educate street food vendors on the importance of adopting good service standards and hygiene practices to enhance tourists' perceptions of street food and increase likelihood of repeat visitation. Some street food businesses are operated in the form of mobile food trucks, which are particularly popular in North America and Europe. For example, the development of food truck gastronomy has been boosted with public events such as concerts, historical reconstructions, sports and recreation events in Italy and Poland (Alfiero et al. 2017; Kowalczyk and Kubal-Czerwińska 2020).

For this chapter, it is useful to trace the development of street food in Hong Kong. Street food has been part of the local cultural heritage and affordable for consumers since 1940s. By 1960s, it was reported that there were 300,000 hawkers including the majority of illegal hawkers. This forced the British government to introduce measures such as non-transferable itinerant hawker licences as illegal hawkers were considered as a serious threat to the city's health, hygiene and development. The effective measure saw the decline in the number of licensed hawkers from 50,000 in 1974 to 6000 in 2007. Next, the local authorities issued 218 fixed-pitch hawking licences (licence transferable to immediate family)

10 Perceptions of Gen Z Tourists on Street Food in Hong Kong   255

Table 10.1 Different modes of street food provision in Hong Kong

Mode of operation	Capacity	Costs	Flexibility	Target customers
Illegal hawking (fish-ball trolley)	Low	Low	High	Cheap food for locals
Fixed pitch hawker (wet market stall)	Low	Low	Medium	Cheap food for locals
Dai Pai Tongs (seafood dai pai tongs)	Medium	Medium	Low	Affordable food for locals
Cha Chaan Teng (Tsui Wah restaurant)	High	High	Low	Local food to locals and visitors
Food Trucks	Low	High	Medium	Local/foreign foods to locals and visitors

Source Adapted from Cheung et al. (2018)

and some Dai Pai Tongs (licence transfer to one's spouse only). As a result, some Dai Pai Tongs gave up their business licences for some monetary compensation while others moved to shops and malls as "Chinese Cafes" and "Cha Chaan Teng" (Hong Kong-style cafes). In 2017, the government collaborated with stakeholders and introduced the new Food Truck Pilot Scheme (FTPS), aiming to create job opportunities for locals and boost attraction appeal for visitors. Table 10.1 shows different modes of street food provision in Hong Kong (Cheung et al. 2018).

Gen Z Tourists

Gen Z, born after 1994 and aged 25 (in 2020) are also called Baby Bloomers, Generation 9/11, Post-Millennials and Tweens. Gen Z are a generation of young people characterized by their usage and adaptation of technology in their daily lives, as well as values, life experiences, motivations and common buying behaviour (Kotler and Lee 2016; Priporas et al. 2017; Rainer and Rainer 2011; Williams and Page 2011). Gen Z is influenced by new media, virtual friends and the power that comes with technology. They are receptive to products emphasizing peer acceptance and they enjoy sharing comments from other peers. For Tweens, they can be using new social and virtual networking sites in building their online communities (Williams and Page 2011; Branwell 2010; Posnick-Goodwin 2010).

Researchers have revealed the crucial importance of Gen Zers not just because of their sheer numbers but also their exceptional set of attributes. It is important to investigate this Generation's unique set of attitudes and beliefs, motivations, expectations and behaviours and this has seen an increase in academic research on understanding the Gen Zs' perceptions (Moreno et al. 2017; United Nations World Tourism Organisation 2008). Numerous studies adopted the approach of identifying general travel motives of the young generation (e.g. Carr 1999; Mohsin and Alsawafi 2011; Thrane, 2008; Xu et al. 2009). Rita et al. (2019) analysed and compared the travel motivations and preferred destination activities of US millennials and UK millennials. The study revealed both groups of respondents have similar push motives and validated the Anglophone phenomenon (English-speaking countries such as UK, US, Australia, New Zealand and Canada shared common roots). The characteristics of millennial generation may be pervasive, but it does not represent a global phenomenon (Leask et al. 2014; Moscardo and Benckendorff 2010). Young generations have unique motivations and personality (Carr 2001) traits in terms of sensation-seeking (Pizam et al. 2004), novelty and excitement seeking, engage in physical risk (Lepp and Gibson 2003). More importantly, young tourists are more likely to adopt risk-taking behaviour (Berdychevsky and Gibson, 2015). It will be useful to examine factors that can influence Gen Z consumers' perceptions of street food in Hong Kong.

Methodology

A survey questionnaire was developed based on the review of literature to determine the perceptions of Gen Z tourists towards patronizing street food in Hong Kong. The constructs used were based on the review of available literature which have been developed in the previous studies and modified to fit the scope of this research (Chavarria and Phakdee-auksorn 2017; Gupta et al. 2018; Henderson et al. 2012; Lee et al. (in press); Yoon and Chung 2018; Yusuf 2017).

The purpose of this study is to identify the perceptions of Gen Z tourists (Kotler and Lee 2016; Rainer and Rainer 2011) aged 18–25 from mainland China and Western countries when they visited Hong Kong. This study examines the similar and unique perceptions of Chinese Gen Z tourists and Western Gen Z tourists. Findings can provide useful insights for destination marketers and policymakers in developing and promoting food tourism to Chinese and Western tourists to Hong Kong.

The questionnaire comprised of three sections. The first section contained questions about respondents' trip characteristics. The second section inquired about respondents' socio-demographic characteristics. The third section initially contained the 26 perception statements (to be rated on 5-Likert scale) of respondents on street food in Hong Kong. To ensure quality and accuracy, a Mainland Chinese business executive translated the original English into Chinese version and then back-translated to English to ensure clarity and consistency. A key benefit of conducting a back-translation is it enables comparison of the original source language version with the version which was back-translated into the source language (Maneesriwongul and Dixon 2004). A pilot study was conducted prior to the actual survey to ensure the content validity and clarity of the questionnaire including the motive dimensions. A pilot study is an exploratory phase that aims to identify and eliminate problems before the full survey is carried out (Nykiel 2007). The pilot study was conducted on two individuals—a Mainland Chinese academic staff and a Taiwanese postgraduate student. And it revealed a couple of the perception statements were quite similar so they were removed from the questionnaire, resulting in 24 perception statements.

The study adopted a convenience sampling method that is affordable and easy, and respondents are accessible. However, this method can be bias and sample size should be carefully treated as a representative of the population (Etikan et al., 2016; Mackey and Ross-Feldman, 2005). A total of 161 Gen Z tourists' (104 Chinese and 57 Western: USA—17, Canada—5, Australia—8, UK—7, Germany—4, Spain—1,

Denmark—1, France—4, Sweden—3, Finland—1, Russia—2, Switzerland—2, Ukraine—1, Italy—1) valid questionnaires were collected at the various tourism attractions and street food venues such as the Central Harbourfront Event Space, Hong Kong Disneyland, Golden Bauhinia Square, Ocean Park, Salisbury Garden, Science Museum and Tsim Sha Tsui Art Square between January and February 2018.

Reliability and Validity of the Measurements

Before proceeding further analysis, a Cronbach's alpha test was conducted to assess the reliability of 24 statements. Cronbach's alpha is used to test the inter-relationship among measurement scales which would tell us if these 24 statements are measuring the same latent variable (i.e. street food). The resulting α coefficient of reliability ranges from 0 to 1 in providing this overall assessment of a measure's reliability. If all of the scale items are entirely independent from one another (i.e. are not correlated or share no covariance), then $\alpha = 0$; and, if all of the items have high covariances, then α will approach 1 as the number of items in the scale approaches infinity. In other words, the higher the α coefficient, the more the items have shared covariance and probably measure the same underlying concept (Goforth 2015). Values of Cronbach's alpha greater than 0.70 were considered to be reliable (Nunnally 1978). The reliability coefficients for the scales on the 24 street food perception statements were 0.827. Considering the minimal acceptable level of alpha coefficient (i.e. 0.70), these values suggested that scales could be considered reliable and used for further analysis.

Results and Discussions

Three stages of analysis were carried on for this study. First of all, a descriptive summary of the 161 responses' key demographic characteristics was provided in Table 10.2. Then the focus of the analysis was given to the 24 perception statements. And at last, a closer look was applied to the respondents' preference over 14 HK street food items.

10 Perceptions of Gen Z Tourists on Street Food in Hong Kong 259

Table 10.2 Demographic characteristics of the respondents ($N = 161$)

Characteristics		Chinese		Western		Total	
		N	%	N	%	N	%
Gender	Female	67	41.6	32	19.9	99	61.5
	Male	37	23.0	25	15.5	32	38.5
Income	40,000 and below	60	37.3	27	16.8	87	54.1
	40,001–60,000	22	13.7	15	9.3	37	23.0
	60,001–80,000	15	9.3	9	5.6	24	14.9
	80,001–100,000	3	1.9	5	3.1	8	5.0
	Above 100,000	4	2.5	1	0.6	5	3.1

Characteristics of Respondents

As shown in Table 10.2, the respondents of this study comprised of 38.5% male and 61.5% female Gen Zs. Most of the respondents (54.1%) answered their annual household income less than 40,000 US dollars. The profile of respondents was consistent with other street food studies in Delhi (Gupta et al. 2018); Yogyakarta (Yusuf 2017); Chavarria and Phakdee-auksorn 2017) as majority of respondents were females with household income below 40,000 US dollars.

Further analysis for this study was carried out on these 161 samples. First of all, the exploratory factor analysis (EFA) was employed to identify the key perceptions towards Hong Kong street food among the Gen Zs. The perception statements were factor analysed using principal component analysis with varimax rotation (KMO = 0.722, Bartlett's Test: Chi-Square = 1087.504, df = 276, Sig. = 0.000). Based on Kaiser's criterion, or the eigenvalue rule, only factors with an eigenvalue of 1.0 or more were retained for further analysis (Pallant, 2007). A cut-off point for factor loadings was set at 0.40 in the interpretation of the final rotated factor pattern (Stevens, 2002). Five factors generated from the EFA were named: Factor 1—etic destination image, Factor 2—local emersion, Factor 3—e-WOM, Factor 4—emic food characteristics and Factor 5—safety/hygiene. The five factors accounted for near 50% of the cumulative variance (Table 10.3).

Table 10.3 Results of the EFA (N = 161 Gen Z Tourists)

Factors and items	Factor loading	Cronbach's Alpha	Mean	S.D	Grand mean	Eigen-value	Variance explained (%)
Factor 1—etic destination image					3.39	5.142	21.424
I have high expectations of HK street foods	0.628	0.817	3.44	0.850			
I have good knowledge of HK street foods	0.613	0.818	3.34	1.006			
I will not feel like I am in HK unless I enjoy eating street foods	0.602	0.822	3.49	1.007			
I prefer to eat street foods than restaurants in HK	0.539	0.818	3.14	0.919			
I perceive HK as a street food destination	0.456	0.820	3.53	0.962			
Factor 2—local emersion					3.93	2.102	8.756
I will recommend my friends to consume HK street foods	0.727	0.819	3.89	0.906			
I had a satisfactory experience with HK street foods	0.699	0.818	3.76	0.779			
HK street foods are delicious	0.553	0.821	3.96	0.782			

(continued)

10 Perceptions of Gen Z Tourists on Street Food in Hong Kong — 261

Table 10.3 (continued)

Factors and items	Factor loading	Cronbach's Alpha	Mean	S.D	Grand mean	Eigen-value	Variance explained (%)
Eating street foods introduces me to unique local culture	0.521	0.822	3.98	0.746			
I am adventurous and keen to try a variety of HK street foods	0.459	0.819	4.04	0.749			
Factor 3—e-WOM					3.39	1.722	7.175
I learned about HK street foods from social media	0.774	0.819	3.62	1.030			
I learned about HK street foods from the internet websites	0.752	0.817	3.52	1.025			
Media is a reliable source of information on HK street foods	0.703	0.822	3.40	0.925			
I learned about HK street foods from TV coverage	0.640	0.821	3.02	1.060			
Factor 4—emic food characteristics					3.75	1.503	6.264
HK street foods offer good range of local cuisines	0.638	0.817	3.88	0.756			

(continued)

262   D. Lee et al.

Table 10.3 (continued)

Factors and items	Factor loading	Cronbach's Alpha	Mean	S.D	Grand mean	Eigen-value	Variance explained (%)
HK street foods offer good range of international cuisines	0.546	0.825	3.54	0.935			
I prefer HK street foods that are presented attractively	0.532	0.821	4.03	0.778			
I prefer to consume HK street foods with my travel companions	0.474	0.822	3.84	0.741			
I consume HK street foods that my travel companions like	0.456	0.821	3.68	0.841			
HK street foods are good for price and value	0.451	0.820	3.55	0.873			
Factor 5—Safety/Hygiene					3.47	1.410	5.875
I prefer HK street foods that are generally good for my health	0.789	0.828	3.27	1.049			
I prefer HK street foods that match with my usual eating habit	0.641	0.821	3.41	0.990			

(continued)

Table 10.3 (continued)

Factors and items	Factor loading	Cronbach's Alpha	Mean	S.D	Grand mean	Eigen-value	Variance explained (%)
I prefer to eat different HK street foods everyday	0.484	0.817	3.46	1.000			
I prefer HK street foods of high hygiene standards	0.459	0.833	3.73	0.994			
Total variance explained							49.494

Factor 1—*Etic Destination Image* contains five items, such as "I have high expectations of HK street foods", "I have good knowledge of HK street foods", "I will not feel like I am in HK unless I enjoy eating street foods", "I prefer to eat street foods than restaurants in HK" and "I perceive HK as a street food destination". The "etic" in this factor name means that the information sources to form the destination image are from the outside of the street food system (Pike 1967). The factor has a grand mean of 3.39, the lowest rated factor together with Factor 3. There is the perception of HK as a street food destination; however, respondents do not consider trying street foods as a must-do tourism activity as they do not value Hong Kong high as a street food destination. HKTB has been working on promoting food tourism in HK; tourists' perception of a street food destination is associated with their expectations and knowledge. It is suggested that the local authorities should develop destination marketing strategies, focusing on providing relevant street food knowledge, in promoting street food effectively to attract visitors to Hong Kong.

Factor 2—*Local Emersion* has five items, including "I will recommend my friends to consume HK street foods", "I had a satisfactory experience with HK street foods", "HK street foods are delicious", "Eating street food introduces me to unique local culture" and "I am adventurous and keen to try a variety of HK street foods". This factor has a grand mean of 3.93, the highest ranked factor. This factor suggests street foods may provide local culture experience (Yusuf 2017), and it is an important element for the Gen Zs to know about HK. This is consistent with Phuket tourists' perceptions of street food in terms of *food quality* (delicious) and *service quality* (authentic local cuisines*)* (Chavarria and Phakdee-auksorn 2017). The high rating on this factor suggests that Gen Z tourists emphasized the importance of street food operators offering quality cuisine and local experience for consumers. This finding is consistent with recent studies on food tourism that hedonic value and utilitarian value (Shin et al. 2019), and hedonic value benefits (Yoon and Chung 2018) can have a favourable influence on young consumers' perceptions. This finding also supported that food experience is positively associated with value benefit (Gupta et al. 2018) and satisfaction (Chavarria and Phakdee-auksorn 2017).

Factor 3—*e-WOM* has four items including "I learned about HK street foods from social media", "I learned about HK street foods from the internet websites", "I learned about HK street foods from TV coverage" and "Media is a reliable source of information on HK street food". The factor had a grand mean of 3.39 and is the least ranked factor, together with Factor 1. The measurement of media is related to the influence of media including social media, the internet and television. This perception is new to the literature but well reflects the key characteristics of this generation: digital natives and social networks (Francis and Hoefel 2018). It is suggested that the role and impact of media exposure are crucial to promoting street foods in Hong Kong (Yusuf 2017), in particular for the young and emerging market. However, the low rating by Gen Zs indicates not sufficient information regarding HK street foods was provided or available in the relevant social media platform or online sources. Social media platforms such as Facebook, Twitter, WeChat can be sources of virtual communication channels for Gen Z in search of reputable online brands (Williams and Page 2011; Branwell 2010; Posnick-Goodwin 2010). Hence, destination marketers and policymakers can focus on promoting street food through social media platforms in boosting awareness and reputation of street food in Hong Kong.

Factor 4—*Emic Food Characteristic* consists of six items, which are "HK street foods offer good range of local cuisines", "HK street foods offer good range of international cuisine", "I prefer HK street foods that are presented attractively", "I prefer to consume HK street foods with my travel companions", "I consume HK street foods that my travel companions like" and "HK street foods are good for price and value". The "emic" here refers to the internal features of the street food. This factor had a grand mean of 3.75 and is the second highest ranked factor. This suggests that Gen Z placed great importance on street food operators offering quality local and international cuisines to consumers. This finding is consistent with sensory appeal in Yogyakarta street food (Yusuf 2017). Gen Zs are also identified as price-conscious foodies (Claveria 2018). Price is the number one element they look for when buying food.

Factor 5—*Safety/Hygiene* includes four items, such as "I prefer HK street foods that are generally good for my health", "I prefer HK street foods that match with my usual eating habit", "I prefer to eat different HK street foods everyday" and "I prefer HK street foods of high hygiene standards". This factor had a grand mean of 3.47. This finding is consistent with the factor of consideration on patronizing healthy/hygienic street foods in Delhi (Gupta et al. 2018), Phuket (Chavarria and Phakdee-auksorn 2017), and Yogyakarta (Yusuf 2017).

Further on, the mean scores for each of the five factors were computed, the 161 samples were divided into two groups—Chinese and Western, and a series of independent t-tests were conducted on these five factors to compare the Chinese and Western groups; according to the independent t-test results, no significant difference was found in all the five factors. Table 10.4 displays the results for the independent t-tests.

The mean scores for each Gen Z group in the table above show the Chinese Gen Z had a slightly lower perception level on factors 2 and 4,

Table 10.4 Results of independent t-test on five factors between Chinese and Western Gen Z's

Factors	Chinese	Westerns	t-value	Sig.(2-tail)
1. Etic destination image	3.45	3.28	1.694	0.092
2. Local emersion	3.90	3.99	−1.026	0.306
3. e-WOM	3.47	3.26	1.651	0.101
4. Emic food characteristics	3.73	3.80	−0.870	0.385
5. Safety/Hygiene	3.50	3.40	0.948	0.344

266   D. Lee et al.

compared to the Western counterparts. This means the Chinese tourists were less satisfied with the street food experience, and were less likely to consider street foods as a cuisine. However, this low difference is not statistically significant. On the other side, the Western peers showed lower level on factors 1, 3 and 5, which means they did not consider HK as a street food destination as much as their Chinese cohort, showed less confidence in food quality provided by street food, and they were less comfortable with the health and hygiene issues. But this difference is near-marginal statistically significant.

To help further understand if any differences between Chinese and Western Gen Zers' perceptions about HK street food, a set of chi-square tests were conducted to explore how much the Gen Zers know about HK street food between these two groups. There were 14 traditional HK street food listed in the questionnaire, and the respondents were asked to rate 1–5 (strongly dislike to strongly like) or 6 (don't know). The responses on these 14 foods were collapsed into 4 categories: dislike (1–2), neutral (3), like (4–5) and don't know (6). Then chi-square tests were performed to compare Chinese and Western groups' knowledge on those 14 HK street foods. The Chi-square results (Table 10.5) indicate that these two Gen Z groups had significantly different knowledge on 10 out of 14 HK street food items, and the cross-tabulation results reveal that

Table 10.5 Chi-Square results of the 14 HK street food items

Street ffood	Chi-square	Sig	Street food	Chi-square	Sig
Baked Waffle	3.860	0.277	Squid	5.707	0.127
Beef Offal	25.980	0.000***	Egg Waffle	3.306	0.191
Pig Intestine	22.856	0.000***	Pineapple Bun	7.917	0.045*
Egg Tart	9.403	0.015*	Put Chai Ko	19.934	0.000***
Fin Soup	29.740	0.000***	Roasted Potatoes	17.555	0.001**
Fish Ball	7.404	0.052	Stinky ToFu	9.900	0.019*
3 Treasures	15.608	0.001**	Sugar Cake	12.233	0.007**

Note * = significance at .05; ** = significance at .01; *** = significance at .001

the Chinese Gen Zs know more about and are more likely to like these 10 street foods, compared to their Western peers.

Conclusion, Future Research and Implications

The street food industry has been growing quickly into a powerful consumer market (Alfiero et al. 2017). The purpose of this study was to identify Gen Z tourists' perceptions of street foods when visiting Hong Kong. Similar to previous literature on street food (Yoon and Chung 2018; Chavarria and Phakdee-auksorn 2017; Gupta et al. 2018), Gen Z tourists are concerned and emphasized on the importance of health/hygiene standards as the key determinant factor in patronizing and visit intention to Hong Kong. This current study also revealed a new finding that Gen Z view e-WOM as a powerful tool in destination marketing. This suggests that HKTB can focus on promoting street food to Gen Z through popular social media platforms to Western tourists (e.g. Facebook, YouTube, WhatsApp and Twitter) and WeChat, QQ and Weibo (Mainland Chinese) in reaching out to targeted Gen Z population effectively. More importantly, this will boost the awareness, image and perceptions of street food. The Gen Z also view that food quality (emic food characteristics) and service quality are important attributes among street food operators.

In contrast to Lee, et al. (in press)'s study where they identified different perceptions between Chinese and Western tourists' food perceptions in HK, this study did not find significant difference between Chinese Gen Zs and Western Gen Zs' views on HK street food. Chinese Gen Zs place a slightly higher value on factors of etic destination image, e-WOM and safety/hygiene than their Western peers. Food safety is a big concern in China; the difference in the factor of Safety/Hygiene indicates the role of social background plays on street food perceptions. However, the chi-square results in this study indicated that the Chinese group have more knowledge on HK street food than the Western group, which might be helpful to understand the slightly different perceptions on the factors of etic destination images and e-WOM. A closer investigation on the cross-tabulation results revealed that those food items with strongly significant difference are more traditional Chinese food (such as Putchaiko and 3 Treasures) or more odd-appealing food (such as Beef Offal, pig intestine) with little to none influence by Western cooking style; and those 4 items with no significant difference are either imported and adjusted Western food (baked waffle and egg waffle) or more normal-looking food (squid and fish ball). Further research is needed to understand how HK delivers its street food and/or destination message to its different target markets, which would help to form more effective marketing strategies. More importantly, destination marketers should adopt an effective Z-generational food tourism marketing strategy by personalizing to the unique needs of Gen Z segment (Williams and Page 2011). For those Western markets that have less knowledge about traditional Chinese food, it would be better to provide more food information, including ingredients, taste, presentation and even the food history; for the mainland Chinese market, the marketing message should focus on high standard of hygiene and cost value of HK street food.

Even though interesting findings are uncovered in this study, the study does possess limitations. First, generalizing findings of this study should be done with caution since a convenience sampling method was applied. Data collected through convenience sampling method may not accurately represent the population (Bougoure and Neu 2010; Kim et al. 2013; Shin et al. 2019). Second, this study used a cross-sectional survey, longitudinal studies are recommended to obtain insights of consumers' perceptions of street food in Hong Kong. Third, this study did not use structural equation modelling (SEM) mainly because of this small sample size. The sample size is relatively small. It is not possible to do an exploratory factor analysis (EFA) on Chinese tourists and Western tourists, respectively, as the recommended minimum sample size is 150 and also meet the ratio—5 cases: 1 item (Hutcheson and Sofroniou 1999). This study comprised of 161 respondents—104 Chinese tourists and 57 Western tourists and a total of 24 items.

Future studies on street food should consider the impact of environmental risks (food wastage, excessive use of disposables) as using environmentally friendly products and fresh ingredients could reduce perceived risks of consumers (Yoon and Chung 2018). It is also recommended that future studies should examine the potential moderating role of demographic characteristics such as gender as it can affect consumers' perceptions in service quality (Maet al. 2011; Shin et al. 2019). Currently, the two Chinese cities—Chengde and Shunde and Macao SAR are identified as "Cities of Gastronomy" of the UNESCO Creative Cities Network. It will be useful to conduct research on examining Hong Kong fulfilling the eight criteria in achieving the status of "Cities of Gastronomy" and boost the city's image as a food tourism destination (Pearson 2017). Gen Zs are health conscious and prefer more sustainable products, it is useful to consider exploring the benefits and costs of promoting local organic products and creating certification programmes on street food industry in Hong Kong can reduce the concerns of food safety/hygiene (Holmes et al. 2018).

In Hong Kong, there are 51 restaurants, 13 hotel restaurants and six theme park restaurants that received halal certification from The Incorporated Trustees of the Islamic Community Fund of Hong Kong. There are halal certified eateries and five mosques listed on HKTB's website and Hong Kong's Ocean Park offers prayer rooms (*The Straits Times* 2018). Researchers emphasized the importance of adopting halal procedures and certification (halal mark/logo) for street food vendors to attract Muslim travellers (Hakeem and Lee 2018). Currently, only Butchers Club is listed in the Michelin Guide. To enhance the awareness and image of street food industry in Hong Kong, the local authorities can consider incorporating the street food operators in the Michelin Guide (Michelin Guide 2018).

Present findings suggest street food could be a potential attraction to tourists. Tourism planners and officials may consider deploying more resources to redesign, redevelop and repackage this potential tourism product. Since to develop quality and yummy street food, it is necessary to involve culinary skills. Therefore, the invitation of culinary experts or restaurant associations to join the task force for developing, designing and planning of the product is seen to be an alternative. In addition, a long-term plan should be written covering all four categories of street food.

Presently the street food offered by food truck operations have been confined to the territory. With continued development in the region, it is envisaged that both local citizens and tourists would love to taste the culinary food products offered by food trucks from the broader region of South China. Especially, the central government of China has recently rolled out a strategic regional development plan called "Greater Bay Area". Besides the socio-economic, transport and technological development, the development of leisure and culinary products are also specified in the national plan. Among the eleven cities in the Bay Area, there are at least four cities are famous for its culinary product including Guangzhou, Hong Kong, Shunde and Macau. It is thus believed that the concept of cross-border food truck can be one of the tools to match the overall development of the region and enhance the attraction of tourism.

References

Acho-Chi, Cletus. "The Mobile Street Food Service Practice in the Urban Economy of Kumba, Cameroon." *Singapore Journal of Tropical Geography* 23, no. 2 (2002): 131–148.

Alfiero, Simona, Agata Lo Giudice, and Alessandro Bonadonna. "Street Food and Innovation: The Food Truck Phenomenon." *British Food Journal* 119, no. 11 (2017): 2462–2476.

Anenberg, Elliot, and Edward Kung. "Information Technology and Product Variety in the City: The Case of Food Trucks." *Journal of Urban Economics* 90 (2015): 60–78.

Berdychevsky, Liza, and Heather Gibson. "Women's Sexual Sensation Seeking and Risk Taking in Leisure Travel." *Journal of Leisure Research* 47, no. 5 (2015): 621–646.

Björk, Peter, and Hannele Kauppinen-Räisänen. "Local Food: A Source for Destination Attraction." *International Journal of Contemporary Hospitality Management* 28, no. 1 (2016): 177–194.

Boniface, Priscilla. *Tasting Tourism: Travelling for Food and Drink*. Routledge, 2017.

Bougoure, Ursula-Sigrid, and Meng-Keang Neu. "Service Quality in the Malaysian Fast Food Industry: An Examination Using DINESERV." *Services Marketing Quarterly* 31, no. 2 (2010): 194–212.

10 Perceptions of Gen Z Tourists on Street Food in Hong Kong   271

Branwell, J. "Technology: Generation XD Uses Internet for Better Social Interaction." *Marketing Week* 14, no. 7 (2010).

Carr, Neil. "A Study of Gender Differences: Young Tourist Behaviour in a UK Coastal Resort." *Tourism Management* 20, no. 2 (1999): 223–228.

Carr, Neil. "An Exploratory Study of Gendered Differences in Young Tourists Perception of Danger Within London." *Tourism Management* 22, no. 5 (2001): 565–570.

Chang, Richard CY, Jakša Kivela, and Athena HN Mak. "Attributes That Influence the Evaluation of Travel Dining Experience: When East Meets West." *Tourism Management* 32, no. 2 (2011): 307–316.

Chavarria, Luis Carlos Torres, and Panuwat Phakdee-auksorn. "Understanding International Tourists' Attitudes Towards Street Food in Phuket, Thailand." *Tourism Management Perspectives* 21 (2017): 66–73.

Chen, Qian, and Rong Huang. "Understanding the Importance of Food Tourism to Chongqing, China." *Journal of Vacation Marketing* 22, no. 1 (2016): 42–54.

Cheung, Ho-mei May, Ka-yiu Cheung, Pui-wing Choi, Po-chun Shun, and Tsz-hin Tang. "The Food Truck Pilot Scheme in Hong Kong: Governance, Stakeholders and Regulatory Responses." *Capstone Project* (2018).

Claveria, Kelvin. "Generation Z Statistics: New Report on the Values, Attitudes and Behaviors of the Post-Millennials." *Vision Critical* (2018). https://www.visioncritical.com/blog/generation-z-statistics. Accessed on October 14, 2019.

Cohen, Erik, and Nir Avieli. "Food in Tourism: Attraction and Impediment." *Annals of Tourism Research* 31, no. 4 (2004): 755–778.

Connelly, M.A. "20 Must-Try Street Foods Around the World." *Fodor's Travel* (2016, November 8). https://www.fodors.com/news/photos/20-must-try-street-eet-foods-around-the-world. Accessed on October 14, 2019.

Creswell, John W., and Vicki L. Plano Clark. *Designing and Conducting Mixed Methods Research.* Sage, 2017.

Dawson, Richard J., and C. Canet. "International Activities in Street Foods." *Food Control* 2, no. 3 (1991): 135–139.

De Vries, Henk J., and Frank M. Go. "Developing a Common Standard for Authentic Restaurants." *The Service Industries Journal* 37, nos. 15–16 (2017): 1008–1028.

DiPietro, Robin. "Restaurant and Foodservice Research." *International Journal of Contemporary Hospitality Management* 29, no. 4 (2017): 1203–1234.

Du Rand, Gerrie E., and Ernie Heath. "Towards a Framework for Food Tourism as an Element of Destination Marketing." *Current Issues in Tourism* 9, no. 3 (2006): 206–234.

Echtner, Charlotte M., and Pushkala Prasad. "The Context of Third World Tourism Marketing." *Annals of Tourism Research* 30, no. 3 (2003): 660–682.

Engeset, Marit Gundersen, and Ingunn Elvekrok. "Authentic Concepts: Effects on Tourist Satisfaction." *Journal of Travel Research* 54, no. 4 (2015): 456–466.

Enright, Michael J., and James Newton. "Determinants of Tourism Destination Competitiveness in Asia Pacific: Comprehensiveness and Universality." *Journal of Travel Research* 43, no. 4 (2005): 339–350.

ETB. "Macao Takes Its Cuisine to the Streets of Sydney." *ETB Travel News*. https://australia.etbtravelnews.global/353027/macao-takes-its-cuisine-to-the-streets-of-sydney/. Accessed on April 19, 2018.

Etikan, Ilker, Sulaiman Abubakar Musa, and Rukayya Sunusi Alkassim. "Comparison of Convenience Sampling and Purposive Sampling." *American Journal of Theoretical and Applied Statistics* 5, no. 1 (2016): 1–4.

Francis, Tracy, and Fernanda Hoefel. *True Gen': Generation Z and its Implications for Companies*. McKinsey & Company, 12, 2018.

Gass, Susan, Alison Mackey, and Lauren Ross-Feldman. "Task-Based Interactions in Classroom and Laboratory Settings." *Language learning* 55, no. 4 (2005): 575–611.

Goforth, Chelsea. "Using and Interpreting Cronbach's Alpha" University of Virginia Library Research Data Services + Sciences. (2015). https://data.library.virginia.edu/using-and-interpreting-cronbachs-alpha/. Accessed May 20, 2020.

Gupta, Vikas, Kavita Khanna, and Raj Kumar Gupta. "A Study on the Street Food Dimensions and Its Effects on Consumer Attitude and Behavioural Intentions." *Tourism Review* 73, no. 3 (2018): 374–388.

Hakeem, AbdulElah, and Hoon Lee. "Understanding Muslim Visitors' Attitudes Towards Korean Street Food." *International Journal of Tourism Sciences* 18, no. 3 (2018): 215–235.

Hall, C. Michael, Liz Sharples, and Angela Smith. "The Experience of Consumption or the Consumption of Experiences? Challenges and Issues in Food Tourism." In *Food Tourism Around the World*, pp. 326–347. Routledge, 2004.

Henderson, Joan. "Food Hawkers and Tourism in Singapore." *International Journal of Hospitality Management* 19, no. 2 (2000): 109–117.

Henderson, Joan C., Ong Si Yun, Priscilla Poon, and Xu Biwei. "Hawker Centres as Tourist Attractions: The Case of Singapore." *International Journal of Hospitality Management* 31, no. 3 (2012): 849–855.

Heinrich Boll Stiftung. "Perspectives—Political Analyses and Commentary Asia Politics of Food." Issue 5, February 2017. https://th.boell.org/sites/default/files/hbs_-_perspectives_-_asia_5_-_en_-_online_-_170321.pdf. Accessed May 10, 2020.

Hinson, T. "Cruising to Asia? Here's the Best Street Food to Try in Each Culinary Capital." *The Telegraph.* https://www.telegraph.co.uk/travel/cruises/articles/best-street-food-asia-cruise/. Accessed May 10, 2020.

Hjalager, Anne Mette. "What Do Tourists Eat and Why? Towards a Sociology of Gastronomy and Tourism." *Tourism (Zagreb)* 52, no. 2 (2004): 195–201.

HKTB Research. "Research and Statistics." *PartnerNet.* HKTB. Accessed on April 27, 2018. https://partnernet.hktb.com/en/research_statistics/latest_statistics/index.html

Holmes, Mark R., Rachel Dodds, George Deen, Anna Lubana, Jessica Munson, and Sarah Quigley. "Local and Organic Food on Wheels: Exploring the Use of Local and Organic Food in the Food Truck Industry." *Journal of Foodservice Business Research* 21, no. 5 (2018): 493–510.

Hutcheson, Graeme D., and Nick Sofroniou. *The Multivariate Social Scientist: Introductory Statistics Using Generalized Linear Models.* Sage, 1999.

Hudson, Simon, and Graham A. Miller. "The Responsible Marketing of Tourism: The Case of Canadian Mountain Holidays." *Tourism Management* 26, no. 2 (2005): 133–142.

IBISWorld. "Food Trucks Industry in the US Market Size 2005–2025." *IBISWorld.* Industry Market Research Report. https://www.ibisworld.com/industry-statistics/market-size/food-trucks-united-states/. Accessed on May 20, 2020.

Kim, Yeong Gug, Anita Eves, and Caroline Scarles. "Building a Model of Local Food Consumption on Trips and Holidays: A Grounded Theory Approach." *International Journal of Hospitality Management* 28, no. 3 (2009): 423–431.

Kim, Sung-Bum, Kyung-A. Sun, and Dae-Young Kim. "The Influence of Consumer Value-Based Factors on Attitude-Behavioral Intention in Social Commerce: The Differences Between High-and Low-Technology Experience Groups." *Journal of Travel & Tourism Marketing* 30, nos. 1–2 (2013): 108–125.

Kivela, Jakša, and John C. Crotts. "Gastronomy Tourism: A Meaningful Travel Market Segment." *Journal of Culinary Science & Technology* 4, nos. 2–3 (2005): 39–55.

Kotler, Philip, and Nancy Lee. *Social Marketing: Changing Behaviors for Good*. Sage, 2016.

Kowalczyk, Andrzej, and Magdalena Kubal-Czerwińska. "Street Food and Food Trucks: Old and New Trends in Urban Gastronomy." In *Gastronomy and Urban Space*, pp. 309–327. Springer, Cham, 2020.

Leask, Anna, Alan Fyall, and Paul Barron. "Generation Y: An Agenda for Future Visitor Attraction Research." *International Journal of Tourism Research* 16, no. 5 (2014): 462–471.

Le, Truc H., and Charles Arcodia. "Risk Perceptions on Cruise Ships Among Young People: Concepts, Approaches and Directions." *International Journal of Hospitality Management* 69 (2018): 102–112.

Le, Truc H., Charles Arcodia, Margarida Abreu Novais, and Anna Kralj. "What We Know and Do Not Know About Authenticity in Dining Experiences: A Systematic Literature Review." *Tourism Management* 74 (2019): 258–275.

Lee, D., Watson, B., Chan, W., and H-W., E. "Culture and Motives of Tourists on Food Consumption in Hong Kong." Special Issue of Tourism Culture and Communication (in press).

Lee, Kuan-Huei, and Noel Scott. "Food Tourism Reviewed Using the Paradigm Funnel Approach." *Journal of Culinary Science & Technology* 13, no. 2 (2015): 95–115.

Lepp, Andrew, and Heather Gibson. "Tourist Roles, Perceived Risk and International Tourism." *Annals of Tourism Research* 30, no. 3 (2003): 606–624.

Lukovitz., K. "Figuring Out Gen Y's Electic Eating Preferences." *MediaPost*. Marketing Daily, January 22. https://www.mediapost.com/publications/article/98919/figuring-out-gen-ys-eclectic-eating-preferences.html. Accessed on February 14, 2019.

Ma, Jintao, Hailin Qu, David Njite, and Su Chen. "Western and Asian Customers' Perception Towards Chinese Restaurants in the United States." *Journal of Quality Assurance in Hospitality & Tourism* 12, no. 2 (2011): 121–139.

Mak, Athena HN, Margaret Lumbers, Anita Eves, and Richard CY Chang. "The Effects of Food-Related Personality Traits on Tourist Food Consumption Motivations." *Asia Pacific Journal of Tourism Research* 22, no. 1 (2017): 1–20.

Maneesriwongul, Wantana, and Jane K. Dixon. "Instrument Translation Process: A Methods Review." *Journal of Advanced Nursing* 48, no. 2 (2004): 175–186.

McKercher, Bob, Fevzi Okumus, and Bendegul Okumus. "Food Tourism as a Viable Market Segment: It's All How You Cook the Numbers!" *Journal of Travel & Tourism Marketing* 25, no. 2 (2008): 137–148.

Miller, L., and W. Lu. "Gen Z Is Set to Outnumber Millennials." *Bloomberg Economic* (2018). https://www.bloomberg.com/news/articles/2018-08-20/gen-z-to-outnumber-millennials-within-a-year-demographic-trends. Accessed on October, 14, 2019.

Michelin. "Michelin Guide Hong Kong Macau 2019 Selection." December 11, 2018. https://guide.michelin.com/sg/en/article/news-and-views/michelin-guide-hong-kong-macau-2019-selection. Accessed on October 16, 2019.

Mkono, Muchazondida, Kevin Markwell, and Erica Wilson. "Applying Quan and Wang's Structural Model of the Tourist Experience: A Zimbabwean Netnography of Food Tourism." *Tourism Management Perspectives* 5 (2013): 68–74.

Mohsin, Asad, and Abdulaziz Mohammed Alsawafi. "Exploring Attitudes of Omani Students Towards Vacations." *Anatolia—An International Journal of Tourism and Hospitality Research* 22, no. 1 (2011): 35–46.

Moreno, Flor Madrigal, Jaime Gil Lafuente, Fernando Ávila Carreón, and Salvador Madrigal. "The Characterization of the Millennials and Their Buying Behavior." *International Journal of Marketing Studies* 9, no. 5 (2017): 135–144.

Moscardo, Gianna, and Pierre Benckendorff. "Mythbusting: Generation Y and Travel." *Tourism and Generation Y* (2010): 16–26.

Namugumya, Brenda Shenute, and Charles Muyanja. "Contribution of Street Foods to the Dietary Needs of Street Food Vendors in Kampala, Jinja and Masaka Districts, Uganda." *Public Health Nutrition* 15, no. 8 (2012): 1503–1511.

Nunnally, Jum C. "An Overview of Psychological Measurement." In *Clinical Diagnosis of Mental Disorders*, pp. 97–146. Springer, Boston, MA, 1978.

Nykiel, Ronald A. *Handbook of Marketing Research Methodologies for Hospitality and Tourism*. Routledge, 2007.

O'Connor, Kieran, Glenn R. Carroll, and Balazs Kovacs. "Disambiguating Authenticity: Interpretations of Value and Appeal." *PloS one* 12, no. 6 (2017).

Okumus, Bendegul, Fevzi Okumus, and Bob McKercher. "Incorporating Local and International Cuisines in the Marketing of Tourism Destinations: The Cases of Hong Kong and Turkey." *Tourism management* 28, no. 1 (2007): 253–261.

Okumus, Bendegul, Sevil Sönmez, Sean Moore, Daniel P. Auvil, and Griffith D. Parks. "Exploring Safety of Food Truck Products in a Developed Country." *International Journal of Hospitality Management* 81 (2019): 150–158.

Özdemir, Bahattin, and Faruk Seyitoğlu. "A Conceptual Study of Gastronomical Quests of Tourists: Authenticity or Safety and Comfort?" *Tourism Management Perspectives* 23 (2017): 1–7.

Pallant, Julie, and SPSS Survival Manual. "A Step by Step Guide to Data Analysis Using SPSS for Windows Version 15." *SPSS Survival manual* 3 (2007).

PATA. "MGTO Promotes Macao's Gastronomy as a Calling Card of the City to Attract More Tourists from Thailand." *Pacific Asia Travel Association.* May 11, 2018. https://www.pata.org/mgto-promotes-macaos-gastronomy-as-a-calling-card-of-the-city-to-attract-more-tourists-from-thailand/. Accessed on October 15, 2019.

Pearson, David, and Thomas Pearson. "Branding Food Culture: UNESCO Creative Cities of Gastronomy." *Journal of Food Products Marketing* 23, no. 3 (2017): 342–355.

Pike, Kenneth. *Language in Relation to a Unified Theory of the Structure of Human Behavior.* 2nd edition. The Hague: Mouton, 1967.

Pizam, Abraham, Gang-Hoan Jeong, Arie Reichel, Hermann van Boemmel, Jean Marc Lusson, Lizl Steynberg, Olimpia State-Costache et al. "The Relationship Between Risk-Taking, Sensation-Seeking, and the Tourist Behavior of Young Adults: A Cross-Cultural Study." *Journal of Travel Research* 42, no. 3 (2004): 251–260.

Posnick-Goodwin, Sherry. "Meet Generation Z." *California Educator* 14, no. 5 (2010): 8-18.

Priporas, Constantinos-Vasilios, Nikolaos Stylos, and Anestis K. Fotiadis. "Generation Z Consumers' Expectations of Interactions in Smart Retailing: A Future Agenda." *Computers in Human Behavior* 77 (2017): 374–381.

Rainer, Thom S., and Jess W. Rainer. *The Millennials: Connecting to America's Largest Generation.* B&H Publishing Group, 2011.

Rane, Sharmila. "Street Vended Food in Developing World: Hazard Analyses." *Indian Journal of Microbiology* 51, no. 1 (2011): 100–106.

Rita, Paulo, Ana Brochado, and Lyublena Dimova. "Millennials' Travel Motivations and Desired Activities Within Destinations: A Comparative Study of the US and the UK." *Current Issues in Tourism* 22, no. 16 (2019): 2034–2050.

Shea, G. "Best 23 Cities for Street Food from Miami to Tokyo." *CNN Travel*. Culinary Journey. August 8, 2018. https://edition.cnn.com/travel/article/best-cities-street-food/index.html. Accessed October 14, 2019.

Shin, Yeon Ho, Haemi Kim, and Kimberly Severt. "Consumer Values and Service Quality Perceptions of Food Truck Experiences." *International Journal of Hospitality Management* 79 (2019): 11–20.

Smith, Stephen LJ, and Honggen Xiao. "Culinary Tourism Supply Chains: A Preliminary Examination." *Journal of Travel Research* 46, no. 3 (2008): 289–299.

Solomon, Micah. "For Small Business Week: All About Millennial Consumers and Millennial-Friendly Customer Experiences." *Forbes*. May 3, 2018. https://www.forbes.com/sites/micahsolomon/2018/05/03/for-small-bus iness-week-all-about-millennial-consumers-and-millennial-friendly-cus tomer-experiences/#d4b49f52f91a. Accessed on October 16, 2019.

Statista. "Value of the U.S. Food Truck Industry from 2014 to 2020 (in Million U.S. Dollars)." *Statista.* Industry Value of Food Trucks in the U.S. 2014–2020. Accessed October 15, 2019. https://www.statista.com/statistics/444 924/industry-value-us-food-trucks/.

Stevens, James P. *Applied Multivariate Statistics for the Social Sciences.* Routledge, 2012.

Su, Ching-Hui Joan, Chin-Hsun Ken Tsai, Ming-Hsiang Chen, and Wan Qing Lv. "US Sustainable Food Market Generation z Consumer Segments." *Sustainability* 11, no. 13 (2019): 3607.

The Economist. "America's Food-Truck Industry Is Growing Rapidly Despite Roadblocks." *The Economist*, Daily Chart. May 4, 2017. https://www.eco nomist.com/graphic-detail/2017/05/04/americas-food-truck-industry-is-gro wing-rapidly-despite-roadblocks. Accessed on October 15, 2019.

The Straits Times. "Plenty of Halal Food Options for Muslim Travelers in Hong Kong." *The Straits Times.* May 28, 2018. https://www.straitstimes.com/lifest yle/food/plenty-of-halal-food-options-for-muslim-travellers-in-hong-kong.

Thrane, Christer. "The Determinants of Students' Destination Choice for Their Summer Vacation Trip." *Scandinavian Journal of Hospitality and Tourism* 8, no. 4 (2008): 333–348.

Timothy, Dallen J., and Geoffrey Wall. "Selling to Tourists: Indonesian Street Vendors." *Annals of Tourism Research* 24, no. 2 (1997): 322–340.

Travel2Next. "Macao is the flavor of September." *Travel2Next*. Best of Macau. September 3, 2018. Accessed October 15, 2019. https://travel2next.com/macau-food- truck-sydney-melbourne/.

United Nations World Tourism Organisation. "Youth Travel Matters—Understanding the Global Phenomenon of Youth Travel." *World Tourism Organisation*. 2008.

U.S. Chamber of Commerce. "Food Truck Nation. Food Truck Index." 2014. https://www.foodtrucknation.us/wp-content/themes/food-truck-nation/Food-Truck-Nation-Full-Report.pdf. Accessed on October 15, 2019.

Vanschaik, Brenda, and Joyce L. Tuttle. "Mobile Food Trucks: California EHS-Net Study on Risk Factors and Inspection Challenges." *Journal of Environmental Health* 76, no. 8 (2014): 36–38.

Wallace, L. "The Foodie Generation: What We're Learning from Millennials." *Food24.com*. January 10, 2018. Accessed on October 16, 2019. https://www.food24.com/News-and-Guides/Features/the-foodie-generation-what-weve-learnt-from-millennials.

Wang, Ning. "Rethinking Authenticity in Tourism Experience." *Annals of Tourism Research* 26, no. 2 (1999): 349–370.

Wang, N. *Tourism and Modernity: A Sociological Analysis*. Oxford: Pergamon Press (2000).

Wijaya, Serli, Brian King, Thu-Huong Nguyen, and Alison Morrison. "International Visitor Dining Experiences: A Conceptual Framework." *Journal of Hospitality and Tourism Management* 20 (2013): 34–42.

Williams, Kaylene C., and Robert A. Page. "Marketing to the Generations." *Journal of Behavioral Studies in Business* 3 (2011): 1.

Wood, J. "Generation Z Will Outnumber Millennials This Year." World Economic Forum. WEForum.org. https://www.weforum.org/agenda/2018/08/generation-z-will-outnumber-millennials-by-2019/. Accessed May 10, 2020.

Xu, Feifei, Michael Morgan, and Ping Song. "Students' Travel Behaviour: A Cross-Cultural Comparison of UK and China." *International Journal of Tourism Research* 11, no. 3 (2009): 255–268.

Yeap, Jasmine AL, Kim Sheinne Galzote Ong, Emily HT Yapp, and Say Keat Ooi. "Hungry for More: Understanding Young Domestic Travellers' Return for Penang Street Food." *British Food Journal* (2019).

Yoon, Borham, and Yeasun Chung. "Consumer Attitude and Visit Intention Toward Food-Trucks: Targeting Millennials." *Journal of Foodservice Business Research* 21, no. 2 (2018): 187–199.

Yusuf, Mohamad. "Measuring Tourist's Motivations for Consuming Local Angkringan Street Food in Yogyakarta, Indonesia." *Journal of Indonesian Tourism and Development Studies* 5, no. 2 (2017): 65–72.

11

Generation Z Active Sports Tourism: A Conceptual Framework and Analysis of Intention to Revisit

Francesco Raggiotto and Daniele Scarpi

Introduction

With an estimated spending power of more than € 140 billion, it is not surprising that Generation Z is by far the tourist segment with the highest potential. Generation Z poses several challenges for tourism marketers, as these consumers are not just merely different from the preceding generations. More importantly, they *want* to feel different.

Considering the tourism industry, this generic behavioral pattern of Generation Z may suggest that leveraging on traditional offerings may not fully unleash the potential of these consumers; instead, it might even lead to the opposite effect. Young travelers are always in search of new

F. Raggiotto (✉)
Department of Economics and Statistics, University of Udine, Udine, Italy
e-mail: francesco.raggiotto@uniud.it

D. Scarpi
Department of Management, University of Bologna, Bologna, Italy

© The Author(s), under exclusive license to Springer Nature
Switzerland AG 2021
N. Stylos et al. (eds.), *Generation Z Marketing and Management in Tourism and Hospitality*,
https://doi.org/10.1007/978-3-030-70695-1_11

and unique experiences to live authentic, lasting sensations in response to the overwhelming availability of virtual experiences that characterizes Generation Zers' everyday life. Generation Z individuals tend to avoid predictable locations in favor of emotional or adventurous types of tourism. This tendency is also apparent regarding Generation Z sports engagement: nontraditional sports events, like action sports, primarily attract Generation Z, reflecting the generational search for authentic, unique sensations. Thus, scholars and practitioners recognize Generation Z as the most profitable consumer segment for the sport tourism industry, rotating around events that are capable of attracting several thousands of young participants, boosting the economy of the host location.

We present a psychological perspective in the study of Generation Z, addressing what leads them to actively participate in an action sporting event. Keeping in mind some key marketing outcomes, such as satisfaction and the intention to visit the tourism location, we develop and test a conceptual model on a sample of 180 Generation Z individuals.

The results provide useful theoretical and managerial insights that we discuss at the end of the chapter. Overall, they add to the current knowledge on Generation Z's tourism behavior by addressing this emerging and high-potential consumer segment, which is increasingly taking the stage—and possibly reshaping—of the sports industry.

Generation Z and Sports

Generation Z constitutes of those individuals that were born between the mid-1990s and the late 2000s (Wood 2013). These individuals are still currently (as of 2019) in their formative years, and are mostly the daughters and sons of Generations X and Y. Marketers are striving to find strategies to capture and retain the Generation Z consumer segment, which is associated with extraordinary potential in terms of direct, and most notably, economic spending power. Several estimates put Generation Z's spending power around 140bn Euros. Even more, estimates say that Generation Z can influence a 560 bn Euros household spending power (Page and Williams 2011). A globalized mindset denotes Generation Z: they have been (or are being) raised in a globalized world, are very marketing-savvy and native digitals (Page and Williams 2011).

Generation Z emphasizes the construction and the affirmation of the self, both from an individual as well as from a social viewpoint: they are strongly self-confident (Berkup 2014), and they emphasize their social belonging and their reference groups. As such, Generation Z strongly values goods and activities reinforcing peer acceptance, like, for instance, social media usage (Fenton et al. 2016) and entertainment products (Dimock 2019). This preference also reflects on their tourism consumption choices. Thus, it is often a symbolic significance that determines the choice of the location or event to visit. In that, sports-related tourism consumption is no exception because it has symbolic importance referred to self-improvement and social belonging (Fenton et al. 2016; Bosnjak et al. 2016). Specifically, from a tourism perspective, action sports participation is usually organized around events taking place—either regularly or occasionally—in a location that becomes the attraction point for Generation Z's members, who flock there for the duration of the event. For instance, the FISE action sports festival is a regularly hold action sports event in southern France, that attracts tens of thousands of Generation Z participants from around the world.

The extensive use of digital technologies that characterizes Generation Z has led to consider often such individuals as passive, apathetic consumers (Boorman 2019). However, being born in a connected, globalized world has instead increased Generation Z lateral thinking, making Generation Z energetic and strongly oriented toward self-improvement and challenges (Berkup 2014). Thus, the massive consumption of digital media has not annihilated but instead modified Generation Z sources of stimulation and arousal. In terms of tourism participation and preferences, this means that the consumption of traditional sports events among Generation Z consumers is rapidly declining while, on the one hand, Generation Z individuals are among the most involved in the tourism for action sports events (InspireSport 2019; Medium 2019).

Action sports events have a high communicative power (Raggiotto et al. 2019) that well suits Generation Z media consumption; they are spectacular to watch, fast, and communicated in real-time on social media or through 1-minutes streaming videos. Furthermore, action sports are relevant to Generation Z because of the social meaning that Generation Z attributes to participation in action sport events. Generation Z sees such a form of tourism as a way to bond with others of the same generational cohort (Canniford 2011). The unique, highly engaging experiences offered by action sports exert an intense fascination on Generation Z, which sees participation in these activities as a way to engage in authentic experiences and live out-of-ordinary sensations that will last over time (Brymer and Schweitzer 2017). In that, action sports events could constitute a unique opportunity for tourism in the eyes of Generation Z.

Finally, Generation Z and action sports appear also linked with regard to the concept of authenticity. Authenticity is crucial in action sports participation (Rickly-Boyd 2012). It is rooted in the psychological mechanisms driving action sports participation, such as the individual search for freedom (Brymer and Schweitzer 2013), and the need to affirm one's uniqueness (Rinehart and Grenfell 2002). Psychological theories on action sports explicitly state that participation is compelling as it represents an *"experience of authenticity"* (Lyng 2014, p. 456). With that regard, Generation Z strongly values authenticity and realness (Page and Williams 2011), and emphasizes the adherence of people (like influencers, opinion leaders), products, and brands to specific values and personalities (Priporas et al. 2019; CNBC 2018). Perceptions of authenticity drive, to a great extent, Generation Z choices also in tourism, and the search for authenticity is grounded in the broader need to search for truth in products and experiences (Mkono 2012). In this vein, the tourism rotating around action sports events offers participants unique opportunities to engage in highly involving, authentic activities. Furthermore, this type of tourism allows Generation Z the opportunity to explore new, authentic places, natural landscapes, and cultures.

Action Sports and Their Relevance

Sport Marketing scholars define action sports as those activities that challenge participants' physical and mental limits, which often entail risks and high sensationalism (Gyimóthy and Mykletun 2004), and in which accidents or mistakes commonly result in severe injury (Allman et al. 2009). BMX, base jumping, snowboarding, kayaking, snowboarding, and free climbing (Brymer and Houge Mackenzie 2016) are all examples of action sports.

In recent years, participation in action sports tourism has experienced outstanding growth (Xtremesports 2008). Since 2014, the number of action sports regular participants has exceeded 22 million people, only considering BMX riding and snowboarding (TBI 2014). Action sports tourists from Generation Z make most of the industry revenues (over 70%, ISPO 2016), thus making them a core target for this tourism industry. Most notably, average income and spending power are higher for Generation Z than the national average (ChronReport 2011). Generation Z almost dominates the vast, appealing market of action sports tourism, as the average age of active (athletes) and passive (spectators) participants below 25 years for disciplines like BMX, skateboarding, and wakeboarding (Statista 2018). These consumers flock to the locations hosting the action sport events and constitute massive revenues for the local tourism.

The market offer of the action sports industry is multifaceted and highly heterogeneous, proposing many different events for every sporting discipline. Such events represent a vital component of the action sports industry, due to its attractive power in terms of participants and sponsors. Furthermore, events hold a energizing experience for action sports participants as well, representing a unique occasion for competitive confrontation, and providing the necessary stimulation to test one's abilities and improve performance.

Many such action sports events have become tourism phenomena worth millions. For instance, the estimated value of the triathlon Ironman is around € 600 million, and generates through active participation, € 800 million revenues with several thousand participants from around the world (Ozanian 2017). Accordingly, from an industry perspective, considering the determinants of active participants' visit intention appears crucial (Shonk and Chelladurai 2008), even more than in the case of other industries (Akhoondnejad 2016; Tanford and Jung 2017). Visit intention concerns the sport tourists' intention to come to the location (Baker and Crompton 2000). Visit intention is a significant proxy of actual tourists' behavior (Loureiro 2014), and thus represents a critical strategic goal for tourism operators (Shonk and Chelladurai 2008).

Basing on these considerations, this chapter addresses participants' visit intention to the location hosting the action sports event as the outcome variable. The concept of visit intention is central in practice as well as in theory. In essence, such centrality is affirmed in academic research by the presence of several studies considering visit intention as their dependent variable, spanning through many different settings, namely: festivals, destinations, and sports events (Stylos et al. 2017).

However, despite the apparent relevance of action sports events for tourism, there are still few studies for Generation Z sport tourists (Priporas et al. 2018; Fotiadis et al. 2020). In the following, we address this gap by looking at possible psychological drivers for the participation of Generation Z in action sports events.

Action Sports Psychology

A fascination with risk and danger typically characterizes Generation Z participation in sports events (Laurendeau 2006), both in active participation and in passive spectatorship (Raggiotto et al. 2019; Bennett and Lachowetz 2004). Academic literature suggests that such fascination is likely to be denoted by complex, underlying psychological mechanisms determining individual engagement in action sporting events, and, accordingly, the willingness to visit the location hosting the sports event. Sensation-seeking attitude is a manifestation of the desire to achieve a better self-image (Dewhirst and Sparks 2003). Sensation-seeking reflects a desire to escape, to move away from personal negative states (e.g., depression or fear) (Taylor and Hamilton 1997).

Further, Generation Z often considers participation in action sports events as a kind of initiation rituals (Lyng 2014). Thus, Generation Z's decision to visit the location hosting the action sports event is highly symbolic, helps one's growth, and also assumes significance in terms of expressing one's social belonging (Kang et al. 2011). Action sports tourism events participation become a means to express the individual self, as well as a way to get close to an ideal self (Gyimóthy and Mykletun 2004).

Sensation-Seeking, Satisfaction, and Intention to Visit

The sensation-seeking theory postulates that individual engagement in action sports can be explained mostly by the presence/absence of a specific personality trait, namely the sensation-seeking personality trait (Schroth 1995). The sensation-seeking trait drives the individual willingness to continually search for "*varied, novel, complex and intense sensations and experiences, and the willingness to take physical, social, legal, and financial risks for the sake of such experiences*" (Zuckerman 1994, p. 27). In other words, the sensation-seeking personality trait urges individuals to seek new experiences, as well as increasing levels of stimulation and intensity of such stimulation. Such a trait also drives the choice of the type of tourism and tourist activities, as sensation-seekers prefer experiences with increasing levels of novelty, intensity, and risk (Roberti 2004). Literature has documented a link between the sensation-seeking personality trait and participation in action sports tourism (Frenkel et al. 2019). The relationship is particularly strong for Generation Z (Chase et al. 2017), and psychology scholars have suggested that a positive, individual attitude toward risk and danger determines an active search for situations entailing such characteristics (Lyng 1990).

If tourism managers can shape the action sports events in line with Generation Z's desire for arousal, positive sensations, perceptions, and reactions are likely to be obtained, turning the tourism experience into a success (Xu et al. 2012). Indeed, satisfaction is crucial in sports tourism: the satisfaction participants feel drawing from the event, is a critical antecedent of their likelihood to participate again sometime in the future (Kaplanidou and Gibson 2010).

The Role of the Event Image Fit

Event image is composed of attitudes, attributes, benefits, and costs related to a brand or event (Kaplanidou and Vogt 2007). Event image is an *"overall subjective perceptions of the [event] activity"* (Gwinner 1997, p. 148). Sport event tourism strives to create compelling, meaningful images surrounding their events, leveraging on the physical effort (Kaplanidou and Vogt 2007), or subcultural significances (Green 2001). Managers of action sports events manage them like brands (Walker et al. 2013) and imbue them with functional, emotional, and symbolic meanings (Filo et al. 2008). Event image is the meaning that participants give to the event, what it represents for them (Gwinner and Eaton 1999). Arguably, action sports events have a strong, iconic image for Generation Z, and are typically associated with sophistication (Bennett and Lachowetz 2004) and innovativeness (Franke and Shah 2003).

The concept of image fit is powerfully relevant (Hosany and Martin 2012). In sports marketing, several studies have emphasized that image fit between the image of oneself and the image of the event affects the decision to participate in the event (He and Mukherjee 2007; Hee Kwak and Kang 2009). Consumers select events and make their tourism choices basing on the level of perceived fit between the image of the event or place and the image of the self. Furthermore, they also evaluate how the event fits the image of one's ideal self. In this sense, image cues help individuals to get close to how they would like to be and to move away from social groups they do not want to be associated with (Lyng and Matthews 2007).

Image fit may assume a particularly relevant significance for Generation Z, as it generally has a strong, energetic self-image (Schreier et al. 2007), and vivid inner life (Coffey 2008). Accordingly, image fit is likely to influence Generation Z's tourism choices. Specifically, the perceived fit between the event image and Generation Z's self-image could help to understand the intention to visit the location hosting the sports event.

An Empirical Investigation of Generation Z Visit Intention for Action Sports Events

The Aims

This section provides an analysis of Generation Z's visit intention toward action sport events, based on the three main factors identified before: sensation-seeking, satisfaction, and event-fit. The purpose is threefold:

1. verify if and how far sensation-seeking is present in Generation Z individuals and how it drives their behaviors;
2. examine Generation Z's revisit intention for action sports events;
3. identify what drives Generation Z's revisit intention to participate in action sports event.

Considerations Guiding the Analysis: The Theoretical Model

Overall, the considerations detailed in the first part of the chapter link the psychological literature on sensation-seeking with the sports marketing literature. Essentially, we advance that individuals in Generation Z display a higher sensation-seeking tendency and develop stronger satisfaction toward the event, particularly when they perceive a fit between the image of the event and the image they have of themselves. In turn, satisfaction toward the sporting event leads to visit intention for the location that hosts it. In summary, we develop the original conceptual model graphically summarized in Fig. 11.1.

As Fig. 11.1 shows, the left side of the model relates to the psychology of the individual. The right side of the model refers to marketing-related outcomes building up the source of revenue for the sport tourism managers.

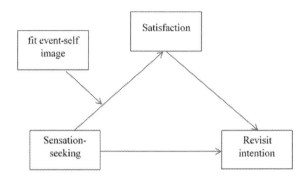

Fig. 11.1 The conceptual model

Considerations Guiding the Analysis: The Research Context

BMX or BMX racing (bicycle motocross racing) is a competitive sport in which participants race off-road bicycles on dirt tracks. The diffusion of BMX racing originated in southern California. The spread of this phenomenon, which originated mostly as a youth hobby, was supported mainly by the action of the media, which rapidly popularized documenting such practice in movies and documentaries (Ryan 2006). Such popularization fueled by media stimulated the development of a market for BMX products, accessories, and other elements devoted to the improvement of the BMX experience.

Furthermore, media coverage significantly contributed to the development of a structuring process of BMX as a professional sport. Gradually, sport governing bodies become a driving force in the development and the organization of mega-events involving BMX racing, culminating in BMX becoming a medal sport at the 2008 Summer Olympics in Beijing under the UCI sanctioning body. All these factors encouraged a massive marketization of BMX. They leveraged, to a great extent, the distinguishing, original subcultural significance of action sports, which played a crucial role in attracting Generation Z to BMX.

Scales and Considerations Guiding the Analysis

Measures come from existing marketing and psychology studies (visit intention: Kaplanidou and Gibson 2010; event image fit: Grohs and Reisinger 2014; sensation-seeking: Hoyle et al. (2002); satisfaction: Picón et al. 2014). Responses to the questionnaire items were provided by respondents using 7-point Likert scales ranging from 1 (*strongly disagree*) to 7 (*strongly agree*). Data were collected using a questionnaire administered to participants in a leading BMX competitive event in Europe during 2018. A total of 180 responses from Generation Z participants were collected. Notably, about 80% were males, reflecting the demographics of a male-dominated world and reflecting well the population of BMX according to media reports (*The New York Times* 2015) and the extant literature (Agilonu et al. 2017). All participants fell within the age range of Generation Z (McKinsey 2018). Trained research assistants administered the questionnaire to consumer-athletes to minimize ambiguity within the survey as well as to ensure understandability (Podsakoff et al. 2003). The model was tested via SPSS 25 PROCESS 3.3 macro (Hayes 2018).

Results

The measurements were found reliable and valid, as they satisfy the psychometric requirements (Cronbach's alphas and composite reliability >0.70, average variance extracted >0.50) (Fornell and Larcker 1981; Hair et al. 2010).

Results provide support for the model in Fig. 11.1. Specifically, the estimates show that sensation-seeking tendency exerts a significant influence on satisfaction (B = 0.27; $p < 0.001$). This result means that the more Generation Z feels that the event it participated in was able to satisfy the thirst for sensations, the higher the satisfaction.

Furthermore, there is empirical support of a positive impact of event satisfaction on visit intention (B = 0.34; $p < 0.001$). In other words, the key to making Generation Z come back to the same tourist location is to satisfy it by quenching the thirst for strong sensations. Nonetheless, the relationship between event satisfaction and visit intention is stronger for those Generation Z individuals who perceive a stronger fit between themselves and the event image ($B_{high} = 0.14$ vs. $B_{low} = 0.06$). More formally, the estimates of the model suggest that image fit significantly moderates the effect of satisfaction on visit intention (B = 0.19; $p < 0.05$). This result means that satisfaction will be a powerful driver of visit intention if Generation Z feels that the sports event "speaks" to it, helps it socialize, and defines itself. In other words, the higher the perceived fit between the image of the event and the image of oneself, the more likely it is that satisfaction will translate into patronage and re-patronage for the tourism location, thus guaranteeing a stream of loyal tourists.

Finally, the model estimates report a nonsignificant direct effect of sensation-seeking on visit intention (B = 0.01; $p = 0.87$). Thus, sensation-seeking influences visit intention only through satisfaction. This result means that sensation-seekers are not more likely or less likely to become loyal tourists: they will be, depending on whether they are satisfied or not with the action sports event. More formally, satisfaction fully mediates the sensation-seeking–visit intention relationship. In other words, the more Generation Z tourists perceive that the event provides strong, compelling sensations, the more they will be satisfied with the experience, and the more they will come to the same event and location in the future.

To summarize, visit intention was stronger for Generation Z participants who displayed high levels of sensation-seeking, and who were also satisfied with the event and perceived a stronger fit between the image they have of themselves and the image they have of the event.

Figure 11.2 summarizes the results of the model.

Conclusions

We addressed a consumer segment, Generation Z, that is becoming more and more important for the tourism industry, at an outstandingly fast pace. We focused on action sport events, a context worth (more than) € 5 billion for tourism managers (Forbes 2014).

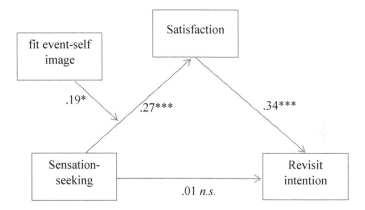

Fig. 11.2 Results of model estimation

The findings might provide some insights to practitioners. First, attracting tourists toward sports events is the main challenge in the action sports industry. Action sports events mostly target Generation Z and try to attract them to the location hosting the event. Thus, understanding the determinants of Generation Z's intention to revisit and participate again in these events is crucial for managing the tourism flow (Raggiotto and Scarpi 2019). Yet, few analyses have considered the specific characteristics of Generation Z (Brymer and Houge Mackenzie 2016) participating in action tourism events, as most scholars investigated traditional sports and traditional tourism settings.

Sensation-seeking tendency served as the trigger for participants' visit intention. In other words, the trend of Generation Z to seeking tourism locations providing strong sensations influences their tourism choices. Looking at action sport events, we highlighted a tight interdependence of marketing-related and psychology-based factors that might be unique for Generation Z.

Event satisfaction enhances the intention to participate again in the event. Furthermore, the perceived degree of fit between the image of the event and the image of oneself influences the relationship between satisfaction and visit intention. Specifically, a higher perceived image fit leads to come back to the event. This result is in line with other research on

Generation Z, which found that this Generation attributes great importance to building a solid self-image, and does so by engaging in social activities (Ek-Styvén and Foster 2018; McCormick 2016).

Overall, this chapter introduced and tested a novel theoretical framework for the analysis of Generation Z by using established variables in the field of psychology, which, however, were rarely used outside their original domain and generational cohort. Besides, the evidence in this chapter provides useful to decipher the complexity of Generation Z behavior within the context of sporting events consumption. Overall, our findings suggest that scholars and practitioners should address Generation Z individuals' decision-making separate to other generations, as their tourism choices differ from those of the other generational cohorts.

Finally, our findings corroborate those of extant research concerning the role of satisfaction and event image in shaping the decision to visit a location (Kaplanidou and Vogt 2007; Kaplanidou and Gibson 2010) and further provide new theoretical insights. From a managerial standpoint, events should strive to align to the desired level of arousal of participants, or, at least, be perceived by participants as a crucial component in sustaining their search for sensation, which is so typical of Generation Z. In this sense, if managers provide incremental levels of challenge, variety, and difficulty in sports events, they could strengthen Generation Z's decision to select it and revisit it.

Our results showed the importance of the perceived fit between event and self-image, which highlights the need to take a customer-based perspective when marketing action sports events to Generation Z sports tourists. Action sports events targeting Generation Z should deliver a compelling image that holds meanings for participants and helps them grow and define themselves. The event would preferable meant to help Generation Z to define and identify their values for driving the intention to visit the location that hosts it. Overall, we contribute advancing knowledge on Generation Z's active sport tourism, addressing one of the most relevant, high-potential consumer segments.

The complementarity of sensation-seeking, satisfaction, and image fit in driving event visit intention for Generation Z should encourage researchers to envision action sports events from a broader perspective and to investigate this generational cohort further.

References

Agilonu, A., Bastug, G., Mutlu, T. O., & Pala, A. (2017). Examining Risk-Taking Behavior and Sensation Seeking Requirement in Extreme Athletes. *Journal of Education and Learning*, *6*(1), 330. 10.5539/jel.v6n1p330.

Akhoondnejad, A. (2016). Tourist Loyalty to a Local Cultural Event: The Case of Turkmen Handicrafts Festival. *Tourism Management*, *52*(March), 468–477. 10.1016/j.tourman.2015.06.027.

Allman, T. L., Mittelstaedt, R. D., Martin, B., & Goldenberg, M. (2009). Exploring the Motivations of BASE Jumpers: Extreme Sport Enthusiasts. *Journal of Sport & Tourism*, *14*(4), 229–247. https://doi.org/10.1080/147 75080903453740.

Baker, D. A., & Crompton, J. L. (2000). Quality, Satisfaction, and Behavioral Intentions. *Annals of Tourism Research*, *27*(3), 785–804. https://doi.org/10. 1016/S0160-7383(99)00108-5

Bennett, G., & Lachowetz, T. (2004). Marketing to Lifestyles : Action Sports and Generation Y. *Sport Marketing Quarterly*, *13*(4), 239–243.

Berkup, S. B. (2014). Working with Generations X and Y in Generation Z Period: Management of Different Generations in Business Life. *Mediterranean Journal of Social Sciences*, *5*(19), 218–229. https://doi.org/10.5901/mjss.2014.v5n19p218

Boorman, A. N. (2019). The New Generation of Students. In P. M. Jenlink (Ed.), *Multimedia Learning Theory: Preparing for the New Generation of Students* (pp. 57–68). Rowman & Littlefield Publishers.

Bosnjak, M., Brown, C. A., Lee, D.-J., Yu, G. B., & Sirgy, M. J. (2016). Self-Expressiveness in Sport Tourism: Determinants and Consequences. *Journal of Travel Research*, *55*(1), 125–134.

Brymer, E., & Houge Mackenzie, S. (2016). Psychology and the Extreme Sport Experience. In F. Feletti (Ed.), *Extreme Sports Medicine* (pp. 3–13). https://doi.org/10.1007/978-3-319-28265-7_1

Brymer, E., & Schweitzer, R. (2013). The Search for Freedom in Extreme Sports: A Phenomenological Exploration. *Psychology of Sport and Exercise*, *14*(6), 865–873. https://doi.org/10.1016/j.psychsport.2013.07.004

Brymer, E., & Schweitzer, R. D. (2017). Evoking the Ineffable: The Phenomenology of Extreme Sports. *Psychology of Consciousness: Theory, Research, and Practice*, *4*(1), 63–74. https://doi.org/10.1037/cns0000111

Canniford, R. (2011). How to Manage Consumer Tribes. *Journal of Strategic Marketing*, *19*(7), 591–606. https://doi.org/10.1080/0965254X.2011.599496.

Chase, H. W., Fournier, J. C., Bertocci, M. A., Greenberg, T., Aslam, H., Stiffler, R., ... Phillips, M. L. (2017). A Pathway Linking Reward Circuitry, Impulsive Sensation-Seeking and Risky Decision-Making in Young Adults: Identifying Neural Markers for New Interventions. *Translational Psychiatry*, *7*(4), e1096. https://doi.org/10.1038/tp.2017.60

ChronReport. (2011). *The Average Income of a Triathlete*. Retrieved August 16, 2017, from https://work.chron.com/average-income-triathlete-13934.html.

CNBC. (2018). There's a Generation Below Millennials and Here's What They Want from Brands. Retrieved November 1, 2019, from https://www.cnbc.com/2018/04/09/generation-z-what-they-want-from-brands-and-bus inesses.html.

Coffey, M. (2008). *Explorers of the Infinite: The Secret Spiritual Lives of Extreme Athletes—And what They Reveal about Near-death Experiences, Psychic Communication, and Touching the Beyond*. Penguin.

Dewhirst, T., & Sparks, R. (2003). Intertextuality, Tobacco Sponsorship of Sports, and Adolescent Male Smoking Culture: A Selective Review of Tobacco Industry Documents. *Journal of Sport & Social Issues*, *27*(4), 372–398. https://doi.org/10.1177/0193732503258585.

Diliberto, S., Tumminello, M., & Lo Verde, F. M. (2019). Household Expenditure on Leisure: a Comparative Study of Italian Households with Children from Y- and Z-Generation. *International Journal of the Sociology of Leisure*, *2*(1–2), 121–146. https://doi.org/10.1007/s41978-019-00037-z.

Dimock, M. (2019). Defining Generations: Where Millennials End and Generation Z Begins. *Pew Research Center*, 1–7. Retrieved from https://www.pewresearch.org/fact-tank/2019/01/17/where%0Ahttps://www.pewres earch.org/fact-tank/2019/01/17/where-millennials-end-and-generation-z-begins/.

Ek Styvén, M., & Foster, T. (2018). Who Am I If You Can't See Me? The "Self" of Young Travellers as Driver of eWOM in Social Media. *Journal of Tourism Futures*, *4*(1), 80–92. https://doi.org/10.1108/JTF-12-2017-0057.

Fenton, S. A. M., Duda, J. L., & Barrett, T. (2016). Optimising Physical Activity Engagement During Youth Sport: A Self-Determination Theory

Approach. *Journal of Sports Sciences, 34*(19), 1874–1884. https://doi.org/10.1080/02640414.2016.1142104.

Filo, K. R., Funk, D. C., & O'Brien, D. (2008). It' s Really Not About the Bike : Exploring Attraction and Attachment to the Events of the Lance Armstrong Foundation. *Journal of Sport Management, 22*(5), 501–525. https://doi.org/10.1123/jsm.22.5.501.

Forbes. (2014). X Games At 20: The Evolution Of Action Sports. Retrieved from https://www.forbes.com/sites/alanaglass/2014/06/07/x-games-at-20-the-evolution-of-action-sports/#7b84752452f6.

Fornell, C., & Larcker, D. F. (1981). Evaluating Structural Equation Models with Unobservable Variables and Measurement Error. *Journal of Marketing Research, 18*(1), 39–50. https://doi.org/10.2307/3151312.

Fotiadis, A., Stylos, N., & Vassiliadis, C. A. (2020). Travelling to Compete: Antecedents of Individuals' Involvement in Small-Scale Sports Events. *Tourism Recreation Research*, 1–17. https://doi.org/10.1080/02508281.2020.1808934.

Franke, N., & Shah, S. (2003). How Community Matters for User Innovation: An Exploration of Assistance and Sharing Among End-Users. *Research Policy, 32*(157–178), 157–178. https://doi.org/10.1016/S0048-7333(02)00006-9.

Frenkel, M. O., Brokelmann, J., Nieuwenhuys, A., Heck, R. B., Kasperk, C., Stoffel, M., & Plessner, H. (2019). Mindful Sensation Seeking: An Examination of the Protective Influence of Selected Personality Traits on Risk Sport-Specific Stress. *Frontiers in Psychology, 10*(July), 1719. https://doi.org/10.3389/fpsyg.2019.01719.

Green, C. B. (2001). Leveraging Subculture and Identity to Promote Sport Events. *Sport Management Review, 4*(1), 1–19. https://doi.org/10.1016/S1441-3523(01)70067-8

Grohs, R., & Reisinger, H. (2014). Sponsorship Effects on Brand Image: The Role of Exposure and Activity Involvement. *Journal of Business Research, 67*(5), 1018–1025. https://doi.org/10.1016/j.jbusres.2013.08.008.

Gwinner, K. (1997). A Model of Image Creation and Image Transfer in Event Sponsorship. *International Marketing Review, 14*(3), 145–158. https://doi.org/10.1108/02651339710170221.

Gwinner, K. P., & Eaton, J. (1999). Building Brand Image Through Event Sponsorship: The Role of Image Transfer. *Journal of Advertising, 28*(4), 47–57. https://doi.org/10.1080/00913367.1999.10673595.

Gyimóthy, S., & Mykletun, R. J. (2004). Play in Adventure Tourism—The Case of Arctic Trekking. *Annals of Tourism Research*, *31*(4), 855–878. https://doi.org/10.1016/j.annals.2004.03.005.

Hair, J. F., Black, W. C., Babin, B. J., Anderson, R. E., Tatham, R. L., & others. (2010). *Multivariate Data Analysis* (7th ed.). Upper Saddle River: Prentice Hall.

Hayes, A. F. (2018). Introduction to Mediation, Moderation, and Conditional Process Analysis Methodology in the Social Sciences. *Guilford Press*. https://www.guilford.com/MSS.

He, H., & Mukherjee, A. (2007). I Am, Ergo I Shop: Does Store Image Congruity Explain Shopping Behaviour of Chinese Consumers? *Journal of Marketing Management*, *23*(5–6), 443–460. https://doi.org/10.1362/026725707X212766.

Hee Kwak, D., & Kang, J. (2009). Symbolic Purchase in Sport: The Roles of Self-Image Congruence and Perceived Quality. *Management Decision*, *47*(1), 85–99. https://doi.org/10.1108/00251740910929713.

Hosany, S., & Martin, D. (2012). Self-Image Congruence in Consumer Behavior. *Journal of Business Research*, *65*(5), 685–691. https://doi.org/10.1016/j.jbusres.2011.03.015.

Hoyle, R. H., Stephenson, M. T., Palmgreen, P., Lorch, E. P., & Donohew, R. L. (2002). Reliability and Validity of a Brief Measure of Sensation Seeking. *Personality and Individual Differences*, *32*(3), 401–414. https://doi.org/10.1016/S0191-8869(01)00032-0.

InspireSport. (2019). *Have Generation Z forgotten the Importance of Sport?* Retrieved November 29, 2019, from https://www.inspiresport.com/have-generation-z-forgotten-the-importance-of-sport/.

ISPO. (2016). *Action Sports: An Industry Searching for the Way Out of Crisis.* Retrieved January 16, 2018, from https://www.ispo.com/en/trends/id_78182622/action-sports-an-industry-searching-for-the-way-out-of-crisis.html.

Kang, J., Bagozzi, R. P., & Oh, J. (2011). Emotions as Antecedents of Participant Sport Consumption Decisions : A Model Integrating Emotive , Self-Based , and Utilitarian Evaluations. *Journal of Sport Management*, *7*(4), 314–325. https://doi.org/10.1123/jsm.25.4.314.

Kaplanidou, K, & Gibson, H. (2010). Predicting Behavioral Intentions of Active Event Sport Tourists: The Case of a Small-Scale Recurring Sports Event. *Journal of Sport & Tourism*, *15*(2), 163–179. https://doi.org/10.1080/14775085.2010.498261.

Kaplanidou, Kyriaki, & Vogt, C. (2007). The Interrelationship Between Sport Event and Destination Image and Sport Tourists' Behaviours. *Journal of*

Sport and Tourism, 12(3–4), 183–206. https://doi.org/10.1080/147750807 01736932.

Laurendeau, J. (2006). "He didn't Go in Doing A Skydive": Sustaining the Illusion of Control in an Edgework Activity. *Sociological Perspectives, 49*(4), 583–605. https://doi.org/10.1525/sop.2006.49.4.583.

Loureiro, S. M. C. (2014). The Role of the Rural Tourism Experience Economy in Place Attachment and Behavioral Intentions. *International Journal of Hospitality Management, 40*(May), 1–9. https://doi.org/10.1016/j.ijhm.2014.02.010.

Lyng, S. (1990). A Social Psychological Analysis of Voluntary Risk Taking. *The American Journal of Sociology, 95*(4), 851–886.

Lyng, S. (2014). Action and Edgework. *European Journal of Social Theory, 17*(4), 443–460. https://doi.org/10.1177/1368431013520392.

Lyng, S., & Matthews, R. (2007). Risk, Edgework, and Masculinities. In K. Hannah-Moffat & P. O'Malley (Eds.), *Gendered Risks* (pp. 75–97). Routledge.

McCormick, K. (2016). Celebrity Endorsements: Influence of a Product-Endorser Match on Millennials Attitudes and Purchase Intentions. *Journal of Retailing and Consumer Services, 32*, 39–45. https://doi.org/10.1016/j.jre tconser.2016.05.012.

McKinsey. (2018). *'True Gen': Generation Z and Its Implications for Companies.* Retrieved November 1, 2019, from https://www.mckinsey.com/industries/consumer-packaged-goods/our-insights/true-gen-generation-z-and-its-imp lications-for-companies.

Medium. (2019). Generation Z Is Transforming How Sports Content Is Watched And Distributed. Retrieved November 29, 2019, from https://medium.com/instant-sponsor/generation-z-is-transforming-how-sports-con tent-is-watched-and-distributed-f46696b800c9.

Mkono, M. (2012). A netnographic examination of constructive authenticity in Victoria Falls tourist (restaurant) experiences. *International Journal of Hospitality Management, 31*(2), 387–394. https://doi.org/https://doi.org/10.1016/j.ijhm.2011.06.013

Ozanian, M. (2017). Andrew Messick is making Ironman a global brand. Forbes, June 29. Retrieved August 1, 2019, from https://www.forbes.com/sites/mikeozanian/2017/06/29/podcast-andrew-messick-is-making-iro nman-a-global-brand/#2d63c43c6b67.

Page, R. A., & Williams, K. C. (2011). Marketing to the Generations. *Journal of Behavioral Studies in Business, 3*(1), 1–17. https://dx.doi.org/10.1080/096 5254X.2017.1291173.

Picón, A., Castro, I., & Roldán, J. L. (2014). The relationship between satisfaction and loyalty: A mediator analysis. *Journal of Business Research*, *67*(5), 746–751. https://doi.org/10.1016/j.jbusres.2013.11.038.

Podsakoff, P. M., MacKenzie, S. B., Lee, J. Y., & Podsakoff, N. P. (2003). Common Method Biases in Behavioral Research: A Critical Review of the Literature and Recommended Remedies. *Journal of Applied Psychology*, *88*(5), 879–903. https://doi.org/10.1037/0021-9010.88.5.879

Priporas, C.-V., Stylos, N., & Kamenidou, I. (Eirini). (2019). City image, city brand personality and generation Z residents' life satisfaction under economic crisis: Predictors of city-related social media engagement. *Journal of Business Research*. https://doi.org/10.1016/j.jbusres.2019.05.019

Priporas, C. V., Vassiliadis, C. A., Stylos, N., & Fotiadis, A. K. (2018). The effect of sport tourists' travel style, destination and event choices, and motivation on their involvement in small-scale sports events. *Event Management*, *22*(5), 745-765.

Raggiotto, F., & Scarpi, D. (2019). Living on the edge: Psychological drivers of athletes' intention to re-patronage extreme sporting events. *Sport Management Review*. https://doi.org/10.1016/j.smr.2018.12.005

Raggiotto, F., Scarpi, D., & Moretti, A. (2019). Advertising on the edge: appeal effectiveness when advertising in extreme sports. *International Journal of Advertising*, 1–24. https://doi.org/10.1080/02650487.2019.1653009

Rickly-Boyd, J. M. (2012). Lifestyle climbing: Toward existential authenticity. *Journal of Sport and Tourism*, *17*(2), 85–104. https://doi.org/10.1080/147 75085.2012.729898

Rinehart, R., & Grenfell, C. (2002). BMX Spaces: Children's Grass Roots' Courses and Corporate-Sponsored Tracks. *Sociology of Sport Journal*, *19*(3), 302–314. https://doi.org/10.1123/ssj.19.3.302

Roberti, J. W. (2004). A review of behavioral and biological correlates of sensation seeking. *Journal of Research in Personality*, *38*(3), 256–279. https://doi.org/10.1016/S0092-6566(03)00067-9

Ryan, J. (2006). Joe Kid on Stingray: The History of BMX. *Aethlon: The Journal of Sport Literature*, *24*(1), 165.

Schreier, M., Oberhauser, S., & Prugl, R. (2007). Lead Users and the Adoption and Diffusion of NewProducts: Insights from Two Extreme Sport Communities. *Marketing Letters*, *18*(1–2), 15–30.

Schroth, M. L. (1995). A comparison of sensation seeking among different groups of athletes and nonathletes. *Personality and Individual Differences*, *18*(2), 219–222. https://doi.org/10.1016/0191-8869(94)00144-H.

Shonk, D. J., & Chelladurai, P. (2008). Service Quality , Satisfaction , and Intent to Return in Event Sport Tourism. *Journal of Sport Management*, *22*, 587–602. https://doi.org/10.1123/jsm.22.5.587.

Statista. (2018). *Number of Participants in Wakeboarding in the United States from 2006 to 2017 (in Millions)*. Retrieved April 29, 2019, from https://www.statista.com/statistics/191342/participants-in-wakeboard ing-in-the-us-since-2006/.

Stylos, N., Bellou, V., Andronikidis, A., & Vassiliadis, C. A. (2017). Linking the Dots Among Destination Images, Place Attachment, and Revisit Intentions: A Study Among British and Russian Tourists. *Tourism Management*, *60*, 15–29. https://doi.org/10.1016/j.tourman.2016.11.006.

Tanford, S., & Jung, S. (2017). Festival Attributes and Perceptions: A Meta-Analysis of Relationships with Satisfaction and Loyalty. *Tourism Management*, *61*, 209–220. https://doi.org/10.1016/j.tourman.2017.02.005

Taylor, R. L., & Hamilton, J. C. (1997). Preliminary Evidence for the Role of Self-Regulatory Processes in Sensation Seeking. *Anxiety, Stress & Coping*, *10*(4), 351–375. https://doi.org/10.1080/10615809708249309.

The New York Times. (2015). High Diving, a Crowd-Pleasing Sport, Pursues an Olympic Platform. Retrieved August 31, 2019, from https://www.nyt imes.com/2015/08/06/sports/diving-a-crowd-pleasing-sport-pursues-an-oly mpic-platform.html.

Triathlon Business International. (2014). *Breaking Down the U.S. Triathlon Marketplace*. Retrieved August 16, 2017, from https://www.triathlonbusine ssintl.com/market-research-survey.html.

VoGo. (2019). *VoGo at the FISE World Series Montpellier 2019*. Retrieved August 30, 2020, from https://www.vogo-group.com/en/at-the-fise-montpe llier-2019/.

Walker, M., Kaplanidou, K., Gibson, H., Thapa, B., Geldenhuys, S., & Coetzee, W. (2013). "Win in Africa, With Africa": Social Responsibility, Event Image, and Destination Benefits. The Case of the 2010 FIFA World Cup in South Africa. *Tourism Management*, *34*(August), 80–90. https://doi. org/10.1016/j.tourman.2012.03.015.

Wood, S. (2013). Generation Z as Consumers: Trends and Innovation. *Institute for Emerging Issues: NC State University*, *119*(9), 1–3. https://doi.org/10. 1002/jcb.27136

Xtremesports. (2008). *Extreme Sport Growing in Popularity*. Retrieved August 16, 2017, from https://xtremesport4u.com/extreme-land-sports/extreme-sport-growing-in-popularity/.

Xu, S., Barbieri, C., Stanis, S. W., & Market, P. S. (2012). Sensation-Seeking Attributes Associated with Storm-Chasing Tourists: Implications for Future Engagement. *International Journal of Tourism Research*, *14*(3), 269–284. https://doi.org/10.1002/jtr.860

Zuckerman, M. (1994). *Behavioral Expressions and Biosocial Bases of Sensation Seeking*. Cambridge: Cambridge University Press.

12

Are Generation Z Ethical Consumers?

Penny Walters

Introduction

Generation Groupings

Generation groupings aren't categorised by exact dates, but are based on groupings of people born during specific trends or around notable historical events. Strauss and Howe (1991), suggested that cohorts throughout history share distinct characteristics and values in their book 'Generations'[1] and expanded on this in their second book, 'The Fourth Turning'. They argued that cohorts have a cycle of about twenty years, and that after four cohorts, there appears a 'turning' whereby, after a period of crisis, a new social, political, and economic climate emerges. But it could be argued that, '*The divisions we use aren't particularly robust. They tend to be imported from North America without much thought… and*

P. Walters (✉)
School of Management, University of Bristol, Bristol, UK
e-mail: penny.walters@bristol.ac.uk

© The Author(s), under exclusive license to Springer Nature
Switzerland AG 2021
N. Stylos et al. (eds.), *Generation Z Marketing and Management
in Tourism and Hospitality,*
https://doi.org/10.1007/978-3-030-70695-1_12

303

capture changes that often don't have clear inflection points, so dates can vary from pundit to pundit.[2]

People grouped by observers into cohorts during the last century include (Fig. 12.1).

- **The Silent Generation**, also called 'Golden Boomers' (born between c1925 and 1945)[3] refers to people who are currently aged in their seventies up to nineties.
- **Baby Boomers** (born between 1946 and 1964)[4] also known as 'boomers' or 'alpha boomers' refer to a member of the demographically large generation born between the end of WWII (1945 onwards) and the mid-1960s.
- **Generation Jones** (born between 1954 and 1965). The term was reportedly[5] first coined by Jonathan Pontell, a social commentator[6] who identified these years as a cohort.
- **Generation X** (born from mid-1960s to 1980) was first coined and later disowned by Douglas Coupland, author of the 1991 book *'Generation X: Tales for an Accelerated Culture'*. Notable businesses founded by Generation Xers include: Google,[7] YouTube,[8] and Amazon.[9]

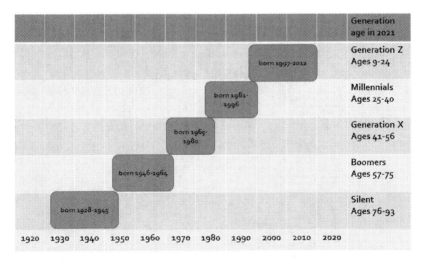

Fig. 12.1 The recent generations (*Source* The Author)

12 Are Generation Z Ethical Consumers? 305

- **Xennials** (born between the late 1970s and early 1980s)[10] which appears to have been coined in 2014[11] and includes **Yuppies** (young urban professionals) who were reputedly rebelling against the suburban lifestyles of their parents.
- **Millennials** (born between early 1980s and mid-1990s). The PEW Research Centre[12] explicitly uses 1996 as the last birth year for Millennials, and anyone born between 1981 and 1996 (ages 24–39 in 2020) is considered a Millennial, and anyone born from 1997 onwards is part of a new generation.
- **Generation Z** born between mid-1990s and late 2000s (currently aged early to mid-twenties) are also termed 'post-Millennials', 'Gen Z', 'zoomers' (a mix of the terms Generation Z and Boomer), 'iGen,[13] or 'homelanders'.[14]
- **GenAA** The final and most recent cohort has been labelled as GenAA, born after 2010, and who are predicted to have a significant impact upon the economy c2045.[15]

Generation Z

Generation Z born between 1996 and 2010 (currently aged early to mid-twenties), are also termed 'post-Millennials', 'Gen Z', 'zoomers' (a mix of the terms Generation Z and Boomer), 'iGen',[16] or 'homelanders'.[17]

Generation Z people are the children of Generation X-ers and the grandchildren of Boomers. They have used digital technology since a young age and are fully familiar with the internet and social media. Zoomer[18] is also a meme character spread on 4chan, mocking Gen Z adolescents and young adults, similarly to how the thirty-year-old boomer is used to mock older Millennials. Fry and Parker's demographic portrait[19] of American Gen Z concluded that 'post-Millennials' are likely to be most diverse, best-educated generation yet. Their key findings were that:

- post-Millennials are more metropolitan and racially and ethnically diverse, less likely to be born abroad,

- majority of post-Millennials are non-white in urban areas and western states,
- post-Millennials more likely to be pursuing college and less likely to be in the workforce,
- post-Millennials are slower to enter the labour force,
- post-Millennials' family lives are similar to those of Millennials when they were young.

Research by The Center for Generational Kinetics[20] found that 46% of Gen Z people follow more than ten online influencers and that 10% follow fifty or more; 73% of Gen Z follow at least one brand on social media compared to 64% of Millennials, and 52% of Gen Z follow three brands or more. Gen Z prefers to interact with companies via Instagram rather than the Millennial-preferred Facebook or Twitter.

Generation Z comprise about one-third of the global population of 7.7 billion, just higher than Millennials, according to a Bloomberg analysis of United Nations data.[21] Gen Z'ers are therefore the largest group of consumers in 2020. Twenge explained that parents, educators, and employers have an urgent need to understand today's rising generation of teens and young adults because, *'iGen is the first generation to spend their entire adolescence in the age of the smartphone. With social media and texting replacing other activities, iGen spends less time with their friends in person, perhaps why they are experiencing unprecedented levels of anxiety, depression, and loneliness'.*[22] This has huge implications for their social skills.

Tourism is one of the fastest-growing industries with one out of eleven jobs being created by the travel and tourism industry (World Travel & Tourism Council 2016). Research[23] has shown that 79% of Gen Z first travelled overseas before the age of fifteen, and that as a generation, they are better travelled than ever before, and therefore want authentic experiences in unique destinations, which make them feel as though they're amongst the first of their peers to 'discover' experiences.

Generation Z are people who are of interest to marketers and market researchers because this group are now starting to enter the workforce, earn their own income, and are becoming consumers. But are they ethical consumers?

Ethical Consumerism

It could be argued that ethical consumerism can be difficult to define exactly. Cooper-Martin and Holbrook succinctly defined ethical consumer behaviour as, '*decision-making, purchases and other consumption experiences that are affected by the consumer's ethical concerns*'.[24] Kirchoff explained that ethical consumerism, '*...is form of political activism based on the premise that purchasers in markets consume not only goods but also, implicitly, the process used to produce them. From the point of view of ethical consumerism, consumption is a political act that sanctions the values embodied in a product's manufacture*'.[25]

Background: The 2030 Agenda for Sustainable Development (Sustainable Development Goals).

Sustainable Development Goals (SDGs) are seventeen global goals that represent an urgent 'call to action' for all countries and citizens to work in global partnership to succeed in achieving them, and which outlines a future scenario for people and the planet adopted by all United Nations Member States in 2015. The SDGs built upon previous work of the United Nations (UN), when, during the 1980s, the UN established the Commission on Environment and Development (UNCED), which was tasked with creating a global agenda for change in order to address major worldwide social and environmental challenges. This culminated in a paper called '*Our Common Future*' (also known as the Brundtland report[26] as it was authored by Gro Harlem Brundtland of Oslo, 20 March 1987). The introduction stated that:

> From space, we see a small and fragile ball dominated not by human activity and edifice but by a pattern of clouds, oceans, greenery, and soils. Humanity's inability to fit its activities into that pattern is changing planetary systems, fundamentally. Many such changes are accompanied by life-threatening hazards. This new reality, from which there is no escape, must be recognized - and managed.[27] (p. 11)

The report outlined three fundamental components to sustainable development: environmental protection, economic growth, and social equity, pointing out that the three are intrinsically linked. This report could be seen as the backbone of the UN's work on sustainable development and has influenced subsequent reports and recommendations published by the UN. Agenda 21,[28] the Rio Declaration on Environment and Development, and the Statement of principles for the Sustainable Management of Forests were adopted by more than one hundred and seventy eight Governments at the United Nations Conference on Environment and Development (UNCED)[29] held in Rio de Janeiro, Brazil, 3–14 June 1992. The full implementation of Agenda 21, the Programme for Further Implementation of Agenda 21 and the Commitments to the Rio principles, were reaffirmed at the World Summit on Sustainable Development (WSSD)[30] held in Johannesburg, South Africa from 26 August to 4 September 2002.

The Rise of Ethical Consumerism

Harrison et al. (2005), identified seven factors in the rise of ethical consumerism[31]:

- globalisation of markets,
- rise of transnational corporations,
- rise of single-issue pressure groups,
- technological change,
- shift in market power towards consumers,
- effectiveness of market campaigns, and
- corporate accountability.

Types of ethical consumption-related activities include the following:

- boycotts (not buying items, for example, aerosols),
- positive buying (such as purchasing items labelled 'fair-trade'),
- fully screened ('green' consumers),
- relationship purchasing (such as leaving unnecessary packaging at the supermarket), and

- anti-consumerism/sustainable consumerism (such as cycling or using electric cars).

The outcomes of each range from having small scale to huge impacts. Awareness of these issues have been raised by overseas travel, and some may have even been exasperated, for example, tourists dropping plastic water bottles. Some examples of pioneering ethical consumer campaigns are:

- **Dolphin-free tuna**—One of the earliest modern ethical consumer campaigns during the 1990s resulted in tuna fleets being obliged to fit all nets with special hatches through which accidentally caught cetaceans (including whales, dolphins, and porpoises) could escape, although the practical realities of this have been debated.[32]
- **Cosmetic products free from animal testing**—Testing cosmetic products and their ingredients on animals was banned in the UK in 1998, and across the European Union (EU) in 2013. However, in some countries, China, for example, it is compulsory for any company that sells cosmetics to pay for the products to be tested on animals.[33]
- **Foods that are free of genetically modified organisms (GMOs)**— Genetically modified (GM) crops were espoused as a solution to the 'global food crisis' manifested in the sudden spike in world food prices during 2007–2008, however, these are now viewed with suspicion and there are calls to end its practice.[34]
- **Sweatshop-free clothing**–Investigations into cheap clothing have revealed that some factory owners pay starvation wages, force employees to work unpaid overtime, deny bathroom breaks and sick leave, and retaliate against workers who seek better treatment, so this has led to people not wanting to purchase items made by these companies.
- **Food waste**—1 in 9 people on the planet who are starving or malnourished could theoretically be sufficiently fed on less than a quarter of the food that is wasted in the USA, UK, and Europe each year.[35]

- **Reducing industrial greenhouse gas emissions**—It includes increasing energy efficiency by, for example, fuel switching, combining heat and power, using renewable energy, and the more efficient use and recycling of materials.[36]
- **Saving energy**—It can include using energy-efficient lightbulbs; purchasing energy-efficient appliances; using less hot water by turn down the thermostat on a water heater, or insulating a water heater; installing energy-efficient windows and insulating your home.[37]
- **Fair-trade products**—The Fair Trade Foundation website states that Fairtrade is about better prices, decent working conditions, local sustainability, and fair terms of trade for farmers and workers in the developing world; Fairtrade aims to address the injustices of conventional trade, which traditionally discriminates against the poorest, weakest producers. It theoretically enables them to improve their position and have more control over their lives.[38]
- **Conflict-free diamonds**—These are diamonds that are mined and shipped without connection to rebel or terror groups. Procedures and agreements like The Kimberley Process[39] are in place to guarantee that diamonds are mined and shipped according to certain ethical standards. 'Blood diamonds' often originate in war-torn areas and are illegally traded, gaining attention during the Sierra Leone civil war in the 1990s.[40]
- **Reducing the prevalence of micro-plastics**—Plastic is the most prevalent type of marine debris found in oceans and Great Lakes; micro-plastics are plastic debris that are less than five millimetres in length, and of recent concern are microbeads which are added as exfoliants to health and beauty products, such as some cleansers and toothpastes.[41]
- **Addressing homelessness**—It includes not just the stereotype of young men, but also including women, seniors, the sick, children, and veterans; and begs the question as to why people are homeless in wealthy countries.[42] A good example of direct action is Help Bristol's Homeless charity[43] whose ethos is that housing must come first, and they provide lorry containers which have been recycled and adapted into a small community of micro flats, and once the residents are more settled, other problems can be addressed.

- **Fracking**—At midnight on 2 November 2019, the UK government announced a moratorium (temporary ban) on fracking in England, which followed eight years of protests, arrests, demonstrations, remonstrations, letters, emails, and community organising.[44]
- **Fur industry**—After banning the use of fur in their company, British luxury fashion house Burberry announced plans to be plastic-free by 2025[45] although it could be argued that this is a marketing ploy.
- **Throwaway coffee cups**—Friends of the Earth explained that the problem with disposable coffee cups is actually three problems: what they're made of, how many there are, and where they end up; with more than four times as many takeaway coffee shops in the UK today as there were twenty years ago; people are using and throwing away at least 2.5 billion takeaway cups a year, and less than 0.25% of those cups, one in every four hundred, are recycled.[46]
- **The bottled water conundrum**—Whilst it is better to drink water than sugary or fizzy drinks, the amount of plastic that is used can be a hidden disadvantage; and there is no evidence that bottled water is any healthier than tap water. Karunananthan, the national water campaigner for the Council of Canadians, pointed out that, *'When the carbon footprint of drinking out of your tap is zero, you can't deny that the environmental impact of bottled water is more harmful'.*[47]
- **Greenwashing**—It is the process of conveying a false impression or providing misleading information about how a company's products are more environmentally sound, and is a term which originated in the 1980s.[48] In the travel industry, greenwashing refers to tour operators who make eco-trips seem more sustainable and ethical than they actually are or who mislead tourists into thinking that by participating in a particular activity they are giving back to the local community or environment.
- **Plastic straws**—The British government confirmed a ban on plastic straws, stirrers, and cotton buds to slash plastic waste will come into force in April 2020[49] citing that annually in the UK, 4.7 billion plastic straws, 316 million plastic stirrers, and 1.8 billion plastic-stemmed cotton buds, with an estimated 105 of cotton buds being flushed down toilets and can end up in waterways and oceans.

312   P. Walters

Some additional ethical consumer campaigns that are explicitly relevant to travel and tourism are:

- **Ecotourism**—It is the advocacy of the principles of: minimising physical, social, behavioural, and psychological impacts; building environmental and cultural awareness and respect; providing positive experiences for both visitors and hosts; providing direct financial benefits for conservation; generating financial benefits for both local people and private industry; delivering memorable interpretative experiences to visitors that help raise sensitivity to host countries' political, environmental, and social climates; designing, constructing, and operating low-impact facilities; recognising the rights and spiritual beliefs of the indigenous people in that community and work in partnership with them to create empowerment.[50]
- **Sustainable tourism**—It involves a commitment to making a low impact on the environment and local culture by reducing your carbon footprint, whilst helping to generate future employment for local people; aiming to ensure that development is a positive experience for local people, tourism companies and the tourists; saying no to illegal trading; and taking care of heritage places.
- **Annual Ecotourism Conference**[51]—Key stakeholders gathered to discuss the future of ecotourism connected with protected areas; focussing on the role of protected areas in ecotourism and sustainable tourism development, which ensure protecting the environment and enabling nearby communities to benefit from growth in tourism.

The UK Ethical Market

The Ethical Consumer organisation has been producing its Markets Reports annually since 1999. Their 2018 report[52] revealed that, in many sectors, consumers are turning towards more sustainable options, as their concern for the environment grows, for example, 'green energy' (which comes from natural sources such as sunlight, wind, rain, tides, plants, algae, and geothermal heat) reportedly grew by 56.3% in 2017. The purchase of ethical clothing increased by 19.9% and buying second-hand clothing for environmental reasons increased by 22.5% and purchase of ethical food and drink grew by 16.3% in 2017. However, two key green markets, sales of solar panels and energy-efficient cars reportedly fell.

The Ethical Consumer survey revealed growing environmental concern, finding that 11% of people reported to be vegetarian and 3% vegan, an increase of 52 and 153%, respectively, since 2016. Over a quarter of those surveyed stated that they had avoided buying a product or using a service due to its negative environmental impact in the past year, an increase of 65% since 2016. Gen Z are the most likely age group to avoid buying or using a product or service that has negative impact on the environment, with 34% of 18–24-year olds, and 29% of 25–34-year olds reporting it was a reason for them to withhold spending. The fast fashion industry (companies such as H&M, Zara, C&A, Peacocks, Primark, Xcel Brands, and Topshop) is reportedly the second largest polluter in the world after the oil industry.[53]

Žnideršić, 1991 pointed out that *the phenomena of ethical consumption and ethical consumer behaviour play a more prominent role in marketing theory and practice research*.[54] However, although these issues are raised by consumers as important to them, are people involving themselves in them? Although consumers are increasingly engaged with ethical factors when forming opinions about products and making purchase decisions, there are significant differences between consumers' intentions to consume ethically, and their actual purchase behaviour, termed an 'ethical purchasing gap'.[55] Gen Z consumers are sophisticated and technologically prepared for different types of actions to protect rights, but sales trends of ethical products and services do not record significant growth and participation in the total consumption.[56] The main ethical consumer trends seem to only be within food and drinks ('fair-trade' items and organic food), and small declines in consumption of cheap clothing from 'sweat shops'.

The broader range of issues (including environmentalism) integrated within ethical consumerism creates complex decision-making processes for ethically minded consumers (Freestone and McGoldrick 2008).[57] Carrington et al. 2010, stated that understanding the gap between what ethically minded consumers intend to do and what they actually do at

Theories of Reasoned Action and Planned Behaviour

Ajzen's now classic 'Theory of Reasoned Action', 1980, was devised in an attempt to predict an individual's intention to engage in a behaviour at a specific time and place. The theory of reasoned action was based on the assumption that human beings usually behave in a 'reasonable way' by taking account of available information and implicitly or explicitly considering the implications of their actions. The theory was intended to explain the behaviours over which people have the ability to exert self-control. The key component to the model is behavioural intent, whereby intentions are influenced by the attitude about the likelihood that the behaviour will have the expected outcome and the subjective evaluation of the risks and benefits of that outcome.[59] The original theory of reasoned action was modified to enable it to predict and explain goal-directed behaviour.[60] The modified theory of planned behaviour differs from the original theory of reasoned action in that it takes into account perceived as well as actual control over the specific behaviour. Ajzen lamented that a frequently voiced criticism of the theory of planned behaviour and other reasoned action models is that they are too 'rational', not taking sufficient account of cognitive and affective processes that are known to bias human judgements and behaviour.[61]

Declared intentions are often not aligned to subsequent behaviours. Attempting to understand the purchase decision-making processes of ethically minded consumers, researchers within have drawn on the established theoretical frameworks from within the consumer behaviour, business ethics, and social psychology domains (Newholm and Shaw 2007).[62] These models tend to be based on cognitive approaches, focussing on the internal (mental) process of decision-making (Fukukawa 2003).[63] Carrington et al. stated that, despite their ethical intentions, ethically minded consumers rarely purchase ethical products, stating that *ethical consumers don't walk their talk*.[64] Kim et al., 1997 termed this an 'Attitude Behaviour Gap'.[65] This intentions-behaviour gap is important to researchers and industry, yet poorly understood (Belk et al.).[66] Cowe and Williams, 2000, termed this a '30:3 phenomenon'[67] explaining that about 30% of consumers state that they care about ethical standards, but only about 3% of purchases reflect these standards.

Nicholls and Lee, 2006, concluded that, *'Focusing marketing efforts on raising (brand) awareness alone, without considering brand image, is clearly not sufficient to turn positive attitudes towards Fair Trade into ethical intent and purchase behaviour. In fact, raising the moral intensity around the Fair Trade proposition to the point where consumers are made to feel guilty about their purchases may actually have a negative effect'.*[68] Bray et al. (2010) concluded, from their focus group research into factors that impeded ethical consumption, that inertia (a tendency to do nothing or to remain unchanged) in purchasing behaviour was such that the decision-making process was *'devoid of ethical considerations'.*[69] They noted post-purchase dissonance and retrospective feelings of guilt. Some participants displayed a reluctance to consume ethically due to personal constraints, a perceived negative impact on image or quality, or an outright negation of responsibility. Those who expressed a desire to consume ethically often seemed deterred by cynicism, which caused them to question the impact they, as an individual, could achieve.

What Are the Determinants of Tourism Demand? The Gen Z Case

A number of factors which can increase travel potential for Gen Z, including easier availability of credit cards and PayPal, ease of booking and connecting trains, buses, and budget airlines, car rental, cheap accommodation, AirBnB, rising per capita income, increased availability of leisure time, reduced travel barriers, visa-free travel, free museums. Many Gen Z will spend more money for immersive, unique, authentic experiences that lets them experience life as a local, rather a typical tourist. The term 'flashpacker' has arisen, whereby a rapidly growing segment of travellers stay in modest accommodation (such as AirBNB) and expressing an interest in meeting locals as well as seeing sights, but spend freely, even excessively, for meals and activities at their chosen destination.

The development of new technologies and social media has helped people help to share tourist experiences by videos, pictures, comments, and likes. Apps can help speed up the time taken to book flights, check the availability of accommodation, or opening times of a preferred attraction beforehand. Conversely, social media can be seen as disruptive, as it could be argued for example, that some Gen Z want a selfie and the background rather than the actual tourist experience. Some tourist experience reputations can be quickly damaged by poor reviews on sites such as Trip Advisor.

Some problems can arise when choosing where to travel to, for example with obtaining visas, language barriers, diet requirements, vaccine requirements, or religious beliefs such as wanting to attend a religious service on specific days. Also, some tourist destinations with a religious focus can create divides where only part of the local population identifies with the heritage promoted for tourism (Uriely N. et al. 2003).[70]

The Coronavirus (COVID-19) Pandemic, Its Impact on the Tourism Industry, and Gen Z Tourists

The coronavirus (COVID-19) pandemic triggered an unprecedented crisis in the tourism economy when many Governments stopped all but essential flights. The OECD (The Organisation for Economic Co-operation and Development—an international organisation that works to build better policies for better lives) estimates that the impact points to 60–80% decline in international tourism in 2020. Domestic tourism, which accounts for around 75% of the tourism economy in OECD countries, is expected to recover more quickly, as it offers the main chance for driving recovery, particularly in countries, regions, and cities where the sector supports many jobs and businesses.[71]

Recovery from the impact of COVID-19 will need to include lifting travel restrictions, applying new health protocols for safe travel, diversifying potential markets, restoring traveller confidence, updated information via apps, new tourism marketing promotion campaigns, that is, a whole rethinking of the tourism sector. Co-operation amongst different countries will need to be fostered to collaboratively develop the tourism industry. Because the pandemic has triggered a global economic crisis, and many economies have fallen into recession, it may be that the travel and tourism industry will never be the same again and more people will only travel domestically, within the country they live in.

COVID-19 Crisis as an Opportunity for Gen Zs Towards Ethical Tourism

Governments need to provide better infrastructure and better protection for the environment. For example, Iceland is recognised as a leading sustainable tourism destination due to its significant efforts to drive green economic growth, preserve and enhance the natural environment as well as improving the quality of life of the people through local involvement and education.[72] In May 2012, Promote Iceland commissioned a master mapping project for the Icelandic tourism industry and to establish its foreign direct investment (FDI) potential.[73] The aim of the project was to create a platform for the government and tourism industry stakeholders to formulate a long-term strategy and goals to maximise tourism's economic contribution. The private sector expanded a lot in recent years to provide services and facilities for the growth of demand in tourism. The report concluded that the focus needs to shift from volume to high yield, low impact visitation, recognising a balance must be struck between the two especially in making the destination a year round visitor attraction.[74]

New laws and new organizations that focus on promoting tourism and investment in the country should be created in order to protect tourism in the country and the people that benefit from it. For example, Tayrona National Natural Park in Colombia,[75] which is located along Colombia's Caribbean coast and is known for its beautiful beaches and biodiversity, is closed to the public and only the indigenous tribes along with the local authorities, either the police or army, can be at the park, three times a year for a period of between two weeks and a month. The closures allow some restoration of the different ecosystems that make up the protected area.

The Travel Project, which is a partnership with creatives and story-tellers from across the globe, seeks to 'inspire, inform, educate and amaze' through a mix of videos, thought-piece articles, and stand-out imagery. Their mission is '*To explore how travel has the ability to change us, shape us and make us into the best possible versions of ourselves*'.[76] Their suggestion is that Gen Z travellers will need to enhance their skill sets, including lateral critical thinking, cultural sensitivity, the ability to work in teams, and knowing how to communicate clearly and effectively.

Conclusions

The Center for Generational Kinetics concluded that '*Rather than hanging posters of TV celebrities or athletes on their bedroom wall, Gen Z is following influencers on social media, and marketers need to urgently shift their efforts accordingly*'.[77] Their findings showed that whilst 95% of Gen Z own a smartphone and over half use it more than five hours per day, online personalities could make an immediate impact on this generation's brand loyalty and purchasing decisions.[78] Influencer-created how-to videos on YouTube are especially effective for engaging Gen Z consumers. Vision Critical[79] reported that Gen Z respond to 'edgy' campaigns and they want to co-create culture. Companies need to embrace these approaches, and utilise them as part of their marketing, because Gen Z won't engage with companies that don't keep up. In fact, it has been argued that, '*the most effective way to attract Gen Z travellers is by taking a more targeted and personalised approach. This even ranks above discounts and perks when it comes to achieving this audience's loyalty*'.[80]

This will inevitably lead to 'smart tourism', derived from the concept of 'smart city' which utilises technology as an enabler of development of tourism destinations. Gen Z are very familiar with technologies and use multiple components for every process in their travel, including reservations systems, weather, maps, public transport via social media, and various communication and connection applications. Smart cities could be seen as the cities of the future, built on a legion of interconnected devices that are constantly analysing, reporting, and evolving to improve and innovate services within their community. The collated data and fast connectivity can be used in collaboration to manage public services and design tools that enhance the visitor experience. This could lead to cities becoming safer, cleaner, and more attractive places to visit. There will also be a ripple effect on businesses within the area, including hotels and hostels, restaurants, gift shops, coffee shops, and retail stores.

Ultimately, the group who influences this generation most are their peers.[81] Gen Z favour user-generated content over traditional influencer content. The influencers who make an impact are the ones who have carved out their niche, know their audience, and tell compelling stories, aligning themselves with relevant brands.

Notes

1. Strauss and Howe, 1991, <u>Generations</u>. The History of America's Future. *William Morrow.*
2. The Conversation. From Boomers to Xennials: We Love Talking About Our Generations, But Must Recognise Their Limits. https://theconver sation.com/from-boomers-to-xennials-we-love-talking-about-our-genera tions-but-must-recognise-their-limits-80679.
3. Richard Fry, Ruth Igielnik, and Eileen Patten. How Millennials Today Compare with Their Grandparents 50 Years Ago. Posted 16 March 2018. https://www.pewresearch.org/fact-tank/2018/03/16/how-mil lennials-compare-with-their-grandparents/.
4. PEW Research. Michael Dimock. Defining Generations: Where Millennials End and Generation Z Begins. Michael Dimock. Posted 17 January 2019. https://www.pewresearch.org/fact-tank/2019/01/17/where-millennials-end-and-generation-z-begins/.
5. *The Chronicle Review.* Jeffrey J. Williams. Not My Generation. Posted 31 March 2014. https://www.chronicle.com/article/Generation-Jones/ 145569.

320   P. Walters

6. Generation Jones. Between The Baby Boom Generation and Generation X. Posted 2016. https://www.generationjones.com/.
7. Google. www.google.com.
8. YouTube. www.youtube.com.
9. Amazon. https://www.amazon.com.
10. USA Today. Ryan W. Miller. Are You a Xennial? How to Tell If You're The Microgeneration Between Gen X and Millennial. Posted 20 D. https://eu.usatoday.com/story/news/nation/2018/12/20/xennials-millennials-generation-x-microgeneration/2369230002/.
11. Good. Reasonable People Disagree About the Post-Gen X, Pre-Millennial Generation. Posted 25 September 2014. https://www.good.is/articles/gen eration-xennials.
12. PEW Research. Michael Dimock. Defining Generations: Where Millennials End and Generation Z Begins. Michael Dimock. Posted 17 January 2019. https://www.pewresearch.org/fact-tank/2019/01/17/where-millennials-end-and-generation-z-begins/.
13. Jean Twenge. iGen. https://www.jeantwenge.com/igen-book-by-dr-jean-twenge/.
14. *Forbes*. Neil Howe. Are Homelander Kids "Overruled"? Posted 17 April 2018. https://www.forbes.com/sites/neilhowe/2018/04/17/are-hom elander-kids-overruled/#33eb032a78b8.
15. *Forbes*. Kurt Cagle. Rethinking Millennials and Generations Beyond. https://www.forbes.com/sites/cognitiveworld/2018/08/22/rethinking-mil lennials-and-generations-beyond/#2810c0721893.
16. Jean Twenge. iGen. https://www.jeantwenge.com/igen-book-by-dr-jean-twenge/. Accessed 26 November 2019.
17. *Forbes*. Neil Howe. Are Homelander Kids "Overruled"? Posted 17 April 2018. https://www.forbes.com/sites/neilhowe/2018/04/17/are-hom elander-kids-overruled/#33eb032a78b8.
18. Know Your Meme. Origin. https://knowyourmeme.com/memes/zoomer.
19. PEW Social Trends. Richard Fry, Kim Parker. Early Benchmarks Show 'Post-Millennials' on Track to be Most Diverse, Best-Educated Generation Yet. A Demographic Portrait of today's 6- to 21-Year-Olds. Posted 5 November, 2018. https://www.pewsocialtrends.org/2018/11/15/early-benchmarks-show-post-millennials-on-track-to-be-most-diverse-best-edu cated-generation-yet/.
20. The Center for Generational Kinetics. The State of Gen Z 2018 Research Findings. New Study Finds Gen Z Creates Digital Celebrities Out

of Social Influencers. https://genhq.com/state-of-gen-z-2018-research-fin dings/.

21. Bloomberg. Lee J Miller and Wei Lu. Gen Z Is Set to Outnumber Millennials Within a Year. Posted 20 August 2018. https://www.bloomb erg.com/news/articles/2018-08-20/gen-z-to-outnumber-millennials-wit hin-a-year-demographic-trends.

22. Jean Twenge. iGen. https://www.jeantwenge.com/igen-book-by-dr-jean-twenge/.

23. CMO. Travel Trends: On the Go with Generation Z. https://cmo.adobe.com/articles/2019/5/generation-z-travel.html#gs.cse7c6.

24. Cooper-Martin, E., and M. B. Holbrook, 1993, 'Ethical Consumption Experiences and Ethical Space', *Advances in Consumer Research* 20 (1), 113–118. P. 113.

25. Britannica. Christopher Kirchhoff. Ethical Consumerism. Political Activism. Posted 17 May 2016. https://www.britannica.com/topic/ethical-consumerism.

26. United Nations. Report of the World Commission on Environment and Development. Our Common Future. 1987. Available at: https://sustainab ledevelopment.un.org/content/documents/5987our-common-future.pdf.

27. United Nations. Department of Economic and Social Affairs, Sustainable Development. https://sdgs.un.org/goals.

28. Sustainable Development Goals (SDGs) Knowledge Platform. Agenda 21, UNCED, 1992. https://sustainabledevelopment.un.org/index.php?page= view&nr=23&type=400&menu=35.

29. Sustainable Development Goals (SDGs) Knowledge Platform, United Nations Conference on Environment and Development (UNCED), Earth Summit. https://sustainabledevelopment.un.org/milestones/unced.

30. World Health Organisation (WHO) World Summit on Sustainable Development. https://www.who.int/wssd/en/.

31. Rob Harrison, Terry Newholm, and Deirdre Shaw, 2005. The Ethical Consumer. Sage Publications Ltd. https://login.microsoftonline.com/b2e 47f30-cd7d-4a4e-a5da-b18cf1a4151b/saml2.

32. *The Independent*. Peter Marren. Dolphin-friendly tuna? Don't Believe It. Posted 12 October 2006. https://www.independent.co.uk/environment/ dolphin-friendly-tuna-dont-believe-it-419728.html.

33. Peta UK, The Easy Way to Go Cruelty-Free. https://www.peta.org.uk/liv ing/easy-way-go-cruelty-free/.

34. Glenn Davis Stone, and Dominic Glover, 2011, 'Genetically Modified Crops and the "Food Crisis": Discourse and

Material Impacts', *Development in Practice*, 21 (4–5), 509–516. DOI: 10.1080/09614524.2011.562876.

35. Olio. The Problem of Food Waste. https://olioex.com/food-waste/the-problem-of-food-waste/.
36. Centre for Climate and Energy Solutions. Controlling Industrial Greenhouse Gas Emissions. https://www.c2es.org/content/regulating-industrial-sector-carbon-emissions/.
37. Energy Sage. Energy Conservation: 10 Ways to Save Energy. Last updated 16 January, 2019. https://www.energysage.com/energy-efficiency/101/ways-to-save-energy/.
38. The Fair Trade Foundation. What Is Fair Trade? https://www.fairtrade.org.uk/what-is-fairtrade/.
39. The Kimberley Process. What Is the Kimberley Process? https://www.kimberleyprocess.com/en/what-kp.
40. The Diamond Pro. Michael Fried. Conflict-free Diamonds: What Are They and Where to Get Them? https://www.diamonds.pro/education/conflict-free-diamonds/.
41. National Ocean Service. What Are Microplastics? https://oceanservice.noaa.gov/facts/microplastics.html.
42. *Huffington Post*. Clarence B. Jones. Homelessness Is Still a Moral and Ethical Issue. Posted 13 April 2016, updated Apr 14, 2017. https://www.huffpost.com/entry/homelessness-is-still-a-m_b_9680706.
43. Help Bristol's Homeless. https://helpbristolshomeless.org/.
44. Friends of the Earth. Jamie Peters, The Fracking Ban: What Does It Mean? Published 6 November 2019. https://friendsoftheearth.uk/climate-change/fracking-ban-what-does-it-mean.
45. MSN. After Banning Fur, Burberry Announces Plans to Be Plastic-Free By 2025. Posted 18 March 2019. https://www.msn.com/en-gb/lifestyle/style/after-banning-fur-burberry-announces-plans-to-be-plastic-free-by-2025/ar-BBUUvvu?ocid=spartanntp.
46. Friends of The Earth. Throwaway Coffee Cups: What Should We Do? https://friendsoftheearth.uk/plastics/throwaway-coffee-cups-what-should-we-do.
47. Heather Kohlmann. 'Environmentally Friendly' Bottled Water? No Such Thing. Posted 15 May 2009. https://this.org/2009/05/15/environment-water-bottle/.
48. *The Guardian Newspaper*. The Troubling Evolution of Corporate Greenwashing. https://www.theguardian.com/sustainable-business/2016/aug/20/greenwashing-environmentalism-lies-companies.

49. Gov.UK. Press release. Gove Takes Action to Ban Plastic Straws, Stirrers, and Cotton Buds. Published 22 May 2019. https://www.gov.uk/govern ment/news/gove-takes-action-to-ban-plastic-straws-stirrers-and-cotton-buds..
50. Ecotourism. Principles of Ecotourism. https://ecotourism.org/what-is-eco tourism/.
51. Ecotourism. Fourth annual Armenia Ecotourism Conference: Key Stakeholders Gather to Discuss the Future of Ecotourism connected with Protected Areas. https://ecotourism.org/ecotourism/fourth-annual-arm enia-ecotourism-conference-key-stakeholders-gather-to-discuss-the-future-of-ecotourism-connected-with-protected-areas/.
52. Ethical Consumer. Clare Carlile. The UK Ethical Market. Posted 17 December 2018. https://www.ethicalconsumer.org/research-hub/uk-eth ical-consumer-markets-report.
53. Sustain Your Style. Fashion's Environmental Impact. https://www.sustainyo urstyle.org/old-environmental-impacts.
54. Kovač-Žnideršić, R., and M. Dražen, 1991. 'Gender Differences and Influence on Ethical Behaviour of Consumers', Marketing (Beograd. 1991). 2013; 44 (1), 29–38. https://doi.org/10.5937/markt1301029K.
55. Bray Jeffery, Nick Johns, and David Kilburn. An Exploratory Study into the Factors Impeding Ethical Consumption Published online: 26 August 2010. https://www.springerlink.com/content/66v3145068161261/.
56. Ethical Consumer. 2011. Ethical Consumerism Report. https://www. ethicalconsumer.org/sites/default/files/inline-files/ethical-consumerism-rep ort-2011-1.pdf.
57. Freestone, O., and P. McGoldrick, 2008, 'Motivations of the Ethical Consumer', *Journal of Business Ethics*, 79, 445–467.
58. Carrington, M. J., B. A. Neville, and G. J. Whitwell, 2010, 'Why Ethical Consumers Don't Walk Their Talk: Towards a Framework for Understanding the Gap Between the Ethical Purchase Intentions and Actual Buying Behaviour of Ethically Minded Consumers', *Journal of Business Ethics*, 97(1), 139–158. Page 140.
59. LaMorte, W. W., The Theory of Planned Behavior, Boston University School of Public Health. Last updated 9 September 2019. https://sphweb. bumc.bu.edu/otlt/MPH-Modules/SB/BehavioralChangeTheories/Behavi oralChangeTheories3.html.
60. Ajzen, I., 1985, From Intentions to Actions: A Theory of Planned Behavior. In *Action-control: From Cognition to Behavior*, Edited by: Kuhl, J and Beckman, J. 11–39. Heidelberg: Springer. P. 12.

61. Ajzen, I., 2011, 'The Theory of Planned Behaviour: Reactions and Reflections,' *Psychology & Health*, 26 (9), 1113–1127. https://doi.org/10.1080/08870446.2011.613995.
62. Newholm, T., and D. Shaw, 2007, 'Studying the Ethical Consumer: A Review of Research', *Journal of Consumer Behaviour* 6, 253–270.
63. Fukukawa, K., 2003, 'A Theoretical Review of Business and Consumer Ethics Research: Normative and Descriptive Approaches', *The Marketing Review* 3, 381–401.
64. Carrington, M. J., B. A. Neville, and G. J. Whitwell, 2010, 'Why Ethical Consumers Don't Walk Their Talk: Towards a Framework for Understanding the Gap Between the Ethical Purchase Intentions and Actual Buying Behaviour of Ethically Minded Consumers', *Journal of Business Ethics*, 97(1), 139–158.
65. Kim, Y-K., J. Forney, and E. Arnold, 1997, 'Environmental Messages in Fashion Advertisements: Impact on Consumer Responses', *Clothing and Textiles Research Journal*, 15 (3), 147–154. https://journals.sagepub.com/doi/abs/10.1177/0887302X9701500303.
66. Belk, R., T. M. Devinney, and G. Eckhardt, 2005, 'Consumer Ethics Across Cultures', *Consumption, Markets and Culture*, 8 (3), 275–289.
67. Cowe, R., and S. Williams, 2000, 'Who Are the Ethical Consumers?' Ethical Consumerism Report, Cooperative Bank. https://www.cooperativebank.co.uk/servlet/Satellite?c=Pageandcid=1139903089615andpagename=CoopBank%2FPage%2FtplPageStandard.
68. Nicholls, A., and N. Lee, 2006, 'Purchase Decision-Making in Fair Trade and the Ethical Purchase 'Gap': Is There a Fair Trade 'Twix'?', *Journal of Strategic Marketing*, 14 (4), 369–386. CrossRefGoogle Scholar. https://www.tandfonline.com/doi/full/10.1080/09652540600956384.
69. Bray Jeffery, Nick Johns, and David Kilburn. An Exploratory Study into the Factors Impeding Ethical Consumption. Published online: 26 August 2010. https://www.springerlink.com/content/66v3145068161261/.
70. Uriely, N., A. Israeli, and A. Reichel, 2003, 'Religious Identity and Residents' Attitudes Toward Heritage Tourism Development: The Case of Nazareth', *Journal of Hospitality and Tourism Research*, 27 (1), 69–84. https://doi.org/10.1177/1096348002238881.
71. OECD. Tourism Policy Responses to the Coronavirus (COVID-19). Updated 2 June 2020. https://www.oecd.org/coronavirus/policy-responses/tourism-policy-responses-to-the-coronavirus-covid-19-6466aa20/.

72. PKF. Promote Iceland. Long-term strategy for the Icelandic Tourism Industry, February 2013. https://www.islandsstofa.is/media/1/final-long-term-strategy-for-icelandic-tourism-industry-270213kh.pdf. Page 58.
73. PKF. Promote Iceland. Long-term Strategy for the Icelandic Tourism Industry, February 2013. https://www.islandsstofa.is/media/1/final-long-term-strategy-for-icelandic-tourism-industry-270213kh.pdf.
74. PKF. Promote Iceland. Long-term Strategy for the Icelandic Tourism Industry, February 2013. https://www.islandsstofa.is/media/1/final-long-term-strategy-for-icelandic-tourism-industry-270213kh.pdf. Page 91.
75. Tayrona National Natural Park Colombia. https://www.ecohabsantamarta.com/tayrona-national-park.
76. Contiki. The Travel Project. https://www.contiki.com/six-two/thetravelproject/.
77. The Center for Generational Kinetics. The State of Gen Z 2018 Research Findings. New Study Finds Gen Z Creates Digital Celebrities Out of Social Influencers. https://genhq.com/state-of-gen-z-2018-research-findings/.
78. The Center for Generational Kinetics. The State of Gen Z 2018 Research Findings. New Study Finds Gen Z Creates Digital Celebrities Out of Social Influencers. https://genhq.com/state-of-gen-z-2018-research-findings/.
79. Vision Critical. Matt Kleinschmit. Generation Z Characteristics: 5 Infographics on the Gen Z Lifestyle. Updated 7 October, 2019. https://www.visioncritical.com/generation-z-infographics/.
80. CMO. Travel Trends: On The Go With Generation Z. https://cmo.adobe.com/articles/2019/5/generation-z-travel.html#gs.cse7c6.
81. CMO. Travel Trends: On The Go With Generation Z. https://cmo.adobe.com/articles/2019/5/generation-z-travel.html#gs.cse7c6s.

Index

A

accommodation 5, 54, 59, 61, 108, 109, 122, 127, 145, 149, 150, 155, 157, 158, 175, 179, 235, 236, 315, 316

airline industry 152, 182, 183

analytics 10, 14

artificial intelligence 5, 74, 173

aspirations viii, xii

attitudes viii, xii, 26, 66–68, 76, 80, 81, 83, 84, 111, 121, 131, 168, 169, 175, 180, 237, 240, 256, 286–288, 314, 315

authentic 13, 35, 108, 109, 145, 160, 168, 169, 173, 183, 195, 225, 227–229, 231, 235, 237, 239, 241, 242, 252, 264, 282, 284, 306, 315

B

behaviour x, 4, 8, 9, 15, 58, 62, 64, 66, 67, 82, 84, 122, 126, 129, 131, 169, 170, 174, 175, 183, 184, 194–197, 199–201, 207, 210, 214, 216, 224, 240–243, 251, 255, 256, 307, 312–315

business ecosystem 54

C

capabilities 3, 29, 34, 36, 43, 44, 197, 211

career ix, 7, 9, 17, 27, 30–34, 37, 43, 45, 54, 55, 70, 74, 76, 78, 79, 81, 83–85, 171

channels 17, 30, 31, 42, 43, 143, 146, 153, 171, 174, 176, 177, 181, 241, 243, 264

© The Editor(s) (if applicable) and The Author(s), under exclusive license to Springer Nature Switzerland AG 2021
N. Stylos et al. (eds.), *Generation Z Marketing and Management in Tourism and Hospitality*,
https://doi.org/10.1007/978-3-030-70695-1

328   Index

characteristics ix, xi, xii, 3, 6–9,
13, 16, 19, 20, 26, 30, 34,
54–58, 62, 66–68, 70, 72,
83–85, 123, 127, 129, 133,
143, 145, 159, 161, 170, 171,
175, 205, 224, 229, 230, 241,
242, 256–259, 264, 265, 267,
269, 287, 293, 303
Charisma 17
cloud computing 153
cohort vii, ix, x, 4, 6, 8, 9, 13, 15,
19, 26–32, 34–36, 38, 43, 45,
71, 102, 103, 106, 108, 111,
112, 122–125, 131, 201, 266,
284, 294, 295, 303–305
collaborative 10, 32, 33, 37, 39–41,
44, 45, 108, 317
collectivistic 128
communication 10, 27, 28, 30–32,
35, 37, 39, 43, 44, 57, 75, 76,
102, 142–144, 146, 147, 151,
153–155, 158, 171, 174, 175,
215, 236, 319
competitive advantage 56, 57, 250
conflict resolution 33, 34, 37
connectivity 11, 31, 32, 39, 102,
319
consumption viii, 11, 54, 57, 108,
110, 111, 130, 143, 149, 178,
207, 224, 226, 227, 236, 239,
241, 250, 252, 253, 283, 294,
308, 313, 315
coronavirus 71, 316
corporate ix, 16, 17, 31–34, 37, 40,
43, 67, 78, 308
Couchsurfing 109, 161
COVID-19 xii, 216, 316, 317
creativity 9, 10, 15, 18, 27, 44, 45,
67, 68, 79, 236, 237

crisis xii, 26, 71, 124, 303, 309,
316, 317
cruise xi, 42, 55, 193–216
cruising market 195

D

data 4, 14, 33, 77, 147, 268, 291,
306, 319
decision-making 32, 37, 39, 68, 69,
129, 130, 154, 155, 171, 174,
175, 194, 199, 307, 313–315
destination image xi, 177, 259, 263,
265, 267
destination marketing 147, 161,
170, 176, 253, 263, 267
diaspora 7
digital natives 5, 7–13, 16, 17,
20, 32, 35, 71, 72, 74, 108,
232–234, 264
digital nomadism 13, 20
disabilities 107
DMOs xii
domestic 231, 316, 317

E

e-commerce 13, 143
efficiency 45, 253, 310
emersion xi, 259, 265
emotions 102, 124, 131
employee retention 80
engagement ix, xii, 38, 41, 42, 76,
169, 173, 174, 181, 185, 282,
286, 287
entertainment 5, 54, 58, 75, 109,
125, 127, 132, 143, 152, 155,
228, 230, 236, 238, 283

entrepreneur viii, ix, 11, 13, 44, 55–69, 80, 81, 83–85, 104, 108

ethical consumer 306, 307, 309, 312, 313

ethical consumerism xii, 307, 308, 313

Ethical Market 312

eudaimonia 110

events vii, x–xii, 6, 7, 16, 26, 31, 103, 104, 126, 131, 145, 158, 170, 181, 182, 184, 225, 227, 231, 232, 252, 254, 282–290, 292–295, 303

experience x, 6, 7, 11, 12, 14, 26, 28, 31, 32, 34–36, 38, 66, 71, 75, 81, 102, 104–106, 108–112, 122, 124–129, 131, 143–146, 148, 150, 151, 153–155, 158–161, 169–171, 174–176, 180, 183, 194, 195, 197, 198, 200–202, 205, 206, 212, 214, 225–231, 235–242, 250–255, 260, 264, 266, 282, 284, 285, 287, 290, 292, 306, 312, 315, 316, 319

F

Facebook 71, 74, 75, 124, 142, 146, 155, 168, 171, 179, 180, 183, 238, 264, 267, 306

feedback 10, 31, 35, 39, 40, 42, 44, 75, 78, 79, 81, 109, 144, 146, 149, 158, 159

fitness 102, 103

flexibility 15, 19, 32, 43, 44, 66, 76, 78, 255

foodie xi, 178, 223–232, 240–243, 251, 265

food tourism xii, 111, 230, 231, 242, 250–253, 257, 263, 264, 268, 269

Functionality 79, 144

G

gastronomy xi, 242, 254

generations vii–xii, 4–11, 13–15, 17–19, 26–43, 45, 54, 55, 70–80, 83–85, 102, 106–108, 110, 111, 121–124, 126, 129, 133, 141–147, 154, 160, 161, 168, 169, 172, 174–176, 180, 181, 195, 206, 224, 232–243, 251, 255, 256, 264, 268, 281, 283–289, 291–295, 303–306, 318, 319

globalisation 3, 249, 308

Governments xii, 308, 316, 317

H

Heterogeneity 57

hotels 12, 14, 44, 54, 55, 59, 61, 65, 82, 103, 107, 109, 111, 128, 131, 132, 153, 157, 169, 170, 174, 175, 179, 180, 184, 253, 319

human resource 10, 20, 37, 54, 83

hygiene xi, 254, 259, 263, 265–269

I

incentive 16, 81

individualistic 9, 13, 28, 39, 72, 233, 241

influencers ix–xi, 11, 12, 168–171, 173–185, 318, 319
innovation challenges 81
Inseparability 57
insights viii, ix, xii, 206, 215, 253, 257, 268, 282, 293, 294
Instagram 8, 71, 74, 142, 146, 160, 168, 171, 173, 176–181, 183, 237, 241, 306
instagrammability 177, 181, 182
Intangibility 57
integration 18, 44, 106, 145
intergenerational ix, 27, 36–38, 44, 45
internationalization 66
internet vii, 4, 9–12, 32, 57, 71–75, 102, 123, 124, 127, 129, 132, 141–144, 147, 153–155, 157, 161, 169, 171, 175, 224, 232–234, 239, 241, 261, 264, 305
Internet of Things (IoT) x, 147, 151, 153, 157, 160
interpersonal 34, 44
intrapreneur ix, 55, 67–70, 83–85

K

knowledge management 3
knowledge transfer ix, 37, 41, 42

L

leadership styles ix, 5, 13, 15–17, 20, 39, 40
leisure tourism 125
LGBT 107
LGBT community 107

lifestyle ix, 4, 27, 55, 57, 58, 60, 62–66, 70, 72, 103, 110, 144, 171, 175, 178, 182, 226, 227, 229, 238, 240–242, 249
local communities 62, 102, 176, 311
loyalty 18, 27, 33, 36, 75, 181, 235, 318
luxury resorts 180

M

machine learning 5
media 9–11, 30, 33, 125, 141, 168, 172, 200, 210, 216, 226, 234, 261, 264, 290
meditation tourism 106
mindful 37
minorities 112
mobile apps 8, 79, 148, 151, 152, 158, 161, 237
motivation(s) x, 5, 17, 34, 42, 58, 62, 65, 66, 72, 76, 79–81, 125–127, 195, 224, 230, 242, 251, 255, 256
multimedia 124, 142, 157, 234
museums 59, 62, 132, 147, 150–152, 157, 158, 160, 235, 315

N

networks 8, 11, 64, 66, 109, 124, 142–144, 146, 149, 152, 158, 170, 171, 202, 203, 224, 238
norms 37

O

Online opinion leaders 174

On-Site x, 153, 156
organic food 65, 228, 239, 313

P

pandemic xii, 71, 216, 316, 317
performance 17, 18, 30, 31, 35–37,
    57, 75, 79, 253, 285
Perishability 57
personality traits 6, 16, 195, 287
personnel 3, 19, 67, 131, 132
piracy xi, 194, 196, 198, 204, 208,
    211–214
platforms 8, 10–12, 14, 16, 37, 41,
    43, 74, 108, 155, 161, 168,
    169, 171, 176, 179, 180, 264,
    267
policy makers 123, 253, 257
politics 76
post-travel x, 147, 153, 156, 158
preferences viii, xi, xii, 13, 27, 31,
    32, 35, 39, 40, 54, 76, 78,
    111, 122, 127, 131, 132, 159,
    226, 228, 229, 235, 241, 242,
    254, 258, 283
pre-travel x, 146, 152–156
productivity 19, 45, 76, 78
pro-environmental behaviors 110

Q

QR codes x, 147, 149, 151–153

R

reservations 107, 109, 146–148,
    158, 159, 234, 319
restaurant 14, 54, 55, 59, 62, 64,
    104, 132, 148, 150, 151,

157, 158, 175, 178, 179,
    184, 203, 206, 207, 212, 214,
    225, 227–230, 234, 236–242,
    251–253, 255, 260, 263, 269,
    319
revisit xii, 37, 289, 293, 294
RFID 153
robotics 5

S

safety xi, 105, 127, 128, 133, 177,
    194, 195, 197–200, 202, 203,
    206, 207, 211, 213–215, 253,
    259, 265, 267, 269
Seasonality 57
security xi, 26, 33, 40, 105, 108,
    143, 152, 194, 195, 198–200,
    202, 203, 206, 207, 211–215
self-esteem 34, 81
service management 57
sharing economy 44, 108, 161
smart x, 144, 146–155, 157–161,
    234, 239, 319
smartphones vii, 5, 8, 11, 103, 123,
    129, 142, 144, 146, 147, 153,
    154, 158, 159, 234
Snapchat 8, 74, 142, 243
social interactions 36, 44, 147, 155,
    161, 229, 235
socialization x, 146, 223, 236
social media x, 8, 10–12, 32–34,
    41, 43, 71, 74, 75, 81, 102,
    123, 126–129, 131, 142, 146,
    147, 153–155, 158, 160, 168,
    170–174, 176–179, 181–183,
    202, 207, 215, 234, 237, 238,
    241, 242, 251, 261, 264, 267,
    283, 284, 306, 316, 319

332 Index

social responsibility 12, 14, 233, 242
sports x, xii, 125, 128, 131–133,
203, 254, 282–290, 292–295
strategy 42, 44, 63, 65, 160,
180–182, 184, 185, 250, 252,
268, 317
sustainability 102, 111, 126, 149,
176, 228, 242, 310
Sustainable Development Goals
(SDGs) 307
sustainable growth 66

talent 11, 26, 43, 54
Telecommuting 78
terrorism xi, 30, 71, 159, 194, 196,
198, 204, 208, 209, 211–214
thematic tourism xii
Tik Tok 168
tourism education 20
transformational leadership 16–19
transportation xi, 5, 54, 59, 61, 108,
147, 149, 158, 170, 182, 183
travel agencies 12, 55, 131
travel bloggers 174
trends xii, 8, 11, 13, 20, 38, 44, 75,
131, 144, 160, 171, 173, 175,
236, 239, 313

Twitter 71, 75, 124, 146, 168, 171,
179, 180, 183, 264, 267, 306

values viii, 4, 5, 8, 17, 26–29, 31,
33, 39, 108, 111, 121, 125,
129, 170, 237, 238, 255, 258,
283, 284, 294, 303
virtual reality (VR) 5, 8, 11, 149,
152, 154, 155, 157–160
visionary 17, 66, 70
volunteering 81, 111, 125

Wearable technologies x, 103, 153
well-being x, 102–106, 108,
110–112, 236
wellness 101–107
wireless 147, 151, 153
workforce ix, 4, 10, 15, 16, 19,
26–29, 34–36, 41, 45, 54, 70,
74, 82–85, 106, 306

YouTube 8, 10, 74, 84, 142, 146,
155, 168, 172, 180, 183, 238,
241, 267, 304, 318